Exploring Speech Communication
AN INTRODUCTION

Exploring Speech Communication
AN INTRODUCTION

Mary Forrest
Eastfield College

Margot A. Olson
North Lake College

West Publishing Company

St. Paul
New York
Los Angeles
San Francisco

DEDICATION

...to Mary Daniel and Sue Cook

...to Beatrice and James Allensworth

PHOTO CREDITS

6 Courtesy of Stock Boston, Mark Antman. **15** Courtesy of Stock Boston, Owen Franken. **20** Bob Gaylord. **26** Courtesy of Stock Boston, Donald Dietz. **36** Courtesy of Stock Boston, Donald Dietz. **39** From Black Star, Ira Berger. **76** Photo by Burt Glinn ©Magnum Photos, Inc. **79** Courtesy of Jeroboam Inc., H.S. Chapman. **90** Courtesy of Stock Boston, Barbara Alper. **94** Photo by Jeff Jacobson ©Magnum Photos, Inc. **104** Courtesy of Stock Boston, George Malave. **107** Courtesy of Jeroboam Inc., Peeter Vilms. **146** Courtesy of Bob Gaylord. **156** Courtesy of Bob Gaylord. **162** Courtesy of Stock Boston, Philip Jon Bailey. **171** Courtesy Bob Gaylord. **176** Courtesy of Stock Boston, Frank Siteman. **191** Courtesy of Stock Boston, Arthur Grace. **230** Courtesy of Jeroboam, Inc., Don Ivers. **234** Courtesy of Jeroboam, Inc., Rose Skytta. **240** Courtesy of Jeroboam, Inc., Peeter Vilms. **252** Photo by Abigail Heyman ©Magnum Photos, Inc. **254** Courtesy of Bob Gaylord. **262** Courtesy of Bob Gaylord. **298** Courtesy of Bob Gaylord. **303** Courtesy of Bob Gaylord. **312** Courtesy of Jeroboam, Inc., Hap Stewart. **319** Courtesy of Jeroboam, Inc., Gregg Mancuso. **324** Courtesy of Jeroboam, Inc., Peeter Vilms. **328** ©1978 from Black Star, Janet Fries. **340** Photo by Cornell Capa ©Magnum Photos, Inc. **347** Courtesy of Bob Gaylord.

COPYRIGHT ©1981 By WEST PUBLISHING CO.
50 West Kellogg Boulevard
P.O. Box 3526
St. Paul, Minnesota 55165

All rights reserved

Printed in the United States of America

Library of Congress Cataloging in Publication Data

Forrest, Mary.
   Exploring speech communication.

   Includes bibliographies and index.
   1. Oral communication. I. Olson, Margot.
II. Title.
P95.F6   001.54'2   81-946
ISBN 0-8299-0381-X

Contents

Preface vii

PART ONE Communication Defined   2

    Overview 2

        1. The Meaning of Communication   7
        2. Language in Communication   21
        3. Perception of Self in Communication   37

    Activities 48

    Additional Readings 70

PART TWO Listening and Nonverbal Messages   72

    Overview 72

        4. Listening Behavior   77
        5. Nonverbal Messages   91
        6. Nonverbal Techniques to Help the Listener   105

    Activities 115

    Additional Readings 140

PART THREE Interpersonal Communication　　　　　　　　　　　　　　142

Overview 142

    7. Taking Responsibility for Oneself　　　　　　　　　　　　　147
    8. Relating to Others　　　　　　　　　　　　　　　　　　　　163
    9. Exchanging Messages in Interpersonal Communication　　　177

Activities 192

Additional Readings 224

PART FOUR Small Group Communication　　　　　　　　　　　　　　　226

Overview 226

    10. Small Group Communication Defined　　　　　　　　　　　231
    11. Important Factors for Group Participation　　　　　　　　　241
    12. Some Applications of Small Group Communication　　　　255

Activities 265

Additional Readings 292

PART FIVE Speaker-Audience Communication　　　　　　　　　　　　294

Overview 294

    13. Planning the Speaker-Audience Message　　　　　　　　　299
    14. Delivering the Speaker-Audience Message　　　　　　　　　313
    15. Informative Speaking　　　　　　　　　　　　　　　　　　325
    16. Persuasive Speaking　　　　　　　　　　　　　　　　　　341

Activities 356

Additional Readings 416

Final Activity　　　　　　　　　　　　　　　　　　　　　　　　　　417

References　　　　　　　　　　　　　　　　　　　　　　　　　　　419

Index 421

Preface

Speech communication—talking with one other person, in small groups, and in front of an audience—is an area of study appropriate for every individual. One cannot exist as a normally functioning individual without engaging in the processes of spoken communication. Skill in speech communication is sometimes taken for granted. College curriculums sometimes ignore the very important area of speech communication or require only a single "speech" course as a graduation requirement. When a single speech course is recommended to students, the selection of content becomes extremely important. Should the more informal speaking situations of day-to-day living be emphasized, should the more formal speaker-audience situation be emphasized, or should a combination of both be presented? This book provides a means of integrating interpersonal and small group communication with speaker-audience communication while allowing the instructor to provide emphases in areas most relevant to specific student populations by selecting appropriate activities and chapters for reading.

It is our philosophy that all individuals require interpersonal communication skills, including small group communication, to function in today's world. We have observed that many individuals fear the experience of presenting a message to an audience. To provide exposure to skills helpful in day-to-day living and to provide experiences in speaking before an audience, activities in speaker-audience communication have been integrated with activities in the interpersonal communication areas. This integration allows the student to gradually move from making a somewhat informal statement before an audience to eventually providing the audience with a formal message, all the while participating in intrapersonal, interpersonal, and small group speaking experiences.

To provide the necessary guidance for making a public speech, the last unit of the book has been designed to provide the traditional coverage of speaker-audience communication. The integrated approach avoids the often frightening impact of the assignment to make an informative or persuasive speech to a formal audience and allows formal presentation skills to evolve gradually. The text can be effectively used for interpersonal communication courses, for the integrated speech communication approach, or for a two-semester or two-quarter course of interpersonal communication followed by speaker-audience communication. It can be used also in public speaking courses where exposure to more general communication skills is desirable. By selecting relevant activities and readings from the introductory, listening and nonverbal, interpersonal, small group, and speaker-audience units, a course can be designed to meet the speech communication needs of most student populations. This book would not have been possible without the dedication of the West Publishing Co. editorial and production staff.

At Eastfield College special thanks are due to Margaret Adams, who typed early copies of the manuscript so that our students could use the material as it was developed. Eastfield College students themselves possibly deserve the greatest thanks since they willingly used the early versions of the manuscript. The following students are recognized and thanked for their excellent work in speech preparation during the period in which we wrote our book. The ideas they presented were adapted to provide examples of speeches in the text.

Marsha Birdsong	Ruby Hunter
Jenny Cossaboom	Jeri Jones
Cathy Diffee	Brian Joyce
Deanna Dobbs	Melody Pieratt
Elizabeth Earle	Valerie Ray
Pat Fisher	Susan Robbins
Sammy Geetch	Marvis Rutherford
Julie Gibbens	Mark Williams
Cheryl Gocher	Carol Terrill
Joe Goodrich	Julie Thomas
Paula Haddock	Ken Williams
Rhonda Hardt	Jeff Wright

We sincerely appreciate their hard work and the opportunity we had to know them well. These students and all others who enrolled in the speech communication classes provided the impetus to begin and complete this project. They all deserve thanks.

We wish to thank our professional peers who provided us with valuable recommendations. We owe the following individuals a deep debt of gratitude for making a major contribution to our professional development over the past few years.

William D. Brooks
University of Oklahoma, Norman
Jeanne Christian
Glendale Community College, Arizona

Cheryl Hamilton
Tarrant County Junior College, Texas
Ann Harrell
McLennan Community College, Texas
John W. Preas
Westark Community College, Arkansas
Dan Robinette
Eastern Kentucky
Gwenn Danielson Schultze
Portland Community College
James I. Walling
Central Michigan University
Chrysti Watson
Pasadena Community College
D. G. Wilson
Mt. San Antonio College, California
Gordon Zimmerman
University of Nevada, Reno

    Finally, we must acknowledge James Forrest and George Olson for their support in our endeavor, and Jason Forrest, Laci Forrest, Stefan Olson, and Tonia Olson for sacrificing time spent with us during the completion of this project.

Mary Forrest
Margot Olson
January, 1981

PART ONE

Overview

Communication is a term to which most readers of this book will have already attached some meaning. In fact, many adequate and informed definitions of the term *communication* could be written without reading further. This is because communication—talking, writing, gesturing—is a part of everyone's life. Communication is as common and natural as sleeping or walking. It is a process taken for granted by most. Consider the following reflections of poet Ric Masten in his poem "Conversation."*

> *i have just wandered back*
> *into our conversation*
> *and find that you are still rattling on*
> *about something or other*
> *i think i must have been gone at least*
> *twenty minutes*
> *and you never missed me*
>
> *now this might say something*
> *about my acting ability*
> *or it might say something about*
> *your sensitivity*
>
> *one thing troubles me though*
> *when it is my turn to rattle on for twenty*
> *minutes which i have been known to do*
> *have you been missing too?*

Through the sensitivities of the poet we can recognize a communication situation we have all experienced. Communication is much more than

*Reprinted from Ric Masten "Conversation," *Speaking Poems,* Sunflower Ink, 1977, p. 58.

Communication Defined

talking; it involves relationships with others and reactions to ordinary day-to-day situations like Masten's "Conversation."

The following three chapters have been written to provide a definition of the term *communication*. The chapters deal with the meaning of the term, the physical and intellectual processes which provide the human organism with the ability to communicate, and the effect on the communication process of the individual's image of self. The chapters are based on the research and thinking of many communicators who have shared their careful reflections with others. Their purpose is to provide the foundation needed not only to acquire knowledge about the communication process, but more importantly, to put into practice techniques and skills that can improve one's ability to communicate with others in a variety of ways.

At this point, many readers are no doubt asking themselves the question, "Why study communication?" Few people take courses on how to improve their sleeping and walking skills. Even in more formal areas of study, it is often difficult to understand the rationale for learning some of the knowledge and skills that are emphasized. Although reasons for some areas of study may seem vague, contrived, or totally unrelated to the processes of living, this is not true of communication. Each person, regardless of goals in life, must achieve a minimum level of competence in communication in order to survive. Communication is so vital to every aspect of a full and rewarding life that it is important to achieve more than minimum effectiveness. Communication can be improved by studying basic concepts of communicating with an audience, in small groups, and on a one-to-one basis. Even study of the listening process can facilitate communication. Communication is definitely an area of study where lifelong learning is especially relevant.

Ability to communicate effectively provides an advantage in reaching personal and occupational goals. Perhaps you have chosen to enter a difficult profession such as law, medicine, or teaching, or to become a skilled tradesperson or public service worker. And perhaps you plan to be a parent and an active community member. In several of your many roles, you may be called on to give a speech, to participate in a small group activity, or even to introduce someone. In all your roles you will need to participate on a one-to-one basis and you will need to listen. Communication involves demanding, complex behaviors that study, practice, and concentration can improve. A study of communication will provide a basis for better understanding oneself and for more effective interaction with others. Communication is an area of study that cannot be removed from the processes of daily living; the study of communication is relevant for anyone seeking to expand opportunities and to maximize competence in all areas of living.

A good speaker is not born a good speaker, just as a good athlete is not born a good athlete. Both are born with potential that must be developed. If a magic formula exists for becoming an effective communicator, it includes practice, awareness, interest, and enthusiasm. As a beginning to what will hopefully develop into a lifelong attempt to become an effective communicator, the reader should be able to demonstrate acquisition of the following objectives.

Attitude Objective: Through discovery that the term *communication* represents a complex interaction of physical, psychological, and intellectual processes, the student will recognize the value of learning about and improving communication skills as a lifelong personal goal for achieving a full and rewarding life. (*Activities 1–10*)

Knowledge Objective: Given objective questions, the student will recall the definitions of the following terms and recognize examples or differentiate among them where appropriate. (*Activity 1*)

    I.   Meaning of Communication
       A.   Communication Model
          1.   Originator, encoding, message
          2.   Communication channel
          3.   Receiver, decoding, feedback
          4.   Noise
       B.   Delivery Systems
          1.   Written
          2.   Verbal
          3.   Nonverbal
          4.   The media
       C.   Communication Encounters
          1.   Intrapersonal
          2.   Interpersonal

PART I Communication Defined

              3. Small group
              4. Speaker-audience
         D. Functions of Communication
              1. Levels of basic needs
              2. Information
              3. Persuasion
              4. Decision making
              5. Entertainment
    II. Language in Communication
         A. Sensation
         B. Perception
              1. Environmental factors
              2. Individual factors
         C. Language
              1. Words
              2. Meaning
              3. Influences on usage
              4. Acceptable usage
              5. Conveying meaning
   III. Perception of Self in Communication
         A. Self-concept
              1. Public and private self
              2. Johari Window
              3. Self-fulfilling prophecy
         B. Defensiveness
         C. Self-confidence
         D. Credibility
              1. Character
              2. Competence
              3. Composure
         E. Intrapersonal Communication

Experiential Objective: The student will participate in communication experiences by following instructions for selected activities in the areas listed below. (*Activities 2–9*)

        I. Speech Communication Skills Inventory
       II. Knowing Your Listeners
     III. Why Study Speech Communication
     IV. Sensation
      V. Perception
     VI. Language
    VII. Self-concept

Speaking Objective: Following the instructions given with Activity 10 for Part I, the student will present a two- to three-minute introduction of a historical figure or a classmate. (*Activity 10*)

CHAPTER 1

The Meaning of Communication

Communication is the sharing of meaning. When one person is able to transmit a thought to another person who attaches some meaning to the thought, communication has occurred. The sharing of meaning between two individuals is not always accurate. Each thought transmitted has the potential to take on one or more meanings. An effective communicator takes great care in choosing the words, and perhaps the gestures, that enable the listener to attach the expected meaning to the thought.

Some insight into the question of whether meaning has been shared may be gained by considering the following question: Does a falling tree create sound in an isolated forest? Some would argue that a tree that falls in a forest devoid of listeners creates no sound, and there are others who would argue that sound is created independently of the presence of listeners. There can be no resolution of the controversy until the two debaters recognize that they have attached different meanings to the word "sound." One of them believes that sound must stimulate the eardrum and be transmitted to the brain of some organism; the other believes that sound results from the movement of air waves. Were the two debaters communicating? It seems safe to assume that they were communicating to some extent, but more effective communication would have resulted from clarification of the seemingly simple term, "sound."

To provide an adequate basis for study, the definition of communication must be expanded by illustrating a model for a simple communication exchange, by discussing common delivery systems and types of communication encounters, and by presenting the functions of communication in today's world. Within these contexts, the concept of communication will take on an expanded, more complete meaning that will form the foundation required to bring about more fulfilling communication encounters.

The Communication Model

A communication exchange is the sending of a message from one person to another. When the message is a part of a conversation, many exchanges will often follow rapidly one after another. The communication exchange between two individuals can be illustrated in a simple form by developing a visual model of the process. To provide a concrete basis for the example, consider the following "conversation."

Person 1: I'm tired.
Person 2: You look dead.

Sending the Message

The communication exchange begins when one person has a thought, a feeling, or perhaps a description of an object or event that needs to be transmitted to another person. The *originator*, that is, the sender in the communication exchange, is the first element of the model. (Figure 1.1)

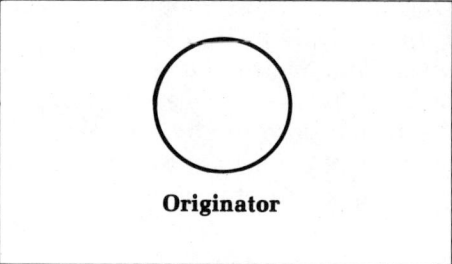

Figure 1.1

The originator must translate the thought, idea, or description into symbols that will convey the intended meaning. Finding the right symbols, usually words, is called *encoding*. (Figure 1.2)

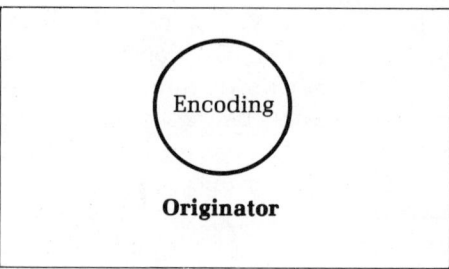

Figure 1.2

Once the encoding process is completed the *message* has been prepared. At this point in the process, message refers to the symbols that the originator will use to send the thought, idea, or description to another person. In the exchange given above, the originator has encoded certain physiological feelings and has used the verbal symbols, "I'm tired," to send the message. (Figure 1.3)

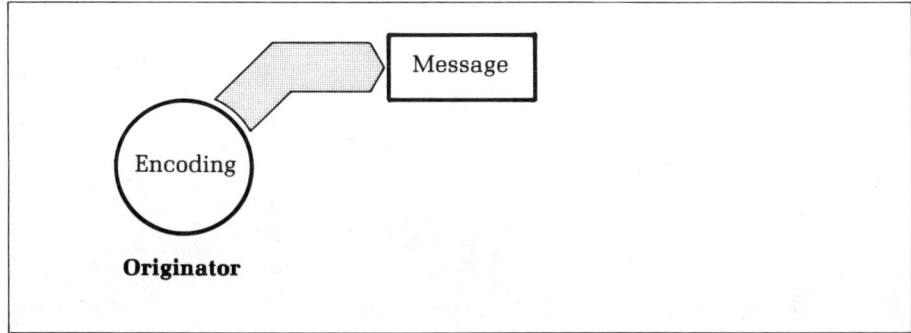

Figure 1.3

The message is sent by the originator via a *communication channel*. There are a number of ways to send messages. Speaking, writing, and gesturing are the most common. (Figure 1.4)

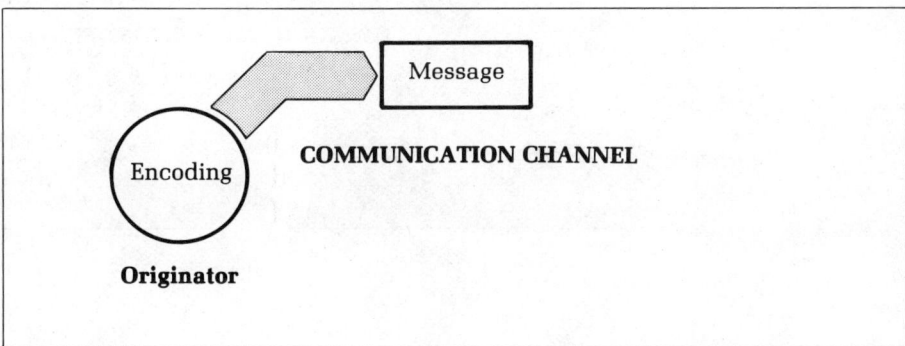

Figure 1.4

Receiving the Message

For communication to take place, there must be a *receiver* of the message. (Figure 1.5)

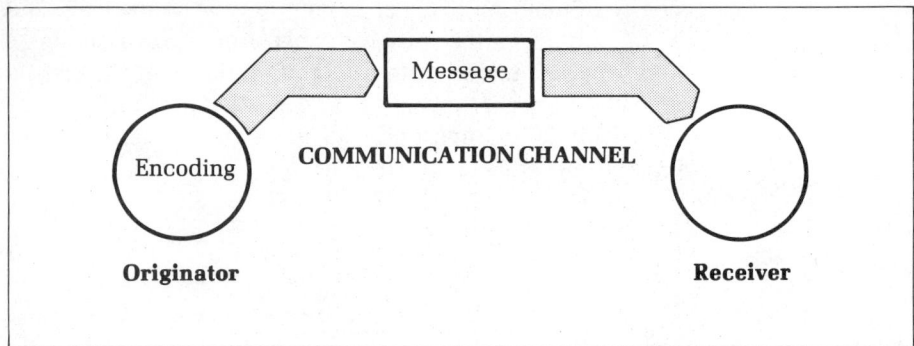

Figure 1.5

The receiver must interpret the symbols used by the originator to transmit the idea, thought, or description. The process of giving meaning to the symbols representing the message is called *decoding*. It is in one sense the opposite process of encoding; it enables the originator and receiver to share meaning and thus to communicate. (Figure 1.6)

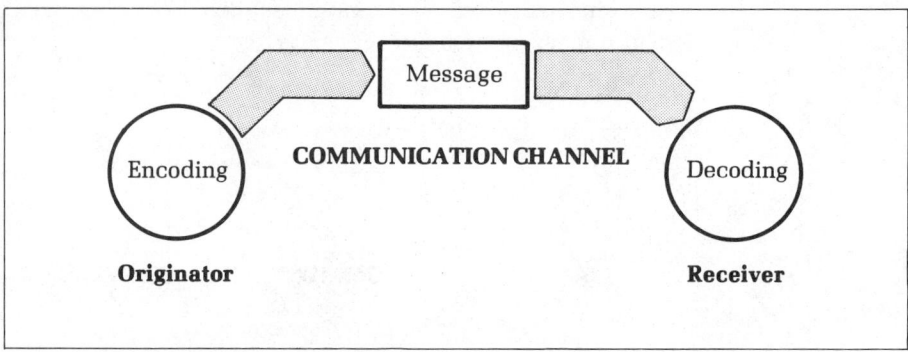

Figure 1.6

Responding to the Message

An acknowledgment that the message was received and decoded is called *feedback*. The feedback may be a frown or a nod, or it may take the form of a question or statement. (Figure 1.7) In the exchange given above, the receiver decoded the message and to show agreement transmitted feedback in the form of a statement, "You look dead."

CHAPTER 1   The Meaning of Communication

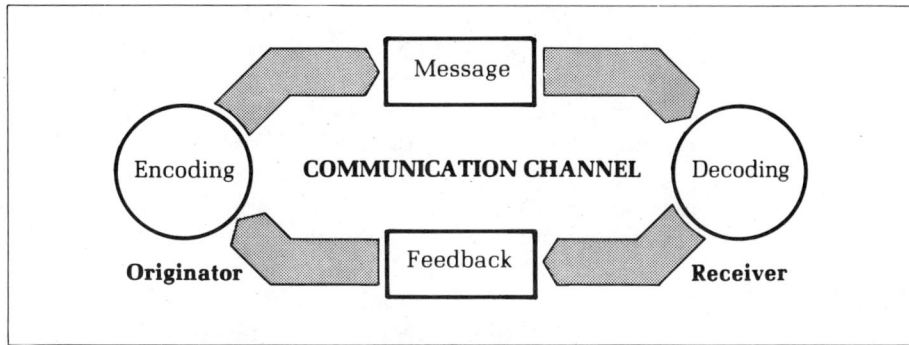

Figure 1.7

If the feedback results in another message from the originator, a continuing exchange of messages and feedback will occur. Both parties involved in the transaction will be originators and receivers and will contribute messages and feedback.

Distortions of the Message

The communication exchange can be upset by interfering stimuli occurring when the message or feedback is sent. The distortion is often called *noise*, and in the communication model illustrates a potential cause of misunderstanding. Noise affecting communication exchanges can be either physical or psychological. (Figure 1.8)

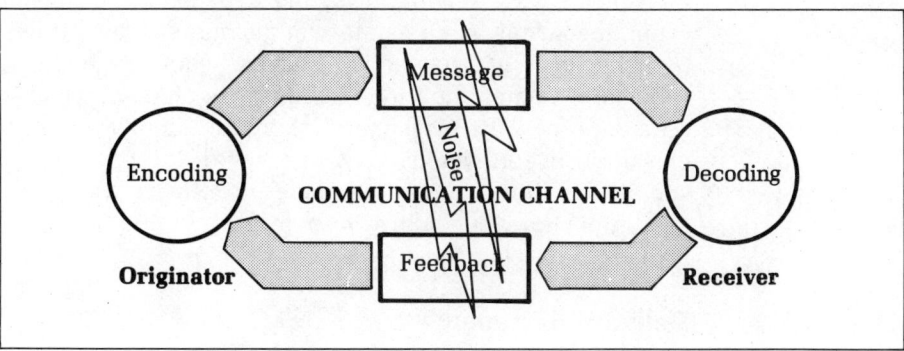

Figure 1.8

Physical noise can be caused by distractions in the surrounding environment or by damage to the sensory receptors. Interference from an environmental factor would include noises from loud machinery, or a television blaring its message through a conversation. Damage to sensory receptors is manifested by impairment of hearing or poor vision. Such physical interference can result in partial reception of a message and can lead to misunderstanding.

Psychological noise is caused by mental characteristics of the individual that make it difficult to encode and decode messages properly. For instance, the originator may have experienced anxiety over expressing a thought and, therefore, selected the wrong words in the encoding process, or social rules may inhibit the originator's ability to express an opinion accurately. Feelings of hostility, conflict, or prejudice will often result in distortion as the receiver gives a different meaning to the message than that intended by the originator. Generally, there is less psychological noise and more effective communication among persons with similar backgrounds, values, language, attitudes, and experiences.

The communication model is a very simple way to demonstrate a very complex process. Its purpose is not to simplify the process. Its value lies primarily in the introduction and illustration of some terms—originator, encoding, message, communication channel, receiver, decoding, feedback, and noise—that will be used as the meaning of communication is further expanded.

Delivery Systems and Communication Encounters

Communication is a constantly occurring series of events. As students read this text, for example, concepts of communication are being transmitted. Reflective students, who stop reading to ponder an idea, are actually communicating within themselves. This example illustrates two ways that a single communication event can be analyzed: according to the type of delivery system used, and according to the type of encounter. The delivery system is the means by which a message can be encoded. There are basically three types of delivery systems: written, verbal, and nonverbal. The delivery systems are used to transmit messages from original sources, such as statements made in conversations between two persons, or from secondary sources such as television or newspaper reports. A communication encounter is characterized by the receiver or receivers of the message. Communication encounters are generally classified in four ways: intrapersonal, interpersonal, small group, and speaker-audience. Both the mode of delivery and the type of encounter are important considerations in developing effective communication skills.

Delivery Systems

The three delivery systems—written, verbal, and nonverbal—are alike in that they rely on symbols to transmit a message. To be effective, the symbols used in written, verbal, and nonverbal communication must be common to both the originator and the receiver of a message. Written and verbal communication both rely on words for the expression of meaning. In nonverbal communication meaning is shared through gestures, facial expressions, listening behaviors, and such artifacts as clothing, hairstyles, and possessions.

The term *speech communication* generally refers to verbal and nonverbal messages. In speech communication, however, writing ability is needed for note-taking, which is an important listening skill, and for the preparation of public speeches. To be an effective communicator it is necessary to acquire special skills in all three of the modes, and to be aware of the power of the media as secondary delivery systems. A brief look at each of the three primary delivery systems and the media as means of transmitting messages may be helpful in expanding the meaning of communication.

Written Communication. In general, written communication requires greater facility with words and language than does verbal communication. The reason for this is the absence of immediate feedback from the receiver to the originator. Often a message is expressed in writing because a spoken message is impossible. To avoid misunderstanding, the originator of the written message must anticipate the decoding process by asking, "What will these words mean to the receiver of the message?" The originator of written communication often has the opportunity to use dictionaries and other writing aids, to ask others to review a message, and to rewrite before sending the message to the ultimate receiver. Interestingly, speech communication skills can sometimes be useful in developing written as well as spoken messages.

Verbal Communication. Just as the study of English composition emphasizes written composition, speech communication generally emphasizes the verbal aspects of transmitting messages. Verbal communication is taken for granted by most people because they acquire the ability to use a spoken language naturally and at a very young age. They fail to realize, however, that many of their day-to-day problems could be lessened by paying greater attention to verbal communication skills. This is not to imply that a speech communication course will solve all life's problems. Even the experts in the field of speech communication suffer the problems of communicating poorly.

Nonverbal Communication. Nonverbal communication occurs simultaneously with verbal communication in face-to-face situations. Even a totally paralyzed person would be communicating nonverbally that a problem with movement exists. Many nonverbal reactions occur spontaneously. Most people in conversation naturally smile, nod, or point without asking themselves each time if the response is appropriate or inappropriate. An understanding of the role that nonverbal messages play in the total communication exchange is useful not only in encoding messages but also in decoding the messages sent by others.

The Media. "The media" are mechanical means of transmitting messages such as television, radio, films, newspapers, magazines, and books. They are considered secondary delivery systems because the receiver of the message does not receive it from the originator in a face-to-face encounter. For most people contact with the media will be primarily as passive receivers of messages. In our roles as passive receivers, the media, especially television, have influenced what we know, what we buy, what we eat, how we live, when we leave home, and even when we go to the bathroom. The media have powerful influences too on personal courses of action and decision making of major consequence in the lives of nearly everyone. Images of professions, fashions, and lifestyles are presented and often form the basis for, or at least contribute to, the goals and aspirations of receivers.

The impact of both print and nonprint media on communication is enormous. There are approximately 120 million television sets in the United States; publishers are reporting higher and higher circulation and advertising revenues. Mass media do much to provide a common bond among and within nations. The receiver, however, must realize first that all messages may not be accurate and unbiased, and then must develop evaluative skills to use in screening messages. The underlying purpose of much of the popular media is sales. Often the sales motivation leads to an overemphasis on subjects that draw attention and to neglect of issues of more importance.

Much that the listener learns in a speech communication course directed toward participation in firsthand sending and receiving of messages can be applied to messages received via some form of media. Listening skills are especially relevant to evaluating any message; a knowledge of purposes of messages and how to construct them helps in understanding and retaining information, and background in interpersonal and small group communication aids in the interpretation of the subtle messages underlying some television entertainment and reading material. The media have an impact on quality of life that most people never consider. Do not be surprised when your child spells relief as R-O-L-A-I-D-S, tells you to buy Downy to soften the clothes, or thinks Aqua Velva can turn anyone into a man.

Communication Encounters

Speech communication is often studied within areas representing the four types of encounters—intrapersonal, interpersonal, small groups, and speaker-audience. The division into the four areas may be viewed as a progression from communicating with oneself, with one other person, with several people, and with large groups of listeners. It should be obvious that the communication situation changes drastically through the

progression from sending messages to oneself to the delivery of a formal message to an audience.

Intrapersonal Communication. Intrapersonal communication, that is, communication that occurs within each individual, is going on continuously. It might be considered the most basic of the four communication encounters because it forms the basis of the messages shared with other individuals. The message must first be established within the individual before it can be transmitted to a receiver. Thoughts, or messages within the individual, need not be shared with others, however. Much time spent in thought has the purpose of developing insights into personal problems, establishing attitudes about issues, or contemplating knowledge that has been gained from personal experiences and the media.

Intrapersonal communication can occur in isolation or in the midst of other people. The distinguishing characteristic of intrapersonal communication is that it is maintained within the individual and is not shared with others. In the study of speech communication, intrapersonal communication is often studied along with each of the other three types of encounters. In interpersonal communication, for example, much emphasis is placed upon individual reflection of attitudes, values, and behaviors. In small group communication, private thought is often given to ways of expressing viewpoints and influencing other members. The planning of the formal message for delivery to an audience is done through careful and reflective study of the material to be presented. Although the study of intrapersonal communication is not always pointed out, it cannot be ignored as an essential element of study in all aspects of speech communication.

Interpersonal Communication. Interpersonal communication occurs when two people recognize the presence of the other and share their thoughts. Interpersonal communication is usually informal and unplanned. The messages are often personal, as when one friend reveals thoughts and feelings to another friend. The messages take the form too of requests for services or information, or of answering the requests of others. Many interpersonal communication techniques have the potential to improve the communication processes that people depend on in fulfilling their day-to-day physical and psychological needs. The many newspaper reports of interpersonal conflicts that eventually result in violence are ample evidence that skill in interpersonal communication is often lacking in American society.

Small Group Communication. Small group communication occurs when several people get together with a specific purpose. The purpose can be social, but often it involves discussion of a particular topic or an attempt to solve a problem. A small group generally forms when meaningful interaction among members occurs because they have something in common. Meaningful interaction in small groups will generally include face-to-face contact, purposeful discussion, a common goal, and an established way of interacting.

Examples of small groups include families, committees in social and work organizations, clubs, and work teams. To be successful, small groups must include people who maintain their individuality while working cooperatively toward achieving group goals. A study of small group communication will reveal information about leadership styles, ways to involve all members of the group, techniques for sharing responsibility, and methods that are useful in reaching conclusions.

Speaker-audience Communication. The presentation of a message to an audience is a more formal situation than interpersonal and small group communication. It generally involves advance preparation and there is little or no verbal interaction between the speaker and audience. The message generally involves a body of material that will be appropriate for a large group of people. The language used to relay the message is more general than it is specific because it must be decoded by a group rather than an individual. It is one speaking situation that permits formulation of thoughts in time to revise and work toward maximizing the effectiveness of the message. There are many specific guidelines available to help the speaker prepare a message for a large audience. Careful preparation in speaker-audience communication increases the chances that the message will be successfully delivered to the listeners.

The communication model can be adapted to fit the four types of encounters. All involve the components illustrated by the model, the major variation being the number of receivers and the extent of feedback. The study of the four types of encounters brings to attention the context variations in speech communication and suggests ways to maximize effectiveness in a variety of situations.

Functions of Communication

The use of speech to communicate evolved first as a survival technique among very early populations of human beings. Today many people take for granted the fulfillment of their most basic needs. According to Abraham Maslow (1954), humans are motivated by the desire to fulfill five levels of basic needs.

1. Physiological—the need for air, water, food, rest, and reproduction of the species.
2. Safety—the need for shelter, clothing, and protection from threats to life and health.
3. Social—the need to belong and to be accepted, appreciated, and loved by others.
4. Self-esteem—the need to respect oneself and be respected by others.
5. Self-actualization—the need to fulfill one's potential and achieve all that is possible.

The more basic needs in Maslow's list must be met before fulfillment of the higher needs can be attempted. Individuals who are concerned about studying and improving speech communication skills have probably achieved adequate physiological and safety needs to survive. They are interested in fulfilling social, self-esteem, or self-actualization needs. Communication will be particularly necessary to gain and give needed information, to persuade or influence others, to consider alternative solutions to problems and make decisions, and for social and entertainment purposes.

Information

To understand and function in the world, human beings must acquire a great store of information. Consider the location of places and things, the procedures for accomplishing specific tasks, and the characteristics of cherished objects and pastimes. Much knowledge is acquired through discovery. Touching a hot flame is one way of acquiring the information that fire burns human skin. Because of the vast quantities of information to be acquired today, however, it is generally more efficient to gain and share information through the written or spoken word—by using the ability to communicate.

Persuasion

Another aspect of contemporary living relates to the influence each person attempts to exert on others. It is important to be able to justify positions and opinions. This does not imply the ability to influence others for personal gain, but rather the ability to supply descriptions of the logic that forms the basis of one's behavior. There are times, too, when personal beliefs lead one to attempt to change the attitudes and values of others. The ability to influence and to judge the influence others exert is an important communication skill. In one word, this important function of communication might be summarized by the term *opinion*.

Decision Making

Decisions are based on knowledge and opinions. The knowledge and opinions that one gathers are often the basis for discussion of alternatives in the decision-making process. An individual's choice of a solution, therefore, depends to a great extent on skill in gathering appropriate information, in evaluating opinions, and in discussing effects of potential solutions. Considering the many decisions facing the individual in contemporary society, communication skill has a tremendous influence on life outcomes.

Entertainment

Last, communication has a social or entertainment function in achieving the fulfillment of human needs. Perhaps skill in this area is not crucial since entertainment is available from the professionals who produce theatre, movies, television, and books. However, greater pleasure is generally gained from such performances when the receiver's ability to decode the message is adequately developed. And nearly everyone interacts at a social level with friends and acquaintances. So again communication skill is an important ingredient in maximizing the benefits of social functions in daily life.

SUMMARY

Communication is the sharing of meaning. To improve one's ability to verbally share meaning with and among others is the goal underlying the study of speech communication. The learning task can be simplified by more fully developing the meaning of the term *communication*. One means of expanding the meaning of communication is to consider and understand the speech communication model, the modes for delivering messages, the types of communication encounters, and the functions of communication in everyday living.

The speech communication model includes the very important concepts of originator, receiver, encoding, decoding, message, feedback, channel, and noise. The three major delivery modes are written, verbal, and nonverbal messages. The media, including newspapers, books, and television, are powerful secondary means for message delivery. The types of communication encounters are intrapersonal, interpersonal, small group, and speaker-audience. Communication serves the functions in everyday living of presenting information, revealing opinions, providing input and discussion for decision making, and creating entertainment.

CHAPTER 2

Language in Communication

Nearly everyone has developed some capacity to communicate verbally with others. Being able to share meaning with others through talking is more or less taken for granted until thought is given to the underlying processes. Just what is it that enables human beings to symbolize meaning and then transmit messages and be understood by others? A brief look at an area of study called language will reveal some of the bases for communication and some of the reasons underlying communication breakdowns.

Language, in very general terms, refers to words and the rules of grammar that determine their usage. A study of language as it relates to speech communication is enhanced by first investigating an area called sensation, then by looking at the relationship of sensation and perception, and finally by noting how language or symbolization depends upon the processes of sensation and perception.

Sensation

Sensation refers to messages sent to the brain via body receptors associated with sight, hearing, touch, smell, and taste. The sensory receptors—the eyes, ears, skin and muscles, nose, and tongue—are the link between the human brain and surrounding environment. The meaning of the messages sent to the brain via the sensory receptors must be learned. One is not born, for example, knowing that the taste of lemon is sour or that the touch of fur is soft.

All the senses contribute to some extent to the speech communication process. Sight transmits nonverbal messages to the brain for interpretation. Since the brain receives approximately two-thirds of its messages from visual stimuli, sight is probably the most important of the five senses. Hearing, of course, transmits verbal messages to the brain for interpretation. Unlike visual messages, where the eye must be directed toward the object, sounds are received from all directions. Smell, touch, and taste sometimes play an important role in the communication process also. Consider, for example, possible messages implied by a strong perfume, a firm handshake, or the taste of salt air at the seashore.

What happens when people find themselves in an environment characterized by a particularly noxious smell (e.g., a chemistry lab after an exercise with sulfur)? At first they are repulsed by the odor, but gradually they become accustomed to the smell and it no longer bothers them. When a newcomer walks into the area, a typical comment might be, "How can you stand this place?" They are able to stand it because of the body's ability to adapt to a constant stimulus. As a stimulus remains the same, fewer and fewer nerve impulses are sent to the brain. The senses of smell and touch more readily adapt to constant stimulation than the other senses. Because the eye is constantly moving, *sensory adaptation* of vision is unlikely.

At any point in time, the body's receptors for sight, sound, touch, smell, and taste are receiving stimulation from many sources. Concentrate, for a moment, on each of your senses—what do you see around you, what are the sounds you can hear, how does your skin feel against your clothes and surrounding objects, are there any distinguishable odors around you, and what tastes are you experiencing? There was probably so much going on around you that you were unaware of most of it. Hopefully you were concentrating on your reading and experienced very little awareness of other stimuli. Focusing on specific aspects of the environment to the exclusion of other aspects is the process of *selective attention*. Fortunately, at least for most people, the neglect of unimportant sensations allows the human mind to focus on and process what is interpreted as the most relevant of the multitude of potential stimuli.

Perception

Sensation and the processes of sensory adaptation and selective attention bring the relevant stimuli from the environment to the brain. What is done with the stimuli and the meanings attached to them is the process of perception. The meanings attached to the stimuli are based on the individual's knowledge, background, and experiences. Thus behavior and the individual's focus on the world are a combination of what occurs in the environment and what has previously occurred within the individual. Further understanding of the perceptual process may be gained by considering some aspects of environment and characteristics of the perceiver that affect perception.

Perception and Environment

To be given meaning, stimuli must be selected, organized, interpreted, and judged. It may be that the chance a given stimulus has to gain mean-

CHAPTER 2　Language in Communication

On Seeing a Policeman

Age 7

Age 14

Age 20

Age 35

Age 50

Age 70

©1974 E.C. Publications, Inc.

ing is similar in probability to the chance a given fish egg has to hatch. Both are dependent on what goes on in the surrounding environment. A dripping faucet, for example, will seldom be heard among the activities of the day. During the quiet of the night it takes on the impact of a steadily beating hammer on a tin roof.

The list below includes a number of factors that affect the chance of a given stimulus to reach the point of being interpreted and judged.

1. Proximity—Stimuli placed closely together are likely to stand out against a less dominant background.
2. Similarity—Stimuli that can be grouped according to some related characteristic will tend to be more dominant than unrelated stimuli.
3. Simplicity—Stimuli that have fewer distinguishing features will tend to be more dominant than those that are quite complex.
4. Closure—Stimuli with gaps that fit into an established pattern will be more dominant than other partial stimuli with no obvious pattern.
5. Intensity—Stimuli that exceed what might be considered the normal range of a stimulus will be more dominant than those within the normal range.
6. Repetition—Stimuli that occur again and again are more likely to become dominant than a single occurrence of a similar stimulus.
7. Change—Stimuli that are new in a somewhat familiar surrounding are more likely to become dominant than whatever preceded them.

The impact of selected stimuli in the perceptual process also depends on their interaction. Seldom does an individual focus attention on a single aspect of a given stimulus. All the senses together react and form a total perceptual experience.

Perception and the Individual

The characteristics of the stimuli themselves affect what is perceived. In addition, the individual's past and present experiences and state of mind affect the interpretation and judgment of stimuli in the perceptual process. It is often said that we see what we want to see. This may be simplified somewhat, but much research has demonstrated that individual perceptions are most certainly related to individual characteristics. Everyone has read about or witnessed different people giving a description of the "same" event. The result is generally as many versions as there are individuals. Perhaps our suspicions should be aroused when two individuals reveal identical accounts of an event!

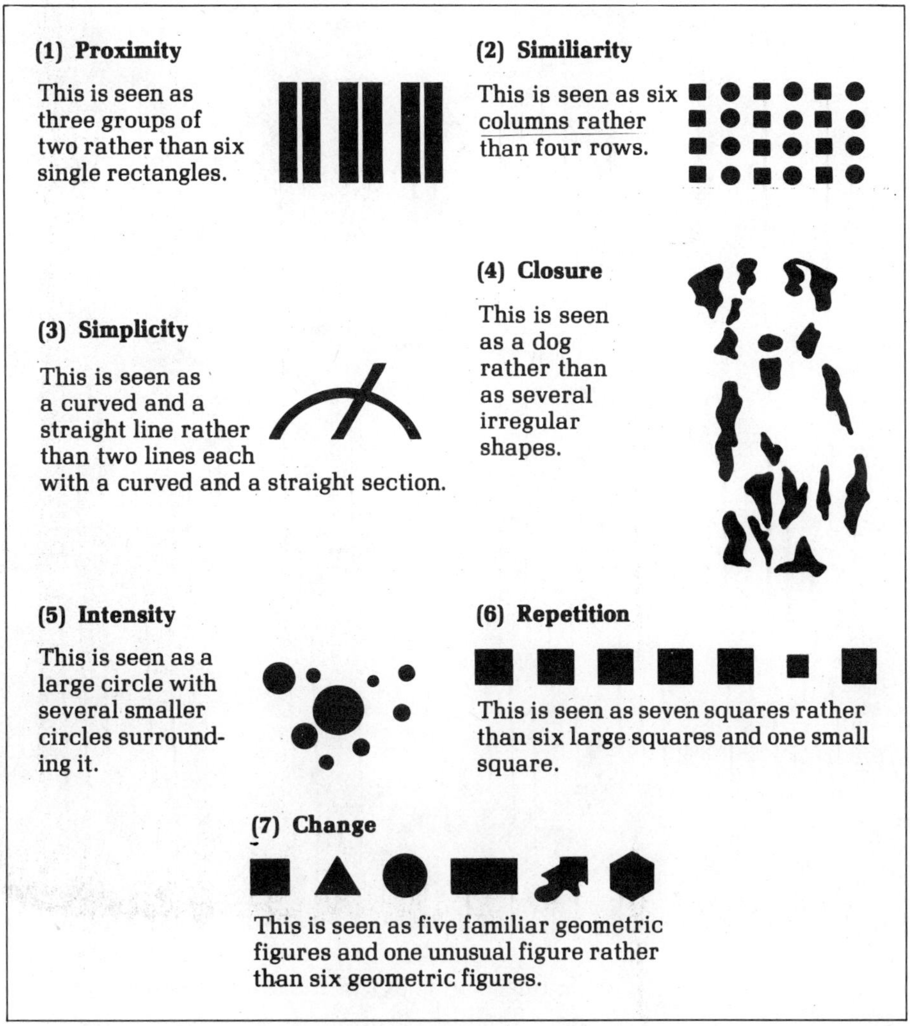

CHAPTER 2   Language in Communication

(1) Proximity
This is seen as three groups of two rather than six single rectangles.

(2) Similarity
This is seen as six columns rather than four rows.

(3) Simplicity
This is seen as a curved and a straight line rather than two lines each with a curved and a straight section.

(4) Closure
This is seen as a dog rather than as several irregular shapes.

(5) Intensity
This is seen as a large circle with several smaller circles surrounding it.

(6) Repetition
This is seen as seven squares rather than six large squares and one small square.

(7) Change
This is seen as five familiar geometric figures and one unusual figure rather than six geometric figures.

Figure 2.1. *Environmental effects on perception.*

Several factors have been shown by researchers to influence an individual's perception of events. These are listed below.

1. Expectancy—Because of prior experience with sets of circumstances that are similar to a set of current circumstances, individuals anticipate what will probably occur and may react according to what is anticipated rather than what is reality. For example, a swimmer ready to begin a race might "jump the gun" at hearing another type of loud noise.
2. Habit—Because of routine ways of reacting to a given stimulus, individuals often fail to perceive subtle differences in a similar

stimulus and react in the way they are accustomed to reacting. For example, even a good student proofing a paper often overlooks misspelled words because of their similarity to the correct spelling.

3. Motive—The dominance of a particular motive will often cause individuals to perceive stimuli associated with fulfilling immediate needs. For example, individuals who become hungry on a motor trip will begin taking notice of signs and other indicators of restaurants and food that would otherwise have been overlooked.

4. Constancy—The world is composed of many features that are uniform. Because of this, individuals automatically adjust a distorted shape to see it as it generally exists. For example, a plate seen from across a table has the shape of an ellipse but would be readily called a circle by most observers.

5. Relativity—Individuals will often categorize stimuli in relation to surrounding stimuli. For example, a basketball player will

seem like a giant among people of average height but will appear normal among teammates.
6. Familiarity—From a group of competing stimuli, individuals are likely to perceive more readily those that they routinely encounter and, therefore, relate to. For example, individuals will readily perceive their own names from among the chatter of a large group of people.

What the individual recognizes from the environment and then interprets is affected by many internal and external factors. The important point to remember, at least in regard to communication, is that people send and react to messages according to their own perspectives, and that many communication breakdowns occur when others make the wrong assumption that everyone sees the world in the same way that they see it.

Extrasensory Perception

Another area of perception that many people find interesting is extrasensory perception, ESP. ESP is the ability to gain information through means that fall outside the realm of scientific law. It includes clairvoyance, knowledge of things that are out of sight; precognition, prediction of future events; and telepathy, the reading of someone else's mind. Most scientists are quite skeptical about extrasensory perception and feel that events attributed to ESP are explainable through coincidence and chance occurrence. Some communicators who are extremely sensitive to their surroundings seem to possess the skills of extrasensory perception. It is likely, however, that such people merely attend to stimuli and perceive their environment with much deeper concentration than the majority of the population.

Language

Language is the use of symbols to convey meaning. Through language humans have been able to make the intellectual, cultural, and technological achievements that set them apart from other animal species. Language provides, as well, the basis for establishing social and emotional ties that are essential for a truly healthy psychological being.

Sensations, primarily sight and sound, allow humans to receive verbal and nonverbal messages from others. Those messages that are perceived are given meaning by the receiver. Verbal messages use language to convey the sender's meaning. To understand language better and to improve speech communication skills, it is useful to consider words, their meanings, the circumstances that influence the ways different people use language, and the acceptable usage of language as a basis for sharing meaning. Finally, several recommendations to facilitate using language to convey thoughts will be presented.

What are Words

Words are the symbols for objects, events, and feelings; they are not the objects, events, and feelings themselves. A problem that occurs in using language is the substitution in an individual's mind of the word for the object, event, or feeling itself. For example, the actual presence of a snake is, perhaps, reason to experience fear. Hearing the word "snake" in the absence of the creature should not cause fear; but it often does.

Words enable humans to translate thoughts and experiences into a form that can be shared with other individuals. What is communicated is based on the combination of words and gestures used to transmit the messages. The words and gestures represent the thought or experience; they are not the thought or experience itself.

Words do create visual images in the minds of both the originator and receiver. The visual image may account for the fear that some people feel when they hear the word snake. For some the visual image is, in effect, the same experience as seeing the object or event itself. Creating strong visual images through verbal communication can be extremely successful as a way of increasing the ability of the receiver to share meaning with the originator of a message. The visual potential of words can create more interesting and successful communication encounters.

Think for a moment of the benefits provided the human race by this amazing ability to use words to represent objects, events, and feelings. Without the symbolic code provided by words conversation would not exist. There would be no way to describe past events or discuss future expectations. Storing memories and experiences would be difficult if not impossible, and transmission of knowledge from generation to generation would probably not exist. Words and their associated visual images, then, enable the human race to describe and represent past, present, and future experiences, thoughts, and expectations.

What is Meaning

Words themselves do not possess meaning. The meanings attached to words exist within the person who is perceiving the words. Many words, in fact, are associated with several meanings, and the same object, event, or feeling may be described in a variety of ways. Words have no meaning until the individuals who use them attach some meaning to them. Each person, through past experiences with a word or combination of words, attaches a unique and personal meaning to every message.

The fact that words do not possess exact meanings common to all communicators is an underlying cause of communication breakdowns. As messages are sent, communicators fail to consider the origin of meaning of the words they select. They fail to consider that the meaning of each word originates in their own experiences with the word in the past. It is unlikely that the receivers of their messages have experienced the same sets of prior experiences with the word. In formulating and interpreting verbal messages, it is important to remember that the same word may

CHAPTER 2   Language in Communication   29

represent more than one thing, that meanings exist within individuals, and that two individuals will often assign different interpretations to the same set of words.

Context, or the interaction of words with one another, is an extremely important way of determining meaning. Context is essential to interpreting words with several meanings, and it is a way to check the meaning that seems to be intended by a message. Many communication

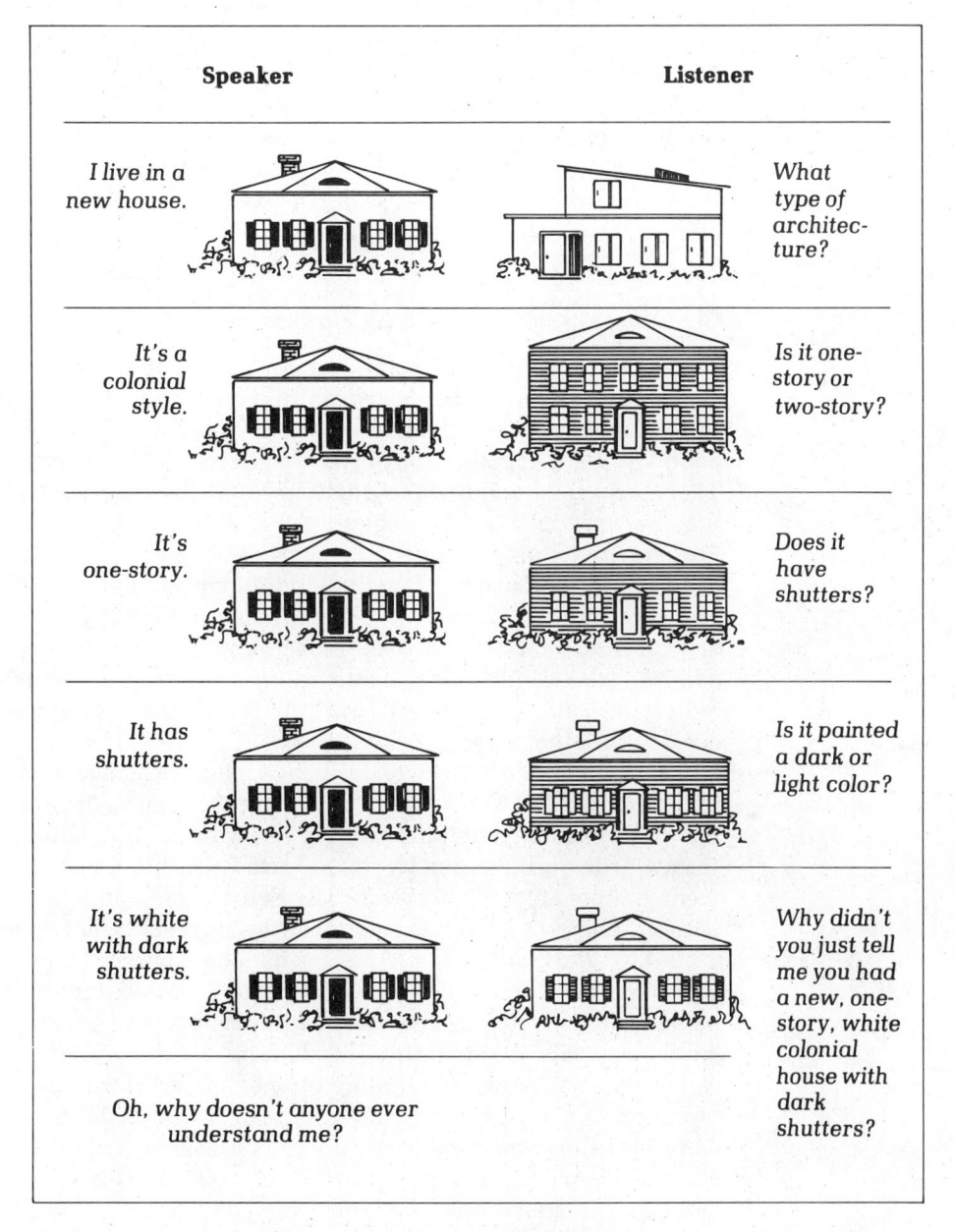

Speaker			Listener
I live in a new house.			What type of architecture?
It's a colonial style.			Is it one-story or two-story?
It's one-story.			Does it have shutters?
It has shutters.			Is it painted a dark or light color?
It's white with dark shutters.			Why didn't you just tell me you had a new, one-story, white colonial house with dark shutters?
Oh, why doesn't anyone ever understand me?			

Figure 2.2. *What is meaning?*

breakdowns occur when words or groups of words are removed from their contexts. This can occur when messages are repeated from person to person, or when the receiver hears a part of the message and then suddenly stops listening.

Another factor to consider in looking at the meanings associated with words is whether the thing represented exists in the real world as well as the mind, or exists only in the mind. For example, the object referred to by the word "table" exists in reality as well as psychologically. It is possible to point at and touch a table. On the other hand, feelings do not exist as actual objects. They exist only within the individual. One cannot locate and see actual objects referred to by words like love, fear, or spirit. Communication breakdown or confusion is more likely to result from words whose meanings exist only internally. Whenever possible, use words that represent concrete objects to add clarity to the communication process.

Circumstances Influencing Language Usage

Language development in the human begins in early infancy. Although cooing and gurgling sounds are emitted earlier, the first words are usually spoken between twelve and eighteen months of age. Young children acquire the language patterns of those with whom they interact. Therefore, they acquire the particulars of their native tongue as well as the characteristics of the region in which they grow up. They acquire certain peculiarities of language that associate them with a particular geographic region. The New England accent of Senator Edward Kennedy and the southern drawl of President Jimmy Carter are very obvious examples of regional variations. More subtle influences are recognized by experts, who notice that one individual "sits in the first row" and another individual "sits on the first row," or that some people use bags for groceries and others use sacks.

A second influence on language usage is socioeconomic position. In fact, many initial impressions of background and education are made on the basis of language, particularly the way the individual uses sounds to form words and chooses words to form thoughts. Eliza Doolittle's change from pauper to aristocrat in *My Fair Lady* could not have occurred without the extensive language training provided by Professor Higgins.

In addition to regional and socioeconomic influences on language, group associations often result in specialized vocabularies and speaking habits. Some occupations, for example, require development of new language skills to understand and to be understood. The use of the CB radio provides a ready example of specialized language skills needed in order to communicate and be accepted in a special group. Not only do words take on new meanings, but verb tenses are modified. Consider the following typical messages heard on the air: "Hey good buddy, how be lookin' over your donkey?" and "Git your hair combed, we got a local takin' pictures and handin' out green stamps."

A fourth influence on language usage is the particular circumstances of each communication encounter. The age, sex, or position of the listener will affect the way the speaker expresses thoughts and feelings. For example, young people often show their respect for an older person by reacting more formally than they would in a similar situation with a peer, and it seems inappropriate to most people to tell dirty jokes to a priest. There are many conventions accepted within subgroups of society concerning what is proper and what is not proper in given situations. As individuals interact interpersonally, in small groups, or with an audience of listeners, their choice of words and use of language is constantly being adapted to provide the most appropriate presentation of the intended message.

A fifth circumstance affecting language usage may be the limitations of the language itself. The Sapir-Whorf hypothesis (Whorf, 1956) was formulated to reflect the notion that our use of concepts to express ourselves is limited to those concepts for which we have words. There are numerous concepts for which words exist in other languages but do not exist in English. For example, one group of people in the Phillippine Islands uses a different name to identify each of ninety-two varieties of rice. To English-speaking people, rice in its raw form is distinguishable in only a few categories by the use of adjectives. Because of its lesser importance to Americans, rice is more or less rice. In contrast, however, consider our vocabulary for describing motor vehicles: coupe, convertible, fastback, pickup, and so on.

Language is a complex system for communicating ideas, thoughts, and feelings to others. Words, with their associated meanings, are the foundation of language, but the ways in which the words are selected and used communicates also. The speaker's native region, background and education, occupation or group membership, the unwritten rules concerning appropriate ways of speaking in given situations, and possibly the limitations of the language itself affect what one individual says and another comprehends.

Acceptable Usage of Language

People are judged by the way they talk. Many inferences, right and wrong, about people are made from their choice and way of saying words. Sophistication of vocabulary, fluency, and the way that words are said can make a powerful impression on the listener. The impression might be one of intelligence, "putting on airs," formality, conscientious preparation, snobbishness, scholarship, and others.

Language is sometimes classified as formal, standard, and slang. Formal language is primarily written or used in professional presentations. It can be found in technical journals, at professional meetings, and in legal reports. Formal language is well organized, follows precisely defined guidelines for preparation, and relies on vocabulary often understood only by members of specific groups. Standard language is the use of language according to generally accepted rules of grammar and pronunciation. It is understood by society as a whole and does nothing to draw particular attention to the speaker. *General American speech* is the term often used to describe the standards of speaking adopted by radio and television announcers, actors, and others with a national image. Slang is primarily language spoken only among persons sharing close personal relationships or common backgrounds. Its use by and clarity for members of specialized groups makes it similar in one way to formal language. Slang is characterized by careless use of language, shortening of words and phrases for ease of speech, and the assignment of new meanings to words considered standard. Consider the following examples of words sharing similar meanings but representing different usage.

Formal	*Standard*	*Slang*
seminar	meeting	get-together
dialogue	conversation	rap session
intoxicants	liquor	booze
error	mistake	goof
theatre	movie	show
residence	home	pad

The different ways of speaking American English within the United States are referred to as dialects. Dialects differ from rules of general American speech in the use of vocabulary, the ways sounds are made and fit together to form words, and the way words fit together to form sentences. There are many dialects in use in the United States. In fact, it might be said that everyone speaks a particular dialect. Examples of obvious dialects include the Southern drawl, Brooklynese, urban Black, and Hispanic influence of Mexican, Puerto Rican, and Cuban cultures. When used in situations where meaning is shared adequately between originator and receivers, dialects cannot be judged as inferior modes of speaking. The difficulty with dialects is that they impair communication when spoken among persons unfamiliar with their use. Not only is meaning lost, but inappropriate impressions of intelligence and individual worth are often made. A speaker's dialect often leads to negative stereotyping by the receiver.

Whether to learn and use the rules of general American speech is an individual decision. Individuals must evaluate goals and determine the audiences with whom they plan to interact. If it appears that messages will be directed toward a broad cross section of American society, then mastery of general American speech will be important. General American speech, as defined by dictionaries and handbooks of grammar, is probably the most common basis for communication in the mobile society of today and will be understood more readily by a cross section of society. Whatever the situation, to maximally share meaning, it is important to realize that individual cultural, social, and economic differences can cause mistaken meaning, or even no meaning, to be attached to a given message by a specific receiver.

Considerations in the Use of Language

In considering individual differences in sensation, perception, and language, it almost seems as if communication among individuals could not exist. Somehow it does and considering everything, it works quite well. There are problems in communication, however, that can often be overcome by careful choice of the best combination of words to represent a message. Eight guidelines for the use of language to convey meaning are given below.

1. Use feedback to check the accuracy of interpretation. This is important to sender and receiver. As sender, pay special attention to the feedback the receiver provides. As receiver, provide feedback that will give the sender an indication of your understanding.
2. Do not react reflexively to what you hear. Remember that words are not the actual objects, events, or feelings, and that meanings given to words are unique within each individual.
3. Remember that you do not know everything there is to know. The message you are receiving may not relate to your prior experience and knowledge. You may need to request additional information to attach personal significance to the message.
4. Keep in mind that situations change. As you send and receive messages, be aware that the prior experiences on which you are basing your descriptions and interpretations might have become invalid.
5. Use context to substantiate the intended message. Many words in the English language have several meanings and many words sound very much like others. As speaker, do not assume the listener is aware of the context: provide the context. As listener, pay attention to context as a means of checking your interpretation of the message.
6. Avoid extreme reactions to messages. Often it is easier to interpret a given message and react as if it were a "yes-no" situation. A less extreme reaction will often more accurately reflect your true perception as well as avoid communication breakdown.
7. Remember that communication is more accurate between two persons sharing common experiences. Therefore, communication is clearer when words are selected that will make sense to the listener. Communication breakdown will be less likely to occur when messages are clear and relevant to the receiver.
8. Avoid intentional distortion of messages. Some communicators are creative enough to manipulate words meaning one thing into thoughts meaning something else. Such use of language is dishonest and really cannot be called communication.

Language is essential to the way our world operates. Misunderstandings are often humorous but can be disastrous. When accurate communication is the goal, it is necessary to consider how the listener will react to the symbols used to transmit the message. It is unwise to assume that symbols will be understood as intended.

SUMMARY

The meaning given to the words used to communicate a thought or feeling is based on the entire set of reactions that occur in the receiver's mind. The meaning is based on the sensations of sight, sound, touch, taste, and smell that reach the receiver's brain. It is based on how the selected sensations are perceived, that is, how the receiver uses experience and knowledge to organize, interpret, and judge the sensations. The basis for understanding is language, or the use of symbols, both verbal and nonverbal, that represent specific objects, events, or feelings.

Communication breakdowns or confusion often occur when the receiver's interpretation of the words used to convey a message is different from the originator's intention. To communicate effectively, both originators and receivers must realize that no two people, no matter how similar their backgrounds, will ever assign exactly the same meaning to a given set of symbols. To communicate effectively, it is important to keep in mind individual differences in the reception of stimuli, in the perception of the interacting stimuli that reach the brain, and in the unique interpretations given to the words of the common language.

CHAPTER 3

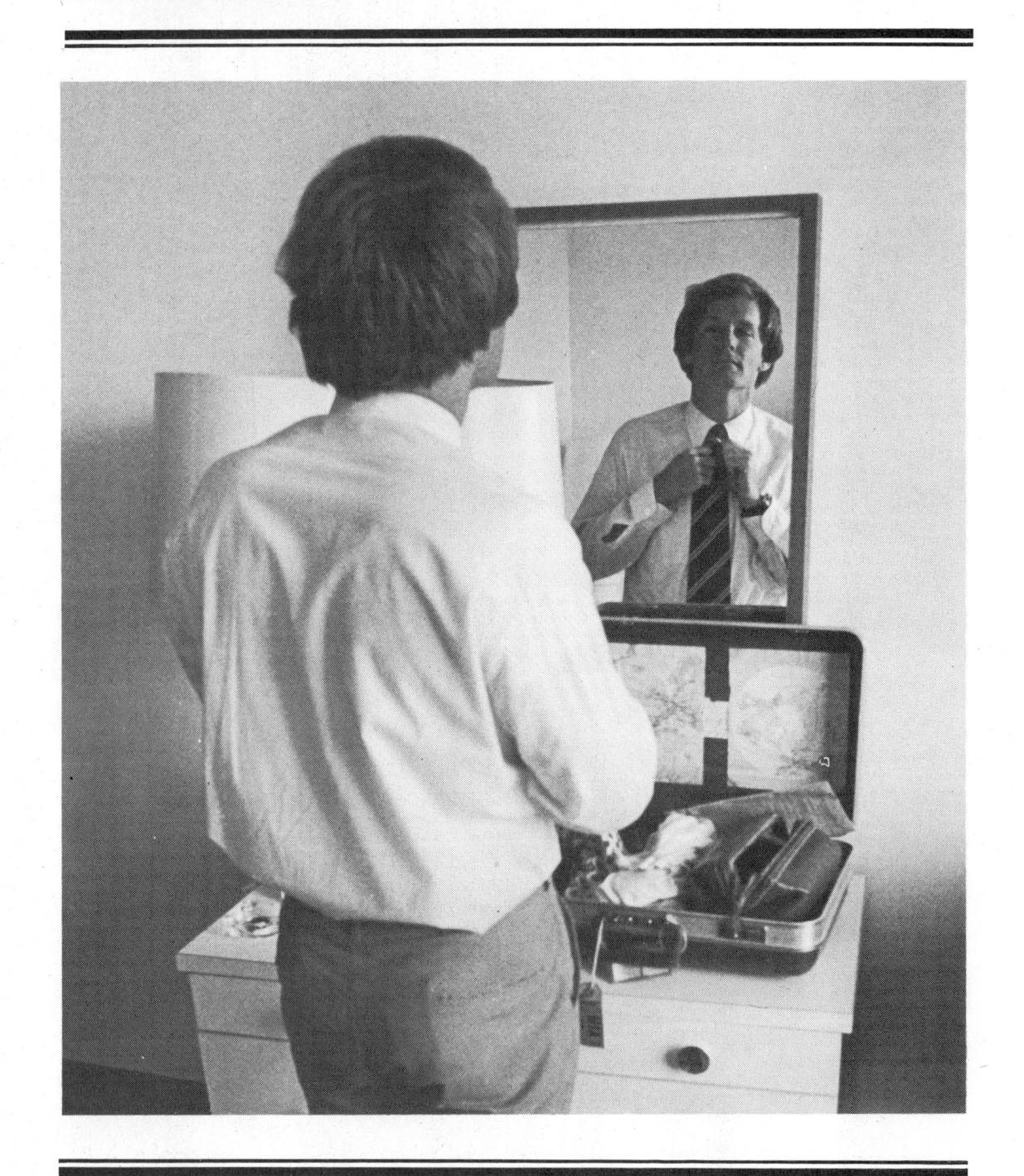

Perception of Self in Communication

The communication process is based on the perceptions of the originators and receivers of messages. These perceptions include stimulation of the sensory receptors for hearing, seeing, tasting, smelling, and touching, as well as the background, experiences, and knowledge composing the communicator's perception of self. Perception of self includes the feelings people have about themselves and the feelings they think others have about them.

After the basic sensory processes, perception of self may be the most important aspect of the communication process. When two persons are communicating, there may be as many as six perceptions of self interacting. Consider for a moment the various perceptions of self diagrammed below, (Barnlund, 1962).

	You		*Other Person*
1.	Your image of the other person	4.	Other person's image of you
2.	Your image of yourself	5.	Other person's image of self
3.	Your impression of the other person's image of you	6.	Other person's impression of your image of him or her

The communication process, as complicated as it may seem, is facilitated when the communicators have accurate impressions of their own self-images. When a clear impression of self exists it is easier to concentrate on the messages being sent and received. Speculation about others' impressions diminishes considerably, and feelings of greater confidence generally exist within the individual. Persons who have accurate and clear perceptions of self will be able to do the best they can with the abilities and characteristics they possess. Number 2 above is probably the most important of the six perceptions.

Figure 3.1. *Perceptions of self.*

It can be a difficult task to analyze one's own self-image. It is probably worthwhile, however, as a part of the process of working toward improvement of communication skill. To assist the process of personal image clarification, it is useful to examine more fully the meaning of self-concept, to contrast self-confidence as a communicator with defensiveness, to review the effect of credibility as it affects the sharing of meaning, and to explore the relationship of intrapersonal communication and self-concept.

Self-Concept

Self-concept is your idea of who you are and what you are. It is much more than name, age, occupation, marital status, eye color, height, and so forth. It is a combination of physical features, intellectual abilities, style of establishing and maintaining relationships, way of expressing thoughts and opinions, selections of clothing and other personal property, and everything else that makes one person unique and distinguishable from every other.

Self-concept begins developing as the infant becomes aware of the world and begins interacting with significant others in the surrounding environment. It is formulated primarily by successes and failures in different types of experiences, by the types of feedback received from others, and by perception of the various roles and behaviors that are expected. The determination of feelings and worth begins early in life but can be modified and even changed radically throughout life.

Self-concept is sometimes measured along a line that is called negative at one end and positive at the other. In theory at least, the many factors contributing to self-concept can be analyzed and, in a sense, weighed to determine where on the line from negative to positive an individual's overall self-concept falls. This is a useful measure. An important point to consider, however, is that nearly everyone possesses some negative and some positive feelings about specific aspects of self-concept. Even the most confident persons harbor some self-doubt; even the most downtrodden individuals should be able to identify something positive about themselves. Before taking a serious look at your own self-concept, a review of information about public versus private self, the self-fulfilling prophecy, and the effect of self-concept on communication might prove helpful.

Public versus Private Self

Each individual has a self that is presented to others and a self that remains hidden from others: the public and private selves. Differing public and private selves may be exemplified by the attitudes towards housecleaning and guests that many families seem to hold. Many individuals present a public image of pride in a neat and orderly home; yet their private image allows for some clutter and disorderliness. The public image is often a combination of the private image and the role the individual is playing in a given situation.

In addition to the public and private selves, there are parts of the self that are known and other parts that are unknown. For example, an individual might be quite aware of a dialect representing a specific regional upbringing, but be totally unaware of habitually coughing before saying something. It is hard to admit or even to realize that there are some aspects of self that are unknown to the individual, but it is probably true.

By combining the public and private selves with the known and unknown selves, a model for analyzing self-concept can be developed. The model, called the Johari Window (Luft, 1969), is shown in the following diagram. The name of the model, Johari Window, comes from the names of the two men who developed the concept, Joseph Luft and Harry Ingham. The four parts of the Johari Window are more fully described below.

1. The *open* section refers to the image that is revealed to others and known by self. Examples of the open section include pride in housekeeping, leisure activities that are selected, profession entered, topics chosen for conversation, and dress selected for special occasions.
2. The *hidden* section refers to those things known to self but not revealed to others. Allowing some disorderliness when no guests are expected is an example of the hidden section. Other examples include writing letters instead of taking notes during a lecture, being friendly to someone you dislike, and accepting committee assignments with a false display of enthusiasm.
3. The *blind* section refers to those aspects of self that are revealed to others but remain unknown to self. Some examples include always coughing before speaking, having a rip in the back of your pants, and feeling confident in a situation where others find you to be inadequate.
4. The *unknown* section refers to those aspects of self that are unknown to both self and others. Reactions to events never occurring in prior experience would comprise the majority of examples. Filling the gas tank at a self-service station for the first time, giving your first public speech, and confronting a dishonest friend are examples of the unknown self.

	Known to Self	Not Known to Self
Known to Others	Open	Blind
Not Known to Others	Hidden	Unknown

Figure 3.2. *Johari window.*

By analyzing what is known and by trying to learn some things that are currently unknown, the self-concept can be studied. Ideally, the open section of the model will grow as one learns more about self and is able to share this knowledge with others. The open section will become more honest, as well, as the individual accepts those facets that were once hidden. A more honestly revealed and a clearly conceived self-concept is described by the following diagram.

Open	Blind
Hidden	Unknown

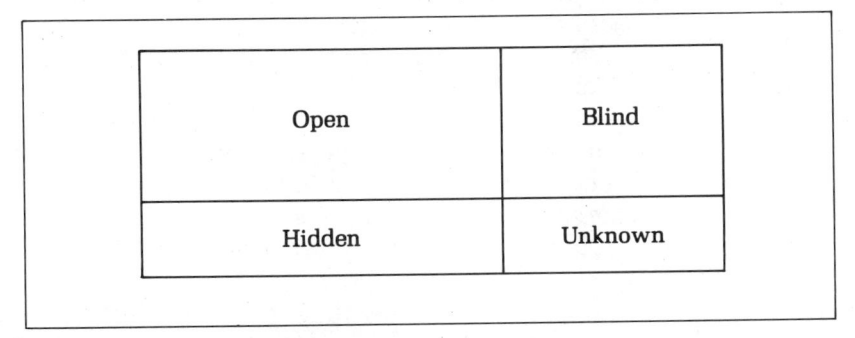

Figure 3.3. *Johari window.*

With different individuals and in different situations, the division of area in the various sections may change. Certainly differences would occur in the size of the open section in conversation with a lifelong friend as compared to conversation with a total stranger. This is to be expected. Generally speaking, however, communication is more successful when both individuals have large "open" areas in their Johari Windows and are able to reveal honest information and avoid role-playing behaviors. One possible contribution to noise in the communication channel (i.e., the hidden self) is thus significantly reduced.

Self-Fulfilling Prophecy

Often individuals will think ahead to possible outcomes of future events. The expectation may be positive—doing well on a test, having fun at a party, or creating interest among the audience for a public speech. Or the expectation may be negative—blowing an important job interview, having a miserable evening with family members, or disliking the food and service at a new restaurant. The expectation often results in behavior that makes the outcome more likely to occur. Confidence in knowledge learned for a test may reduce test anxiety significantly and, therefore, make that high grade more probable. Nervousness about an important interview may mask true potential and make an otherwise promising candidate appear incompetent. The expectation and the resulting increased likelihood of its occurrence is known as the self-fulfilling prophecy.

The self-fulfilling prophecy works in two ways. First, perception of self may result in behavior on the part of the individual that influences outcomes. The preceding examples typify this effect. The self-fulfilling prophecy may occur also when others' perceptions of individuals influence outcomes. This commonly occurs when labels are attached to individuals by significant others. For example, average children may progress slowly in school because they have been told they are slow learners; or a beautiful young woman, having been teased and taunted for years because of braces on her teeth, may perceive herself as ugly. Outcomes, then, may be significantly influenced by the individual's perception of self as well as others' implied perceptions of the individual.

The self-fulfilling prophecy is helpful when it works in positive ways. Consideration of potential negative outcomes can be an important means of changing the direction of events that depend very heavily on the expectations and attitudes of those involved. The effect of self-fulfilling prophecy on communication is significant. Preconceived ideas that an interpersonal relationship, a small group activity, or a public speech would go well or poorly will often contribute to the outcome.

Effects of Self-Concept on Communication

Two effects of self-concept on communication have just been discussed: the importance of openness in facilitating the communication process, and the role of expectations in affecting outcomes in communication encounters. In addition, there are some general characteristics that seem to be associated with communication experiences of individuals possessing healthy positive self-concepts.

A positive self-concept or lack of it has a direct effect on both verbal and nonverbal communication. Fear can cause the vocal pitch to rise, the body to shake, the hands to get clammy, the knees to knock, and the stomach to churn. Fearful individuals are hesitant to speak out before an audience or in a group, and often stammer or speak incessantly in conversation.

Persons with positive self-concepts act differently. Although sometimes hesitant in new situations, they gradually begin to feel relaxed, to find ways to participate, and to enjoy themselves. Self-accepting persons participate in life. They are objective, spontaneous, and emotionally and intellectually honest. They do not brood about lost opportunities, lost causes, errors, and failures. They profit from mistakes and try to do things differently in the future.

Persons with positive self-concepts have their own values and principles, which they are willing to defend even in the face of strong opposition, but they are secure enough to modify their ideas if new evidence suggests a better way. They are capable of acting on their own judgment even when others disapprove. Persons with strong self-concepts see themselves as equals, not as inferior or superior persons. They realize that they are of value to other people. To be an effective communicator in speaker-audience, small group, interpersonal, and probably even intrapersonal situations, it is important to feel good about oneself.

Self-Confidence versus Defensiveness

Perception of self influences behavior in nearly every situation. From perception of self comes an individual's feelings about what can and cannot be accomplished. These feelings about the potential for success versus failure in a situation can be called self-confidence. Whether an individual will take a flying leap off the diving tower of the campus pool is dependent to a large extent on confidence in survival. Applying for jobs, meeting new people, or volunteering for a special task are all based on self-confidence or perception of ability to meet the challenge. Because nearly every aspect of living involves some form of communication, self-confidence plays an important role in communication. To assess the importance of self-confidence, a look at defensive behaviors and ways of improving self-concept is useful.

Defensiveness

Defensive behavior, a way of covering up inadequacies, often arises when self-confidence is low. Just as the word implies, it is a way of defending or protecting oneself when seemingly under attack. It is a means of justifying behavior perceived to be inadequate in a given situation and, therefore, eliminating any threat to self-concept. Defensive behaviors, then, result from the degree of confidence perceived appropriate by the individual for a given situation. They are a way to distort reality so that it appears to be congruent with the perceived self-image the individual holds in that situation.

The problem with defensive behaviors is their detrimental effect on the communication process. They add noise to the communication process and make sending and receiving messages either difficult or impossible. Defensive behaviors involve either avoidance or attack. In avoidance the individual "flees the enemy" by withdrawing from or ignoring the situation. In attacking, the individual finds a way to threaten the other individual's self-concept. Some common defensive behaviors are described below.

1. Fantasy—To avoid facing a threatening situation, we dream of an unreal world that is more pleasing.
2. Repression—Instead of accepting a situation that seems threatening, we ignore it.
3. Apathy—Rather than face a threatening situation, we pretend that it does not matter.
4. Helplessness—Rather than admit that a task or situation may be difficult for us, we avoid it by concluding that it is impossible.
5. Compensation—We may perform some action in an attempt to make up for a shortcoming, or to draw attention away from it.
6. Rationalization—To avoid accepting the truth about an inade-

quacy, we create an explanation that makes it appear acceptable.
7. Verbal Aggression—To avoid a threatening situation, we sometimes draw attention from ourselves by verbalizing another's apparent or contrived shortcomings.
8. Displacement—Rather than face the individual who threatens our self-concept, we turn our hostility toward another individual or object that we feel will be less harmful.

Defensive behaviors are sometimes healthy. There are times when the self-concept must be protected in one of the above ways. In general however, it is probably more productive for the communicator to attempt to reduce such behaviors.

Improving Self-Concept

One way to reduce the avoidance and attacking behaviors associated with defensiveness is to develop and maintain a strong self-concept. When changes in self-concept are desirable, there must be a certain amount of analysis and knowledge to determine realistic personal goals. In addition, the will to work toward the desired objective must exist. It may not be an easy task to replace long-established negative self-images with more positive images. In evaluating progress, it may be more rewarding to judge gains made toward a goal rather than to make success or failure dependent on achieving the goal itself.

A certain amount of self analysis is required to determine areas of self-concept that are inaccurately perceived. It is important for individuals to have realistic expectations of what they are able to do. Negative aspects of self-concept are often the result of setting expectations too high. It is important, too, to have accurate perceptions of self. Many competent individuals have negative self-images, not from inadequacies, but because of inability to make clear and accurate judgments of their own worth. A boost in self-concept might result from a more realistic judgment of self.

Feedback is a good way to determine the reliability of self-perception. Feedback from others that is always more positive than personal perceptions is a good indicator that personal perceptions have been unrealistically low. To develop a positive self-concept it is important to interact as often as possible with others. Through interaction with others feedback about behavior is readily acquired. Most people are striving for praise and recognition. Those with positive self-concepts realize that they may not always receive praise in situations involving communication. They are not destroyed by this realization and often try repeatedly to achieve important personal goals. Self-concept can be realistically built by attending to the comments on actions, ideas, beliefs, and mannerisms received from others.

Self-Confidence

No matter where on the continuum of ability an individual falls in regard to a specific task or situation, a realistic yet positive self-concept will result in self-confidence. Self-confidence is knowing what can be done and then giving it a good try. A negative self-concept distorts reality and can result in inaccurate decisions about what should and should not be attempted. Failures can result because no attempt was made, or because there was little chance of accomplishing a given task.

Just as no one has a totally positive and perfect self-concept, no one is totally self-confident in every situation. There will be times when individuals with generally positive self-concepts feel a lack of confidence in a given situation. Yet a person who is self-accepting will experience a minimum of such situations, and approach even difficult situations with as much confidence as possible. Self-confidence in communication encounters can be improved by experience. Often it takes only one successful experience to alleviate the self-doubt that produced anxiety and possibly even avoidance in the past.

Credibility in Communication

In all communication it is extremely important that listeners perceive the speaker as believable. If for some reason the speaker is perceived as untrustworthy, the intended message will be distorted as it is decoded by the listener. A speaker's goal is to transmit a specific message to another person. A listener is not likely to place much value in messages from speakers who are disliked, distrusted, or disbelieved.

The confidence of the listener in what a speaker has to say is termed credibility. It is the believability of a message in a given situation. The speaker must have an accurate perception of self and listener characteristics if credibility is to be maximized. An analysis of listener qualities and expectations allows the speaker to present a message in a way that will seem credible. Credibility is important in both informative and persuasive communication situations. Listeners find it hard to accept information from speakers who do not seem knowledgeable about what they are saying. Likewise, it is difficult to convince others of an opinion if they lack trust in the speaker.

Credibility can be maximized by considering the perception by the listener of the speaker's character, competence, and composure. Character refers to the personal characteristics a speaker represents. Sincerity, honesty, and reliability are especially important for establishing credibility. Competence refers to the authority, wisdom, and knowledge demonstrated when a speaker communicates. To establish credibility, it is important to be accurate, to document information with other sources, and to quote trustworthy sources. Composure refers to the speaker's ability to appear confident. Speakers will be more readily accepted by listeners if they are able to project an image of enthusiasm and poise in speaking style. Ability to be credible is tied very closely to both self-concept and self-confidence. To be sincere, accurate, and enthusiastic in presenting a message to one other, a small group, or a large audience, it is important for speakers to perceive themselves as projecting a credible image.

Intrapersonal Communication and Self-Concept

Intrapersonal communication refers to the conversations speakers have with themselves. In developing communication skills, the self-analysis that is required involves intrapersonal communication. Individuals can take courses and read books about communication to no avail. Unless they deal with their own speaking strengths and weaknesses they are wasting their time. Positive change in communication skill takes, rather it requires, application of the content and skills to personal habits and characteristics. Knowing what self-fulfilling prophecy means is not the same as realizing how self-fulfilling prophecy affects behavior. Your attempt to understand how you react to situations where preconceived outcomes may affect behavior requires intrapersonal communication.

As you consider your self-concept through the process of intrapersonal communication, try to look at yourself as if you were outside your body. You may discover habits and speech patterns that are comfortable but not necessarily effective. Change, if you realize its necessity, is never easy because it involves the risks of disappointment and failure. Becoming an effective communicator is likely to require determination, perseverance, discipline, and effort—intrapersonally. It depends on the person and how important the desire to improve communication skills becomes. It requires conversations within the individual and the setting of unique personal goals.

To become a more effective communicator, capitalize on your strengths but identify your weaknesses. You may have to convince yourself to discard negative perceptions of self resulting from past experiences. You will need to expose yourself to new situations in spite of the risks they might involve. Let the self-fulfilling prophecy work in your favor by considering positive outcomes and projecting a positive image. In formal speaking situations, this may require some preparation and practice; in more informal speaking exchanges, this may require new reactions to familiar situations.

Increasing your self-awareness or developing a positive self-concept is the most vital result of intrapersonal communication. To become an effective communicator, you must do more than learn what it takes to organize a speech, improve your listening skills, work in small groups, and react effectively in interpersonal situations—you must involve yourself in the process. It means taking a close look at the way you see yourself. It means many intrapersonal communication encounters.

SUMMARY

The communication situation is affected by the perceptions and expectations of all concerned. Participants bring their own values and attitudes to the situation. Further, the physical states of participants affect their role in the communication situation. And self-concept, the way individuals feel about themselves, is a critical factor in the communication experience.

Self-concept is determined by the value individuals place on their own worth. This value affects what is said and how things are said in one-to-one situations, small group discussions, and even speaker-audience situations. A clear perception of self often leads to greater openness and self-confidence in communication situations. There is less distortion from defensive behaviors, and speaker credibility can be established more easily and effectively. Success as a communicator depends to a very great extent on intrapersonal communication—the application of the knowledge and skills to the behavioral patterns of the individual.

Activity 1
Information about Communication

Preparation: Read Part I: Communication Defined. Prepare yourself for a test by reviewing the "Knowledge Objective" included in the Overview for Part I and by answering the practice items given below.

PRACTICE ITEMS FOR PART I

Instructions: Select the best answer for each item.

1. The originator of a message becomes aware that the message was received through
    a. noise
    b. transmission
    c. decoding
    d. feedback
2. The communication model includes
    a. visual, audio, and written components
    b. originator, message, and receiver
    c. content, organization, and delivery
    d. sensation, perception, and language
3. A communication encounter including eight to ten persons would be called
    a. intrapersonal
    b. interpersonal
    c. small group
    d. speaker-audience
4. The basic need to belong and to be accepted, appreciated, and loved by others is called
    a. safety
    b. social
    c. self-actualization
    d. communication
5. What process has occurred when a noxious (i.e., bad) odor no longer appears unpleasant?
    a. selective attention
    b. tactile stimulation
    c. perceptual breakdown
    d. sensory adaptation

Activity 1 continued

6. The use of knowledge, background, and experience to give meaning to sight, sound, taste, smell, and touch is called
   a. perception
   b. sensation
   c. language
   d. intelligence
7. Symbols used in the communication process to represent objects, events, and feelings are called
   a. meanings
   b. feedback
   c. words
   d. messages
8. The term "self-concept" refers to the ways people
   a. describe others' feelings
   b. perceive themselves
   c. view the world
   d. achieve long-term goals
9. What is the name for the seemingly undesirable behaviors that occur as a means of protecting the self-concept?
   a. defensive
   b. perceptual
   c. aggressive
   d. intrapersonal
10. Credibility is a concept in communication that refers to the
    a. similarity of attitudes held by speaker and listener
    b. ability of speakers to convince listeners of their views
    c. clarity of language used by the speaker
    d. believability and trustworthiness of what a speaker says

Key: 1.d 2.b 3.c 4.b 5.d 6.a 7.c 8.b 9.a 10.d

Group Activity: Attend class and complete objective test items for Part I: Communication Defined.

Individual Activity: Make arrangements with your instructor to complete objective test items for Part I: Communication Defined.

Activity 2
Speech Communication Skills Inventory

Preparation: As you begin your study of speech communication, you have a set of feelings about your present skill in various speaking situations. It is an interesting exercise to record these initial feelings and to compare them to your feelings about your speech communication skills at the end of the the course.

For each statement below, rate yourself as you feel at this moment. Indicate your feelings by circling the appropriate number to the left of the statement.

    1 = very strong   2 = strong   3 = don't know   4 = weak   5 = very weak

Think carefully and be honest with yourself. These results are for you alone.

1.   1 2 3 4 5   I feel good about myself when meeting people.
2.   1 2 3 4 5   I feel adequate when I talk to people.
3.   1 2 3 4 5   I project a positive self-image.
4.   1 2 3 4 5   I use words that are well suited to my listener.
5.   1 2 3 4 5   I use correct grammar.
6.   1 2 3 4 5   I find the right words to express my thoughts.
7.   1 2 3 4 5   I use natural gestures when speaking.
8.   1 2 3 4 5   I understand nonverbal feedback from others.
9.   1 2 3 4 5   I look at people when I talk to them.
10.   1 2 3 4 5   I give others a chance to speak.
11.   1 2 3 4 5   I listen attentively to what others have to say.
12.   1 2 3 4 5   I say words clearly when I speak.
13.   1 2 3 4 5   I am comfortable in conversations with others.
14.   1 2 3 4 5   I let others know my true feelings.
15.   1 2 3 4 5   I consider the feelings of others.
16.   1 2 3 4 5   I am open in considering others' opinions.
17.   1 2 3 4 5   I am comfortable admitting that I don't understand.

Activity 2 continued

18.   1 2 3 4 5   I contribute when I participate in small groups.
19.   1 2 3 4 5   I work well in group activities.
20.   1 2 3 4 5   I am relaxed when I give a speech.
21.   1 2 3 4 5   I hold the audience's attention when I give a speech.
22.   1 2 3 4 5   I am able to write an organized speech.
23.   1 2 3 4 5   I am able to convince others to accept my opinion.
24.   1 2 3 4 5   I use evidence to back up what I say.
25.   1 2 3 4 5   I appear to know what I am talking about.

Group and Individual Activities: The statements above can be viewed in one sense as general goals for speech communication improvement. You probably discovered some areas where you feel weaker than others. Keep these in mind as you attempt to improve your communication skills.

Another copy of the Communication Skills Inventory will be included as a final course activity. Make it your goal to gain confidence as you study speech communication skills.

Activity 3
Getting to Know Your Listeners

Preparation: Prepare yourself to make a number of new acquaintances. Your classmates will be your listeners as you practice and learn speaking skills in the contexts of interpersonal, small group, and speaker-audience communication. Getting acquainted with each of your classmates often makes the task of practicing new communication skills easier and more enjoyable.

Group Activity:

Option 1 — Introducing Yourself
Form a large circle including everyone in the class. As a part of the circle, you will introduce yourself four times. During the first time around the circle, state your name and your present or planned occupation. The next time around the circle, give your name and your favorite leisure activity. Next, give your name and the reason you enrolled in the speech communication course. Finally, give your name preceded by an adjective beginning with the same letter as your first name.

Example: Nancy Falk, insurance adjuster
Nancy Falk, tennis
Nancy Falk, requirement for graduation
"Noble" Nancy Falk

As a final part of the activity, rotate around the circle again. When it is your turn, give the adjective and first name of each of your classmates.

Option 2 — Introducing a Classmate
Form groups of two by pairing with people you have not known previously. Include the instructor, too. During the next twenty minutes take turns interviewing each other. As interviewer, ask questions to get to know your partner. Try to learn at least three unique things about the interviewee. The following ideas could be used.

1. What is something in which you take pride (e.g., making the debate team)?
2. Who are the three most important people in your life?
3. What two activities do you like to do best when money is no object?
4. What are two things that you would like people to remember about you?
5. What would you do if given a gift of $100,000?

Prepare to introduce your partner to the group by giving your partner's name and several of the unique characteristics you discovered.

Activity 3 continued

After completing the interviews, form a large circle including everyone in the class. When it is your turn, introduce your partner to the group.

Individual Activity: Before, during, or after class, introduce yourself to your classmates. As your classmates introduce themselves to you, write down their names, present or planned occupations, favorite leisure activities, and the reasons they enrolled in the speech communication course. Learn all their names so you will begin to become well acquainted with your classmates.

Activity 4
Why Study Speech Communication

Preparation: Why did you enroll in a speech communication course? Was it a requirement for your degree program? Or is it an elective selected for its personal growth potential? Now that you are enrolled, what do you want to accomplish in regard to your intrapersonal, interpersonal, small group, and speaker-audience communication skills?

Consider the questions listed below. What do you specifically plan to do to improve your communication skills in each of these areas? Briefly write out your expectations.

1. In what ways do you expect your study of speech communication to help your understanding of yourself (i.e., your intrapersonal communication)?

2. In what ways do you expect your study of speech communication to help you as a social being (i.e., interpersonally)?

3. In what ways do you expect your study of speech communication to improve your ability to make more accurate perceptions of events?

4. In what ways do you expect your study of speech communication to improve your use of symbols (i.e., language) to send messages at each of the four levels of communication?
    a. Intrapersonally—
    b. Interpersonally—
    c. Small Group—
    d. Speaker-Audience—

5. In what ways do you expect your study of speech communication to help you improve your self-concept?

6. In what ways do you expect your study of speech communication to help you improve your credibility as a speaker?

Group Activity: During class discuss what you expect to gain from your study of speech communication. Refer to your answers given for the questions above. Through the discussion, formulate some specific goals you hope to achieve. To express your goals, modify, add to, or delete from the answers you gave above. Save your answers to these questions. At the end of the course, examine your progress in reaching your goals in each of the areas.

Activity 4 continued

Individual Activity: Discuss your answers to the above questions with your instructor. Through discussion, formulate some specific goals you hope to achieve. To express your goals, modify, add to, or delete from the answers you gave above. Save your answers to these questions. At the end of the course, examine your progress in reaching your goals in each of the areas.

Activity 5
Sensation

Preparation: People view the world and what is in it from their own points of view. Many communication problems occur because people forget that differences exist. They forget to see the world through the eyes of others and not just their own.

There are many physiological factors that shape perception. To demonstrate individual differences in regard to the senses, locate items representing pleasant and unpleasant examples of each of the following categories: taste, smell, sound, sight, and touch.

Group Activity: Divide into five groups prior to the day of the group activity. Each group will be assigned a "sense" and will be responsible for bringing items to class representing pleasant and unpleasant examples of their assigned sense. To provide a variety of examples to share, each individual should bring both a pleasant and unpleasant example. Those in the taste group should be certain that the examples are in forms that all class members can experience (e.g., bring one peppermint candy per student). One member of the sound group should bring enough cotton balls for each class member to have two. To avoid overlap of examples, discuss what each group member will try to bring. When all students have brought examples to class, discuss the various senses one by one. As each item is passed around the class, consider how your impression of pleasant and unpleasant sensations differs from those of others. Discuss the following questions after experiencing each group of examples.

1. Taste — your sense of taste may differ from that of your classmates.
    a. Which items did you like to taste?
    b. Which items did you dislike?
    c. Did the items taste sweet, sour, bitter, or salty?
    d. Did any of the examples seem to have no taste at all?
2. Smell — what is true of taste is often true for smell. Smells pleasing to one person can be disagreeable to someone else. Consider the many perfumes, for example, and the variety of fragrances available.
    a. Which items did you find pleasing to smell?
    b. Which items did you enjoy smelling least?
    c. What other odors do you find pleasing and displeasing?
    d. Was there agreement among the group as to odors that were liked and disliked?
3. Sound — continue the discussion of sensation by examining again the examples of sound. First, however, have everyone place cotton balls in their ears. After

Activity 5 continued

experiencing the various sounds again, remove the cotton balls and discuss the following questions.
   a. Which sounds did you find pleasant?
   b. Which sounds did you find irritating?
   c. Has increased noise in today's world caused you to hear fewer pleasing sounds?
   d. What effect does hearing loss have on the communication process?
4. Sight — people who have uncorrected vision problems probably experience great difficulty relying on sight as a part of the communication process.
   a. Which objects were visually the most pleasant to you?
   b. Which objects were visually the least pleasant?
   c. How would people with sight problems react to the objects?
   d. What is your impression of the effect of poor vision on communication?
5. Touch — consider differences in reaction to the feel of different objects.
   a. Which objects were the most pleasant to touch?
   b. Which objects were the least pleasant to touch?
   c. What effect does touch have in an interpersonal communication encounter?
   d. What effect might touch have in a speaker-audience communication situation?

Last, draw a conclusion about similarities and differences in individual reactions to various sensory experiences. Is it important at times to attempt to view the world "through another's eyes"?

Individual Activity: Gather together the pleasant and unpleasant examples you identified above for each of the sensory categories and include six cotton balls with the examples. Locate at least two friends to join you in discussing the questions below.

1. For each category, ask your friends to identify the example representing the pleasant and unpleasant sensation. Do they agree with you? If so, identify at least one example for each sense upon which you and one or both of your friends disagree. How does your impression of pleasant and unpleasant sensations differ from the impressions of others?
2. Place the cotton balls in your ears and ask your friends to do likewise. Spend at least five minutes discussing a topic of interest to all of you. What effect did the partial hearing loss have on the communication process?
3. Discuss the value of viewing the world "through another's eyes." Make certain you include the effect of viewing the world through the other senses also. Is it important in communicating to consider what others are sensing?

Briefly summarize in writing your reactions to the three items immediately above.

Activity 6
Perception

Preparation: From a magazine or newspaper, select a picture that is likely to be misinterpreted without its caption. Remove the caption from the picture. Be certain, however, to save the caption for future reference.

Group Activity: The class should form groups of four or five students who seat themselves in a circle. Beginning with a volunteer, the group members should consecutively number their pictures as they are seated from left to right in order around the circle.

The members of the group should pass their pictures to the group members on their right. Each member should study the picture received and write a four to five sentence interpretation of it. When the group has completed the first round, the pictures should be passed to the right once again, studied, and interpreted in writing. The rotation of pictures should continue until all members have received their original pictures. Each person should have a written description of each picture contributed by the other group members. It is useful to number the descriptions to match the number on the pictures.

Discussion of each picture should follow. Group members should each read their interpretations of each picture. Then the member who contributed the picture should read the original caption. Throughout the discussion, emphasis should be placed on similarities and differences in the perceptions of the various group members. Do individuals seem to relate events to their own backgrounds of knowledge and experience?

Individual Activity: Take your picture without its caption to at least five of your friends. Ask them to make an interpretation of what they see and to explain their reasoning. Write down their interpretations and rationales. Then show them the original caption and write down your perception of their reaction to it.

Consider the similarities and differences in the perceptions of your five friends. Do individuals seem to relate events to their own backgrounds of knowledge and experience? Write a brief summary of your reaction to this experiment.

Activity 7
Use of Language to Convey Meaning

Preparation: On a sheet of 8½-by-11-inch paper, construct an abstract line drawing that you can describe to another person. Practice your description several times. Be certain that you can accurately describe the drawing in no more than two minutes.

Group Activity: Choose a partner you want to work with in class. Sit in chairs with your backs turned. Describe your drawing to your partner. Your partner must reproduce the drawing by relying on the verbal description. Your partner can ask questions but cannot look at the drawing. The more accurate the communication of the description of the abstract drawing, the better the duplication will be. Your ability to select appropriate language to convey the description will determine your success.

When the person attempting to duplicate the drawing has exhausted all possibilities, compare the two drawings. Discuss how the communicator could have been more specific. How could the person reproducing the drawing have asked better questions? In general, was communication good between the two participants?

Now change partners and repeat the exercise exactly as before. Discuss once again the importance of specificity in language when trying to explain any idea or subject to another person.

Individual Activity: Find at least one person who will act as your partner as you follow the instructions to the group exercise above. Briefly summarize in writing an experience describing your drawing and the conclusions you made concerning the questions included in the paragraph above.

Activity 8
Perception of Self — Your Life Line

Preparation: You have a choice as to how you will spend your future years. Hopefully you will make the most of them. The intent of a long life should be positive. How you live your life is vital.

Take a piece of paper and draw a line across it. The dot at the left end represents your birth; write the date under it. The dot at the end of the line signifies the date of your death. Over this date write the number of years you hope to live. Under this dot write the estimated date of your death. Let us hope you want a long life and a useful one. Place a dot that represents where you are now on the line between your birth and death. Then write today's date under this dot.

This line is your life line. To the left of today's date, above the line, write down your accomplishments up to this point. To the right of today's date below the line, indicate some things you would like to do or experience before your death.

Examine your life line. Study it and think about it. How much time are you willing to invest for a life of meaning?

Group Activity: During class share life lines with each of your classmates. To keep track of those you have seen, place your initials on the bottom of each life line. Use the experience of viewing others' life lines as you more fully consider your own perception of past accomplishments and future expectations. Then discuss the following questions with the entire class and revise your life line if you wish.

1. Have others indicated accomplishments and expectations which you considered too trivial to list? What are they?

2. Were you honest in listing your accomplishments and expectations? Which would you change? Are there additions and deletions you would make? If so, what are they?

3. Did the comparison of your life line with those of your classmates help to clarify your perception of your own past accomplishments and future expectations? Explain.

Activity 8 continued

Individual Activity: For several days, either before or after class, share life lines with at least half your classmates. To keep track of those you have seen, place your initials on the bottom of each life line. Use the experience of viewing others' life lines as you more fully consider your own perception of past accomplishments and future expectations. Then write your answers to the series of questions included above with the group activity and revise your life line if you wish.

Activity 9
Analysis of Self-Concept

Preparation: Self-concept may be assessed in many ways. All approaches to the analysis require a deep and honest look at oneself. It is useful to "step outside the body" and take a detached and objective look. It is not a question of "what I want to be" but "what I am."

Option 1 — The Standardized Survey
There are several standardized surveys available to measure self-concept (e.g., Tennessee Self-Concept Scale). These contain statements of behavior that require self-ratings.

For example: I enjoy making new acquaintances. Yes or No

The surveys include methods for combining ratings from the specific statements to produce a single rating of overall self-concept. Generally they provide information, based on prior research with the survey, that is useful in interpreting the score.

Through your instructor or counseling staff, make arrangements to complete one of the self-concept surveys and to be guided through the process of interpreting your score.

Option 2 — The Open-Ended Survey
The open-ended survey generally designates a number of personal reactions or characteristics to be described by the respondent.

For example: How do you feel when you make new acquaintances? Explain in detail.

Although open-ended surveys might be based on formal research, they are generally designed to include a sampling of reactions or characteristics that seem particularly relevant for a specific group.

Answer the questions below as they relate to your own self-concept. Develop the last question yourself—make certain that it allows you to address a specific quality that you find particularly important.

1. How would you describe your appearance?
2. How would you describe the primary ways that you use your time?
3. How would you describe those things at which you excel?
4. How would you describe your personality or disposition?

Activity 9 continued

5. How would you describe your interpersonal relationships?
6. (Your own question.)

Group Activity: As a class or in smaller groups, take turns revealing insights about your self-concept that you may have achieved from the above surveys. Then discuss the questions below with your classmates.

1. Was it difficult or easy to detach yourself and objectively analyze your self-concept?
2. Does knowing yourself take time or can you accomplish the task by completing a survey?
3. How can positive feedback from important people in your life reinforce your self-concept?
4. How does observation of communicators with good self-concepts help you become a better communicator?
5. How does your self-concept affect your confidence in handling a variety of communication situations?

Individual Activity: Discuss the results of your self-concept survey with your instructor. Then write your answers to the five questions listed in the group activity.

Activity 10
Introducing Another Person

Preparation: There may be occasions when you will have to introduce another person to a group. You may introduce a speaker to a group, or you may bring a new member into an already established group.

A formal introduction of another person should be made with confidence and without hesitation. This implies preparation and rehearsal. It is hard to make a speaker or guest comfortable if you forget relevant information and have to count on the person being introduced to fill in the parts you have forgotten.

An introduction of another person should include the types of information shown in the outline below.

I. Attention device — Capture the attention of the listeners by mentioning something about the individual that is especially catching. It need not be humorous. Include also a statement of purpose for your introduction.

II. Factual details—This section of the introduction will depend on the specific occasion. It is the place to list accomplishments and specific information about the person's life.

III. Summary—Briefly review the most relevant of the factual details and let your listeners know that the introduction of the person is complete.

To create an even flow of information, parts of the introduction should be designed to complement the personality of the person being introduced and to have relevance to the listeners.

Option 1 — Introducing a Famous Person
Research the life of a famous person, either living or dead. To find information, consult the library catalogue to locate biographies, use an encyclopedia, or check some of the *Who's Who* publications.

When your material has been gathered, prepare an outline like the one above with attention device, factual details, and summary. Limit your material to what can be presented in two to three minutes. The factual information on a famous person will probably be an overall listing of accomplishments or a more detailed analysis of a single outstanding accomplishment. When the outline is complete, have it reviewed by your instructor and then practice it in front of an imaginary audience until you are comfortable with the presentation. To help in your preparation, an example of an introduction of a famous person follows.

Activity 10 continued

An Introduction of Agatha Christie

Topical Outline	*Script*
I. Attention device	
A. Attention statement	Who was Agatha Mallowan and why should she be classified as a famous person even though she considered herself simply to be Mrs. Max Mallowan?
B. Purpose statement	It is my purpose to answer this question and in doing so introduce you to a lady who has brought me many hours of sheer entertainment.
II. Factual details	
A. Identification	Being the wife of one of Britain's foremost archaeologists has not been Agatha's only claim to fame as Max Mallowan has not been her only husband. Agatha was formerly married to Archibald Christie, making her name Agatha Christie the most widely read detective-mystery writer of our time.
B. Accomplishments	When she died at the age of eighty-three she had produced sixty-eight novels, more than 100 short stories and seventeen plays. She had published in 103 languages throughout the world—truly accomplishment enough to be famous.
	In her autobiography she gives some insight into why she considered herself simply to be Mrs. Max Mallowan. She says when filling in her occupation on a form it never occurred to her to fill it in with anything but "married woman" because she says, "I was a married woman, that was my status and that was my occupation. As a sideline I wrote books."
C. Agatha Christie characters	Within her works she created many characters but none so well remembered as Hercule Poirot, the meticulous Belgian detective with the magnificent mustache and excellent little grey cells.
	Agatha was to regret not having made him younger when she created him because by the time she wrote her last book about him he would have been well over a hundred years old.

Activity 10 continued

Introduction continued

Another of her memorable characters was Miss Marple, a spinster, full of curiosity, knowing everything and hearing everything, whom Agatha referred to as the complete detective service in the home.

III. Summary
    A. Personal appreciation

At present I am still working my way through her many books and the characters Hercule Poirot and Miss Marple are very much alive to me.

    B. Conclusion

I am not looking forward to ending this enjoyable task and I am sure many other Agatha Christie enthusiasts share my enjoyment and my sentiments.

Option 2 — Introducing a Classmate

Choose a person in the class that you would like to get to know better. Arrange a specific time outside of class when you can interview the person. During the interview find out as much as possible about the person.

You may want to describe the person in relation to a single outstanding accomplishment or according to some of the characteristics listed below.

1. Age
2. Marital status
3. Children
4. Occupation
5. Religion
6. Geographic location (e.g., native Texan)
7. Hometown (e.g., Dallas)
8. Dwelling (e.g., apartment)
9. Major (e.g., music)
10. Class (e.g., freshman)
11. Ambition (e.g., architect)
12. Political (e.g., Republican)
13. Clubs (e.g., P.T.A.)
14. Sports (e.g., tennis)
15. Friends (e.g., card players)
16. Hobbies (e.g., reading)
17. Interests (e.g., family)
18. Talents (e.g., writing)
19. Admire (e.g., educated people)
20. Dislike (e.g., Communist party)

Activity 10 continued

When your material has been gathered, prepare an outline like the one above with attention device, factual details, and summary. Limit your material to what can be presented in two to three minutes. When the outline is complete, have it reviewed by your instructor and then practice it in front of an imaginary audience until you are comfortable with the presentation.

To help in your preparation, an example of an introduction of a student is given below.

An Introduction of Kooky Karen

Topical Outline	*Script*
I. Attention device	
A. Attention statement	I want to boggle your mind and that is just exactly what this introduction is going to do.
B. Purpose statement	I am going to describe a fascinating personality—one of our own classmates—Kooky Karen.
II. Factual details	
A. Early life	Karen was born December 18, 1955. She graduated from Lancaster High School in May, 1974. The next fall, she entered Stephen F. Austin University and became, as you might expect from looking at her, a Mam'selle Model.
B. Recent events	In her second year at Stephen F. Austin, she continued as a Mam'selle Model. But a young man named Richard won her heart. Karen and Richard were married in August, 1976, and moved to Nacogdoches. After a year, they returned to Mesquite and Karen entered East Texas State University. Then in January, 1979, she enrolled here at Eastfield.
C. Future events	Karen's future looks promising. Karen and Richard are going to make room for a permanent guest this August. Her name will be Amanda Marie.
	If parenthood doesn't block the path, Karen will receive her B.S. in home economics in August, 1981. And, if all goes well, Jason Cory will be born in September, 1982.
III. Summary	
A. Review	With a beautiful and intelligent person like Karen involved, Richard, Amanda, Jason, and Karen will live happily ever after.

Activity 10 continued

    B. Conclusion   Oh, I forgot to mention, Richard and Amanda are expecting another new arrival—they'll be grandparents in 2002.

Group Activity: During class, make your two- to three-minute introduction of a famous person or classmate. You may use note cards and visual aids if you wish.

Individual Activity: Make an appointment with your instructor to plan a specific time to present a two- to three-minute speech to introduce a famous person or an individual from your class. You may use note cards and visual aids.

Evaluation Form
Introducing Another Person

(Points are given to the right of each criterion.)

I. Attention device
   _____ Captures attention (4)
   _____ States purpose of presentation (4)

II. Factual details
   _____ Statement of factual details (4)
   _____ Effectiveness of factual details (4)

III. Summary
   _____ Review of relevant details (4)
   _____ Conclusion (4)

IV. Personal qualities
   _____ Can be heard (2)
   _____ Conversational style (2)
   _____ Control of fillers—ah's, you know's (2)
   _____ Speaker enthusiasm (2)
   _____ Looks at listeners (2)
   _____ Speaker confidence (2)
   _____ Warmth and friendliness (2)
   _____ Speaker credibility (2)

V. Presentation
   _____ Completed two-to-three minute introduction (10)

Additional Readings in Introductory Communication

In addition to books and articles cited in these chapters, the following books are excellent sources for further study of communication.

Holtzman, P. D., and Ecroyd, D. *Communication Concepts and Models.* Skokie, Illinois: National Textbook Co., 1976.

> Models of communication are explained in a detailed and simplified manner.

Newman, M., and Berkowitz, B. *How To Be Your Own Best Friend.* New York: Random House, 1973.

> A very short book that is useful in evaluating self-concept and developing an awareness of personal strengths and accomplishments.

Thomson, D. S. *Language.* New York: Time, Inc., 1975.

> From the Time-Life series on human behavior, this book covers important concepts about language in a very readable format.

Ziglar, Z. *See You At the Top.* Gretna, California: Pelican Publishing Co., 1979.

> Writing in a conversational style, Ziglar teaches the principles and procedures of positive thinking as they relate to all aspects of living and all types of people.

PART TWO

Overview

The human race communicates with verbal and nonverbal symbols simultaneously. Verbal symbols are the sounds and combinations of sounds that form the words that comprise spoken messages. Nonverbal symbols are all communication techniques other than the actual words used by a speaker. These include facial expressions, vocal qualities, and all forms of body movement.

Jonathan Swift was a master at describing nonverbal messages. Although Swift is better known for his satire of eighteenth century political and social customs, in *Gulliver's Travels* he skillfully described the adventures of a man lost first among tiny human creatures, then giants, and later other variations of the human race. Gulliver was able to communicate effectively enough in these foreign lands to save his life and fulfill his basic needs.

> *I answered in a few words but to no Purpose, and made a Sign with my Hand that was loose, putting it to the other, and then to my own Head and Body, to signify that I desired my Liberty. It appeared that he understood me well enough; for he shook his Head by way of Disapprobation, and held his Hand in a Posture to shew that I must carried as Prisoner.....I gave Tokens to let them know that they might do with me what they pleased.*

Imagine yourself in a foreign land, among strange creatures, and with no knowledge of the language. Your only option, save fainting, would be to call on your ability to send accurate nonverbal messages.

Jonathan Swift was a keen observer of another aspect of communication: listening, or the processing of verbal messages. He recognized the poor listening skills that some of his countrymen seemed

Listening and Nonverbal Messages

to demonstrate. He created a country of people of the same body proportions as Gulliver but who had great difficulty communicating.

> *I observed here and there many in the Habit of Servants, with a blown Bladder fastned like a Flail to the End of a short Stick, which they carried in their Hands. In each Bladder was a small Quantity of dried Pease, or little Pebbles (as I was afterwards informed). With these Bladders they now and then flapped the Mouths and Ears of those who stood near them, of which Practice I could not then conceive the Meaning. It seems, the Minds of these People are so taken up with intense Speculations, that they neither can speak, or attend to the Discourses of others, without being rouzed by some external Taction upon the Organs of Speech and Hearing; for which Reason, those Persons who are able to afford it, always keep a Flapper in their Family.*

How many of us need a "Flapper" to keep our minds off "intense speculations" when supposedly listening to some form of verbal communication?

The study of communication often excludes many aspects of nonverbal communication and emphasizes only speaking and other verbal skills. This does not seem rational when such nonverbal messages as postures, facial expressions, and gestures form a second language that everyone uses; and when even the best message given through the eloquent lips of a practiced speaker is lost when the receivers are without their Flappers. Nonverbal communication then, is defined here as those aspects of communication that require skills other than those involved in the formation and sending of verbal messages. These two basic areas of communication, listening and nonverbal messages, are critical to the development of adequate skill in sending verbal messages in interpersonal, small group, and speaker-audience communication situations.

After studying the material on nonverbal communication, the reader should be able to demonstrate acquisition of the following objectives.

Attitude Objective: By applying skills and concepts associated with nonverbal messages and listening behaviors, the student will recognize the value of developing nonverbal as well as verbal communication skills. (*Activities 1-10*)

Knowledge Objective: Given objective test items, the student will recall the definitions of the following terms and recognize or differentiate among them where appropriate. (*Activity 1*)

I. Listening behavior
   A. The listening process
      1. Some definitions
         a. Listening
         b. Not listening
      2. Types of listening
         a. Passive, active
         b. Social, serious
         c. Critical, discriminative
      3. Listening characteristics
      4. Listening habits
   B. Developing listening skills
      1. Listening improvement
         a. Social and serious listening
         b. Critical listening
         c. Discriminative listening
      2. Distorted messages
         a. Environmental distraction
         b. Physiological and semantic problems
         c. Psychological and social problems
         d. Communication chains
II. Nonverbal messages
   A. Types of nonverbal messages
      1. Body motion
      2. Personal space
      3. Touching
      4. Paralanguage
      5. Physical characteristics
      6. Artifacts
      7. Environment

PART II   Listening and Nonverbal Messages   75

        B.   Implications of nonverbal messages
            1.   Conflicting messages
            2.   Awareness of one's own nonverbal messages
            3.   Body language
                a.   Openness
                b.   Cooperation
                c.   Frustration
                d.   Confidence
                e.   Nervousness
                f.   Courtship
   III.   Nonverbal techniques to help the listener
        A.   Body motion
            1.   Posture
            2.   Movements
            3.   Gestures
            4.   Eye contact
            5.   Facial expressions
        B.   Vocal expression
            1.   Volume
            2.   Pitch
            3.   Rate
            4.   Articulation and pronunciation
            5.   Vocal quality
        C.   Appearance
            1.   Grooming
            2.   Demeanor

Experiential Objective: The student will participate in nonverbal communication experiences by following instructions for selected activities in each of the areas listed below. (*Activities 2–9*)
    I.   Listening
        A.   Myths
        B.   Types of listening
        C.   Listening behavior questionnaire
        D.   Listening log
   II.   Nonverbal messages
        A.   Body motion
        B.   Personal Space
        C.   Touching
        D.   Paralanguage

Speaking Objective: Following the instructions given in Activity 10 for the fantasy trip or the demonstration, the student will prepare a four-minute presentation designed specifically to facilitate the listening process of the audience. (*Activity 10*)

CHAPTER 4

Listening Behavior

If communication is to exist, an internal process called listening must occur. Most communicators take listening for granted. Originators of messages assume that their receivers are paying attention; receivers of messages assume that their attending skills are adequate. But listening is much more than the sensory process of hearing. It means processing what is heard so that meaning can be determined and a reaction can be made.

Communicators often hear but do not listen. For example, listeners will routinely say, "I don't care" to a question about dinner or a television program, and later react with surprise because their opinions were not considered in the choices made. Or the receiver of a message will appear to be giving full attention to what is being said, only to inquire about a specific point just made by the speaker. The receivers of the messages clearly heard but failed to give the attention required at the perceptual level to change hearing to listening. Listening is a skill that can be studied, practiced, and improved. Through effective listening, it is possible to learn more, be more appreciative of pleasant sounds in the environment, and be more sensitive to messages received.

The Listening Process

To appreciate the significance of listening in the communication process, it is useful to make clear distinctions between the concepts of hearing and listening and between the concepts of not hearing and not listening. Basically, the two pairs of concepts are distinguishable as sensory versus perceptual processes. Hearing and not hearing are sensory processes; listening and not listening, perceptual processes. For listening to occur, then, a message must not only be transmitted to the brain via sensory processes but also be attended to and interpreted. The listening process in action is influenced by the type of situation and by the characteristics and habits of the listener.

Some Definitions

Listening. Listening depends on the ability of the potential receiver of a message to hear what is said and then to perceive the message as relevant enough to decode. Listening can be defined concisely as the attachment of meaning to spoken words. In greater detail, listening is defined as the selective process of giving attention to the spoken words, attaching meaning, and responding with understanding. Listening is the prerequisite to the decoding process referred to in the communication model.

Not Listening. Not listening does not imply failure to hear but failure to attend to stimuli and to attach meaning to spoken words and, therefore, failure to respond with understanding. Think for a moment about the concepts of listening, not listening, hearing, and not hearing. Communicators will sometimes claim that they failed to hear when, in fact, they failed to listen. In general usage, the two concepts, not hearing and not listening, are often inappropriately used to mean the same thing: failure to attend to and attach meaning to relevant stimuli.

Types of Listening

Assuming that listening takes place at all, it occurs with different intensities within the receiver of the message. The intensity will depend on the importance of a particular message as it competes for the listener's attention. A major distinction in listening intensity can be made between passive and active listening.

Passive Listening. Passive listening refers to those forms of listening in which many people engage simply because they happen to be present. This can occur, for example, when someone is talking or when music is playing. The potential receiver of the message is minimally, if at all, concerned about the listening process. This type of listening is barely more than hearing.

Active Listening. Active listening involves listening with a purpose, such as understanding, evaluation, or enjoyment. It can occur while listening to a lecture, judging a television commercial, or watching a movie. The main goal of active listening is to understand the meaning intended by the speaker. There must be a willingness to listen and a desire to try to understand the message as it is intended. Active listening is dependent to a great extent on acquiring desirable listening skills. Active listening can occur in either a social or a serious setting.

Social listening refers to situations where enjoyment of what is to be heard is the primary objective. Social listening, for example, takes place during casual conversations or while attending to messages meant to entertain. Social listening enables individuals to enlarge experiences, expand interests, develop an awareness of cultural and ethnic influences, and mature socially. Being an effective listener in social situations can improve the image others hold of a person as well as result in increased self-confidence. A good listener is always in demand in social situations.

Serious listening is appropriate for situations where it is important to expand knowledge or gather information for decision making. Serious listening, for example, occurs when a friend gives a detailed set of instructions or a boss tells an employee how to complete a task. The goal of serious listening is usually to attend to as many details and receive as much information as possible. Language facility and vocabulary can be improved by close attention to the ways that other people report information and analyze situations. Serious listening can be either critical or discriminative.

Critical listening occurs when the receiver of a message attempts to analyze evidence presented by the speaker and make critical judgments about the accuracy and quality of the material. Critical listening involves the abilities to distinguish between fact and opinion, to distinguish between emotional and logical arguments, to detect bias and prejudice, to evaluate a speaker's arguments, to recognize propaganda, to draw inferences, to make judgments, and to evaluate sales "gimmicks." Critical listening is extremely important in gathering information needed to make decisions. Messages must be heard, listened to, and then screened for appropriateness to the decision at hand.

The purpose of discriminative listening is understanding and remembering. In discriminative listening, such skills as understanding meanings of words from context, understanding the relationship of details to main points, following steps when given directions, following the sequence of the message, listening for details, listening to a question with an intent to answer, recognizing repetition of the same idea in different words, repeating what has been heard, taking notes, and outlining are emphasized. Discriminative listening is particularly important for students who find themselves in learning situations where the bulk of course content is given in lectures.

The types of listening situations reveal a wide range of attending behaviors—from barely more than hearing through general conversation to understanding and evaluation of sometimes complex messages. The listener must exert various degrees of energy in the various situations. It is not appropriate to use passive listening skills when taking notes in an important meeting or class.

Listening Characteristics and Habits

There are many different ways to listen. Ability to listen effectively in the different serious listening situations is acquired in part by practice. In addition to skill developed through practice, listening effectiveness is determined to some extent by physical characteristics, demographic variables, and by experiences of the listener. Habits, that is, responses that are automatic for an individual, also affect listening skill. Many listening habits result in effective attending behaviors, but many others result in ineffective attention to the message being received. Several poor listening habits may even be practiced simultaneously.

Characteristics Affecting Listening. If a person has normal hearing, there is little relationship between age and ability to listen. However, there are some age-related variables, the primary one being attention span. Young children have considerably shorter attention spans than young adults. Also, when a person reaches old age, listening ability may be negatively affected by reduced reception within some ranges of sound.

Personality characteristics of the listener can affect listening effectiveness. Understanding of verbal messages can be reduced by defensive behaviors, whereas objectivity tends to increase understanding. Listeners who have personal worries, feelings of insecurity, or a sense of failure tend to be poorer listeners than those who are optimistic and free from momentary worries. Interests and attitudes toward the material affect listening effectiveness too, since people are more likely to attend to material they perceive as interesting or important.

Fatigue is another characteristic that often affects listening ability. When a listener is mentally or physically tired, reduced attention span proportionately decreases ability to listen. Fatigue can cause a temporary loss of desire to attend to and understand the message sent by the speaker. It is wise to be rested when important messages require attention.

Listening Habits. Daydreaming is probably the most troublesome listening fault. A speaker will mention a person or thing that will trigger an association in the listener's mind. The association will divert attention from the speaker and cause some of the message to be lost. When the listener returns attention to the speaker, what is heard no longer seems to relate to the original message. Consider your own behavior as you attempt to listen to a group discussion. You may hear the word "travel" as it applies to payment for local expenses and begin dreaming about your summer vacation. By the time you return, the group may be discussing a menu for a party. Off you go again, thinking about what you plan to eat for your evening meal.

Closed-mindedness is another serious listening problem. Closed-mindedness operates when positions listeners hold dear are threatened. Closed-minded people refuse to listen to ideas, viewpoints, and values that are different from their own. If one has a strong belief that credit spending leads to financial doom, then it is difficult to listen to a message arguing that borrowing money can be a useful practice. There is a tendency to think, "I know all I want to know on this subject," and then to think about something else. Important facts are shut out whether they are right or wrong. Generally a speaker is not seeking agreement on the issue, but is seeking close attention and fair appraisal on the part of the listener. If listeners are aware of their biases and convictions, they can attempt to have open minds when such topics are discussed.

Faking attention is a protective device that listeners use from time to time. They pretend to listen by showing an alert facial expression, maintaining eye contact, and occasionally nodding the head. Actually their minds are somewhere else. Listeners who find themselves having difficulty remembering what has been said should check themselves to determine if they have been faking attention. How many times have you asked a question only to realize that you missed the answer by faking attention and failing to listen?

Failure to attend to an uninteresting or difficult message is a common listening problem. Listeners who find themselves in such communication situations should try to make the best use of their time by actively listening, discussing material where appropriate, and asking questions if possible. Something might be learned and prove useful in the future. Certainly there is no potential for gain if listeners fail to attend to the message. The difficulty in maintaining attention is often related to the challenge of sifting the useful material from the total message. This problem will often occur when messages have been designed with a different audience in mind and are thus "over the head" of the listener.

Distractions often affect listening effectiveness. A poor listener habitually fails to attend to messages when distractions occur. Untrained listeners will be disturbed by poor speaker delivery, traffic noise, noise in adjoining rooms, or even visual stimuli like glaring lights. When distractions occur, the effective listener will modify internal behavior in an attempt to attend fully to the message sent by the speaker. Rather than dwell on that interesting conversation across the room, for example, it is wise to concentrate on the message of immediate concern.

Some people listen only for facts and avoid evaluation of the message. If facts are important, the listener should attend to them. If it is more important to analyze the message, evaluation should occur as the message is processed. A similar problem occurs when the listener attempts to outline or take note of everything said by a speaker. It is often more effective to listen for several minutes and then make note of key ideas and concepts rather than attempt to outline the message point by point. Such emphasis on specific facts often results in retention of insignificant details rather than knowledge of an entire process.

Developing Listening Skills

Now that the distinction has been made between the processes of hearing and listening, the various types of listening situations have been introduced, and characteristics and habits that affect listening have been discussed, it is relevant to consider ways to improve listening skills, and some ways that the listening process leads to distortion of messages.

Listening Improvement

Because so much time is spent in listening, it seems reasonable to attempt to improve listening behavior. Through effective listening, it is possible to learn more, to become better informed, and to gain in sophistication. In direct communication with others, an improvement in listening will likely lead to a widening circle of friends. In attending to speaker-audience and small group messages, an improvement in listening can lead to increased knowledge and ability to make decisions. Good listening habits result in greater dependability and fewer embarassments since fewer errors are made, directions are more clearly followed, and more informed responses can be made.

Social and Serious Listening. There are ways to improve the listening that occurs in interpersonal relationships at the social level. The following list includes some hints that can be used to improve ability to listen in a more informal setting. Many of the recommendations make sense in both serious and social listening situations. The important point is to practice them where appropriate.

CHAPTER 4 Listening Behavior

1. Do not make it appear that you have all the answers. Some listeners always appear to want to win an argument rather than to solve a problem or receive information.
2. Avoid the attitude that you are superior to the speaker in power, position, wealth, or intellect. Try to make others realize that you respect their opinions.
3. Try not to appear uninterested or show a lack of concern. On the other hand, do not pass judgment on others for their ideas. Avoid blaming or praising based upon your own values.
4. Be willing to reconsider your own attitudes, ideas, and values based upon the rationales you have been given. Be willing to consider all possibilities.
5. Be spontaneous, straightforward, and honest with other communicators. Do not base your reactions on hidden motives.
6. Avoid nonverbal behaviors that create a negative climate. Try not to avoid eye contact, turn the body away, shake the head, wring hands, or engage in other nonverbal movements with negative meanings.

The following list includes a number of hints that can be practiced to improve serious listening behaviors. These can be practiced until they no longer require direct thought but occur almost automatically.

1. Be physically prepared to listen. Evaluative listening especially takes energy and it is important to be rested for the experience.
2. Set listening goals. A message will make more sense if there is an understanding of how the input can be useful.
3. Recognize any potential prejudices you might have and determine how the message relates to your values. Keeping an open mind is essential to the listening process.
4. Try to understand the meaning of the message even if it is unclear. When the message is difficult to understand, it is useful to write down questions to be asked after a speaker has completed presentation of the message.
5. Be a responsive listener. Nonverbal expressions such as nods, smiles, or puzzled expressions can reveal understanding or lack of understanding.
6. Always shut out distractions. Noises, other people, or daydreaming often take the listener's attention away from the message.
7. Be alert to the nonverbal language of the speaker. Movements, posture, and facial expression all contribute to the speaker's message.

Improving listening behaviors at both the social and serious levels can be accomplished. The suggestions for social listening emphasize the interpersonal contact of listener and speaker; those for serious listening emphasize getting the most from the message. It takes some effort at first to develop good listening behaviors that eventually become good listening habits.

Critical Listening. Critical listening is especially important in communication since it permits the assessment of evidence or ideas that are essential in making valid decisions. It is more than just receiving and understanding a verbal message. It is an attempt to analyze verbal messages received. All suggestions and instructions from others are based upon their values, knowledge, and experiences. Listeners cannot accept uncritically what they hear. They must take responsibility for evaluating the information they receive.

Different people have different values. When listening critically, it is essential to be aware of the speaker's values and to be ready to reconsider one's own values. If the speaker's values reflect a specific position on an issue, then it may be that the message reflects the same position. Values are seldom verbalized but are definitely implied. It is sometimes useful to point out differences in values and to discuss them openly.

It is useful too in developing critical listening skill to learn to recognize differences in statements of facts and statements of opinions. Communicators rarely specify whether their messages are facts or opinions and some develop great skill in making opinions sound like facts. A factual statement must be backed by evidence. This evidence can be directly observable, or can be found in written reports, books, or documents.

Some questions you might try to answer as you critically listen, analyze, and evaluate are given below.

1. Is the speaker's opinion backed by evidence (e.g., quotations, examples, statistics, facts that support the main idea of the message)?
2. Are the conclusions based on relevant facts?
3. What does the speaker have to gain from your acceptance of the conclusion (e.g., a salesman)?
4. Is the speaker qualified to draw the conclusion?
5. Can the evidence presented be countered by opposing evidence?
6. Does the speaker use correct reasoning (e.g., moving from specifics to more general statements, emphasizing similarities and differences, or showing that one event was the cause of another)?
7. Is propaganda used to gain acceptance for the message?
8. Is the message of value to you personally?

Attention to these questions might prove helpful in situations requiring critical listening. Critical listening is a part of the critical thinking process. Critical listening is the evaluation of verbal messages; critical thinking, the evaluation of all types of input relating to a particular issue. Thus, critical listening is essential in judging the worth of verbal input used to make decisions.

Discriminative Listening. In discriminative listening, a major goal is to understand and remember. Note taking is an extremely useful tool in discriminative listening. Without a photographic memory it is often difficult to remember the key ideas of a message, not to mention less important details or supporting evidence. Notes can provide an adequate stimulus for recall of important details of lectures and speakers. When a complete record seems important and the speaker does not object, however, it may be appropriate to record the message on audio tape.

Since note taking is the more usual course of action, an awareness of some note-taking techniques that facilitate discriminative listening can be useful. First, notes should be brief; it does not seem reasonable to attempt to take down every word. Second, it is useful to try to make clear and well-organized notes so that review will be easier. Soon after the listening experience, it is wise to review the notes and fill in from memory any important missing information.

In taking notes from lectures in a formal classroom setting the steps listed below are suggested.

1. Be prepared for the lecture by completing reading assignments and reviewing previous notes.
2. Immediately before the lecture, write down the date, the topic heading, and any other information you have.
3. Use the same format each time; listen for words like first, next, important, and significant to indicate main ideas; jot down important details and examples; leave space between main ideas so that other notes can be added; and be sure to make notes of the conclusion or summary.
4. Review the lecture notes and include any omissions, spell out unusual abbreviations, and coordinate them with notes from the text.

Even in situations where someone gives you a brief set of instructions, careful note taking will improve your chances of retaining and understanding important information.

Distorted Messages

Internal or external interference with the communication process is often called "noise." The interference can be caused by environmental distractions, physiological impairment, semantic problems, psychological and social problems, and chains of communication. When noise interferes with the communication process it becomes more and more difficult to send and receive accurate messages. Therefore, one means of improving listening is to eliminate factors that cause noise and distort messages.

Environmental Distractions. Environmental distractions are the result of outside interference that makes it difficult for the listener to receive the message. Have you ever tried to listen to a news broadcast while someone was vacuuming the rug? If so, you have experienced noise in the communication channels. Such physical noise may not be so important in listening to a television broadcast. It is probably much more important when listening to an instructor describe the questions for an upcoming test. When environmental distractions affect reception of a message it is essential to attempt to eliminate the interference. This might be done by moving closer to the message source, by increasing the volume of the message, or by removing the distraction from the immediate surroundings.

Physiological Impairment and Semantic Problems. Deaf people cannot receive messages in the way that a person with normal hearing can. People with speech impediments may be difficult to understand. These are examples of physiological impairments that make the listening process more difficult. Semantic problems, on the other hand, occur because of word choice. It is often difficult to find just the right words to express a thought. Differences in language use, culture, experience, and education affect meanings that both the communicator and receiver assign to different words. The listener who has difficulty interpreting the words used in a message may be forced to ask for clarification. With tact, such requests can be made without causing embarrassment to other participants in the communication encounter.

Psychological and Social Problems. Sometimes people have difficulty communicating because of their prior experiences or backgrounds. For example, people often become nervous in unfamiliar situations and both their listening and speaking skills are likely to suffer. A low self-concept may affect speaking and listening skills as well. These are examples of psychological problems that make it difficult for the listener to receive a clear message. Social problems in listening result from preconceived and unchangeable ideas about individuals or groups of people. Thoughts like "nice girls don't do things like that," or "all women belong at home," can get in the way of open and honest communication. We tend to "not listen" if the ideas expressed are those to which we are violently opposed. The conscientious listener must learn to keep an open mind as a message is listened to and to remain nonjudgmental until the message has been totally delivered.

Communication Chains. Within organizations and among members of groups, information is constantly being transmitted from person to person. At work the most remote person in the company eventually hears about the boss's interpretation of the new telephone policy. At home the teenage children often spread news of the new telephone policy among themselves. Chains of communication are the ways that messages can be transmitted from individual to individual. The three most common ways of spreading information are the single-strand chain, gossip chain, and branching chain.

A single-strand chain is the process where person "A" tells person "B," person "B" tells person "C," person "C" tells person "D," and so on. A single-strand chain can be pictured as a single line of people, each hearing the message from only one person and telling it only to one other person. A great deal of distortion will result in the original message if the single-strand chain is very long.

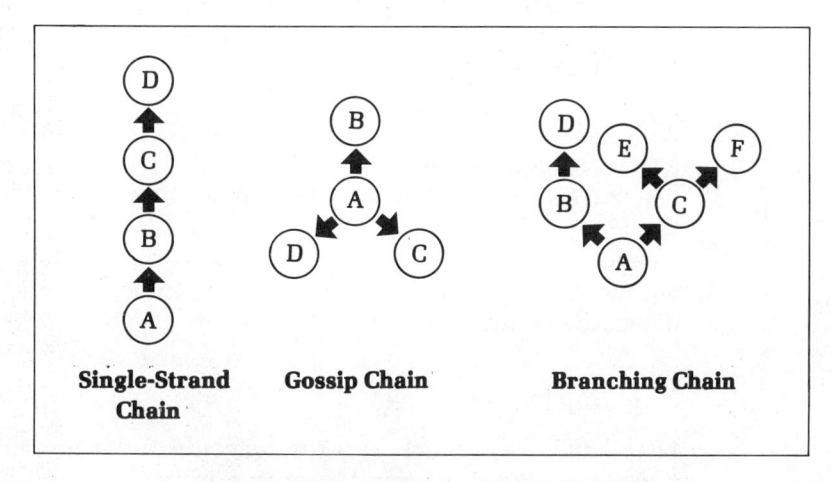

Figure 4.1. *Communication chains.*

The gossip chain occurs when person "A" tells person "B," person "A" tells person "C," person "A" tells person "D," and so on. The gossip chain can be pictured as a circle of listeners with the gossiper in the middle. The person who transmits the message will often distort the message as it is told over and over to many different individuals.

The branching chain is a combination of the single-strand and gossip chains. In the branching chain, person "A" tells person "B" and "C," person "B" tells person "D," person "C" tells persons "E" and "F," and so on. The originator of the message can be pictured in the center of a number of ropes leading outward. Some of the ropes are short, some long, and some indicate further branching as they radiate outward.

Designated chains of communication often exist in organizations. Bosses, for example, are expected to provide their employees with certain information. In contrast to the more formal chains of communication, informal chains exist where individuals somewhat randomly pass messages on to others. The number of times the message is repeated, whether by the same person as in the gossip chain, or by different people as in the single-strand chain, increases the amount of distortion that occurs as details are changed, omitted, or added.

In looking at distortion that occurs along the different types of communication chains, it is important to note that the message exists (a) as the speaker thinks of it, (b) as the speaker says it, (c) as the listener perceives it, and (d) as the listener remembers it. To increase the accuracy of a message as it is transmitted, keep the following in mind.

1. Take notes to help recall specific details.
2. Make the message as simple as possible.
3. Arrange details in a logical order.
4. Emphasize the important details.
5. Repeat the major details in a review process after the message has been relayed.

Noise in the communication process, whether physical, social, psychological, or caused by repetition of a message, interferes with the listener's ability to comprehend and understand with accuracy. The listener must make a conscious effort to compensate for distortion by moving away from physical noise, by asking questions to clarify what is not understood, and by remaining open-minded when the message does not match values.

Avoiding Distractions

Listening is hard work. It takes concentrated effort to eliminate distractions and to keep the mind from wandering away from the message. It is an easy way out to place the blame for poor listening on the speaker's "worthless message." The listener must take responsibility for attending to the message.

One problem that occurs when concentrating on a spoken message is that the mind of the receiver is working faster than the speaker is able to talk. People are able to think about four times faster than they are able to speak. Speakers comfortably talk at about 125 words a minute; thinkers can easily process about 500 words a minute. The mind that is merely receiving a message is underutilized and often directs unused potential toward other interests, then returns to the message, strays again, and so forth.

Some suggestions for keeping the mind actively involved in a message are listed below.

1. Evaluate the support and rationale underlying the speaker's message.
2. Make mental summaries of each part of the message as it is presented.
3. Relate each part of the message to parts that preceded it.
4. Try to anticipate the speaker's next point.

5. Determine what parts of the message are more important than others.
6. Remind yourself to be open-minded and pay attention even when you disagree.
7. Reflect on vocabulary and sentence structure as they supply the context for validating your impressions.

In one sentence, the idea is to develop techniques you can use to stay tuned to the speaker's message and avoid the cycle of straying off, coming back, straying off, and so forth. Effective listening requires an actively involved mind, not just a passively receptive mind.

SUMMARY

Listening and hearing are different processes in the individual. Hearing goes little beyond awareness of sound. There is practically no personal involvement in the hearing process. It is through listening that verbal messages are perceived, processed, and reacted to. If one gets tired of listening to a classroom lecture, for example, the instructor can be "tuned out" and participation can be reduced to the level of hearing. Input that arrives via the process of hearing only has minimal imprint on one's memory. Very little conscious decoding occurs.

Types of listening can be distinguished as shown in the following outline.

A. Passive listening
B. Active listening
   1. Social listening
   2. Serious listening
      a. Critical listening
      b. Discriminative listening

The different types of listening require different degrees of concentration, are appropriate for specific types of situations, and are affected to some extent by interest, fatigue, and personality traits.

Listening skills can be developed and improved at both the social and serious levels. To make effective use of time spent in serious listening situations, it is particularly important to develop good critical and discriminative listening skills. To be a good listener it is useful to be aware of ways that messages can be distorted by environmental factors; physiological impairment; and semantic, psychological, and social problems, as well as the ways that repetition of the same message changes its meaning. Finally, one means of improving listening may be as simple as keeping your mind actively involved in the message.

CHAPTER 5

Nonverbal Messages

There is much more to the communication process than speaking. In addition to speaking, communicators are involved in listening to others and in sending and interpreting nonverbal messages. To receive meaning from a spoken message it is necessary to listen, of course, and to read movements, facial expressions, gestures, and other nonverbal signs that add meaning to the spoken message. Listeners are senders of nonverbal messages also. Without uttering a sound receivers of messages can respond, thereby giving feedback to the speaker.

Think of your own experiences as a speaker. You may have been in the middle of a conversation that you had planned to go one way and, because of a movement, a look, or a gesture on the part of the receiver, changed what you intended to say. As a receiver of a message you have, no doubt, frowned or looked confused and caused the speaker to clarify what was said. Nonverbal messages are sent continually by all persons involved in the communication process. Even the seeming lack of a nonverbal message can communicate the "cold shoulder" type of impression with which all communicators are familiar.

For most speakers verbal messages are essential for communicating information about concrete objects and relationships. Nonverbal messages are generally more appropriate in enhancing or reinforcing expressions of feelings and emotions. Think about the difficulty many communicators have in verbally expressing emotional reactions. Such expression is made more easily and clearly with the aid of nonverbal expression. Consider someone saying "I love you" without the aid of nonverbal messages, and someone explaining a complex formula in mathematics without verbal messages. In the study of communication it is useful to recognize the many types of nonverbal behavior that contribute to the formulation of the total message and to consider some implications of nonverbal messages in the processes of sending and receiving messages.

Types of Nonverbal Messages

Included among those aspects of nonverbal communication that convey messages are (a) body motion, (b) personal space, (c) touching behavior, (d) paralanguage, (e) physical characteristics, (f) artifacts, and (g) environment (Knapp, 1972). Many important messages are transmitted through nonverbal language. Although people differ to some extent in meanings associated with specific types of nonverbal language, researchers have concluded that common meanings are associated with many expressions and movements. In spite of the fact that nonverbal messages are easily misunderstood and must be interpreted within the context in which they occur, they play an essential part in communication. One can usually decide not to send verbal messages but cannot choose to cease sending nonverbal messages. Even silence says something.

Body Motion

Body motion includes facial expressions, whole head movements, gestures, trunk movements, and posture (Eisenberg and Smith, 1971). Although communicators spend much less time speaking than in using body motions to communicate, they give little thought to how they move as they send and receive verbal messages.

Each message sent to a potential receiver is actually a set of messages. A sender may say a few words, point to something, and frown. The receiver must interpret the words as well as the pointing and frowning behaviors. The same words and pointing movement accompanied by a smile might have an entirely different meaning and interpretation. As the sender of the verbal and nonverbal messages is in the process of transmitting, the listener, although silent, is revealing reactions via nonverbal messages.

There is no firm consensus on whether body motions and their associated meanings are natural human characteristics or whether they are learned responses unique to specific groups of people. Much evidence points to the conclusion that body motions are learned behaviors. This is supported by observations that people of different backgrounds assign different meanings to the same body motions. For example, one individual might attract the attention of a waiter in a restaurant with a nod and direct look in the eye, whereas another individual might slightly raise an arm and point at the waiter.

Most communicators have a good intuitive knowledge of those behaviors that are common within their specific cultures. According to some researchers, for example, crossed arms generally suggest defensiveness and indicate negative communication. Anxiety and lack of confidence are indicated by cuticle picking, nail biting, pencil chewing, and fidgeting with jewelry or hair. Rapid movements often express fear.

Aggressiveness or dominance is suggested by a pointing finger. Boredom and impatience are indicated by tapping of fingers or clicking of a ballpoint pen. A flirtation might be enhanced by arranging the hair or smoothing a dress. Confidence is displayed by an erect posture with shoulders held back.

Certain physical behaviors are sometimes associated with occupations. Professional people like lawyers or professors often seem to be evaluating or thinking. They might lean forward, sit on the edge of a chair, or support the head with a hand on the cheek. Athletes often seem to display their strength. They might stand with legs apart, feet solidly on the ground, and muscles flexed. Some body motions are subtle and some are quite obvious. Whatever, they merit conscious attention by the communicator who strives to be perceptive and to clarify the meaning of the total message.

Personal Space

It has been said that each person has a personal space that can be conceptualized as an invisible bubble (Sommer, 1969). The invisible bubble defines the territory that individuals claim as their own. Others should not enter the invisible bubble without an invitation. Consider the somewhat common situation where two people in a casual conversation tend to move very slowly across the room. In such cases the individual who is backing away is experiencing an invasion of personal space and is attempting to restore the boundaries of the bubble.

Edward Hall (1959, 1966) has concluded that comfortable distances between persons in communication situations are related to the

Figure 5.1. *Everyone has an invisible bubble around them that defines their personal space.*

nature of the message. In the American population, he has identified eight distances that correspond to certain types of messages.

1. Very close (3 to 6 inches)—soft whisper, secretive, intimate.
2. Close (8 to 12 inches)—audible whisper, very confidential.
3. Near (12 to 20 inches)—soft voice, confidential.
4. Neutral (20 to 36 inches)—soft voice, personal information.
5. Neutral (4½ to 5 feet)—full voice, impersonal.
6. Public distance (5½ to 8 feet)—full voice.
7 and 8. Stretching the limits of distance (up to 100 feet)—greeting and departure distance.

These classifications may be reduced by calling 1 and 2 the intimate zone; 3 and 4 the personal zone; 5 and 6 the social zone; and 7 and 8 the public zone.

Communication occurs most effectively when the personal space of the individuals involved is not invaded. In general, the intimate zone

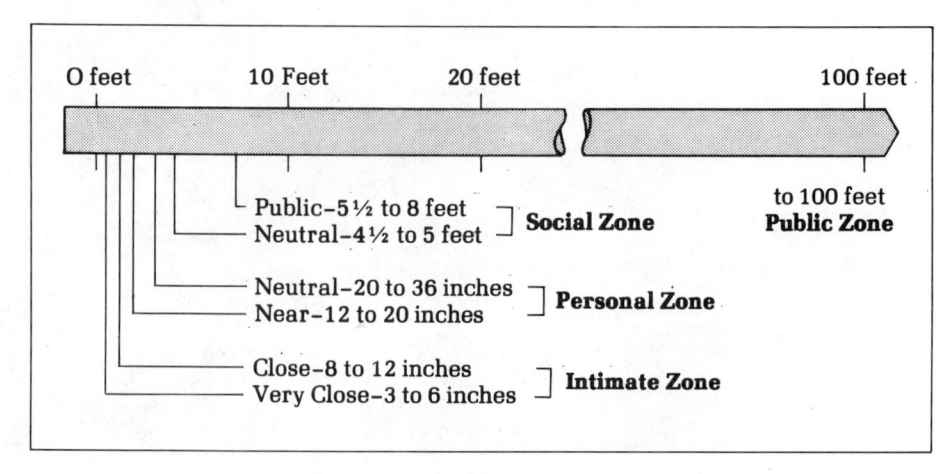

Figure 5.2. *Zones of distance.*

should not be violated by those who are not intimate. Persons in a crowded bus are probably having their intimate zone violated and find the closeness uncomfortable. By avoiding eye contact in such close situations, crowded individuals are sometimes attempting to maintain a sense of control over personal space. The personal zone is acceptable for party conversation, for talk among classmates, and for discussion among close friends. It generally connotes a close and trusting relationship. More general conversation and business transactions will occur at the social distance. The public distance is established between the public speaker or actor and the audience.

Personal space has much to do with the ways that furniture is arranged and buildings are designed. It affects the choice of seating within groups and the comfort that individuals feel in certain situations. Members of a family will often display ownership of territory within their homes by claiming a specific chair or room. Consider the behaviors of people in public places. In a nearly vacant library, for example, few people would select a chair immediately next to one of the other patrons. Most individuals would select a seat that allowed them to maximize their personal bubbles. Or consider a student who visits an instructor's office for a conference. Many students are more comfortable when both the instructor and student sit on easy chairs rather than when the instructor sits behind and the student across the desk.

It has been established that different cultures have special space requirements. For Americans, the comfortable and appropriate distance to stand for conversation is about an arm's length. Arabs, however, stand very close and look intently into each other's eyes. Americans will sometimes interpret such violations of their personal space as pushy, overbearing, and aggressive. Others may interpret an American's backing away as cold and standoffish. Try invading the personal space of others and note the verbal and nonverbal communication that results.

Touching

Communication by touch has always had a special significance to human beings. It is certainly the earliest form of communication available to the human infant. Orphaned babies placed in institutions have died for lack of cuddling and holding. Through the experience of touching, a child is reassured, comforted, accepted, and made to feel loved.

Early touching experiences of the infant and child may be directly related to the effectiveness of adult interpersonal communication. Early experiences establish the first patterns of interpersonal relationships. They often determine individuals' confidence in themselves and amount of trust in others. For adults touching is one of the most valuable forms of nonverbal expression. Through touch, one can communicate such emotions as fear, coldness, anxiety, love, warmth, and security.

Paralanguage

Paralanguage refers to qualities or tones of the voice and speaking styles not directly related to the specific words that are said. It includes the sounds associated with laughing and crying. The loudness, pitch, rate, and rhythm of the voice are the vocal qualities most obvious to the average communicator. The concept of speaking styles refers to pauses, fillers like "ah," "uh," "anda," and drawling or clipping of words.

Specific reactions to messages often result more from the tone of voice of the sender than from the actual words said. Loudness or softness of voice conveys meaning by providing emphasis to certain verbal messages. Shouting is often associated with anger; quietness, with disappointment. Pitch describes the highness or lowness of the voice. A high-pitched voice is often associated with whining, fear, or anxiety. A low-pitched voice conveys relaxation and calmness. Pitch differs, too, at the end of statements and questions. Listen carefully at the end of a question—normally pitch will rise. Rate refers to the speed of what is said. Quick speech generally indicates urgency; slow speech, a hesitation. Rhythm refers to the way that loudness, pitch, and speed are varied. With little variety a monotone effect will result.

Each individual develops a speaking style, or a pattern, of pausing, using fillers, and drawling or clipping words. Pausing often conveys a message of thoughtfulness and reflection. If done with skill pauses allow the speaker to formulate thoughts and give appropriate emphases. Pauses accompanied by "ah's" and "er's," however, can have a nearly opposite effect, revealing a lack of decisiveness or preparedness. The third quality, drawling versus clipping, might be exemplified by a resident of the deep South in the United States and a resident of London. Such "accents" communicate an individual's heritage and background to some extent.

Physical Characteristics

Physical characteristics are those qualities of an individual that generally stay the same. Physical characteristics are in part acquired through heredity. For example, individuals can do little to alter permanently height, bone structure, or eye color. Other physical characteristics are acquired as one passes through the developmental phases of life, or as one makes decisions about physical appearance. For example, length of hair, posture, and aspects of appearance related to grooming can be determined to a considerable extent by the individual.

Both types of physical characteristics—those over which an individual has control and those over which little control is possible—provide nonverbal messages in a communication situation. For example, the condition of a person's hands communicates something about the type of work in which the person is involved. The length, style, and condition of a person's hair reveal information about the person's lifestyle—casual versus structured, progressive versus conservative. Physical characteristics and their corresponding messages interact with what, in communication, are called artifacts.

Figure 5.3. *The way we dress and the things we own send messages to others about our values and life styles.*

Artifacts

Artifacts are those objects which communicators display while sending and receiving messages. These include such items as clothing, jewelry, makeup and perfume that directly interact with physical appearance. First impressions of individuals are often relayed via the nonverbal messages associated with an individual's overall appearance. Such judgments can relate to a person's socioeconomic status, values, and interests. First impressions made on the basis of physical characteristics and artifacts, however, are often proved to be very inaccurate.

Recently the topic of clothing as it relates to success has received attention in the popular press. John T. Molloy (1975, 1977) has been called "America's first wardrobe engineer" by Time Magazine. He has conducted numerous investigations of reactions to specific ways of dressing that create desired images. He feels that most men and women who seek to advance in the corporate structure dress for failure. Molloy (1975; p.15) makes the following statement as he expresses the effect of dress on image.

> *I can help you look successful, fatherly, honest, sexy, or even use clothes to mask or overcome detrimental physical characteristics or quirks. I have successfully applied these techniques on behalf of national political figures of both parties, executives of many of America's leading corporations, diplomats of foreign governments stationed in the United States, foreign executives seeking to do business here, television personalities, salesmen, courtroom lawyers, defendants in major criminal trials, professional associations, and, of course, private individuals.*

Molloy is convinced that people who look successful and educated receive better treatment in nearly all business and social situations. He bases his conclusions on studies where reactions to individuals wearing different types of clothing have been recorded. His message is quite persuasive and leaves the reader feeling that such artifacts as clothing can, in fact, make a strong statement to others.

Environment

In addition to the objects that create the outward appearance of an individual, choices of other objects such as cars and furnishings, room arrangements, and preferences for specific places provide nonverbal messages. Communicators make inferences from the make and model of a car, the type of architecture of a home, and choice of a restaurant for an evening meal. For example, the message seems different when a couple selects a quiet, small, dimly lit restaurant for their date in contrast to a noisy, large, brightly lit restaurant. And does not the choice of a small economical car versus a mid-sized sportier model reveal something about the purchaser's values?

Numerous studies have been conducted over the years in an attempt to relate choices of environmental factors to other traits. The relationships, however, are so complex that it is difficult to make specific conclusions. Many factors, preferences, and constraints interact. Nevertheless such choices do provide information in a communication situation and, right or wrong, contribute to perceptions of what is going on.

Some Implications of Nonverbal Messages

The study of nonverbal messages has intrigued scholars for years. Nierenberg and Calero (1971) have bibliography in their book, *How to Read a Person Like a Book*, with references dating as far back as 1822 (e.g., *Practical Illustration of Rhetorical Gestures*, by Henry Siddons). Other books contain extensive bibliographies and reviews of research and opinions concerning nonverbal messages. For purposes of this review, information about conflicting verbal and nonverbal messages, awareness of one's own nonverbal messages, and body language will be covered.

Conflicting Messages

The major goal of communication is to send and receive messages that are clear and accurate. This requires speaking ability and listening ability as well as the ability to receive and interpret nonverbal messages. If you notice a gesture, an article of clothing, or a facial expression, it might be a planned action of the communicator meant to send a message, a subconscious movement of the communicator, or a random motion of no importance. One problem with nonverbal messages is that we are not sure if they are intended or not. Another problem in interpreting nonverbal messages is the possibility that verbal and nonverbal messages may conflict.

Consider the person who has just had a foot trampled while sitting on a bus. The trampler, with face set in a worried manner, might say, "I'm sorry." The person with the crushed foot is likely to be grinding teeth in pain while saying, "No problem. My foot is fine." The actual message of pain was communicated fairly clearly. Conflicts between verbal and nonverbal messages can go much deeper. There are situations where it is hard to determine which message, the verbal or nonverbal, is the more accurate.

Examples of verbal and nonverbal messages that are hard to interpret often occur during heated discussions, arguments, or what might be called personality clashes in situations where appearances of friendship must be upheld. For example, a mother and daughter in the company of friends might have a discussion over a matter on which they disagree. The verbal messages might mask the true extent of the problem while the nonverbal messages may be subtly revealing that a conflict situation exists. Unfortunately for the sender who tries to mask the conflict, not only the intended receiver but everyone observing the transaction can give meaning to such sometimes not so subtle nonverbal messages.

In situations where verbal and nonverbal messages seem to conflict, it is generally the nonverbal message that is the more truthful (Nierenberg & Calero, 1971). To clarify situations where conflicting messages occur, it is useful to try two things. First, interpret the total nonverbal message or the cluster of individual signs that follow one another. Often more accurate meanings can be gathered from nonverbal messages that seem to go together. Isolated movements and gestures that result from an individual's habits do not necessarily carry the meaning normally assigned them (e.g., blinking eyes may be due to a physical impairment). Second, initiate a verbal response by asking a question aimed at clearing up the confusion. Such questions as, "are you certain about that," "let me see if I understand what you've said," or "could you expand on that," are useful to clarify a message that includes conflicting verbal and nonverbal components. Understanding nonverbal messages is a difficult task. Each can be contradicted, made clearer, or confused by the verbal and other nonverbal messages it accompanies.

Awareness of One's Own Nonverbal Messages

Have you ever thought about the nonverbal messages that you send and the meanings others might attach to them? If communicators become aware of the nonverbal messages they are sending, they become more aware of their own reactions to situations and are able to communicate better. Very often nonverbal messages cause receivers of messages to react in specific yet unanticipated ways.

Each movement or motion is, in a sense, a word in a nonverbal language. It is a language that is hard to speak fluently. It contains a great deal of "noise" that distorts messages. Although it is hard to see oneself speak in nonverbal ways, like other languages, practice makes it easier to understand. Try looking at yourself as you speak to other people, in small groups, and to large audiences. What do you see? Do you have habits that might interfere with the nonverbal messages you send? What type of messages do you send? What does your clothing say? What messages do you send through the qualities of your voice? How close do you get to people in different kinds of situations? Do you ever communicate through touch?

People who become aware of their own nonverbal messages can sometimes improve the clarity of the messages they convey. Consider an individual who sits somewhat rigidly with arms folded in conference with another individual. Realizing this and the message of resistance that it probably conveys, the first individual might change posture to indicate an attitude of openness toward the topic of discussion. It seems only logical that the communication process will be more effective if both parties feel that each is receptive and open to discussion.

Like learning a foreign language, the process of self-observation and conscious knowledge of nonverbal messages will take time. It seems a hard task to concentrate on both the content of a message and how to express it both verbally and nonverbally. It might be easier to begin noticing your own nonverbal behaviors as you listen in situations that do not require total concentration. For example, take a look at yourself as you chat with a close friend and as you chat with an authority figure. Are your nonverbal behaviors different? If so, should they be different?

Body Language

Body language has been a prevalent topic in the popular press for several years. Books like *Body Language* (Fast, 1970) have been best sellers and popular periodicals have included many articles on body language or, as it was called earlier in this chapter, body motions or movements. The scientific community has done much work in this area of communication too. Psychologists, sociolgists, anthropologists, and communication theorists have studied the meanings attached to gestures, facial expressions, posture, eye movement, and other nonverbal expressions. Of the areas differentiated in the earlier section on nonverbal messages the area of the body language (i.e., body motion) has probably received more attention and created wider interest than any of the others.

Because of the popularity of the study of body language by both scholars and the general public, perhaps it deserves further discussion here. It is impossible in this limited space to cover the entire domain of body language. Therefore, a few of the more common and possibly the more interesting generalizations about body language will be presented. Nierenberg and Calero (1971), in *How to Read a Person Like a Book*, discuss a number of different behavioral states and the body language associated with them. Among these behavioral states are openness, cooperation, frustration, confidence, nervousness, and courtship.

Openness. The human behaviors associated with openness are similar to those behaviors of animals that communicate submissiveness by lying on their backs and exposing their stomachs and necks. Open arms with palms exposed are a particularly common and easily observable indication of openness. It is, in fact, a posture that is commonly displayed in religious statues. An unbuttoned coat is another symbol of openness. A general demeanor of being relaxed often expresses openness. In group situations openness may be shown by members drawing closer together.

Cooperation. The state of being cooperative is similar to that of being open. It seems that true cooperation requires an openness to exploring the situation. A cooperative attitude is demonstrated by a posture that can be described as a "sprinter's position." It is a nonverbal indicator of being ready for action by leaning forward with feet on tiptoes. The cooperative gesture is further demonstrated by such behaviors as sitting on the edge of a chair, hand-to-face gestures, unbuttoning of the coat, and tilting the head in an attentive position. It can be especially useful to recognize behaviors that indicate a change from a cooperative attitude to a noncooperative attitude so that the situation can be restructured before it results in irreparable changes in attitude.

Frustration. Frustration is a behavior communicated nonverbally by most people at one time or another. It is communicated by a wide range of behaviors like short breaths, hands tightly clenched, wringing of hands, fistlike gestures, pointing index finger, palm to the back of the neck, and kicking the ground or an imaginary object. Frustration seems to be a mental state that is openly communicated both to oneself, even when alone, and to others. Frustrated people are generally seeking solutions. When reacting to others' frustrations, it is often helpful to send nonverbal messages that communicate reassurance and confidence.

Confidence. Confidence is demonstrated by a proud, erect stance that can be achieved by squaring the shoulders and straightening the back. A confident person also seems to have longer, more frequent eye contact and to blink less. Steepling (joining of the fingertips and wrists), hands joined together behind the back with chin thrust upward, claiming territory by placing feet on a desk or one leg over the arm of a chair; or by placing personal articles in desired space, elevating oneself to a higher plane than others, and leaning back with hands supporting the head are other behaviors that communicate confidence. Many of these characteristics can be associated with authority figures who must display confidence as part of their role.

Nervousness. Nervousness is the opposite of confidence. We've all noticed what might be called "uptight" messages from those around us. This is an instance where the verbal messages usually contradict the nonverbal messages. Most people resist admitting anxiety and often take offense when asked a direct question about how they seem to be feeling. Several indicators of nervousness are the following: clearing of the throat, the "whew" sound, extinguishing or leaving a cigarette burning, fidgeting in a chair, hands covering the mouth while speaking, tugging at clothing while seated, jingling money in pockets, and ear-tugging. When such behaviors are observed, it is sometimes useful to pause briefly and analyze the situation that is causing nervousness. Sometimes an objective look at a situation can greatly reduce anxiety.

Courtship. Persons engaged in courtship behaviors can be identified by a state of firm muscle tone, attempts at improving appearance, and a feeling of being at ease with each other. The posture of a couple in love seems to be less slumped than usual. The skin seems to take on a firmer look. There is an attempt to smooth the hair, straighten the clothing, and check reflections in mirrors or windows. Some gestures like crossing and uncrossing the legs and direct eye contact are used to express an interest in involvement. Normally men and women who are romantically interested in each other have little difficulty expressing this emotion via nonverbal messages.

SUMMARY

Human beings rely heavily on verbal communication to transmit and receive messages. Nonverbal messages also play an essential role in the total communication process. Verbal communication is particularly appropriate for transmitting knowledge. Nonverbal messages are particularly appropriate for sharing emotions, feelings, and attitudes. Love, for example, can be communicated verbally but is more effectively communicated with the addition of nonverbal messages.

Nonverbal language is expressed through body motions, personal space, touching, paralanguage, physical characteristics, artifacts, and environment. Through nonverbal language, power, trustworthiness, status, love, affection, acceptance, hostility, and other emotions and attitudes can be communicated. Some individuals are more adept at both sending and receiving nonverbal messages than others. Hopefully, through an awareness that nonverbal messages are important aspects of communication, a greater sensitivity to one's own nonverbal messages and those of others can be developed.

CHAPTER 6

Nonverbal Techniques to Help the Listener

Listening is a complex process. To be an effective listener it is necessary to select and process those elements in the environment that provide the most important information. By studying and practicing good listening habits individuals can do much to improve their own skill as listeners. Speakers can do much also to help the listener attend to and retain the important aspects of a message.

By considering the effects of nonverbal stimuli on the receiver of the message, the speaker can facilitate the listening process in interpersonal, small group, and speaker-audience communication situations. The goal of the speaker in facilitating listening is to eliminate factors that might be distracting and to present the message in a manner that maintains attention. The speaker's body motions, vocal expression, and appearance are extremely important nonverbal factors in facilitating the listening process.

Body Motion

Body motions that contribute to the effectiveness of speakers as they send messages include posture, movements, gestures, eye contact, and facial expressions. Skill in facilitating the listening task of intended receivers can be developed by paying attention to the nonverbal messages sent with the verbal messages.

Posture

Posture can be described along dimensions from relaxed to rigid and erect to stooped. A relaxed posture indicates informality; a rigid posture, formality. An erect posture indicates pride and confidence; a stooped posture, timidness or lack of concern. In communication situations interest and confidence are two states that have direct effect on the attentiveness of the listener. Interest in the listener can be indicated by a somewhat rigid and erect posture. Lack of interest is indicated by a totally relaxed or stooped posture. An especially good example of posture as it relates to interest occurs as an instructor ends a somewhat dull lecture and says, "Now, let me tell you what to study for the test." The relaxed and possibly slouched postures of the students suddenly change to indicate attention.

In speaker-audience and small group situations, an erect but relaxed posture is probably the appropriate stance. The erect posture provides a look of preparedness and confidence that helps to establish credibility. The somewhat relaxed posture removes the look of tenseness and nervousness that speakers often feel. Hands rattling change, kept in the pocket, or held behind the back tend to keep the speaker from being free and spontaneous. If standing, speakers should have weight distributed about equally on both feet. It is recommended that they not lean on a lectern or table. In fact, it is often better not to use a lectern since it can create a barrier between the speaker and listeners.

In interpersonal situations, the appropriate posture can be quite varied. If passive listening is appropriate, a totally relaxed posture might be most effective. If a very serious dialogue is occurring, a rigid and upright posture might communicate the appropriate concern. In all speaking situations, a change in posture from somewhat passive to more alert is a good way to indicate readiness to speak or change roles. It should be noted that postures are acquired, in many cases, by copying the postures perceived to be used effectively by others in communication situations.

Movements

A speaker's movements can enhance and hinder the communication process. Movements are probably most effectively used as a nonverbal emphasis of verbal statements—that is, telling the listener that a particular part of a message is especially important. By moving the body closer to the listener, for example, the speaker can send the nonverbal message that the upcoming verbal statements are particularly significant. By moving away from the listener, emphasis can be drawn to a message that indicates a cautionary or doubtful reaction. Constant movement, however, may be so distracting that it will weaken or "throw away" the entire message.

A public speaker's movements in most cases should be free and uninhibited. The speaker should feel free to move around in front of the audience. The speaker can emphasize points by moving toward the audience or by taking a step and pausing. The statement or word that comes immediately after the movement is the point that receives the emphasis. When a speaker's stand is used, the speaker should not hide behind it but should feel free to move around it to the side or even to the front. It is acceptable too to move away from the speaker's stand to refer to a chart or diagram on an easel or blackboard. In less formal small group and interpersonal communication situations, seemingly routine movements will not be as noticeable as they are in a speaker-audience situation. In all situations, a speaker's movement should be used to enhance and not to interfere with the message.

Gestures

Gesturing is a type of nonverbal expression that most speakers use quite naturally. Gesturing that is spontaneous and unplanned is generally the best. Forced gestures alert the receiver of a message to the speaker's uneasiness. Gestures are particularly important in pointing out relevant visual elements of the surroundings, and as a way of reinforcing parts of the spoken message. The listener often relies on gestures to add specificity to somewhat vague verbal messages. For example, gardeners might reinforce messages concerning huge tomatoes by pointing out one of particularly large size, by making emphatic gestures as they say the word "huge," or by using their hands to show the approximate size.

Beginning public speakers often complain that they do not know how to use their hands effectively in making gestures. They prefer to put them in their pockets or hide them behind their backs. If hands are left by the side, there is often a natural, free, and uninhibited gesturing that comes as the result of involvement in what the speaker is saying. If gesturing is difficult, the public speaker may consciously want to plan a gesture at a certain place in the speech. This can seem awkward to the speaker in the beginning, but as experience increases the gestures will seem more natural. It is helpful to speak as often as possible before an audience so that gestures can be practiced. This will lead to a more relaxed feeling and eventually gesturing will become entirely spontaneous in speaker-audience situations. In small group and interpersonal communication situations gestures are generally second nature. The speaker can, however, develop skill in the use of gestures as a means of reinforcing or further defining important concepts.

Figure 6.1. *To be authentic in communication, eye contact with your listeners is essential to show that you care about them.*

Eye Contact

Even more important than gesturing in facilitating the listening task is eye contact. Some speakers tend to look at the ceiling, floor, or anyplace but the eyes of their listener or listeners. Avoidance of the listeners' eyes sends a message of extreme discomfort or lack of interest that does nothing but hinder communication. Ignoring the listener by failing to establish eye contact reduces the speaker's credibility and the chance to convince or inform the listener of anything.

Public speakers should maintain good eye contact as much of the time as possible by looking directly into the eyes of various members of the audience and not over their heads or at their feet. Staring at one particular person in the audience or one area of the audience should be avoided also. Any part of the audience that is constantly ignored will feel less and less involved with the message and find it more and more difficult to listen effectively. In small group communication, eye contact can be established with every group member at various points in a discussion. This is effective in helping each group member feel that the message is intended personally. In communication with one other person, constant eye contact becomes a stare and causes the listener to feel discomfort. In interpersonal situations, it is best to lose and reestablish eye contact in a way that seems natural for the situation.

Facial Expressions

Another important aspect of nonverbal communication and a definite way to help the listener is through facial expression. Facial expression should be consistent with the speaker's message. Without appropriate facial expression, the listener will doubt the sincerity of the speaker. When this occurs the ability to listen either critically or discriminately can be affected. A good example of the importance of facial expressions to the message occurs in films where a second language has been dubbed over the native language. The facial movements often seem inappropriate for the verbal message. Nonverbal expressions like frowns, smiles, grimaces, and appearances of excitement, happiness, or concern help the listener feel that the speaker is sincere. The feeling of sincerity generated by the speaker helps create interest in the message.

Speakers who are new to public speaking are sometimes nervous at first and find it difficult to present an expressive face. As speakers gain experience and appear before more groups, they become more relaxed and more expressive. As the speaker reveals involvement with the subject by facial expression as well as other nonverbal movements, the audience often senses the interest and becomes equally involved. It is generally unwise, however to laugh or "break out of character" in a formal speaking situation. In general, public speakers should concentrate on the message so intently that they remain in control of the situation even when the audience laughs or smiles. Certainly it is acceptable to smile and look happy but it is better not to lose composure completely by laughing on the platform because of something in the message. In less formal communication situations facial expressions, like gestures, occur more naturally. A face that expresses involvement in the message can be a useful tool for creating a similar involvement in the listener.

Vocal Expression

The ways that speakers use their voices make a difference in whether or not one listener or an entire audience pays attention to what a speaker has to say. A listener does not pay attention to ideas, supporting materials, or language as much as to the sounds that are heard. These sounds are uttered with a particular volume, pitch, rate, articulation, pronunciation, and vocal quality which affect the listener's reaction to the message. Inadequate volume, monotonous pitch, rate that is too rapid, sloppy articulation, mispronounced words, a voice quality that is heavily marred by regionalisms, and other facets can cause the listener's ear to turn away from the message. For this reason a person who is trying to communicate should pay close attention to the vocal aspects of speech.

$$\begin{pmatrix} \text{Volume + Pitch + Rate + Articulation} \\ \text{+ Pronounication + Vocal Quality} \end{pmatrix} - \begin{pmatrix} \text{"Er" + "Uh"} \\ \text{+ "You Know"} \end{pmatrix} = \begin{matrix} \text{Vocal} \\ \text{Expression} \end{matrix}$$

Figure 6.2. *Vocal expression.*

©1961 United Feature Syndicate, Inc.

Volume

Volume refers to the loudness and softness of the communicator's voice. It is determined by the amount of air supporting the sound production. When there is a considerable amount of air to support a sound it will be loud. When there is little air, the sound will be faint. When communicators speak so softly that they cannot be heard, they waste their own time as well as that of their listeners.

Often speakers, especially public speakers, will barely speak above a whisper. This may be caused by a poor self-concept resulting from a feeling that the message has little value. If the intended listener does not hear what is being said, then no communication can take place. A flexible variation in volume is also important to the listening process. Without variation in volume, the speaker places the same emphasis on everything. This makes the message appear dull. Emphasis and contrast may be achieved by speaking softly or by stating an idea with increasing volume. The pattern of beginning a sentence with adequate volume and then fading at the end should be avoided, however.

Pitch

Pitch variation is also important. Pitch refers to the highness and lowness of the voice. As air passes over tensed vocal folds they vibrate and sound is formed. The amount of tension present as the vocal folds vibrate determines the pitch of the speaker's voice. When tension is great, pitch will be high. Less tension creates a lower pitch. Common errors for speakers, especially public speakers, are a sameness of pitch that produces a monotonous voice, or a pitch that seems to strain the voice. A strained voice in a speaker-audience situation often results from a beginning speaker's nervousness before an audience and passes as confidence is gained. Feelings of insecurity often lead to improper pitch usage.

A speaker's optimum pitch level refers to those tones best suited to the individual's voice. Nothing, however, is more boring than a speaker who remains at the same pitch throughout a message. To create variety, a speaker should deviate both four or five pitches above and below the optimum pitch level. Creating variety is easier if the speaker has chosen a topic in which both personal and audience interest can be developed. If a speaker is eager to discuss the subject with the listeners it is likely that an energetic and animated voice will result.

Rate

Rate refers to the speed at which a message is delivered. A desirable rate of speaking is one that permits the listener to grasp what the speaker says. If the rate of speech is too slow, the listener's interest will wander; if too fast, much of the message will be lost. Rate of speech, within understandable ranges, can be used to alert the listener to certain behavioral states of the speaker. Rapid rate of speech indicates excitement or urgency; slow rate of speech, boredom.

Because of insecurity before an audience, beginning public speakers often tend to present their messages too rapidly. This causes them to be less interesting because they lack variety in speaking rate. Speakers who are sure that they know what they are talking about are better able to vary rate. By recording a speech on tape before the delivery date, the speaker can practice varying rate. If the speaker will listen objectively to the recording, corrections and improvements can be made. If it seems too fast to the speaker, who knows the subject, then it is sure to be too fast for the average listener. A speaker who tends to get nervous and talk too fast should make a conscious effort to slow down. Remember too that every second does not have to be filled with sound. Speakers in all situations can pause to get their breath or collect their thoughts.

Articulation and Pronunciation

Articulation is the process of forming individual sounds and joining them together. Pronunciation is the way that a whole word should be said. Articulation is primarily a matter of habit. Many people say "jist" instead of "just," or "git" instead of "get" because they are in the habit of articulating these words incorrectly. When speakers say "Illinois" with an "s" sound at the end, however, it is probably because they do not know the correct pronunciation.

When sounds are articulated correctly they do not need to sound overly precise or affected. Each sound is uttered to be distinct and easily recognizable, without adding sounds that should not be there (e.g., "warsh" instead of wash), without omitting sounds (e.g., "swimmin" instead of swimming), without substituting incorrect sounds (e.g., "git" instead of get), and without reversing the order of sounds (e.g., "hunderd" instead of hundred). When people learn to form sounds incorrectly, articulation problems like omissions, distortions, and slurring result.

Because mistakes in pronunciation are the result of lack of knowledge, many errors can be eliminated once the speaker learns the correct way to say the words. It is important to learn which letters or letter combinations are spoken or silent, how a word is correctly pronounced, when a syllable is accented, and which regional variations are acceptable. If a speaker knows the correct way to say a word but continues to err, then the problem is one of articulation, not pronunciation. When speakers include words unfamiliar to them in their messages, they are wise to consult a dictionary, a book called *A Pronouncing Dictionary of American English* (Kenyon and Knott, 1953), or a person known to be expert in pronunciation.

Vocal Quality

Finally, a speaker's vocal quality is significant to the way that listeners receive the message. Vocal quality is that special characteristic in a speaker's voice that makes it unique. The vocal quality can be defined as the resonance, or vibration, of the sounds formed in the vocal folds. The sounds pass through the resonating cavities—the throat, mouth, and nose—and are altered and modified before being emitted. Size, shape, and texture of the resonating cavities determine the sound the listener hears. A voice with good quality is free from nasality, harshness, huskiness, hoarseness, breathiness, and shrillness. It is in general a voice that is pleasant and easy to listen to.

To listen to your own vocal quality, record it on tape. It will probably *not* sound the way you think it should, but it will be you exactly as others hear you. The difference is caused by hearing yourself through bone rather than air as others do. Most people are so accustomed to their voices that they fail to hear them as others do. It is useful as a speaker to develop an awareness of how you sound and to change your voice if it is unpleasant. If you need help in improving the quality of your voice, you may want to consult an expert in the field such as a speech therapist.

Appearance

Grooming

Appearance can and often does contribute to the effectiveness or ineffectiveness of a speaker. In general, appearance becomes more and more important as the communication encounter moves from the intimate relationships of family and friends to that of the casual acquaintance, or the complete stranger. Speakers present a better appearance if they are groomed and dressed in a manner suitable to their listeners. Appearance should in no way detract from the message. An extremely short dress, a low-necked blouse, a sweatshirt with comments printed across the front, or dirty tennis shoes can distract listeners.

Some people react negatively to certain types of dress and grooming. Every minute that a listener spends dwelling on the speaker's appearance is valuable time taken away from concentration on the message. Although many listeners will be quite tolerant of dress and grooming, it is important to give thought to the effect that appearance will have on the communication situation. If there is some question about what will be appropriate dress, it is probably safer to dress conservatively. In general, attention to grooming and dress is definitely more important in formal speaking situations than in casual interpersonal encounters.

Demeanor

Demeanor refers to the manner in which individuals present themselves. Like grooming, a speaker's demeanor can have a definite effect on the first impressions of the listener. For example, public speakers who hesitate and shuffle up to the platform, appear overly nervous, self-conscious, bored, or indifferent, or spend too much time getting organized, tend to make the audience feel ill at ease. Public speakers who wish to attract the interest of their audiences should be ready to get out of their seats as soon as they are introduced and walk to the front of the group without greeting friends or shaking hands. Public speakers should appear confident but not smug, go directly to the platform, adjust notes, survey the audience to see if they are ready to listen, take a deep breath, and begin. When speeches are complete, speakers should give their conclusions. Without saying thank you (the audience should thank the speaker!), speakers should pause to allow the audience a moment to collect their thoughts and reflect, and then they should return to their seats. Demeanor will affect listeners in less formal situations too. Small groups and individuals will react to the manner in which speakers present themselves and will listen more or less effectively because of it.

For example, a parent or spouse must often adopt an authoritarian demeanor to get household members to attend to a "clean up the house" message.

In general then, the speaker's appearance should be such that it does not distract listeners as they attempt to attend to the message. The speaker's demeanor should be confident so that the listener is at ease with the speaker's presence. The entire speaking process will be more effective if it is designed to enhance the receiver's ability to listen.

SUMMARY

The listening process is especially difficult in critical and discriminative situations when attention must be maintained and important points must be retained. The listener, of course, must take responsibility for attending to messages and can do much to improve attending and retention skills. In addition, the speaker who particularly wishes a message to have a significant effect can facilitate the listening process by paying particular attention to body motions, vocal expression, and appearance.

Such body motions as posture, movements, gestures, eye contact, and facial expressions can be used to draw emphasis to particular points of a message. The aspects of vocal expression that require special attention by the speaker are volume, pitch, rate, articulation, pronunciation, and vocal quality. Lack of vocal energy, lack of emphasis and variety, monotony in pitch, and a rate that drags can be dull and cause the listener's mind to wander. A speaker's appearance can be distracting to the listener if inappropriate for the situation.

When an attempt is made to emphasize a point, accomplished speakers will often change their volume; slow their rates of speaking; pause before and after a point; change body position; step toward the audience; or maintain eye contact for a longer, steadier length of time. Combinations of several of these nonverbal aspects of communication can be used effectively to place emphasis on a special point. The listener who is aware of such techniques is then cued to pay attention to particularly important points.

> **Activity 1**
> **Information about Listening and Nonverbal Messages**

Preparation: Read the textual material for Part II: Listing and Nonverbal Messages. Prepare yourself to take a test by reviewing the "Knowledge Objective" included in the Overview for Part II and by answering the practice items given below.

PRACTICE ITEMS FOR PART II

Instructions: Select the best answer for each item.

1. Failure to attach meaning to verbal messages is a definition of
    a. listening
    b. not listening
    c. hearing
    d. not hearing
2. Which is an example of discriminative listening?
    a. evaluating the sales pitch of an insurance man
    b. detecting bias in a decision made by your boss
    c. analyzing the evidence presented from performance tests of new cars
    d. learning the meaning of a new concept from the context in which it is presented
3. Which is a poor listening habit?
    a. jumping ahead of the speaker in anticipation of what will be said
    b. making notes of only key ideas and concepts
    c. waiting until a question has been asked to formulate an answer
    d. being open-minded toward the opinion of others
4. To improve message transmission via communication chains, the speaker should
    a. omit some details of the message
    b. add details to the message
    c. rephrase the details of the message
    d. emphasize important details in the message
5. Which is not a type of nonverbal message?
    a. touching
    b. hearing
    c. gesturing
    d. eye contact

Activity 1 continued

6. Confidence is indicated by
   a. sagging shoulders
   b. lack of eye contact
   c. erect posture
   d. shortness of breath
7. What has probably occurred in a conversation where one individual continues to move away from the other individual?
   a. The two communicators are having an argument.
   b. The retreating individual is emotionally upset by the conversation.
   c. The personal space of the retreating individual is being invaded.
   d. The retreating individual finds the other individual's voice too loud.
8. When verbal and nonverbal messages seem to conflict, which is generally the more truthful?
   a. verbal
   b. nonverbal
9. The knowledge of the correct way to say specific words is called
   a. expression
   b. vocal quality
   c. articulation
   d. pronunciation
10. Which type of body movement is very effective in helping listeners feel that a message is meant for them?
    a. posture
    b. demeanor
    c. eye contact
    d. touching

Key: 1.b   2.d   3.a   4.d   5.b   6.c   7.c   8.b   9.d   10.c

Group Activity: Attend class and complete objective test items for Part II: Listening and Nonverbal Messages.

Individual Activity: Make arrangements with your instructor to complete objective test items for Part II: Listening and Nonverbal Messages.

Activity 2
Listening Myths

Preparation: Contrast the assumptions and facts given below about the listening process.

The following assumptions about the listening process have often been made.

1. You need to be intelligent in order to be an excellent listener.
2. You listen well automatically.
3. You will hear exactly what other people say to you.
4. Neither the personality of speaker or listener affects the listening process.
5. You listen automatically so it is not necessary to study to acquire listening skills.

From research findings, the following conclusions have been verified about listening.

1. A person of average intelligence can be a good listener.
2. Because they are not trained to listen, most people listen poorly most of the time.
3. What is heard is affected by many variables including values, prejudices, and past experiences.
4. Listening is affected by the personalities of the communicators and the way they present themselves visually and orally to the listener.
5. Listening is a learned response that can be practiced until adequate skill is acquired.

Group Activity: The instructor will read an excerpt from literature to the group. As you listen make a conscious effort to be a good listener. Try to become aware of how well you listen. Do you need to overcome certain habits that are interfering with your ability to hear accurately what is being said?

As you listen, record single words or phrases that have some special meaning to you. What type of response does the excerpt from literature elicit from you? Are some of the words or phrases related to something in your life?

Discuss your reactions to the listening process with the entire group. Do you agree more with the assumptions or the facts about listening?

Individual Activity: Select an excerpt from a textbook for a college literature course. Ask a friend or classmate to spend at least ten minutes reading the selection aloud to you. Be aware of any problems that you have in concentrating as you listen.

Activity 2 continued

Is the material interesting to you? Are you daydreaming about something else? Are bad listening habits interfering with your ability to comprehend accurately what is being read?

As you listen, record single words or phrases that have some special meaning to you. Does the selection elicit a particular response from you? Do you relate to specific words or phrases and forget about the overall content of the selection?

Write a one-page report of your reaction to the listening experience you had. Refer to the questions in the two paragraphs above. Relate your reaction also to the assumptions and facts listed in the preparation section for this activity.

Activity 3
Types of Listening

Preparation: You will experience three different listening situations in this activity. For each, you will be required to listen to a specific type of message and complete the questions about the experience.

1. **Social Listening Exercise**

With at least one other person, watch a variety or comedy program on television.

1. Name of the program:
2. Name(s) of the person(s) who joined you:
3. Did watching the program provide an enjoyable social experience for you? Explain.
4. Did watching the program result in an opportunity for you to engage in social listening? Explain.
5. How can you grow socially from such experiences?
6. Were you primarily an active or passive listener in this situation? Cite several examples of why you actively and passively listened during the program or to those who joined you.

2. **Serious, Discriminative Listening Exercise**

Select a person who is making an address or lecture on some topic (e.g., a campus speaker, an instructor's class presentation). Try to select a situation where the primary purpose will be the presentation of information. After listening to the speaker, complete the following items.

1. Topic of address or lecture:
2. Name of speaker:
   Position of speaker:
3. State the purpose of the message in your own words.
4. Did the speaker provide details or speak only in generalities? Cite specific examples from the speech.
5. Did the speaker repeat ideas to give emphasis? If so, list several examples.
6. Were you primarily an active or passive listener in this situation? Cite several examples of why you actively and passively listened during the presentation.

Activity 3 continued

3. **Serious, Critical Listening Exercise**
Go to your library and locate a recording of a speech made by a famous speaker or listen to a news commentary presented on television. Try to select a situation where the primary purpose is to influence your opinion about an important issue. After listening to the speaker, complete the following items.

1. Topic of speech or commentary:

2. Name of speaker:
   Position of speaker:

3. Summarize the message.

4. Was the message based on evidence or on opinion? Explain.

5. Did the speaker present emotional or logical arguments to make the point? Explain.

6. Did you detect bias or prejudice in the presentation? Explain.

7. Were you primarily an active or passive listener in this situation? Cite several examples of why you actively and passively listened during the presentation.

Group Activity: Using your answers to the questions on the three listening situations, discuss the different degrees of concentration you experienced in each. Compare the degree of active and passive listening necessary to be an effective listener.

Individual Activity: Write a one-page summary of your reactions to the three listening situations. Discuss the different degrees of concentration you experienced in each. Compare the degree of active and passive listening necessary to be an effective listener.

Activity 4
Listening Behavior Questionnaire

Preparation: One way to improve listening is to develop an awareness of how you listen on a day-to-day basis. Observe yourself as you listen for a day. Write down the habits that make you a more or less effective listener. Then complete the following "Listening Behavior Questionnaire."

LISTENING BEHAVIOR QUESTIONNAIRE

Instructions: Statements describing twenty listening habits are given below. Indicate whether or not you perceive the statements to be characteristic of your listening habits.

Select the T for "true" if the habit characterizes your listening behavior all or most of the time.

Select the F for "false" if the habit seldom or never characterizes your listening behavior.

Be sure to read each statement carefully as you evaluate your listening habits. The only person you can deceive in this analysis is yourself.

T or F   1. I listen primarily for the facts and evidence provided by a speaker.
T or F   2. I appear to be listening to a speaker's message even when my mind has wandered.
T or F   3. I privately evaluate the delivery style and physical appearance of of those I listen to.
T or F   4. I experience great difficulty listening when the environment includes noise or other distractions.
T or F   5. I do not attempt to listen to messages that are difficult to understand.
T or F   6. I listen primarily for the speaker's overall purpose and reasoning patterns.
T or F   7. I attempt to keep my mind on the speaker's message by relating it to my own interests.
T or F   8. I concentrate on the message and not the delivery style and physical appearance of those I listen to.
T or F   9. I attempt to overcome noise and other distractions that interfere with listening.
T or F   10. I try to relate difficult messages to what little information I might have on the subject.
T or F   11. I accept as truth nearly anything a speaker has to say.

Activity 4 continued

T or F   12. I tune out a message that reflects attitudes, customs, or values different from my own.
T or F   13. I have acquired appropriate and adequate listening skills through natural processes of maturation.
T or F   14. I think about other topics as I listen to messages that do not require total concentraton.
T or F   15. I find emotional arguments to be the most convincing.
T or F   16. I use my evaluative skills to assess speaker credibility and truth of the message.
T or F   17. I remain open and objective to messages reflecting a different background from my own.
T or F   18. I realize the importance of improving listening skill through study and practice.
T or F   19. I attempt to relate a message to my own interests as I listen.
T or F   20. I avoid being taken in by arguments that are not based upon careful reasoning.

To score your questionnaire, give yourself one point for the T's you circled for items 6-10 and 16-20 and give yourself one point for the F's you circled for items 1-5 and 11-15. Your score should fall between 0 and 20. A low score indicates poor habits; a high score, good habits. You might consider changing your behavior on those items for which you failed to earn a point.

To check your own honesty in evaluating your listening skills, compare your responses to the following pairs of items.

 1 with 6   11 with 16
 2 with 7   12 with 17
 3 with 8   13 with 18
 4 with 9   14 with 19
 5 with 10   15 with 20

Since the paired statements represent opposite extremes of the same listening habit, most people will mark one of the pair true and the other false. Consider again any paired items to which the same response was made.

Group Activity: Form small groups of about six people. Using the data from your day of observation, your knowledge of the reading material from Chapter 4, and the completed questionnaire, discuss your listening habits and characteristics with your group. At the end of the discussion follow the instructions on the next page to construct a strategy to improve your listening behavior.

Activity 4 continued

1. List at least ten of your listening habits and characteristics and explain their effect on your ability to listen effectively.

2. Summarize your performance on the "Listening Behavior Questionnaire."

3. For the five habits or characteristics that have the greatest negative effect on your listening skill, list a strategy for improvement.

Individual Activity: Use the data from your day of observation, your knowledge of the reading material from Chapter 4, and the completed "Listening Behavior Questionnaire" to analyze your listening behavior. In addition, ask several close friends and relatives to express their evaluation of your listening skill. Then complete the three items from the group activity above to construct a strategy to improve your listening skill.

Activity 5
Listening Log

Preparation: Record your listening experiences for five days in a log. Draw a chart like the one shown at the end of this explanation. Keep the chart or a note pad with you at all times so that you do not forget to analyze your listening behavior. Note under the columns entitled "Effectiveness of My Listening" whether or not the listening was passive, active, social, serious, critical, or discriminative. Continue your log until you have recorded twenty-five activities. Some activities might include several listening topics. Be sure to record each one. The log is an exercise designed to increase your awareness of your listening behavior. Unless you conscientiously observe yourself and record and analyze your behavior, your time will be wasted.

Example of Listening Log

Date	Activity	Person(s) Involved	Listening Topic	Effectiveness of my Listening	Improvement Needed
7/13	1. Lecture on World History	Classmates and Instructor	World War II	Passive listening through class except during outline of next exam and then it became active, serious, and discriminative.	Use more self-control and better note-taking to keep my attention on lecture.
	2. Lunch with Friend	Friend	Dating Problems	Excellent active, social listening while talking about my problem; mind wandered occasionally during friend's problem.	Place myself in the other person's position to keep me attentive.

Activity 5 continued

Date	Activity	Person(s) Involved	Listening Topic	Effectiveness of my Listening	Improvement Needed
	3. Homework in Library	None	Audio tape on Churchill's speeches	Active, serious, and discriminative listening since instructor gave specific questions to answer.	None

Group Activity: Bring a finished copy of your log with twenty-five entries to class. In groups of six and in round robin fashion discuss your most interesting entries. Did the log increase your awareness of your listening behavior? Analyze your listening behavior and what you know about yourself as a result of the activity.

Individual Activity: Write a one-page paper examining the value of this activity. Did the log increase your awareness of your listening behavior? Analyze your listening behavior in some detail and discuss what you know about yourself as a result of the activity.

Activity 6
Body Motion

Preparation: As we communicate, nonverbal cues reveal specific information about other people. We can develop an awareness of and sensitivity to these cues so that we are able to recognize certain consistencies and discrepancies in the behavior of others. To prepare for this activity relating to the observation of nonverbal messages, review the different ways that body motion can be used to communicate.

Group Activity: To observe the nonverbal behavior of your classmates as expressed through body motion, form groups of approximately eight. Be seated at a table with half the members of the group on each side. Toss a coin to decide which group will start the actvity . Keeping their hands hidden beneath the table, members of the beginning group should pass something small like a penny among themselves.

When a person on the opposite side of the table supposedly knows who has the object, the movement should cease and the group of observers should discuss who has the coin. When the majority of the team agrees, the person who is suspected should be named and the location of the coin revealed. If the suspected person does have the object, the side doing the guessing receives a point. The object is then passed to the other side. The game continues until the instructor halts the action.

At the end of the activity, discuss the nonverbal cues that revealed who had the coin.
1. How did you feel when you were passing the object back and forth?
2. Was it difficult to act as though you did not have the object? Explain.
3. Are you a person who reveals yourself nonverbally in a noticeable way? Explain.

Individual Activity: Gather at least three of your family members or friends together. Introduce them to the types of body motions that provide nonverbal messages and explain how to observe nonverbal messages. Then seat yourselves at a table with your three friends on one side and you on the other. Keeping their hands hidden beneath the table, the group of three should pass something small like a penny among themselves.

Activity 6 continued

When you supposedly know who has the object the movement should cease. The person who is suspected should be named and the location of the coin revealed. The group of four should then rotate and repeat the process until everyone has had two or more turns.

At the end of the activity, discuss the nonverbal cues that revealed who had the coin. Then write out your answers to the three questions at the end of the group activity above.

Activity 7
Personal Space

Preparation: When you intrude on the personal space of others by moving closer, they may feel uncomfortable and move farther away. If they tend to remain close, then they may have some message to share in confidence. Sometimes as people gain interest and enthusiasm over something they tend to move closer to those with whom they are communicating. Those whose personal space is invaded may become uncomfortable and back away almost as if being pursued. The enthusiastic person is often unaware that others are backing away. It is important to be aware of how others feel about personal space. Nonverbal cues given by others dictate whether to remain close or back off. To prepare for this activity, review the descriptions of the eight distances and the types of messages appropriate for each distance.

Group Activity: With your speech class, go to the library or cafeteria and deliberately intrude on the personal space of someone seated alone at a table. Notice if the person tries to restore an appropriate distance by moving away, turning sideways, or building a barrier with books. If this happens move your chair closer to the retreating victim. Notice if the victim chooses to move from the table or asks you to move. Most people will choose to find another place when their personal space is violated in this way.

Return to the classroom and discuss your experience.

Individual Activity: Follow the instructions for the group activity but go on your own. After your experience, write out the answers to the following questions.

1. What type of situation did you create as you invaded someone's personal space? Describe the location, the person, and any other relevant factors.
2. How did you feel as you invaded someone's personal space?
3. How do you think the other person felt?

Activity 8
Touching

Preparation: Some generalizations about touching patterns in our society have evolved over recent years. Several of these are included below in the form of questions. Be prepared to discuss your reaction to each question.

1. Do you tend to allow those with whom you have visual contact to have tactile contact as well? Explain.
2. With which body regions do you allow greater and lesser frequency of contact (e.g., hands, arms, neck)?
3. Are there persons whom you must not touch? If so, what are their characteristics?
4. What messages do you try to send via tactile communication channels?
5. What is your opinion of the following generalizations?
    a. Male and female norms differ in regard to touching behaviors.
    b. People who like and accept their bodies invite more physical contact than those who do not.
    c. American touch vocabulary is limited only to sexual meanings.
    d. Touch can bridge the gulfs that may open between people.

Group Activity: Using your answers to the questions above, participate in a discussion about touching behaviors. Then practice acceptable touching behaviors by walking around the classroom and having physical contact with as many people as time permits. At the end of the exercise discuss your reactions to the following questions.

1. How did it feel to touch the people in your class?
2. How did it feel to be touched by them?
3. Did the experience embarrass you?
4. Does it embarrass you when people you know well touch you?
5. How much space do you need to be comfortable with people around you?

Individual Activity: Review your answers to the questions in the preparation section of the activity and give thought to your normal touching behaviors. Then locate five adults who span a range from intimate family member to new acquaintance. Make physical contact in an acceptable manner with each of the five persons. At the end of the exercise, write out your answers to the questions included with the group activity and your answer to the additional question listed below.

6. Who were the five persons who participated with you in the exercise? Describe each briefly.

Activity 9
Paralanguage

Preparation

A speaker's voice is basic to the art of public speaking and communication in general. Foremost, the speaker's voice should be audible and the listener should have no trouble hearing and understanding it. The voice should be flexible so that variation in pitch, inflection, and rate can be used to communicate a variety of ideas, meanings, and emotions. Unless serious vocal problems exist, practice and experimentation with different ways of expressing thoughts will improve speaking ability.

To practice, select a folk story that you or a small group might practice and share with children at a day care center. Children enjoy a good story but they enjoy it more if it is told in a voice that is energetic and uses variety. Your selection should have an interesting beginning, a logical sequence of events, a spirited conflict, a definite climax, and a satisfying conclusion. The story should increase your listener's understanding of life, contain universal emotions, and show respect for character (e.g., *The Bremen Town Musicians, Rumpelstiltskin, The Ugly Duckling, The Wonderful Pear Tree*).

Read the story silently for enjoyment. Then reread the story slowly once or twice to visualize each scene. Try to visualize each event and character in the story until you feel you have lived the experience. Close the book and think silently through the story. Then read the story aloud using as much vocal variety and energy as possible.

Now prepare the story to be told, not read. Use the outline below to help in preparation.

1. List the sequence of events.
2. Who are the characters?
3. What is the problem?
4. What is the complication?
5. What is the solution?

Practice telling the story by rehearsing your presentation seven or eight times. Keep the language simple. Make the story come alive. Try to keep your voice flexible as you express each character's thoughts. Vary the rate. Variety is essential if your goal is to communicate feeling and thought. As the action progresses, the tempo should increase and build toward an exciting climax. Use the pause to gain suspense or to allow a thought to sink in before continuing to the next event.

Activity 9 continued

Overlearn your story. Think it through whenever you have a moment so that you will have no difficulty remembering the sequence of events when you stand before your audience. Try to make your presentation to a group of children.

Group Activity: When you get to class, form groups of three students. Each member of the group should present the story or a segment of the story taking approximately five minutes. The other two members of the group should serve as audience, trying to listen as a child might listen to the story.

After all have finished their stories, the small groups should discuss vocal variety and paralanguage of the speakers. For each speaker identify several positive and several negative examples of vocal variety and paralanguage.

Return to the larger group, and discuss the positive and negative effects of vocal variety and paralanguage in making the presentations.

Individual Activity: Locate a group of children to whom you can present the story you have rehearsed. As you present the story, observe the children's reactions and your own skill in making the presentation.

Prepare a one-page report describing your experience. Include the following points: the title of the story, an overview of your presentation, the children's reaction, and your impression of the experience with vocal variety and paralanguage.

**Activity
10
Speaking Activity**

Preparation

Option 1: Fantasy Trip

On a sheet of paper, list the five things you like to do most of all. Big things or little things—it does not matter as long as they are important to you. You might associate these five things with certain people, places, things, or seasons. Look at your list as something that tells a great deal about you at this time in your life.

Now imagine yourself in the future, anytime from tomorrow to several years from now, and devise one day that would be ideal for you. Use your list of five things to help you imagine twenty-four hours of the best possible use of that time for you. Fantasize whatever you want within a 24-hour period.

Using what you have learned about listening effectiveness, prepare a three- to four-minute description of your ideal day. In your description, you might include such details as what you would be doing, where you would be, and with whom you would be. Be as descriptive as possible as you capture the complete experience. Use your knowledge of what the speaker can do to help the listener. Remember, too, that all presentations need an attention-getting introduction, main points in the body, a summary, and a conclusion.

Example of a Fantasy

A Look at Heaven

Topical Outline	*Script*
I. Introduction A. Attention device	Stop. Close your eyes. Come with me and you'll be in a world of pure imagination! Just beyond the horizon is a dream world. Follow me into this magical, mystical fantasy.
B. Purpose of presentation	We'll explore a world of which we have little understanding. The people are different; their ways and ideas are far beyond ours.
C. Relate to audience	But first we must find a place for our fantasy to begin. Pure imagination. Search and see this beauty with me.
II. Body A. First main idea	We must fly first to a deserted island somewhere in the South Pacific. Once we've arrived a small row boat will be waiting. We need not worry about the

Activity 10 continued

      direction, for the current of the blue waters will lead us. We drift for an hour before we see anything but blue. We then notice something in sight. A cave is soon revealed. Our boat enters the small opening and instantly the light diminishes and nothing can be seen. It is as if we had lost our sight. Pitch black is everywhere. We can hear the tinkling of water all around us. All of a sudden, the sound is gone and fear sets in. We close our eyes tightly only to find when we open them nothing but blue sunny skies, beautiful trees and flowers, and the sounds of birds chirping and children singing in the distance. The tropical setting creates a feeling that says, "Welcome to the land of enchantment." It is as if this land has been tucked away and isolated from the rest of civilization. We venture out of our boat and begin to take in all this land has to offer. The laughter and singing draw nearer and nearer.

B. Second Main Idea

      The people must have known we were coming for soon we were covered in leis and warm welcomes. They are all so happy. They show us their beautiful paradise and tell stories of their home. Everywhere people are singing and being joyous. We come to a river and see pebbles of gold beaming through the clear water. Very early we learn money and gold mean nothing to these people. They simply do not exist.

C. Third Main Idea

      These people live together, grow together, but never age past forty. They live in this beautiful place forever. They learn as children to appreciate all people and belongings, to sing and dance, and always be happy. There is no knowledge of greed, money, unhappiness, or anything else that tends to be bad. These people know how to love and share that love with one another. There is no need for money for there is nothing to buy. It is just as if anything and everything had already been provided for everlasting life. The beauty of everything

Activity 10 continued

                                                        could be easily seen and always seen because the sun never sets. Enjoyment of life, people, and nature echo all around. No need to worry about time because time has no measure. We learned a song that said, "Living together, growing together, just being together. . ." As we looked all around this tropical paradise with paths cut through the flowers and trees, birds perched high above, rivers and waterfalls that were crystal clear, and people dancing and singing everywhere, we were taken in by the magic. We never knew anything so heavenly could exist, or could it?

III. Conclusion
    A. Summary   We were there, and if only for a short time. It was a mystery for an unguided boat to take us to an isolated tropical paradise where beauty was not only in the setting but also in the people who were so happy and full of life. People who were set apart from a monetary world filled with self-centeredness and greed.
    B. Novel wrap-up   All this beauty was there. . .it was part of our fantasy.

Option 2: Demonstration

In a demonstration bodily actions are used deliberately because the subject matter insists on it. It would be impossible to demonstrate karate without showing the different stances, hand and arm movements, and head positions. A great deal can be said about karate but even more can be shown.

Since the purpose of presenting a demonstration is to use gesture and bodily motion to enhance communication, it is important to choose a subject in which you are interested and about which you would feel confident talking and showing. Almost any topic will be suitable if you become skilled at explaining and demonstrating. Some possibilities are listed below.

Topics for Demonstration

Archery	Brushing teeth	Feather flowers
Baton twirling	Breathing exercises	Fencing
Bottle art	Contact lenses	Fishing
Ballet	Christmas decorations	Flower arranging
Basketball	Decoupage	Guitar playing
Bowling	First aid	Golf

Activity 10 continued

Jogging	Papier mache	Skin diving
Judo	Pool	Soap art
Karate	Puppets	Tying a tie
Knitting	Package wrapping	Tennis
Life saving	Polishing silver	Tissue paper art
Magic	Scarf tying	Tuning out
Modeling	Shaving	Weaving
Paper airplanes	Shoe shining	Wine tasting
Paper mats	Shots	Your choice

After you have chosen a topic it is best to stay with it even if you feel the subject is more difficult than you thought. We often think we know more about a subject than we really do. Often additional information on a topic is available at the library.

In preparing, first list the phases of the process in a step-by-step fashion that you can present in about four minutes. Remember that your audience may know little about the subject. Don't make assumptions about what you think they know. Explain and show every aspect of the process you are demonstrating. You may want to rehearse both the verbal and nonverbal messages in front of a mirror. Body actions should be spontaneous and never memorized. They should be motivated by a desire to help the listeners understand you. Practice the body actions until they become a natural part of your presentation. Be certain to introduce briefly the topic to be demonstrated and to summarize the process as you end your presentation.

Example of a Demonstration

Chisanbop

Topical Outline

Script

I. Introduction
   A. Opening statement

   B. Relate to audience

   C. Statement of main purpose

   D. Preview of first main point

   E. Preview of second main point

Remember when you were in grade school and how you were reprimanded for counting on your fingers?

Well, now you can do it legally. And those in this class who are going to be teachers may even be encouraging their students to do it.

The main purpose of my speech is to teach you how to use finger math.

I would like to begin by telling you a little history of Chisanbop or finger math.

I would also like to show you the basics of using finger math in counting and in simple addition.

Activity 10 continued

    F. Preview of third main point   And finally, I would like to tell you what you can do using the Chisanbop math with time and practice.

II. Body
    A. First main idea   Chisanbop is a fairly recent method of calculating answers to math problems.

        1. Support (definition)   The word "Chisanbop" translated from the Korean language means Finger Calculation Method.

        2. Support   The method was developed twenty years ago by Sung Jin Pai in Korea.

        3. Support   He had a mind capable of solving boggling computations without the benefit of using electronic devices, yet invented such a simple method of math that it is done fantastically by children.

        4. Support (example)   My daughter's kindergarten class was shown this method, so it has to be simple.

    B. Second main idea   I am going to show you how to count using the Chisanbop method and also how to do simple addition.

        1. Support (handout for visual aid)   I am handing out a diagram of the right and left hand and what number unit each finger stands for. This might help you to more easily understand the technique.

        2. Support (visual aid)   I will use this chart so you can count with me.
        3. Support (example)   Each finger on the right hand stands for a single unit. The right thumb represents five units. Therefore, when all fingers on the right hand are "used," the total will be nine. Each finger on the left hand represents ten units and the left thumb represents "50." So when all the fingers on the left hand are "used," the total will be "90." Therefore, combining both hands, you can see that with our ten fingers we can achieve a total count of "99." Nine on the right hand and "90" on the left.

        4. Support (example)   When not in use the fingers are raised, like this. As we use them to count we press them down. For example, "7" would be the right thumb down for "5" and the first two fingers for "6" and "7." Using both hands we can count double digit numbers such as "24" by pressing down the first two ten-unit

Activity 10 continued

        C. Third main idea

            1. Support

            2. Support

            3. Support

III. Conclusion
      A. Summary

      B. Wrap-up

fingers on the left hand and four single unit fingers on the right. In simple addition such as "2 + 1" we press the first two fingers of the right hand for the "2" and then press one more to add the "1" which makes the answer "3."

In the initial stages of Chisanbop, it is very hard to get the action of the fingers down, but when you do your hands become a portable calculator.

Your fingers can be read as clearly as if numbers were on a screen. This lets you know your "place" at a given point in a problem.

Multidigit addition can be done as fast as a calculator. For example, "3 + 4 + 2 + 1 + 3 + 2."

From counting to addition to algebra, all can be done using this method.

I have told you what Chisanbop is and have tried tried to show you how to use this method in counting and simple addition. I have also told you how it can be used in more difficult math.

In conclusion, I would just like to tell you that I think everyone would enjoy learning more about the Chisanbop Finger Math whether you use it yourself or teach it to a child who is learning math. So take your diagram with you and while you are sitting in your car at a red light, practice: right thumb "5" – left thumb "50."

Group Activity: After you have drawn for speaker places relax and enjoy the other presentations. When it is your time to speak approach the front of the room with confidence, and allow your gestures to occur naturally. Your objective in this presentation is to help your audience listen effectively.

As you present your ideas, try to make them clearer by showing the audience as well as telling them. If you use drawings, models, or objects, make certain that everyone can see them. For example, if possible, place drawings on the board as you speak, draw quickly and turn your body toward the audience as often as you can. Remember to stand to the side of the drawing and use the hand next to the

Activity 10 continued

poster to explain a point. Always erase your drawings or gather your other materials quickly after you complete the presentation.

Individual Activity: Make an appointment with your instructor to plan a specific time to make your presentation. Remember to do all that you can to make the listening task easy for your audience.

Evaluation Form
Speaker Facilitation of the Listening Process

(Points are given to the right of each criterion.)

I. Introduction
   _____ Attention-getting device (5)
   _____ Establishes rapport with the audience (5)
   _____ States purpose of presentation (5)

II. Body
   _____ Organization easy to follow (5)
   _____ Creates fantasy or shows process (9)
   _____ Well-planned message (9)

III. Conclusion
   _____ Summary (5)
   _____ Novel wrap-up (5)

IV. Nonverbal speaker characteristics (to facilitate listening)
   _____ Appearance (4)
   _____ Posture (4)
   _____ Free, uninhibited movement (4)
   _____ Spontaneous gestures (4)
   _____ Eye contact (4)
   _____ Facial expression (4)

V. Verbal speaker characteristics (to facilitate listening)
   _____ Volume (4)
   _____ Pitch (4)
   _____ Rate (4)
   _____ Fillers (4)
   _____ Articulation (4)
   _____ Pronunciation (4)
   _____ Vocal quality (4)

Additional Readings in Nonverbal Communication

In addition to books and articles cited in these chapters, the following books are excellent sources for further study of communication.

Beier, E. G., and Valens, E. G. *People-Readings: How We Control Others, How They Control Us.* New York: Stein and Day, 1975.

> Many examples of both listening behaviors and nonverbal messages are given with an interpretation of their meanings.

Morris, D., Collet, P., Marsh, P., and O'Shaughnessy, M. O. *Gestures.* New York: Stein and Day, 1979.

> The authors hope to create an interest in conscious body movements, those expressions of talking bodies that we all use to communicate with each other.

Nichols, R., and Stevens, L. A. *Are You Listening?* New York: McGraw-Hill, 1957.

> Much of the information accepted today as common knowledge about listening was first introduced in this book.

Rosenfeld, L. B., and Civikly, J. M. *With Words Unspoken: The Nonverbal Experience.* New York: Holt, Rinehart and Winston, Inc., 1976.

> This book covers body movements, touch, paralanguage, personal space and artifacts, and provides interesting and varied examples from all parts of society.

Shirley, J. L. *Body Watching is Fun.* Austin, Texas: Best Printing Company, 1979.

> This book deals primarily with body types and implications for communication.

PART THREE

Overview

The emphasis in interpersonal communication is on the interaction of two individuals, that is, the face-to-face exchange between persons who are aware of each other's presence. Each person in the interpersonal communication situation becomes both a sender of messages and a receiver of messages (Patton and Giffin, 1974; p. 5). Interpersonal communication situations can exist when two people are alone, or in group situations where each person is paired with several others as the group as a whole interacts.

Many variables affect the outcomes of interpersonal communication. Such things as appearance, movements, facial expressions, meanings of words, values, and tone of voice affect what is sent on the one hand and received on the other. Interpersonal communication is affected too by the current states of mind of the two individuals. Consider the following poem, "Encounter," by Ric Masten, as he describes a state of mind that can destroy the potential of an interpersonal encounter.*

> *it was just that i was*
> *very touchy that day*
> *and really that's*
> *all i can say*
> *to explain why*
> *while walking through*
> *the sears & roebuck department store*
> *i happened to get into*
> *this fist fight with a mannequin*

*Reprinted from Ric Masten, "Encounter," Speaking Poems, Sunflower Ink., 1977, p. 34.

Interpersonal Communication

Problems in interpersonal communication often originate within individuals and are not caused by the "other" individuals or innocent mannequins who often receive the blame.

Many people feel uncomfortable in their interpersonal relationships. It may be that those individuals feel uncomfortable because they lack experience in skills needed for effective and rewarding interpersonal relationships. Imagine yourself as a person hired to operate a computer. Would you not feel inept if you began your job with little or no training and tried to learn through trial and error? The situation in interpersonal communication for most of us is not as severe as that of an uninformed computer operator. Through the processes of maturing and modeling the behavior of others, people acquire some skill in developing and maintaining interpersonal communication skills. However, professionals in fields of contemporary psychology and communication have, in recent years, published many guides, manuals, texts, and other reading materials in areas related to interpersonal communication. To discover these materials one need only visit the psychology and human development sections of any bookstore or open the covers of many popular periodicals.

To provide an introduction to several popular theories of psychology and communication related to interpersonal relationships, brief overviews of such areas as assertiveness training, transactional analysis, values clarification, and related communication skills will be presented. If there is a common theme throughout these concepts in regard to interpersonal communication, it is the following: that all persons must identify their own position in every situation and take responsibility for that position. Stated somewhat differently, each person must assume responsibility for every action taken and in so doing, eliminate judgmental responses in dealing with the behavior of others. These thoughts will be clarified, expanded, and demonstrated on the pages that follow.

The material is presented as a stimulus. It is presented to develop awareness in the reader of ideas espoused by scholars and practitioners in the fields of communication and human relations. However, inclusion of the material is not meant to imply that the suggestions and techniques are appropriate for everyone. The ideas have been helpful to some people but not to others. It is the responsibility of every reader to become aware of the materials and to evaluate the material in regard to personal needs. The reader is provided with information and experiences and must independently decide to discard the ideas or change behavior in interpersonal encounters.

After studying the various interpersonal communication skills the reader should be able to demonstrate acquisition of the following behaviors.

Attitude Objective: By applying skills and concepts associated with assertiveness training, transactional analysis, values clarification, and related communication skills, the student will experience more fulfilling and rewarding communication at the interpersonal level. (*Activities 1-12*)

Knowledge Objective: Given objective test items, the student will recall the definition of the following terms and recognize examples or differentiate among them where appropriate. (*Activity 1*)

I. Taking responsibility for oneself
   A. Some skills
      1. Owning feelings and thoughts
      2. Self-disclosure
      3. Assertiveness
   B. An application: the interview
      1. Purpose, structure, roles
      2. Employment interview
II. Relating to others
   A. Some skills
      1. Values clarification
      2. Behavioral flexibility
      3. Descriptive listening
      4. Empathy
   B. An application: conflict resolution
III. Exchanging messages in interpersonal communication
   A. Structural analysis
      1. Parent ego state

PART III Interpersonal Communication

        2. Adult ego state
        3. Child ego state
    B. Transactional analysis
        1. Parallel transaction
        2. Crossed transaction
        3. Ulterior transaction
        4. Stroking
    C. Psychological games
        1. Victim, persecutor, rescuer
        2. Titles of games (e.g., alcoholic, harried, blemish)
        3. Trading stamps
        4. Game stoppers
    D. Life scripts
        1. Winners
        2. Losers

Experiential Objective: The student will participate in interpersonal experiences by following instructions for selected activities in each of the areas listed below. (*Activities 2–11*)

     I. Owning feelings and self-disclosure
    II. Assertiveness
   III. Values
   IV. Behavioral flexibility
    V. Descriptive listening
   VI. Empathy
  VII. Conflict resolution
 VIII. Structural analysis
   IX. Stroking
    X. Psychological games

Speaking Objective: Following instructions given in Activity 12 for an inspirational message or for role playing an employment interview, the student will prepare a five-minute presentation designed to motivate listeners to improve some positive personal characteristic, or will work with one other student to demonstrate to an audience effective interview behaviors. (*Activity 12*)

CHAPTER 7

Taking Responsibility for Oneself

It is probably reasonable to assume that most communicators are striving to achieve rewarding interpersonal relationships with others. A common problem, however, is to determine responsibility for the causes of unsatisfactory encounters. Often individuals place the blame for unsatisfactory encounters on the other communicator, thus removing themselves from responsibility. It may well be that many "other" communicators do cause problems in interpersonal encounters. There are some techniques, however, that all communicators can use in presenting themselves as they attempt to achieve successful interpersonal relationships in informal settings as well as such formal settings as the employment interview.

Some Interpersonal Skills

In taking responsibility for oneself, three interpersonal skills are particularly useful: owning feelings and thoughts, self-disclosure, and assertiveness. These skills enable communicators to place the responsibility for effective communication in interpersonal situations on themselves and not on the "other" persons. They are skills that many individuals use quite naturally and effectively as they relate to others.

Owning Feelings and Thoughts

To take responsibility for their behavior communicators must be able to own their feelings and thoughts. Owning feelings and thoughts means accepting them rather than blaming others for them, or pretending they do not exist. When feelings, thoughts, and ideas are owned, complete responsibility for them is accepted.

Owning shows a willingness to accept responsibility for self and a commitment to being nonjudgmental toward others. Therefore, it is the direct opposite of blaming others for the way one feels. Several examples of "owned" and "not owned" feelings and thoughts follow.

Owned: I need to call my friends more often.
Not-owned: My friends don't pay enough attention to me.

Owned: People at this meeting are not listening to me.
Not-owned: The people at this meeting are too irresponsible to listen.

When feelings are owned, it becomes easier to identify and communicate attitudes and thoughts to others. When blame is placed on or projected to someone else, communicators are attempting to transfer responsibility for negative actions from themselves to others.

Denial of feelings refers to a refusal to acknowledge the existence of personal thoughts or intents. Adding denial to the types of reactions from which communicators can select in a given situation results in the three possibilities illustrated below.

Owned: I am upset.
Not-owned: He upset me.
Denied: I am not upset.

A goal for effective communicators then is to take responsibility, "to own up to" the messages they communicate verbally and nonverbally. Messages do not arise without purpose. Persons delivering messages have feelings and goals. In formulating messages in interpersonal relationships, it is useful to consider communication on three levels: the *message*, what was said or done to communicate; the *feelings* that accompanied the origination and delivery of the message; and the *intent*, what the sender intended to accomplish through delivery of the message. As each component of the message is considered, the important choice of behavior is ownership, projection, or denial.

Taking responsibility for one's own behavior can be made easier by looking at events in literal terms, that is, by speaking operationally instead of abstractly (Narciso & Burkett, 1975). To make communication clearer, in other words, the actual circumstances associated with an event or happening can be described specifically, rather than expressed in abstract words like trust, love, tolerance, loyalty, or other constructs. Note the following examples.

Operational: Since I haven't eaten for twenty-four hours, I would like to be served dinner.
Abstract: Since I am hungry, let's eat right now.

Operational: He arrives at work punctually at 8:00 A.M. or he has never stolen materials from the warehouse.
Abstract: He's a loyal employee.

The operational description provides the factual information necessary for assuring clarity. Thus, it is important not only to own feelings and thoughts but to express feelings and thoughts in operational terms. Consider the example below in owning feelings and thoughts and translating them to operational terms.

Owned and abstract: I am an unhappy person. Because of my attitude toward work and family, I find it difficult to cope with the constant pressures of day-to-day living.

Owned and operational: I seldom smile or talk pleasantly to my family and coworkers. I dread getting up in the morning to face the chores ahead of me. I have nothing to look forward to but the same routine. I yell at my family and complain at every opportunity. I avoid speaking at work unless someone addresses me. I always point out the flaws in the behavior of my family and coworkers.

Compare these examples to the one below, which illustrates not owned feelings expressed in abstract terms.

Not owned and abstract: My children make too many demands of me give nothing in return. Even though I work, my husband irritates me by expecting me to be solely responsible for maintaining our home and taking care of the children. The people I work with upset me by being totally inconsiderate.

In considering relationships with other people, the use of first person singular (i.e., I, my, me, etc.) is appropriate because it places responsibility clearly; and the use of operational terms is appropriate because they express the meaning intended by the speaker.

First person: I am upset because my watch was broken.
Second person: You upset me when you broke my watch.

It may be that maturity, true friendship, and emotional honesty cannot be attained until one realizes that judgment of others' actions is inappropriate. Most communicators, however, have learned to place emphasis on the other person in their relationships and strive to change the other person's behavior rather than their own. When feelings and thoughts are owned, individuals can more readily take responsibility for their own behavior. Effective interpersonal relationships often result when communicators are responsive to the feelings and thoughts of others, yet responsible for their own feelings and thoughts.

Self-disclosure

Once individuals have owned feelings and thoughts, thereby taking responsibility for their own behavior, to engage in interpersonal communication they must be able to reveal their feelings and thoughts, or to self-disclose. Self-disclosure can be defined as a willingness to make one's feelings known to others, or as the revelation of personal information by one person to another person. When communicators are able to self-disclose, that is, reveal personal information, they increase their awareness of their own personalities through feedback received from others. Self-disclosure requires courage, however, since feedback can be threatening as well as favorable.

From research on self-disclosure (Jourard, 1971), it has been concluded that persons with healthy personalities will have the ability to self-disclose to at least one other significant person. The fact that men have a shorter life expectancy than women may even be attributable in part to the interpersonal environments of men. The male role is often perceived as one of toughness, objectivity, ambition, unsentimentality, and lack of emotion. This male role prohibits the disclosure of inner experiences, thoughts, and feelings to others. Some men appear to hide their real selves both from themselves and others, and thus must bear the added stress and expend the energy required to keep their feelings hidden.

Self-disclosure can occur at several levels (Fensterheim and Baer, 1975; Lazarus, 1971; Powell, 1969). The levels of self-disclosure can be conceptualized as five concentric circles of increasing diameter with the smallest circle representing complete disclosure to one or a few significant others, and the largest circle representing disclosure at a superficial level to many people. Depending on ability to self-disclose, each person develops a configuration of circles for the various types of circumstances likely to be encountered. The five levels have been described in the following way (Powell, 1969).

Level One: Based on absolute openness and honesty between two intimate friends or marriage partners, self-disclosure is required for a close relationship

Level Two: Revelation of unique feelings that correspond with ideas, judgments, and convictions

Level Three: Communication of ideas and judgments but with caution of the recipient's reaction

Level Four: Reporting of facts with little or no revelation of personal feelings

Level Five: Conversation without communication, no sharing of anything of value

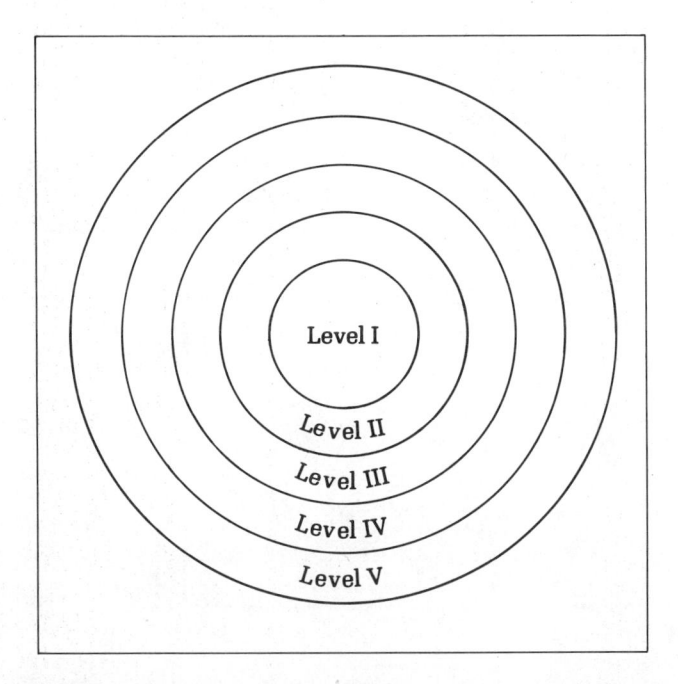

Figure 7.1. *Each individual has a series of circles representing ability to self-disclose to others at various degrees of intimacy. Level I represents absolute openness; Level V represents random chatter of little value.*

When new acquaintances are met, communication generally begins at level five. As the relationship develops the two persons progress to a mutually satisfactory level of communication. Communication problems sometimes arise, however, when an individual is unable to communicate at the different levels when appropriate, or at the same level as the other person.

Self-disclosure of varying degrees can be useful at all five levels of communication. Even starting a conversation at the most superficial level involves self-disclosure. The sometimes difficult situation of beginning a conversation can be made easier by following the steps below, which are based on the concept of free information (Smith, 1975).

1. Ask a question about any topic that you feel may elicit an informative response from the other person.
2. Follow up by expanding on any information that the other person has included in the answer. As a coparticipant in the

©1956 United Feature Syndicate, Inc.

conversation, provide the other person with information to keep things going.
3. Continue the conversation based on information obtained from the responses of the other person and by providing information of your own.

For example, note the cues utilized by the conversants below.

Jake: Hello, have you had an exciting day?
Lynn: Yes, I attended a really interesting speech class.
Jake: I didn't know you were taking speech this semester. Have you made any speeches yet?
Lynn: Yes, I've made two so far.
Jake: What topics did you research?

Compare this conversation with one where the other person fails to provide information.

Jake: Hello, have you had an exciting day?
Lynn: No.
Jake: What class did you just attend?
Lynn: Speech.
Jake: Have you made any speeches yet?
Lynn: Yes.

Jake: How many speeches have you made?
Lynn: Two.
Jake: What topics did you research?

Jake, on the other hand, might have facilitated the conversation by providing Lynn with some information.

Jake: Hello, have you had an exciting day?
Lynn: No.
Jake: Well, I have. I just came from speech class. One of the students gave a presentation on vitamin therapy.
Lynn: That does sound interesting. I've read...

Self-disclosure requires a willingness to accept responsibility for thoughts and feelings as well as taking the risk of revealing such feelings and thoughts to others. Honest self-disclosure in interpersonal communication situations can eliminate possible noise from the communication channel and result in more fulfilling relationships. It requires an orientation where denial of feelings or placement of blame on others is unacceptable personal behavior.

Assertiveness

Because of preconceived notions about what others expect of an interpersonal communications encounter, many people have difficulty expressing their thoughts and feelings. The risk of a negative or adverse reaction on the part of the receiver of the message seems too threatening to allow honest self-disclosures. Such thoughts as, "he won't be interested in my opinion," "she looks like a tough person to convince," or "I'll look stupid if I say what I really think," interfere with an individual's ability to communicate. Several authors (Bloom, Coburn and Pearlman, 1975; Fensterheim and Baer, 1975; Smith, 1975) have composed lists of assertiveness rights that they feel belong to everyone. Some common elements from the lists of assertiveness rights are the following:

1. Saying no when you want to
2. Making requests of others (who also have the right to say no)
3. Discussing problems that arise
4. Having your own opinion
5. Expecting to receive respect from others
6. Answering honestly about your feelings
7. Changing your mind
8. Admitting that you do not know or understand something

Since the purpose of assertive behavior is to facilitate honest and direct relationships with others, these rights form a basic framework for effective interpersonal communication.

Being assertive is different from being aggressive. Assertive behavior does not mean being pushy, being unruly, or exhibiting distasteful behavior. It is a quality related to belief in oneself and control over one's life. It means standing up for oneself. Four aspects of an assertive personality have been identified (Fensterheim & Baer, 1975, p. 20): (a) the freedom to let others know feelings, thoughts, and wants; (b) the ability to talk openly and honestly with strangers, friends, and family; (c) the capacity to make things happen rather than to wait for things to happen; and (d) acceptance of limitations while always striving to make a good effort.

Assertive behavior requires a look at oneself and the belief that individuals do have the right to change their own behavior. As a first step in becoming more assertive, individuals can examine their own behavior and make decisions about positive changes that might be made. They can take responsibility for present behavior. For example, persons who cannot hold jobs should not place the blame on others but should examine their own behavior to determine what they must do to keep their jobs. Individuals who are always angry with their families might analyze their own participation in the unpleasant situations rather than blaming other family members. Persons who are intimidated by salesclerks might try to determine the types of behavior they exhibit that allow them to be intimidated. An assertive person takes responsibility for behavior and therefore has the potential for revealing true feelings and thoughts, rather than masking them because of inhibitions and fears of repercussion.

Several recent books on assertiveness training (Bloom, Coburn, and Pearlman, 1975; Fensterheim and Baer, 1975) offer many suggestions for developing or improving the skill of assertiveness. The techniques have been tried and proved successful in some situations. Communicators who feel uncomfortable with the list of assertiveness rights might consider investigating one or more of the sources described below.

In *The New Assertive Woman* (Bloom, Coburn, and Pearlman, 1975), the authors provide information about the meaning of assertiveness and include many specific examples of assertive responses that have been effective. They stress evaluating the current situation, making decisions about areas in which to become more assertive, and establishing goals to accomplish. Often the overall goal is preceded by a series of exercises or easier goals to lead up to the overall goal. The authors make a contribution by building a case for developing assertive behavior and by providing a rationale for dismissing many of the games and excuses people use to avoid asserting themselves.

In the book *Don't Say YES When you Want to Say NO* (Fensterheim and Baer, 1975), the authors review many aspects of everyday living— social relationships, close relationships, and work relationships—and describe positive approaches for changing ineffective behavior through assertiveness training. The book provides many case studies of situations where assertive behavior was effective and provides laboratory exercises for developing assertive behavior in those areas where difficulty is experienced.

In the book *When I Say No, I Feel Guilty* (Smith, 1975) assertiveness training is approached by providing the reader with descriptions of skills that can be used to develop assertive behavior. The concepts of self-disclosure and free information, discussed earlier, are examples of assertive skills described in this book. Numerous dialogues are provided as examples of the verbal skills often used in many different everyday situations.

An Application: The Interview

One very important and common situation in which interpersonal communication occurs is the interview. An interview is a communication encounter that has the general purpose of collecting information to be used either for reporting or decision-making purposes. The interview can be distinguished from general conversation by its more purposeful objective of collecting specific information and its generally predetermined format. All communicators will find themselves in interview situations at one time or another and many will fulfill the role of interviewer (i.e., the one who asks the questions) as well as interviewee (i.e., the one who answers the questions). It will be helpful to have some general knowledge of the various purposes of interviews and their structure as well as more detailed information about the employment interview.

Basics of Interviewing

Purpose. Within the context of gathering information for reporting and decision-making purposes, three distinct types of interviews can be distinguished: opinion, diagnosis, and employment. Interviews that seek to establish the viewpoints of either individuals or groups have the specific purpose of collecting opinions. These interviews often sample the opinions of specific populations of individuals or focus on the views of one or a few experts in an area. Examples of interviews for collecting opinions would include questioning the parents of children in a particular school about their satisfaction with the reading curriculum, or recording the statements made by the principal in regard to reading achievement at the school.

The diagnostic interview has a somewhat different purpose. It is designed to collect information that permits some prescription to be made in regard to the needs of an individual or group. A very common example occurs between physician and patient as information is sought to determine an appropriate treatment. An example involving a group might include the gathering of information among individuals in a particular work unit with the objective of improving interpersonal relationships among peers.

The employment interview is used by those who hire to assess the potential of an applicant for a job, and by those seeking jobs to determine the desirability of the position. Although the common perception is that the applicant is being interviewed by the employer, often the applicant is interviewing the employer as well.

Structure. In nearly all interview situations the interviewer has given some prior consideration to the type of information being sought and the use it will be given. Based on such considerations, a format for collecting the information is determined. In general, interviews may be classified as structured or unstructured. The highly structured interview is one where all questions have been predetermined and the interviewer's dialogue has been written out and rehearsed almost like a script. The unstructured interview allows the interviewer to say nearly anything that will elicit the type of information desired. And of course, there are many variations between the two extremes.

The structured interview is needed to provide consistency of information when there are several interviewers and many interviewees. When data from a number of individuals are to be combined, it is especially important that the responses be collected from all respondents under nearly identical conditions. This is the case in many scientific investigations that rely on interview data. The unstructured interview is probably most useful when there is only one interviewer and one interviewee and spontaneity is sought, as in a celebrity interview on television. Thus, the amount of structure given an interview is determined primarily by the use the information will have.

Within the general structure of an interview there is some variety in the way that questions are asked. The interviewer will usually ask a question, wait for a response, and make some written record of the response. In less structured interviews, the interviewer can interact with the respondent by restating questions for clarity and by restating some of the responses. Generally questions will be open or closed, neutral or leading, and general or specific. An open question has no predetermined alternative answers. The interviewee is free to formulate the answer. A closed question provides the respondent with specific choices from which to select the answer. Neutral questions are stated without biasing the respondent's answer in one way or another. Leading questions are stated in ways that suggest an answer to the respondent. General questions permit the interviewee to formulate answers from a broad domain. Specific questions direct the respondent to particular aspects of an issue. With the exception of the leading question, a well-constructed interview might include some of each type of question. To clarify the distinctions among question types, note the examples below.

Open: How would you describe the condition of the city's public parks?
Closed: Have you found the city's public parks to be poorly kept or well kept?
Neutral: Which should receive priority—city park maintenance or city park construction?
Leading: Is it wise to maintain existing city parks before building new city parks?
General: What can be done to improve the city's public parks?
Specific: What can be done to improve the playgrounds in the city's public parks?

The Employment Interview

A job applicant wishes to make the best possible impression on the potential employer. Three things are especially important in creating a positive image in the potential employer's eyes: the letter of application, the resume, and the interview. It is important to tailor the application, resume, and interview behaviors to the specific situation. To be hired for a specific job, the applicant must often present the image that fits the job, and not expect the job to be adapted to fit the image.

Letter of application. The letter of application is a written communication with the purpose of convincing the prospective employer that the applicant has the potential for the job. The letter of application should be based on the following general rules.

1. The letter should display such positive characteristics as confidence, dignity, and courtesy.
2. The letter and envelope should be addressed to a specific person and should include both name and title. Do not address letters to President, Personnel Manager, To Whom It May Concern, and so forth.
3. The letter is generally divided into three paragraphs: the reasons for wanting the particular position; personal qualities, education, and experience relevant for the position; and request for an interview and how to be reached.
4. The letter of application should be brief, specific, businesslike in tone, and clearly written.
5. The letter of application should be checked very carefully to ensure correct grammar, spelling, and punctuation; should be neatly typed; and should not include slang, jokes, or unusual stylistic practices.

The applicant might ask, as a final check, "What type of impression would this letter make on me if I were an employer?" See Figure 7.2.

Dana Smith
6300 Fifth Street
Dallas, Texas 75214

Dr. A. J. Robins
Chief of Staff
City Hospital
114 Second Avenue
Dallas, Texas 75206

Dear Dr. Robins:

Your August 10 ad in the <u>Dallas Morning News</u> described your need for a laboratory technician. I am very much interested in this position since it would provide an excellent opportunity to begin my career in the medical field.

My recent training at Dallas University Medical School and internship at the Veteran's Administration Hospital as well as my strong desire to work in the field qualify me to perform successfully in such a position and contribute to your organization. My resume is enclosed.

I would appreciate the opportunity to meet with you. My current address and telephone number are listed on my resume.

Very truly yours,

Dana Smith

Figure 7.2. *Letter of application.*

Resume. Again, in preparing the resume, the applicant is attempting to catch the eye of the potential employer. The resume should include the following types of information.

1. Personal—name and address.
2. Position Objective.
3. Education—relevant high school, college, and special training.
4. Experience—chronological listing of previous jobs with dates and activities.
5. References—permission should be obtained from those listed.

The resume should be neatly typed with parallel construction of sentences and phrases and with parallel spacing of headings and margins. The resume of persons entering a field or beginning a career is best presented on one page. The ten-page resume is more appropriate for established professionals with many experiences and outstanding contributions. See Figure 7.3.

Resume of John Jones
(–Address–)
(–Telephone–)

Position Objective:

Position leading to management and administrative responsibilities in sales division of a major industrial corporation.

Education:

Associates of Arts and Science Degree in Mid-Management from City Community College, June, 1970

Bachelor of Science Degree in Business Administration from Central Texas State University, June, 1972.

Employment History:

1972 to Present: Sales manager for soft drink division of Lone Star Beverage Company. Responsible for personnel, distribution, and sales of over $500,000 in product.

References:

Mr. Jack Andrews
Vice President of Marketing
Lone Star Beverage Company

(–Address–)
(–Telephone–)

Dr. Ann Rogers
Professor of Business
Central Texas State University

(–Address–)
(–Telephone–)

Figure 7.3. Resume.

Interview Behavior. The employment interview is an example of an interpersonal communication situation where owning feelings, self-disclosure, and assertiveness (not aggressiveness) are useful skills. It is important to begin with appropriate greetings (e.g., a firm handshake and "how do you do"). Although interviewers sometimes try to make applicants uncomfortable to note their reactions to stress, most will probably attempt to put the applicant at ease by offering a chair and making casual conversation. The interviewee should relax, maintain good posture, avoid chewing gum, and refrain from smoking unless given permission. When the interviewer does begin to talk about the position, the applicant should keep the following in mind.

1. Be sincere, natural, friendly and relaxed if possible.
2. Be specific and concrete in answering.
3. If unsure of a comment say, "I'm not sure I understand your question."
4. Articulate and pronounce words clearly and distinctly. Avoid using slang. Speak conversationally. Be personable and energetic by varying vocal rate, pitch, and volume meaningfully.
5. Look the interviewer in the eyes during the conversation and address by name occasionally.
6. Smile occasionally and show a pleasant personality. Be alert and spontaneous when the interviewer is speaking. React by using appropriate nonverbal expression.
7. If still interested in the position after the interview, consider writing a follow-up letter immediately. In the letter thank the interviewer and mention something positive about the company. Remark that you would like to be associated with such a company. Type the letter in business format and sent it to the interviewer immediately.

The interviewer will ask quite a variety of questions. Applicants may refuse to answer questions that invade the privacy of their personal lives (e.g., how many children do you plan to have). Some questions applicants should be prepared to answer relate to short and long range goals; rewards expected from career; why the career was chosen; what motivates them; how they will fit into the company; are they willing to travel or move; how they are affected by pressure; are they planning further education; what qualities will make them successful in the job; and so forth. Applicants will want to learn such things as the usual work routine, philosophy and objectives of the company, opportunity for advancement, types of interpersonal relationships operating in the company, evaluation policies, incentives for innovation, management of company, pay and benefits, and so forth. Both potential employer and employee use the interview as a means of collecting information for decision making. Both must be prepared to provide and collect the relevant information.

SUMMARY

An understanding of such communication skills as owning feelings, self-disclosure, and assertiveness are relevant for interpersonal encounters as informal as a conversation between two friends or as formal as an employment interview. Assertiveness training provides an experience in self-discovery that leads to a greater respect and appreciation for oneself. If individuals recognize and believe that they do have basic assertive rights, and that honesty with oneself and others is important, then the potential exists to develop effective relationships with others.

During and after discovery of oneself, interpersonal relationships are facilitated by speaking in the first person singular, by speaking in specific rather than abstract terms, and by self-disclosing personal information at a level appropriate for the situation. The interview is a specific example of an interpersonal communication encounter where owning feelings, self-disclosure, and assertiveness are very relevant. Since most individuals will participate in an employment interview at some time in their lives, an understanding of the purposes and structures of interviews is very important.

CHAPTER 8

Relating to Others

All individuals possess sets of values that affect their abilities to share meaning with others in interpersonal relationships. To communicate effectively, speakers must consider not only their own values but also the values of those with whom they communicate. All too often people stop listening when persons with whom they are communicating display values contrary to their own. To share meaning with others, individuals must continue to listen even when messages seem contrary to their values. Effective communication requires a willingness to listen openly to what others are saying, especially in situations where hostility and conflict are apt to occur.

Some Interpersonal Skills

In addition to knowledge of one's own values and willingness to consider the values of others, three additional skills useful for relating to others are behavioral flexibility, descriptive listening, and empathy. Behavioral flexibility is the ability to select appropriate behaviors to fit given situations. It provides some latitude in communicating with persons whose values differ from one's own. Descriptive listening is a technique useful in helping others think through their problems and arrive at their own conclusions. It requires the listener to be nonjudgmental. Empathy is the ability to put oneself in the place of another. By empathizing one can, perhaps, better understand the values that motivate others.

Values Clarification

What exactly are values? Values are constructs and do not exist as concrete objects like books, cars, furniture, or food. They can be inferred by behavior and, perhaps, by self-disclosures of the individuals who hold them. When convenient they can be easily faked. Values affect self-concept, and they contribute to the impressions held by others. Values are firmly held attitudes used in making choices among alternatives. They represent aspects of living that hold some worth or receive priority.

An example of a value is the importance many people place on pursuing higher education. People who value higher education give it priority in their lives. This importance of the value of education can be identified by observing the individual's contribution of time and resources to achieving the goal and by asking the individual to describe feelings about education. The dedication can be faked, too, by displaying false behavioral clues and self-disclosing false evidence of the attitude.

Figure 8.1. *These illustrations do not represent values; they reflect values. Values do not exist as concrete objects.*

People acquire values in several ways (Adell, 1976): experimentation, authority, rational thinking, personal decision, or intuition. Through experimentation, values are acquired by comparing the results of various ways of approaching similar situations. Behaviors associated with outcomes providing maximum benefits are likely to become a part of the value system. With the authoritarian approach to values, one accepts standards imposed by such important others as parents and leaders of society and religion. Values are acquired also through rational thought and selection on an intellectual level according to a set of moral standards. Or values can be acquired by thinking through what is important only to the individual and without regard to authority or a set of moral standards. Last, it is thought by some that values are acquired through intuition, or some insight, that leads people to select good rather than bad outcomes. Thus it seems that values can be acquired through comparison of results, authoritarian directives, rational thinking, personal decision, or perhaps intuition. It may well be that values acquired from combinations of several of these general methods.

In considering the role of values in the communication process, the following points should be remembered.

1. Since they are internal states values cannot be seen. They do affect reactions to situations, events, and other people. For example, love of family cannot be seen but is an important value to many.
2. Behavior is influenced by an individual's set of values. A knowledge of values will contribute to an understanding and prediction of behavior. Knowing that one values fast cars may explain an individual's choice of a specific type of car.
3. The intensity of values varies. Some values are very strongly held, whereas others are less important. Reactions to situations are affected by the value itself as well as the intensity of the value. For example, music perceived as too loud might be tolerated if liked and eliminated if disliked.
4. The specificity of values varies. Some values are quite specific and others are very general. One might value a more general area, like education, but see little value in taking specific groups of courses.
5. Behavior is often affected by the relative importance of the value. Some situations require choices among outcomes related to several important values. For example, one might feel that travel and education are extremely important. Given a limited amount of income, however, it might be necessary to choose between a trip or a semester in school.
6. The situation will affect the role of a specific value also. The chance to study with a famous professor might make the choice between travel and education much easier to make.

Thus, values are internal states that affect observable behavior in various ways depending on the situation as well as the intensity, specificity, and relative importance of the value.

Values are an important aspect of interpersonal communication. A clearer picture of one's own values can be a useful tool for achieving more fulfilling relationships with others. A popular movement called values clarification has been evolving in recent years. Values clarification (Howe and Howe, 1975; Simon, Howe, and Kirschenbaum, 1972) provides a process, comprised primarily of exercises that lead one to think through feelings, for discovering values. It does not tell a person what values should be held, but provides techniques for self-discovery. The process of values clarification leads to a better understanding of what is important and a better understanding of how to make choices. Do individuals value studying and striving for college degrees? Or do they place more value on partying or other leisure activities? Depending on the relative value of studying versus leisure, priorities can be assigned and choices can be made. Do they play golf or do an assignment? Can they do one or both? Given a limited amount of money, do they pay golf club fees or college tuition?

Being aware of one's own set of values, decision-making processes, ways of setting priorities, and ways of reacting is important since values are directly related to self-concept. One's image of self includes the things that are valued. A clarification of values helps one better perceive self, and therefore, enables self-disclosure. A better defined self-concept has a direct relationship to communication abilities. Values determine topics for conversations, influence choices in work and leisure activities, and affect relationships with others.

Persons with whom one communicates are in the same position. Their skills in interpersonal communication are related to some extent to their perceptions of their own values. Their values will affect their own self-concepts, their behaviors, and their reactions to others' behavior. All messages and the resultant reactions to those messages are influenced by the values held by each participant in the communication situation.

In considering others' values communicators should try to recognize how closely they relate to their own. Perhaps a message from someone with different values should be given deeper consideration than a message from someone with the same values. An attempt to determine the values that motivate a message will provide added information for sharing the intended meaning of the message. Values are seldom verbally stated; they are implied. Recognition of the values motivating a message is an important interpersonal skill. Acquisition of this skill can begin through a better understanding of one's own values.

Behavioral Flexibility

When people are behaviorally flexible they possess the ability to adapt readily to any situation. They are open-minded and able to keep channels of communication open. Behaviorally flexible persons are especially adept at successfully adjusting to new communication situations and at relating to people in new and different ways. They are able to behave in ways appropriate for the situation; they are not at a loss when past behavioral patterns are inappropriate.

When dealing with situations where different values are evident, behavioral flexibility encourages a continuance of dialogue rather than an embarrassed or flustered end to communication. Behavioral flexibility does not imply that communicators accept or appear to accept values or behavior of which they disapprove. It means only that they allow communication channels to remain open by displaying behavior that will maintain an exchange of both similar and different opinions. Consider the following example of a flexible and a judgmental response to the same situation.

Speaker: People in this city are going to have to begin using their cars less. They need to plan fewer trips and carpool more. We need a law to limit driving.

Judgmental response: You are wrong. Freedom of choice is a right in our country. People have the right to drive their cars when and where they want. A law to limit driving would be ridiculous and unconstitutional.

Flexible response: You expressed the need for people to change driving habits. That may be, but freedom of choice has always been a right of the individual. A law to limit driving would cause many hardships and limit the choices of those who wish to allocate their personal resources to driving their own cars as they please.

To gain competence in behavioral flexibility it is useful to identify and focus on ways to behave differently in difficult or irritating situations. It is important also to recognize the behavioral choices available for a given set of circumstances. In many situations alternative reactions are possible. Behaviorally flexible individuals select the most appropriate behavior, not the habitual behavior. To provide experience in the area of behavioral flexibility, attempt to increase the number of times interaction is initiated and dialogue is maintained with someone with whom frequent disagreements have occurred. Another suggestion is to increase the number of owning statements made and to decrease the number of blaming statements. The interpersonal skills of owning feelings and self-disclosure often facilitate attempts to become more behaviorally flexible in difficult situations.

Descriptive Listening

Descriptive listening is the ability to provide feedback in a manner that is not evaluative or judgmental. It is particularly useful in interpersonal relationships when individuals are seeking to understand their own feelings about matters of important concern. The descriptive listener serves as a sounding board, in a sense, as the troubled individual seeks a solution. The individual practicing descriptive listening will react to what is heard by paraphrasing the speaker's message (i.e., saying it in a different way).

Since the goal of descriptive listening is to help the speaker make decisions about specific issues of concern, descriptive messages from the listener must focus on behaviors that can be seen directly. Concrete, specific, and descriptive messages from the listener are encouraged. For example, note the following two approaches to the same situation.

Speaker: I've just found the car that I have to buy, but it's about $5,000 more than I can afford.

Judgmental feedback approach

Listener: John, you shouldn't try to buy such an expensive car.
Speaker: Who are you to try to tell me what car I shouldn't buy?

Descriptive feedback approach

Listener: John, the car you like so much will cost more than you originally budgeted.
Speaker: I can't really spend more unless I give up something else; the cost of the car is almost twice what I wanted to spend.

The descriptive approach does not include a command but allows the receiver of the message to make an independent decision about how to react.

Nondescriptive feedback goes beyond, or adds to, what is directly observable by interpreting, judging, or drawing conclusions. The major drawback in using nondescriptive feedback is the negative effect on the communication process caused by responding in an evaluative or judgmental manner. Gordon (1970) has identified twelve ways that nondescriptive verbal responses can be classified.

1. Commanding—Telling a person to do something, giving an order or a command. For example: Don't buy the expensive car.
2. Warning—Telling a person what consequences will occur if something is done. For example: If you buy the expensive car, you'll go broke.
3. Preaching—Telling a person what should or ought to be done. For example: You ought to buy a car that you can afford.
4. Advising—Telling a person how to solve a problem. For example: It's my opinion that you should buy a cheaper car.
5. Teaching—Trying to influence a person with facts, logic, information, or opinions. For example: The insurance and upkeep on the expensive car will cost you much more than it would for a cheaper car.
6. Criticizing—Making a negative judgment or evaluation of a person. For example: You must be out of your mind to think you could afford that expensive car.
7. Praising—Offering a positive evaluation or judgment. For example: You are smart to realize that the expensive car is too costly for you.

8. Shaming—Making a person feel foolish, putting a person into a category. For example: When you cannot afford to pay for your own lunch, how can you think of spending that much for a car?
9. Analyzing—Determining the motivation for why a person is doing or saying something. For example: The only reason you want that expensive car is to show your old college friends that you've really made it big.
10. Sympathizing—Trying to make a person feel better. For example: Don't be upset by not being able to buy the car; most people can't afford a car like that.
11. Questioning—Searching for more information to help solve the problem. For example: Why can't you be happy with a car that you can afford?
12. Humoring—Trying to get a person away from the problem. For example: There's more to life than cars; aren't you planning to go to London this spring?

In helping a person explore feelings and arrive at conclusions, responses based on the above list are in many cases best avoided. Such responses cause the speaker to react to the feedback rather than face the problem.

Descriptive listening is not a technique that fits all situations. In using the technique, the listener must determine whether or not paraphrasing makes sense. Consider the following examples.

Inappropriate: I wonder where I should park my car when I get to school.

You're concerned about finding a place to park your car.

Inappropriate: My biggest problem is knowing how to pronounce these unusual words.

You seem to be very concerned about knowing how to pronounce some unusual words.

Some statements are just not appropriate for a response based on the descriptive listening technique. To be effective, a listener should refrain from overdoing descriptive reactions and avoid making responses that appear trite or thoughtless.

Agatha Christie's sleuth, Miss Marple, was an expert at descriptive listening. She solved many crimes by attentively listening to and drawing out information from persons associated with the crimes. Because she did not contribute any information to the conversation, she was able to learn a great deal from those to whom she spoke. Consider the following excerpts from *A Murder is Announced* (Christie, 1950).

"Yes, indeed." Miss Bunner sighed. "Very few people would be as loyal to their old friends as dear Miss Blacklock is. Oh, dear, those days seem a long time ago. Such a pretty girl and enjoyed life so much. It all seemed so sad."

Miss Marple, though with no idea of what had seemed so sad, sighed and shook her head.

"Life is indeed hard," she murmured.

"And sad affliction bravely borne," murmured Miss Bunner, her eyes suffusing with tears. "I always think of that verse. True patience; true resignation. Such courage and patience ought to be rewarded, that is what I say. What I feel is that nothing is too good for dear Miss Blacklock, and whatever good things come to her, she truly deserves them."

"Money," said Miss Marple, "can do a lot to ease one's path in life."

She felt herself safe in this observation since she judged that it must be Miss Blacklock's prospects of future affluence to which her friend referred.
(pp. 151–152)

"I'm sorry," she said. "It—it just came over me. What I've lost. She—she was the only link with the past, you see. The only one who—who remembered. Now that she's gone I'm quite alone."

"I know what you mean," said Miss Marple. "One is alone when the last one who remembers is gone...."

"You understand very well," said Letitia Blacklock.
(pp. 193–194)

Descriptive listening is a useful skill in helping others arrive at their own solutions to their problems. It allows the individual to search out a solution while receiving support from a concerned listener. Descriptiveness requires careful listening and rephrasing without being judgmental. It encourages people to open up, it shows that the listener is indeed paying attention, and it forces the person with the problem to take responsibility for any decision made.

Empathy

Empathy is the ability to put oneself in the place of others and experience some of their feelings. One can empathize with positive as well as negative feelings. Empathy involves not only the emotional response of sympathy but also the sharing of joyful experiences. It is easier for individuals to empathize with emotional states that they have experienced than to empathize with unfamiliar emotional states.

Observations of the actual behavior of the other person, what the other person says, and personal experiences with similar situations provide the information required to empathize. It is useful also to listen with eyes as well as ears and to note such nonverbal clues as facial expression, body position, posture, and gestures. An analysis of the match between verbal and nonverbal behavior will be helpful in determining the true meaning of the other's feelings. It is very important, also, in empathizing with another to attempt to remain objective and avoid emotional reactions. Empathic listening, a skill very similar to descriptive listening, is very appropriate for receiving another's self-disclosures in situations where individuals attempt to put themselves in the place of others.

Empathic listening involves making noncommittal responses like the following in an attempt to draw information from another person.

I see.	Really.
Oh.	You don't say.
Mm Hmm.	No fooling.
How about that.	You did?
Interesting.	Is that so.

These are responses that do not communicate ideas, judgments, or feelings that might change the meaning of the message. The responses do, however, invite the other person to share judgments, ideas, and feelings. The responses open the door and invite the person to talk. Other useful, more explicit responses include the following.

"Tell me about it."
"I'd like to hear more about it."

"Tell me more."
"I'd be interested in your point of view."
"Would you like to talk about it?"
"Let's discuss it."
"Let's hear what you have to say."

Often people are more than willing to share their joys and sorrows if only given the chance; and to empathize, the listener needs information. Descriptive listening, where the speaker's ideas are restated in other words by the listener, can be useful too in gaining the information needed to empathize.

Listed below are some basic attitudes that must be present when one is attempting to empathize. When these attitudes are present one can more readily experience the feelings of another person.

1. You must want to hear what the person has to say. This means you are willing to take the time to listen. If you do not have time, you need only say so.
2. You must genuinely want to share the other's experiences at a given time. If you do not want to share at that time, wait until you do.
3. You must be genuinely able to react without judgment to feelings, whatever they may be or however different they may be from your own feelings and from the feelings you think a person "should" have. This attitude takes time to develop.
4. You must have a deep feeling of trust in the person's capacity to handle feelings, to work through them, and to find solutions to problems. You'll acquire this trust by watching the person solve a given problem, not by trying to take responsibility for solving the problem.
5. You must appreciate that feelings are transitory, not permanent. Feelings change—hate can turn into love, discouragement may quickly be replaced by hope. Consequently, you need not be afraid to express feelings, since they will not become forever fixed.

Empathy implies caring and understanding.

In addition to caring and understanding, empathy is dependent on recognition of others' values. If the empathizer can identify the values of the other person, data are gathered that contribute to other past observations and personal experience. The feelings of the other person can be more readily experienced if it can be assumed that the person's behavior results in part from a specific set of values. Generally individuals can more readily experience the feelings of others when their own experiences and values are similar to those of the other person. The question might arise as to how individuals empathize with others whose values differ significantly from their own. The interpersonal skill of behavioral flexibility can be quite useful in such situations. When two individuals do not share similar values, behavioral flexibility allows the empathizers to leave their own frames of reference and more accurately perceive the feelings experienced by others. It is a nonrigid response to an unusual or different experience.

An Application: Conflict Resolution

All communicators have experienced conflict, that is, situations where the alternatives seem to force one of the persons into a losing position. Everyone can relate to previous experience with parent/child conflict, public authority conflict, conflict with rules, supervisor/subordinate conflict, or professional conflict among peers. Consider the examples of conflict situations given below.

> A child wants to stay up and watch TV; the parents want the child to go to bed.
>
> The city bus company will not provide service on Sundays; some residents of the city will not be able to go to church.
>
> Girls cannot wear shorts to school; they want to wear shorts so that they can participate in active sports in physical education.
>
> A supervisor wants an employee to take a morning break at 10:15; the employee's friends take their breaks at 10:45.
>
> One teacher believes that students should receive credit for class participation; another believes that grades should be based only on examination scores.

With the exception of hermits who isolate themselves from society, no one has been able to eliminate conflict from life. Most people feel that conflict is a bad and unhealthy state. Children are told to be polite and not to get angry or no one will like them. In some television and literature, the ideal family is portrayed as living happily ever after. In reality, every interpersonal relationship of any depth has conflict at some points in time. No matter how close two people seem to be, there will be times when their ideas will not match.

Conflict is generally viewed as a negative experience. Feelings often associated with conflict are anxiety, stress, tension, resentment, anger, disappointment, depression, and frustration. However, some positive outcomes can result from conflict situations. Conflict can provide a stimulus for the development of new and creative ideas and can, in fact, tend to strengthen interpersonal relationships. Therefore, learning to deal positively with conflict is one of the most important skills a communicator can acquire.

The common approach in conflict situations is for each participant to strive to defeat the other. This generally results in the win-lose situation where one individual is pleased with the outcome and the other is displeased. A more appropriate outcome would be a win-win situation where both individuals are pleased with the solution. Although the previous win solutions for which both parties were striving might not be realized as originally conceived, both parties will leave the situation with positive feelings and channels of communication will remain open. Consider the following example.

> Ed travels in his job and is home only on weekends. His wife, Susan, stays home all week with their two children. Susan does work part-time while the children are in school, but looks forward to going out or having guests on Friday and Saturday evenings. Ed would like to spend his weekend evenings at home alone with his family. The win-win solution on which they decided was to spend one evening out and one evening at home alone. The evening at home alone, however, would be planned with the same care as evenings with guests and would, therefore, deviate from the normal routine that Susan found so boring.

The key to positive outcomes in conflict situations is a form of compromise. It requires a willingness to consider the values motivating the involved individuals, the ability to empathize with the other person's position, a desire to be behaviorally flexible in reacting to the expectations of the other individual, and accepting a modification of one's own expectations.

One way to handle conflict situations is to look at the problem objectively, that is, as if it belonged to someone else, and then to list as many solutions as possible. To provide meaningful alternatives the two parties in conflict must be willing to abandon their original objective and to attempt to develop some creative solutions. Once the possibilities have been identified they should be discussed for their possibilities as win-win solutions. That is, can the two parties in conflict be happy with the outcome? If so, then the proposed solution can be tried with both parties maintaining flexibility as the situation is worked out in a positive manner.

Much has been written on conflict as it occurs in a variety of settings. *Parent Effectiveness Training* (Gordon, 1970) treats parent-child conflict; *The Intimate Enemy* (Bach & Wyden, 1968) introduces the "fair fight" as a technique marriage partners might use to reduce conflict; and *Interpersonal Conflict Resolution* (Filley, 1975) treats conflict as it relates to business relationships. As in all communication situations, these authors and others stress the importance of keeping open the channels for exchange of feelings and ideas. There can be no resolution of conflict if communication stops. When people fail to deal with conflict in a positive way a great deal of hurt can result. By using interpersonal skills and keeping communication channels open, the possibility of a suitable solution for both parties exists.

SUMMARY

Recognition and awareness of one's own values and those of persons with whom communication takes place are important interpersonal communication skills. Messages sent and received are determined by the values—those things recognized as important—of both parties. Communicators can improve their interpersonal relationships by recognizing their own values and those of others and using this knowledge to interpret messages sent and received.

The skills of behavioral flexibility, descriptive listening, and empathy affect interpersonal communication also. Behavioral flexibility refers to the skill involved in adapting to unfamiliar and possibly distressing situations rather than allowing habitual behavior to be the guide. Descriptive listening relies on paraphrasing to provide nonjudgmental responses to messages from individuals self-disclosing a problem situation. Empathy refers to the ability to put oneself in the place of another and thereby develop an understanding of the other's feelings. Behavioral flexibility, descriptive listening, and empathy are affected by the values of participants brought together in communication situations.

Values, behavioral flexibility, descriptive listening, and empathy are all important skills in relating to others. They have special importance in the positive resolution of conflict situations. By using appropriate interpersonal skills to keep communication channels open, the win-lose outcome common to most conflict situations can possibly become a win-win outcome.

CHAPTER 9

Exchanging Messages in Interpersonal Communication

Communication in interpersonal relationships does not just occur. Interpersonal communication is the result of one complex person expressing something to another complex person. To communicate effectively, individuals must not only acquire the ability to express themselves as they wish to be understood by others, but must also acquire the ability to interpret correctly the messages sent by others. In addition to skill in presenting oneself and relating to others, a knowledge of the processes that occur as messages are exchanged in interpersonal relationships can be a decided advantage in effective communication.

Transactional analysis is a popular approach to the study of interpersonal relationships. Eric Berne (1961; 1964; 1972) is responsible for the early development of the theory; others (Harris, 1967; James & Jongeward, 1971; Meininger, 1973; Steiner, 1974) have expanded his work. It was the intent of Berne and others to develop a method of describing communication that everyone, not just psychologists and psychiatrists, might understand. Even a brief introduction to transactional analysis can contribute to effective communication by providing a greater understanding of psychological processes that affect what is said, heard, and interpreted. Transactional analysis, or TA as it is often called, is composed of four parts: structural analysis, transactional analysis, psychological games, and life scripts.

Structural analysis is the study of three ego states, or aspects of personality, labeled the parent, adult, and child. The three ego states are contained within each person and with some practice can be easily recognized. Transactional analysis, the name of a part of the theory as well as the theory as a whole, refers to the interaction of one individual's ego states with the ego states of another individual. Transactions can be analyzed to determine the effect, for example, of a person reacting as a child to another person reacting as a parent. The part of TA called psychological games refers to a series of transactions that appear to be one thing at the social level but have a different meaning at the psychological level. A game often represents a segment of a script. A life script is a plan that a person decides on during childhood and plays out during a lifetime. The idea that some people are winners and that others are losers is a part of script analysis.

Transactional analysis can provide a basis for more effective interpersonal relationships. Communicators can become aware of why others react in certain ways and why they themselves react as they do. It involves an analysis of what was said and what it really means. Skill in using the voice and ears in communication must be developed as well as skill in understanding the feelings and motivations that underlie what is said or heard. To increase awareness of how personality affects communication patterns, a more detailed description of the four parts of TA follows.

Structural Analysis

Structural analysis provides a way of classifying behavior according to whether it is parental, adult, or childlike. It helps in answering such questions as who we are and why we act as we do. The major purpose of structural analysis is to help communicators recognize which of the three ego states they represent and which ego state is represented by the person with whom they are interacting. The ego states are identifiable by observing such verbal and nonverbal behaviors as demeanor, gestures, voice, and vocabulary.

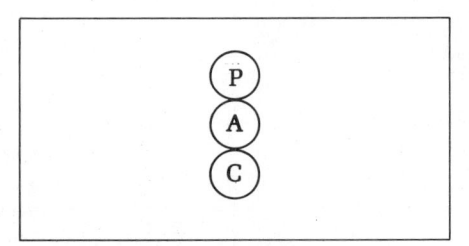

Figure 9.1. *Parent, adult, and child.*

Parent Ego State

The parent ego state resembles the personality of one's own mother and father and possibly that of other parent figures, like grandparents, siblings, teachers, doctors, actors, and actresses. The parent ego state is both kind and nurturing as well as bossy, critical, and prejudiced. The parent ego state can be identified by the following characteristics.

Demeanor: stern, upright, and tense posture of a parent giving directives; or the open arms of an understanding parent.

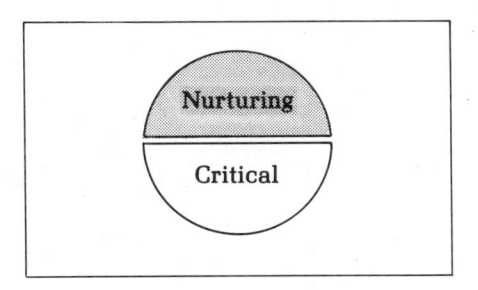

Figure 9.2. *Parent ego state.*

Gestures: a pointing finger, upheld arm, wrinkled brow, and movements signaling refusal; or the opposite gestures signaling a comforting embrace, a pat on the back, and a gentle smile.
Voice: stern, shrill, loud tones of parental wrath; or soft tones of comfort and caress.
Vocabulary: words like naughty, low, disgusting, ridiculous; or helpful, cute, precious, adorable, loving.

Outwardly the parent ego state is very likely to be elicited by the childlike behavior of someone else. Inwardly it can be experienced as a replay of something said or done by an authority figure from the past. For example, a person might spill a drink on a newly cleaned carpet and another person, perhaps the one responsible for the carpet's upkeep, might blurt out in a stern voice, "Why aren't you more careful? I just cleaned the carpet." On the other hand, the person who is about to set his drink on the carpet might hear a voice from the past saying, "Put your glass on the table. Don't you know it will be knocked over on the floor?"

The parent ego state can be described as a tape recording of all the do's and don'ts, rules for living, and how to's that a person needs to function effectively. The recording includes behaviors appropriate for parenting and automatic responses to a wide variety of situations typical in everyday living. The latter include such things as dangers to watch for; reactions to issues like religion, sex, and politics; courtesies and manners; and relationships that reflect the way things are generally done.

Child Ego State

The child ego state is preserved through recordings of childhood experiences. It tends often to be obscured in adults because of the general feeling that childlike behavior is inappropriate. However, it is evident in situations like sporting events and parties. The child ego state is the source of many emotional responses like joy, surprise, fear, and agony. It knows how to have fun and often displays spontaneity, openness, charm, curiosity, and creativity.

The child ego state is composed of three parts. The natural child emerges at birth and relies on the senses without concern for people or

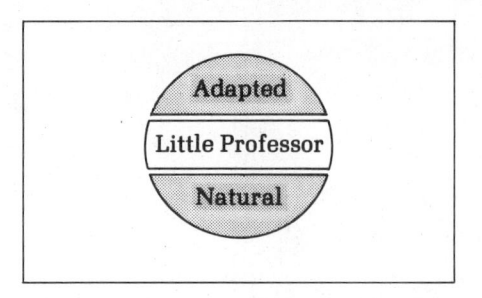

Figure 9.3. *Child ego state.*

places. The adaptive child is a free spirit who changes behavior for the reward of parental approval. The little professor emerges as the infant is able to account for the behavior of others and to sense what is occurring. The child ego state can be identified by the characteristics below.

Demeanor: coyness, cuteness, sulkiness, wiggling, restlessness, helplessness, downward tilt of the head, upturned eyes, and pigeon-toed stance.
Gestures: warding off gesture with an arm, finger in mouth, hugging.
Voice: crying, whining, laughing, screaming, angry, playful.
Vocabulary: short words; exclamations; name-calling; slang; submissive statements like "but I can't," and "I'm so sad"; and emotional statements like "I love you," and "I'm lonely."

The child ego state contains feelings, attitudes, and behavior patterns experienced and learned usually by the age of five. The behavior patterns are often elicited by someone in the parent ego state. The child ego state, because of its emotional and pleasure-seeking inclinations, is perhaps the most valuable aspect of the personality.

Adult Ego State

The adult ego state is comparable to a computer that processes information and provides objective data for decision making. The parent ego state is a recording of things learned from authority figures, whereas the adult ego is a newer recording of unique thoughts and conclusions. The adult ego state gathers data from the parent and child ego states as well as from outside observations. The adult ego state is nonjudgmental, nonbiased, deals strictly with facts, and can be identified by the following characteristics.

Demeanor: attentive, thoughtful concentration, upright posture.
Gestures: pointing index finger, direct eye contact, pursed lips, and arched eyebrows.
Voice: level tone, even loudness, casual, and unemotional.
Vocabulary: phrases like "I think," "what do you think?" "why"; nouns and verbs; and sharp, descriptive, factual statements.

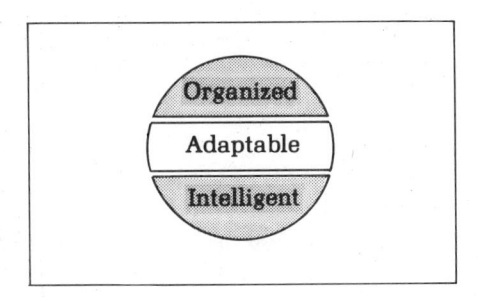

Figure 9.4. *Adult ego state.*

A calm, rational parent ego state is often mistakenly identified as the adult ego state. However, the adult ego state, unlike the parent ego state, is not swayed by prejudices, is nonjudgmental, and maintains an unemotional frame of reference. The adult ego state can update data stored in the other ego states and provide a sense of reality. It can test the information filed away in the other ego states and accept it or reject it. Probability estimation is another function of the adult ego state. It is able to assign weights to available alternatives and make decisions based on available facts. The adult ego state is responsible also for studying, learning, and gaining knowledge.

The adult ego state can be contaminated by the child and/or parent ego states. The contamination occurs when the information from the child and parent ego states is interpreted as factual by the adult ego state. When prejudices from the parent ego state are accepted by the adult ego state without evaluation, the parent ego state has contaminated the adult ego state. When the adult ego state adopts a distorted perception of reality or a delusion from the child ego state, it has been contaminated by the child ego state. The adult ego state will often rationalize the prejudices and delusions and interpret them as factual information.

The Whole Personality

The parent ego state contains values and rules that influence behavior as they are played back from old memories. The child ego state is the seat of emotions and feelings. The adult ego state is like a computer as it gathers information, processes it, and reaches conclusions based on fact. Although differing in proportion in different people, the three ego states together form the personality of nearly every individual. In some people, who seldom have fun, the adult ego state probably predominates; the parent ego state might dominate in a person constantly in a position of authority; and the child ego state might dominate the personality that fails to achieve independence. It is only occasionally that one ego state will compose a personality to the exclusion of the others.

To develop further the concepts of the three ego states, consider the following reactions to the same situation by persons in the three ego states.

The offer of an ice cream while dieting.

Parent: Go ahead and eat it; you need the energy.
Child: Ice cream is so good on a hot day.
Adult: I must resist. That is one-third of my allowed caloric intake.

The late arrival of a teenager from an evening out.

Parent: Where have you been? I've been worried.
Child: Out having a good time again, I see.
Adult: You are thirty minutes late. It is now 11:30 P.M.

Violent scene on television during family viewing.

Parent: Turn that off. Children shouldn't watch shows like that.
Child: This is really exciting.
Adult: What I've read recently is true. Violent shows are available for viewing by children.

Thus structural analysis is a way of classifying reactions so that they can be better understood. When exchanges occur between people, the analysis of the ego states of both parties leads to transactional analysis.

Transactional Analysis

Transactional analysis is the analysis of transactions and chains of transactions between two people. The transactions are analyzed by identifying the ego states of the two persons. The process of analyzing transactions involves a look at what one person says to another, what the other person says in return, and what the exchange means. In interpersonal relationships the ability to make such analyses aids the communication process by reducing misunderstandings.

There are three types of transactions: parallel, crossed, and ulterior. Parallel transactions occur when the ego state of one person is responded to by the addressed ego state of another person. A crossed transaction occurs when the ego state of one person is responded to by an ego state different from the one addressed. In ulterior transactions conversation has one meaning at the social level but in reality has an underlying meaning.

Another important concept in transactional analysis is stroking. Stroking refers to the need people have for receiving attention, that is, the need to be recognized by others. Many transactions occur because of this basic need. Strokes are transactions that let people know that they exist, that they matter, and that they are important.

Parallel Transactions

In parallel, or complementary transactions, the sender of a message receives the expected type of response. The desired ego state of the message receiver is reached successfully and communication continues as the message receiver addresses the ego state from which the message originated. During parallel transactions two people may communicate as parent to parent, child to child, adult to adult, or any one of the six combinations of ego states—parent to child, parent to adult, child to parent, child to adult, adult to parent, and adult to child. Lines of communication are open and conversation can continue indefinitely as parallel transactions follow one another smoothly.

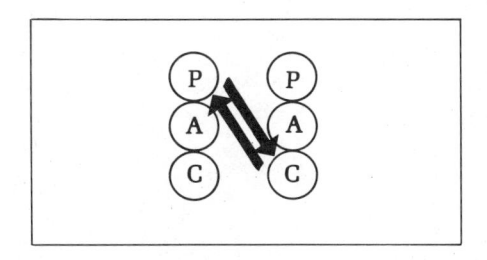

Figure 9.5. *Parallel transaction.*

Examples of the nine types of parallel transactions are given below.

Parent: Some people just don't want to work.
Parent: Yes, they seem to want something for nothing.

Parent: If you are ill, go to bed and get some rest.
Child: Then I'll feel better, won't I?

Parent: My family doesn't eat balanced meals.
Adult: There are four basic food groups which should be included in most diets.

Child: Let's paint the town red tonight!
Child: That will be fun!

Child: I'd like to throw this calculus book in the trash.
Parent: Now, what has you so upset about that book?

Child: I'm sure to fail this test tomorrow.
Adult: You have successfully completed all your assignments.

Adult: Where is the closest grocery store?
Adult: At the corner of Main and Elm streets.

Adult: I need help to stop smoking.
Parent: That's right. I've just thrown away your cigarettes.

Adult: You are angry. What seems to be the problem?
Child: With this messy house, I'll never be ready for our guests.

The parallel transactions that occur most often are the parent to parent, child to child, adult to adult, and parent to child transactions.

Crossed Transactions

When the sender of a message receives an unexpected or inappropriate response, a crossed transaction occurs. In such situations persons tend to glare at each other, withdraw, turn their backs, walk away, or change the topic of conversation. The original line of communication is broken and interpersonal relationships are strained. Communication is likely to stop.

There are seventy-two types of crossed transactions. Examples of the four most common types are provided below.

Adult-Adult: It is 8:00. We are late for the movie.
Child-Parent: I've been hurrying but no one will help me.

Adult-Adult: It is 8:00. We are late for the movie.
Parent-Child: If you had helped, I would be ready.

Child-Parent: I'm not ready. I need some help.
Adult-Adult: To receive help, you need only ask for it.

Parent-Child: If you expect me to be ready on time, clean up the dishes.
Adult-Adult: You seem upset. I have time to help you with the dishes.

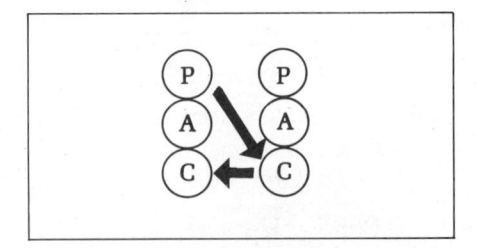

Figure 9.6. *Crossed transaction.*

A crossed transaction can be used in a positive way to end an interpersonal situation perceived to be nonproductive. Once communication has stopped, however, there is no assurance that productive communication can be reestablished.

Ulterior Transactions

When hidden meanings are implied, an ulterior transaction has occurred. Ulterior transactions are overtly disguised as socially acceptable transactions. To understand the transaction and predict the other person's behavior, the covert or psychological meaning of the transaction must be known. Nonverbal clues like tone of voice, facial expression, and posture are important in deciphering ulterior messages. Misunderstandings sometimes occur when one participant thinks an ulterior message is being sent when, in fact, it is not.

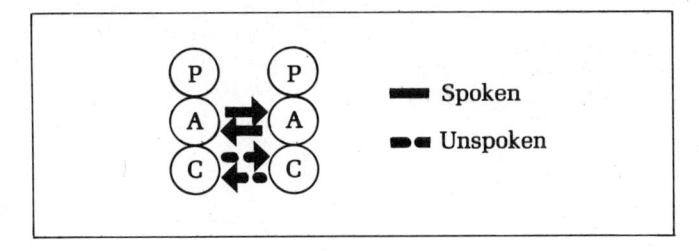

Figure 9.7. *Ulterior transaction.*

The example below is provided to demonstrate the social and psychological messages of an ulterior transaction.

Social level (spoken)
    Adult-Adult: We have to work late on this report, Jane.
    Adult-Adult: Yes, the report must be completed by tomorrow, John.

Psychological level (unspoken)
    Child-Child: (Let's spend the evening together, Jane)
    Child-Child: (I'd love to spend the evening with you, John.)

From the nature of the verbal message, it should be obvious that the psychological meaning of the message is transmitted through nonverbal symbols. The social message covers the real meaning of the message. During ulterior transactions the sender of a message is operating at both a social and psychological level and the message is sent and responded to at two levels. Successful ulterior transactions occur when messages are interpreted and responded to at the psychological level. They are identified when a person says one thing and means another.

Stroking

Stroking is a part of all transactions where individuals feel their existence as persons. Strokes can come from any ego state and be received by any ego state. Strokes are necessary for survival. Infants require much physical stroking. As they mature, physical stroking is replaced by verbal and psychological stroking. Strokes are either positive or negative.

Positive strokes usually occur as a result of a parallel transaction that leaves a person feeling happy, rewarded, and important. Positive strokes come in such forms as compliments, affection, judgments, and listening. Note the following examples of positive strokes.

Compliment: You served an excellent meal today.
Your dress fits beautifully.
Your golf swing makes you look like a pro.
Affection: You are a wonderful husband.
We always enjoy evenings spent with you.
I'll never find a better boss than you.
Judgment: That report was excellent.
Your work on that painting is better.
Your use of resources revealed good thinking.
Listening: Avoid interruptions.
Take time to stop whatever you are doing.
Give feedback.

Positive strokes may take much simpler forms than the examples above. A nod of the head, a comment about the weather, or a "how are you?" are often interpreted as positive strokes. Positive strokes let people know in pleasurable ways that their existence counts.

Negative strokes let people know that they exist also, but in a generally unpleasant way. Negative strokes can be physical, such as a slap in the face, or verbal, such as a complaint about service. Negative strokes often result from ignoring, teasing, humiliating, and laughing at others. Too many negative strokes cause emotional damage. When positive strokes are unavailable, however, people often seek negative strokes. It seems that there is more appeal to receiving negative strokes than to being completely ignored.

In addition to being positive or negative, strokes can also be conditional or unconditional. Conditional strokes occur when one must do something before receiving a stroke. Three primary conditions for stroking are performance, accommodation, and conformity. For example, a parent may imply that a child will receive positive strokes if elected class president, chores around the house are completed, and a neat appearance is maintained. Unconditional strokes occur without a prior behavior and let receivers know that they are being stroked just for being themselves. Unconditional positive strokes are the best kind to receive. Unconditional negative strokes, or abuse for no apparent reason, are probably the worst to receive.

Each of the three ego states needs to be stroked. The child ego state needs positive strokes for being creative and fun loving; the parent ego state, for being nurturing; and the adult ego state for being an effective processor of information. People require different amounts of stroking. Some people are satisfied with an occasional notice; others require almost constant attention. People can learn to give themselves strokes, a process which often leads to more independent and assertive personalities.

People generally develop a routine for gathering strokes. Some people feel that they must impress others with accomplishments, exploits, and successes; others are satisfied with the strokes they give themselves and do not appear dependent on the opinions of others; others need a parent figure to give approval; others seek to make people happy by telling jokes or doing favors; and still others exhibit behavior, like complaining, that generally results in negative strokes. Once individuals recognize their patterns of stroking behavior, they have the capacity to change. They can observe themselves in transactions with others and consciously attempt to establish new patterns.

Psychological Games

Human beings also have a need to do something with their time. In the overall theory of transactional analysis this need is called time structuring, and consists of experiences like withdrawal, rituals, activities, pastimes, games, and intimacy. One means of structuring time, psychological games, has been given much attention in the literature on transactional analysis. Games are a series of ulterior transactions that result in a payoff for both players. The parallel nature of the duplex transaction allows a game to continue indefinitely. It generally involves negative or conditional positive strokes.

There are many different games, all with several common elements: (a) several people, often playing the specific roles of victim, persecutor, or rescuer; (b) a series of seemingly parallel transactions that seem plausible on the surface; (c) an ulterior transaction, sometimes called a hidden agenda; (d) a negative payoff that concludes the game and is the real purpose for playing. Most games begin with a crossed transaction that stops the original line of communication and moves the players into the game. Games prevent honest, intimate, and open relationships. Since they appear to represent one thing on the surface and another in reality, games distort the communication process.

In the following paragraphs, several of the most common psychological games (Berne, 1964) are described. In reading the descriptions note the roles of victim, the one who gets picked on; persecutor, the one who does the picking; and rescuer, the one who tries to intervene. Also note the elements of the hidden agenda and negative payoff.

    I. Life games
       1. Alcoholic: A drunk makes a fool of himself and someone tries to counsel him. The drinking may be pleasurable but the payoff results from the attention, problems, and forgiveness that occur afterwards. A similar game, Dry Alcoholic, has the same moves, leads to the same payoff, but is played without a bottle.

2. Now I've Got You, You S.O.B.: One person catches another making a mistake and makes the other person suffer because of the mistake. The initiator generally looks for errors, discovers them with delight, and vigorously exploits them.

II. Marital games
1. Corner: This is a game where one player wants attention and the other player refuses to give the attention. It might begin with a wife suggesting to her husband that they go out to dinner and then "unconsciously" reminding her husband about broken plumbing. Her intention is that he will feel guilty and take her out, but he becomes annoyed and refuses.
2. Harried: Harried persons fill many roles. Often they take on everything they can find and ask for more. When the going gets too rough, they take advantage of the game by collapsing and letting everyone down. The harried housewife is a common role for women who overextend themselves.

III. Party games
1. Blemish: Players do not feel comfortable with new acquaintances or new events until they have discovered a flaw. The game generally begins with a need to change a feeling of personal failure into a feeling that the failure is associated with the other person or event.
2. Why Don't You—Yes But: A person presents a problem and then rejects the suggested solutions. The idea being that no one can suggest an acceptable solution.

IV. Sexual games
1. Let's You and Him Fight: A woman sets up a competition for her favors between two men. Several outcomes are possible. She might surrender herself to the winner, whether she wants him or not, or she might run off with a third man.
2. Rape: A woman is flirtatious with a man and implies that she is sexually interested in him. When he accepts her seemingly obvious offer, she rejects him.

V. Consulting room games
1. I'm Only Trying To Help You: A person gives advice to someone else. When the suggestion does not result in the desired outcome, the person being helped sometimes blows up by saying, "See what you made me do." The giver of advice becomes defensive and tries again to correct the situation.
2. Wooden Leg: One player uses some physical condition such as pregnancy as an excuse for not doing something.

They often say, "What do you expect from someone in my condition?"

VI. Good games
1. Cavalier: This game is played by a man who is attempting to build a woman's ego. Sex is not the anticipated payoff but rather the satisfaction of having given an effective compliment. The man achieves satisfaction from his own creativity and originality.
2. Happy to Help: A person who plays this game is consistently helpful to other people. The player is motivated by a need to repent for past wickedness, cover present wickedness, or plan for future exploitations. Credit should be given for taking a helpful rather than a harmful approach to achieving the goal.

There are many more recorded and unrecorded games. In looking at the games, two questions are relevant. Why do we play games? How can we stop playing games?

There are several reasons why we play games. One reason, stated earlier, is to pass time. Unfortunately some people spend their entire lifetimes playing games rather than participating in more productive ways to structure time. Another reason for playing games is to gather negative strokes. When positive strokes are unavailable, people often seek negative strokes rather than be ignored. A third reason for playing games is to collect bad feelings. People collect bad feelings as they collect trading stamps. Each time they are hurt by someone they add stamps to their collection. Eventually they might trade their stamps for crying, depression, drunkenness, divorce, or even suicide. A fourth reason for playing games is to avoid intimacy. Since games stop open, honest communication, they stop the type of communication necessary for intimate relationships.

In order to give up games it is necessary to become aware of the games people play and then refuse to initiate them. One can stop games initiated by someone else by refusing to participate in the expected way, that is, by denying payoff or ceasing parallel transactions. Some examples of behaviors that will stop a game are listed below:

1. Give an unexpected response
2. Stop exaggerating your weaknesses or strengths
3. Stop exaggerating the weaknesses or strengths of others
4. Give and receive positive rather than negative strokes
5. Structure more time with activities, intimacy and fun
6. Stop assuming roles of rescuer, persecutor, or victim

For clearer and more honest interpersonal relationships, it seems obvious that games must be eliminated from our interactions with others.

Life Scripts

Psychological games and other aspects of time structuring relate to the moment; life scripts, in contrast, represent the structure of an entire lifetime. A script is a fairly rigid plan adopted during childhood for use throughout life. It implies that many important decisions are made early in life. It is similar to a script used in a theatrical production in that there is generally a cast of characters, a theme, dialogue, and movement toward a conclusion.

Even though unaware of the drama being enacted, each individual compulsively follows a script. Analysis of scripts includes such things as determining why different ego states predominate in different individuals, tendencies to depend on ulterior transactions, techniques used to give and receive strokes, and choice of games. Analysis involves a look at the individual's life plan and self-concept.

The development of the script begins with nonverbal messages received by newborn infants. The messages received at an early age help to determine what children eventually think of themselves, what they think about others, and what they are determined to do with their lives. Scripts are determined in part by such factors outside the family as cultural, social, and religious experiences. Once they are consciously discovered scripts can be changed to be more productive and fulfilling.

In very general terms, life scripts can be classified according to the two broad categories of winners and losers. A winner is associated with success and survival; a loser, with failure and defeat. People who are winners are not necessarily the best at everything. They are people who have successfully made the transition from dependence to independence to interdependence. They are themselves and develop to their fullest potential. Losers, at some point in their development, fail to make a successful transition to interdependence, and to compensate they learn techniques of manipulation. A winner tries to be free of manipulative strategies; a loser hangs onto them.

Most people possess some characteristics of both the winner and loser. The proportion of time spent in each role is related to what happened during childhood and is thus a part of the script. Losing is associated with the negative experiences of childhood and the devices developed for coping. Losers are unaware of their potential and the options available for a more productive life. Through analysis of life scripts, one can determine ways to change a negative script to one with more positive associations. Structural analysis, transactional analysis, and psychological games often deal with the present; script analysis is more appropriate for a review of the past with positive changes determined for the future.

SUMMARY

Transactional analysis is a study of the communication exchanges that occur in interpersonal relationships. It includes aspects of personality referred to as parental, adult, and childlike in behavior; types of interactions that keep communication lines open, that stop lines of communication, and that involve double meanings; games people play; and life scripts that possibly account for successes and failures as adults.

Even a brief introduction to transactional analysis can contribute to effective communication by providing greater understanding of processes involved in sending messages to and receiving them from another person. Understanding the basis of transactions involved in communication is a first step in changing behavior to strive for more fulfilling and rewarding interpersonal relationships.

Activity 1
Information about Interpersonal Communication

Preparation: Read the textual material for Part III: Interpersonal Communication. Prepare yourself for taking a test by reviewing the "Knowledge Objective" included in the Overview for Part III and by answering the practice items given below.

PRACTICE ITEMS FOR PART III

Instructions: Select the best answer for each item.

1. To take responsibility for their own behavior, people need to
    a. self-disclose feelings and thoughts
    b. project responsibility for outcomes to others
    c. communicate in abstract terms
    d. own feelings and thoughts
2. A person reveals feelings about the pressures of being both a student and a salesman.
   The person has displayed ability to
    a. self-disclose
    b. be assertive
    c. be behaviorally flexible
    d. play psychological games
3. Which of the following adjectives is most appropriate for describing an assertive individual?
    a. pushy
    b. rude
    c. independent
    d. angry
4. One friend says to another, "Stop eating so fast; you'll get an upset stomach." This person is revealing the
    a. child ego state
    b. parent ego state
    c. adult ego state
5. What makes people become "losers"?
    a. They are born to be independent.
    b. They learn to cope with negative experiences.
    c. They avoid becoming self-responsible.
    d. They reveal their true personalities.

Activity 1 continued

6. Person 1: "Go away and leave me alone; I'm sick."
   Person 2: "Then you should get some rest."
   This parallel transaction (Person 1 to Person 2) represents
   a. child to parent
   b. child to child
   c. adult to parent
   d. parent to child
7. During which stage of life does one generally develop most of the life script?
   a. childhood
   b. adolescence
   c. young adulthood
   d. middle adulthood
8. A conversation between two strangers gradually becomes more and more heated; one gets angry and the other maintains composure.
   The person who maintained composure displayed ability to
   a. empathize
   b. self-disclose
   c. own feelings and thoughts
   d. be behaviorally flexible
9. In considering values, which of these is false?
   a. Intensity of values varies.
   b. Values cannot be seen.
   c. Values are independent of behavior.
   d. Some values are specific and some are general.
10. A girl hears about the robbery of a friend's home and feels the loss the friend must feel.
    The girl has demonstrated ability to
    a. play psychological games
    b. empathize
    c. own feelings and thoughts
    d. be nonjudgmental

Key: 1.d 2.a 3.c 4.b 5.c 6.a 7.a 8.d 9.c 10.b

Group Activity: Attend class and complete objective test items for Part III: Interpersonal Communication.

Individual Activity: Make arrangements with your instructor to complete objective test items for Part III: Interpersonal Communication.

Activity 2
Owning Feelings and Self-Disclosure

Preparation: Some techniques that many people use to get their ways include crying, pouting, shouting, screaming, pushing, announcing things like "I don't feel good," or saying something like, "If you had a childhood like mine, you'd drink, too." Most get-my-way techniques can be lumped under three broad headings: helplessness, suffering, and anger. These are learned responses to interpersonal communication situations that do not seem to go the way they should be going.

Helplessness, suffering, and anger are not appropriate responses because they involve demands and manipulation of other people and often end in frustration and broken relationships. When a get-my-way tool is used individuals are setting up situations where others are forced to be responsible. Conversely, when others respond to someone else's get-my-way tools, they permit themselves to become responsible for the way the other person feels. All persons are responsible for their own behavior and they alone can change their behavior. When one person in a relationship changes behavior, the others involved in the relationship have the opportunity to evaluate their behavior and perhaps modify it.

Suggestions have been provided below for you to give examples of get-my-way kinds of behavior that you have demonstrated. After you have "owned" each behavior, describe how this behavior could have been changed so that there would no longer be a payoff. An example would be when a father comes home from his office and sees his child crying. Instead of asking, "Why are you crying?" he might say, "Honey, what do you want to happen?"

Part I: Helplessness—not taking responsibility for dealing with difficult situations.

1. Describe one interpersonal situation in which you got your own way be being helpless.

    How could your behavior have been different?

2. Describe one way that you have been physically helpless.

    How could your behavior have been different?

3. Describe one occasion when you used sickness as a form of helplessness to get your own way.

    How could your behavior have been different?

Activity 2 continued

Part II: Suffering—when you imply that another person has hurt you.

1. Describe one situation when you said, "You've hurt my feelings," and have in effect admitted control by the other person.

   How could your behavior have been different?

2. Describe one situation when you have exhibited suffering through withdrawal.

   How could your behavior have been different?

3. Describe one occasion when you have used worry, jealousy, depression, or suffering to prevent someone from acting in a certain way.

   How could your behavior have been different?

Part III: Anger—a last resort technique which includes some forms of overt behavior, silence, and/or physical attack.

1. Describe one situation where you displayed anger by shouting, gesturing, slamming a door, driving discourteously, throwing things, or other similar behavior.

   How could your behavior have been different?

2. Describe one situation in which you manipulated another person and got your own way through anger.

   How could your behavior have been different?

Option 1 — Discussion

Group Activity: With the above examples of get-my-way behavior from your own life, join with others in a circle and self-disclose about one situation. Describe how you could or would change the behavior if you had a chance to participate in that particular situation again.

Individual Activity: With the above examples of get-my-way kinds of behavior from your own life, self-disclose with a friend or family member about one of the situations. Ask the other person to give an opinion about how you might have taken responsibility for your own behavior. Compare this opinion with the one you recorded. Discuss the similarities of your opinions and develop a solution that you both agree would be best. Briefly summarize in writing the solution suggested by your confidant and your mutually agreed upon solution.

Activity 2 continued

Option 2 — Role Playing

Group Activity: In class choose a partner and begin to discuss your get-my-way behaviors. From yours and those of your partner, select one of the situations to role play for the class. After role playing, talk to the class about the behaviors. What attitudes were revealed by the two people in the scene? Was there a communication breakdown between the people? What might have been done to avoid the conflict? What is being disclosed about the people involved?

Individual Activity: Write out a brief dialogue between two communicators who are experiencing get-my-way behaviors. At the end of the dialogue answer the following questions. What attitudes were revealed by the two people in the scene? Was there a communication breakdown between the people? What might have been done to avoid the conflict? What was being disclosed about the people involved?

Activity 3
Assertiveness

Preparation: One way of becoming noticeably more assertive is to establish definite goals. Without goals there is little sense of purpose in life. Goals keep us motivated and when accomplished, reinforce self-esteem. Feeling good about oneself often increases assertive abilities and leads to improvement of interpersonal communication skills.

As a preliminary step to becoming more assertive answer the following questions about your personal goals.

1. What long-term goals do you want to accomplish?
2. What subgoals do you need to accomplish first?
3. What kind of life do you want to lead?
4. What do you want to accomplish professionally?
5. How much money do you want to make in your lifetime?
6. What hobbies or sports do you wish to pursue?
7. How do you want to look?
8. What idealized self-image would you like to acquire?

Now select one of your goals or subgoals that can be achieved in a reasonably short amount of time. As a beginning to your attempt to achieve the goal, complete a worksheet using the following format.

Worksheet for Achieving a Personal Goal

1. I want to achieve the following goal.
2. What might keep me from reaching this goal? (*Check those which apply.*)
    - _____ I don't have the ability, skills, and/or knowledge needed.
    - _____ I don't want it badly enough to work hard for it.
    - _____ I am afraid that I might fail.
    - _____ I am afraid of what others might think.
    - _____ Others don't want me to reach the goal.
    - _____ The goal is too difficult to accomplish.

   Some other reasons are the following.
3. What can I do to reduce the possibility that the reasons given above will prevent me from reaching the goal?
4. Who can help me achieve my goal?
   _____ Name _____ Kind of Help

Activity 3 continued

5. What are my chances for successfully achieving my goal?
   _____ Good   _____ Fair   _____ Poor
   Why do I feel this way?

6. What are some good things that might happen if I reach the goal?

7. What are some bad things that might happen if I don't reach the goal?

8. What are the chances that the bad things might happen if I don't reach the goal?
   _____ High   _____ So/So   _____ Low
   What can I do to reduce the possibility of an unfavorable outcome?

9. Do I still want to reach the goal?

10. What are the first steps I can take to reach the goal?

11. What else can I do to improve the chances for success?

12. Am I going to take the above steps?
    _____ Yes   _____ No   _____ Undecided

13. If the answer to question 12 is yes, I commit myself to the following contract:
    I _____, have decided to try to achieve the goal of _____
    _____. The first step I will take to reach this goal will be to _____
    _____ by _____. My target date
    for reaching the goal is _____.

Group Activity: Bring your completed worksheet to class. With one or two other students, go over your plan and try to strengthen your strategy for reaching your goal. Contribute to the development of the plans prepared by the other student or students in your group.

Individual Activity:

Follow-up: Achieving a Personal Goal

1. My plan for achieving a personal goal
   _____ worked well, since I reached my goal.
   _____ worked somewhat, since I nearly or partially reached my goal.
   _____ did not work, since I failed to reach my goal.

2. How do I feel about my success or failure?

3. The following events contributed to my success or failure.

4. If I were to attempt to achieve the goal again, I would do the following things differently.

Activity 4
Values Clarification

Preparation: Use the format below to express some of your values.

1. In column 1, list ten areas that you value. Examples might be money, love, sex, marriage, family, freedom, education, religion, leisure time, and health.
2. In column 2, describe what you learned about each value as you were growing up.
3. In column 3, write the name and relationship of the person from whom you learned the information in column 2. If you learned on your own through experience, write "EXP."
4. In column 4, indicate the extent to which you now agree with the statement in column 2 by writing strongly agree (SA), partially agree (PA), neutral or don't know (DK), partially disagree (PD), or strongly disagree (SD).

1 Value	2 Statement about Value	3 Name & Relationship	4 Agreement
Example Education	It is essential to obtain a college degree.	Ms. Rogers, teacher	PA
1.			
2.			
3.			
4.			
5.			
6.			
7.			
8.			
9.			
10.			

Group Activity: In groups of four discuss the areas that you value and the reasons you acquired the value. Did someone moralize to you about the issue? Was the belief imposed on you by someone? Did you adopt the belief from someone who serves as a role model for you? Did you acquire the value from your own experience?

Activity 4 continued

Did you weigh several alternatives and make your own free choice? Did you acquire many of your values in the same way? Discuss with your group similarities and differences that you identify within your own list and through comparisons with your list and the lists of your group members.

Individual Activity: Give your list of ten areas that you value to someone who knows you well. Ask that person to provide the information about you for columns 2, 3, and 4. Briefly describe in writing the similarities and differences in the two perceptions of the areas you value.

Activity 5
Behavioral Flexibility

Preparation: Describe on paper in some detail an interpersonal conflict situation that you have recently experienced.

Group Activity: Form dyads in class and discuss the interpersonal conflict situations. Role play one of the conflict scenes. Demonstrate behavioral flexibility by attempting to resolve the problem using the five-step process given below. You and your partner are to resolve the conflict so that you feel happy or satisfied with the mutually agreed upon solution.

Step 1: Either make or write out a statement about the conflict as you and your partner view it. Most important, do not blame, criticize, judge, ridicule, shame, or name-call.

Step 2: Define the dimensions of the conflict by providing areas of agreement and disagreement between you and your partner.

Step 3: When the areas of agreement and disagreement are defined, brainstorm as many solutions to the conflict as possible. Evaluation of the alternative solutions is not permitted.

Step 4: Once the brainstorming is completed, turn your attention to identifying the consequences of each of the best solutions. Both the pros and the cons of each alternative should be listed.

Step 5: Finally, evaluate each of the alternative solutions and attempt to select the one that is most satisfactory to both you and your partner. If a solution that is mutually acceptable cannot be agreed upon, return to steps two and three and repeat the process until a mutually acceptable solution is determined.

At the close of the class return to the main group, share the conflict situation with the class, the solutions you and your partner considered, and the one finally chosen by the two of you.

Individual Activity: Ask the person with whom you have been in conflict to discuss the conflict situation with you. Demonstrate behavioral flexibility by attempting to resolve the problem using the five-step process described above. The two of your are to resolve the conflict so that you feel happy and satisfied with the mutually agreed upon solution. At the close of the experience, describe in writing the conflict, the solutions you and your partner considered, and the solution you finally chose to resolve the conflict.

Activity 6
Descriptive Listening

Option 1 — Interpersonal Communication Situation

Preparation: What areas in your life are you willing to share with others? Listed below are subjects you may or may not feel comfortable discussing.

1. Religious doubts
2. A first love
3. Problems with parents
4. Negative feelings about best friends
5. Weight control
6. Innermost desires
7. Present salary
8. A personal problem
9. Health problems
10. Thoughts of suicide
11. Taking drugs
12. Abortion
13. Marriage problems
14. Financial problems
15. Cost of your house
16. Racial prejudices
17. Jealousy
18. Birth control
19. Cheating
20. Child discipline

You may not wish to share your feelings on many of these topics. Some you would share only with an intimate friend. If someone chose to confide in you on one of these topics, would you be able to listen without passing judgment? Nonjudgmental listening is a skill that is difficult to develop.

Give some thought to several of the topics above so that you can express your feelings to a listener who will attempt to be nonjudgmental in reacting to what you say.

Group Activity: Choose a class member to whom you feel you can relate well. Ask your partner to listen to your feelings about one of the topics from the above list. Watch your partner for signs of making judgments about your feelings on the topic.

Activity 6 continued

Encourage your listener to be nonjudgmental. Pause as you speak to let your listener paraphrase what you have said. Was your listener able to be descriptive or did opinions and judgments enter the conversation?

Then reverse roles so that your partner can express feelings about one of the topics and you can serve as listener. Use your descriptive listening skills; paraphrase what the speaker says. Be especially careful not to evaluate or give your opinion about what was said.

If time allows, change partners and topics until you have talked on several topics and to several people. Remember the purpose of descriptive listening is to help others investigate their feelings and come to their own conclusions. After you have practiced descriptive listening return to the full group and discuss the experience. How do you feel as a speaker? How do you feel as a listener? When would this skill be useful?

Individual Activity: Choose someone in your life with whom you can be honest and who will be sensitive to your feelings. Ask the person you select to listen as you explain your feelings about one of the topics from the above list. Ask the listener to be especially careful not to evaluate what you say but simply to listen and then paraphrase what you say in slightly different words. Watch your listener for signs of having made a judgment. Pause as you speak to allow the listener time to describe what you have said. Was the listener completely accurate in describing, or was judgment passed on your ideas?

Now ask your partner to let you reverse roles and allow you to be the listener. Does your partner feel open enough with you to discuss feelings on a subject from the list? As you listen to the explanation, be especially careful not to give your opinion about what is said. Your task is to paraphrase what you hear. This will allow your partner to hear it in slightly different words.

Write a one-page paper in which you describe the dialogue and the paraphrasing experience. Include your feelings and thoughts about the success of the experiment. You may want to tape the paraphrasing activity so you can record it accurately. Be sure to include your opinion about the advantages and disadvantages of descriptive listening.

Activity 6 continued

Option 2 — Group Communication Situation

Preparation: Your instructor will assign a controversial topic that can be debated in class. You may choose to be either for or against the topic. Take about fifteen minutes to think through and jot down your ideas about the topic.

Group Activity: With the entire group, begin debating the topic informally. There will be no specific speaking order except that the affirmatives and negatives should alternate. Everyone should get a chance to speak at least once. Each new person who speaks may give ideas and feelings about the issue only after restating accurately what was just said. That is, the speaker must use paraphrasing and descriptive listening skills before stating an opinion.

After the debate discuss the following questions about the descriptive listening experience.

1. How did you feel when you tried to listen objectively and understand the debaters? Do you usually try this hard to listen accurately?
2. How did the listening you did compare with the kind you do every day? Do you usually try to evaluate the messages you receive?
3. As a listener, were you able to paraphrase accurately the other debater's statements?
4. How did you feel when you were the one speaking and the other debaters were trying to understand you? Were you relieved that they could not make critical judgments of your message?

Individual Activity: Find several people who are willing to debate the controversial issue with you. Allow them time to complete the preparation for the activity. Group members will take opposite sides in debating the issue. Once everyone is prepared, take turns stating opinions. However, before you state your opinions each should rephrase what was just heard. Use your descriptive listening and paraphrasing skills. Do not make judgmental reactions to the other debaters' statements.

Write a short report of the debate. Present the major arguments for and against the issue. Describe your role as speaker and listener. Then write out brief answers to the questions following the group activity.

Activity 7
Empathy

Preparation: Write several summary statements about the following aspects of your personality.

1. What are the things (at least five) that really interest you?
2. What, ultimately, do you want to accomplish?
3. What are your primary commitments in life?
4. Specifically, what things do you most value about life?
5. What conflicts or problems are you experiencing?

Group Activity: In class select a friend, someone for whom you can feel empathy, and spend at least five minutes reviewing two of your partner's summary statements. Remember to be understanding as attitudes are revealed to you. Attempt to crawl inside your partner's frame of reference and experience another's feelings.

Totally absorb all of the data, both verbal and nonverbal, that are being communicated. By "hearing" both content and effect of each statement, you can assist your partner to express thoughts and feelings in a clear and complete fashion. Resist the temptation to judge or evaluate the comments. Strive to listen with empathy to what is being said. Then repeat the process as you reveal your responses to the questions above and your partner empathizes with you.

Individual Activity: Locate a friend or relative to serve as your partner. Ask your partner to reveal attitudes about the five questions listed above. Remember to be understanding as you listen. Attempt to crawl inside your partner's frame of reference and experience another's feelings.

Totally absorb all of the data, both verbal and nonverbal, that are being communicated. By "hearing" both content and effect of each statement, you can assist your partner to express thoughts and feelings in a clear and complete fashion. Resist the temptation to judge or evaluate the comments. Strive to listen with empathy to what is being said. Then repeat the process as you reveal your responses to the questions above and your partner empathizes with you.

Finally, prepare a written report of both sets of answers to the five questions and your experience at self-disclosure and empathizing.

Activity 8
Conflict Resolution

Preparation: All individuals who involve themselves with others on a day to day basis find themselves frequently involved in interpersonal conflicts. Some of them come about because of inability to communicate ideas, because someone refused to listen, or, perhaps, because a message was not understood. When a conflict does occur in your life there are several alternatives you can take. For instance, you can avoid it completely by just ignoring it. You can change the subject, or distract, or even joke your way through it.

Adler and Towne (1978) in their communication book, *Looking Out/ Looking In,* provide an excellent list of personality types who choose various alternatives rather than being completely honest and meeting a conflict situation directly. Their list, with a short description of each personality type, is given below.

1. Avoiders — People who demonstrate refusal to fight by finding other activities to take up time
2. Pseudoaccommodators — People who pretend that there is no conflict
3. Guilt Makers — People who make others feel responsible for causing pain
4. Subject Changers — Like avoiders, they shift the conversation away from the subject of the conflict
5. Distracters — People who avoid conflict by attacking unrelated aspects of others' lives
6. Mind Readers — People who attempt to analyze others' feelings and ignore their own feelings
7. Trappers — People who arrange circumstances so that others will react in a certain way, and then attack them for acting that way
8. Crisis Ticklers — People who hint at the problem but never fully divulge it
9. Gunnysackers — People who do not respond immediately to conflict but store up resentment and then release it all at once
10. Trivial Tyrannizers — People who avoid the real issue but do many insignificant things aimed at irritating the people causing them resentment
11. Jokers — People who "kid around" when seriousness is more important
12. Beltliners — People who avoid the conflict issue by focusing on other subjects that they know are very sensitive to others—hitting below the belt
13. Blamers — People who find fault with others instead of attempting to resolve conflict
14. Contract Tyrannizers — People who refuse to adjust their relationships with others but insist on maintaining them as they always have been

Activity 8 continued

15. Kitchen Sink Fighters — People who talk about everything but the kitchen sink in order to avoid the real issue
16. Withholders — People who avoid expressing anger honestly by keeping something important from others
17. Benedict Arnolds — People who do things to degrade others behind their backs

> Do you see yourself or someone you know in one of these roles? Using the list above as a guideline, in one page describe a conflict situation from your own life or from the life of someone with whom you are involved. In the closing paragraph, evaluate whether the conflict was dealt with effectively and discuss how interpersonal communication skills could have been used to arrive at a more satisfying resolution.

Group Activity: In small groups of four to six discuss the conflicts you described. Also discuss your evaluation of the conflicts. Decide which of the seventeen descriptors given above best fit the people involved in the conflicts.

Choose the most interesting conflict from each group to role play for the class. After each scene discuss the way the conflict was dealt with and how you feel it should or could be handled differently. In dealing with conflict situations, which interpersonal skills could you use to keep open communication channels?

Individual Activity: Ask someone you know well to role play on a cassette tape the conflict scene you described on paper. At the end of the tape discuss the incorrect or correct way the conflict was handled and how it might have been handled differently. Decide which of the seventeen descriptors given above best fit the people involved in the conflict. In dealing with conflict situations in your own life, what interpersonal skills could you use to keep open communication channels? Discuss this on the tape.

Activity 9
Structural Analysis

Preparation: Complete the following exercise on structural analysis.

1. Analysis of verbal and nonverbal language associated with the three ego states.
   a. Develop a list of words or phrases that are representative of the vocabulary of the parent ego state (e.g., should, don't).
   b. Develop a list of gestures, postures, tone of voice, and facial expressions that are representative of the nonverbal behavior of the parent ego state.
   c. Develop a list of words and phrases that are representative of the vocabulary of the child ego state (e.g., wow, I wish).
   d. Develop a list of gestures, postures, tone of voice and facial expressions that are representative of the nonverbal behavior of the child ego state.
   e. Develop a list of words or phrases that are representative of the vocabulary of the adult ego state (e.g., probability, estimate).
   f. Develop a list of postures, gestures, voice tones, facial expressions, etc., that are representative of the nonverbal behavior of the adult ego state.

2. Getting to know your parent ego state.
   a. Write three things your parents did that you liked.
   b. Write three things your parents did that you did not like.
   c. Now ask yourself, "Do I do any of these things myself?" If so, with whom?
   d. Write down two important parental messages that you still hear as you communicate intrapersonally.
   e. Are these parental messages negative or positive?
   f. Do they still influence your behavior in any way? Where? With whom?

3. Your opinion of yourself.
   a. Were you told you were just like your father, mother, blacksheep uncle, brother, sister, or someone else? To whom were you compared? What types of comparisons were made?
   b. Say in one sentence what you imagine each of your parent figures thought of you when you were a child.
   c. What do you think of yourself now?
   d. In what way is your current self-appraisal related to your parents' opinion of you as a child?
   e. When you have "taken enough" from people, how do you cash in? Whom or what do you cash in on?
   f. Now explore alternatives to "taking it." Could you have handled the situation in a different way so you did not collect?
   g. Try to discover any pattern of stamp collecting and redeeming that you have learned from your past experiences that may be a hindrance to you now.

Activity 9 continued

Group Activity: Share the above analysis of your ego states with your classmates. Does structural analysis apply to you or does it seem to be a theory that does not fit your personality?

Individual Activity: Reflect on the above analysis of your ego states. Also answer the question, does structural analysis apply to you or does it seem to be a theory that does not fit your personality? Justify your answer to the question by referring to the information you have learned about ego states.

Activity 10
Stroking

Preparation: Write out your reactions to the situations and questions about stroking.

1. *Negative Strokes:* Recall several situations in which you were involved in a negative transaction that caused you to collect a negative feeling.
   What were the situations? Describe them.
   Who was involved?
   How did you feel?

2. *Positive Strokes:* Recall several situations in which you were involved in a positive transaction that made you feel good.
   What were the situations? Describe them.
   Who was involved?
   How did you feel?
   In what way does the memory of it make you feel good now?
   What good things do you do to provide yourself with positive experiences?

Group Activity: Reveal to your classmates a positive and negative experience from your descriptions. Who was involved? How did it make you feel? What can you do in life to have more positive interpersonal experiences?

Individual Activity: After your responses to the stroking experiences are completed, list five ways to create more positive interpersonal experiences for yourself by giving and accepting positive strokes.

Activity 11
Games

Preparation: Review the descriptions of the games that were included in the text.

Group Activity: Choose a partner and turn to the description of games included with the reading material. Discuss a game that the two of you can role play. Rehearse the game first just as it is described. Now discuss ways that two people can stop playing games. Refer to the reading material to familiarize yourself with these. Rehearse the game again, incorporating a game stopper. Demonstrate both role-playing situations for the class. Let the class guess the game that you are playing.

Individual Activity: Select two of the games from those described in the reading material. Write a dialogue that demonstrates how each game might be played. Then rewrite each dialogue with a game stopper included.

Activity 12
Speaking Activity

Option 1 — Inspirational Message

Preparation: An inspirational message is designed to provide the listener with a stimulus to further develop some positive personal characteristic. It is an original message to motivate individuals to live their lives on higher planes. The message can be based on a person's life, a book, or an idea. The speaker's goal is to inspire with optimism, hope, and encouragement to reach for a life of greater achievement.

The area of interpersonal communication offers many possibilities for topics for inspirational messages. The concept of winners versus losers, for example, might be an appropriate topic. The books on assertiveness provide many ideas for encouraging listeners to develop more active roles in the directions their lives will take. Actually, all aspects of life provide a basis for inspiring messages.

After selecting a topic use the outline below as a guide for preparing your message. Use definition, examples, and quotations to support your main points. Use visual aids to create and hold audience interest. Prepare your message to be presented in no more than five minutes. Rehearse your message so that you can deliver it with confidence. Note cards may be used. Remember that the image of the speaker is critical in convincing a group of listeners to change their life styles. Evaluation criteria are presented at the end of the activity.

Outline for Inspirational Message

I. Introduction
   A. Opening statement to gain attention
   B. Relate to audience
   C. Statement of main points
   D. Preview of main points

II. Body
   A. First main point
      1. Support:
      2. Support:
      3. Support:

Activity 12 continued

    B. Second main point
       1. Support:
       2. Support:
       3. Support:
    C. Etc.
III. Conclusion
    A. Summary
    B. Transition statement
    C. Concluding statement (quotation, startling statement, poem, question)

To help in your preparation, an example of an inspirational message is given below.

Developing a Personality

Topical Outline	*Script*
I. Introduction	
A. Opening statement to gain attention	In my hand I hold a mirror. Take a good look at yourself. Are you what you want to be? Have you set a goal for your life?
B. Statement of main purpose	The main purpose of my speech today is to stimulate you to take a look at yourself and to help you develop a stronger personality.
C. Preview of main points	First I will describe some general personality characteristics. Then I will give you the three ingredients that influence a positive personality. I will include examples of persons in history who have developed strong personalities.
D. Relate to audience	Then I will expect you to take a good look at yourself and examine your personality.
II. Body	
A. First main point	Psychologists say that most cases of emotional maladjustment are due to the fact people will not accept themselves. They resent their limitations. They constantly daydream of what they would do if only they had another chance. They disregard their own possibilities and never make anything worthwhile out of themselves.
1. Support	The most stimulating successes in history have come persons who, facing limitations and handicaps, took them as part of life's

Activity 12 continued

	game and played splendidly in spite of them. As soon as people begin to accept this positive technique for handling their handicaps, they discover opportunities, always challenging and sometimes fascinating.
2. Support	Self pity and rebellion against oneself get you nowhere. You must accept yourself as a bundle of possibilities and undertake the most interesting game in the world, making the most of your best points. Take charge of your life, develop some plans and organize your living around a purpose. Set a goal.
3. Support	Many people fail to develop their personalities because they think life is something we find instead of something we create. The big business of being a person is to take existence and so organize it around our plans and purposes that it becomes life.
B. Second main point	There are three things that influence a personality: imagination, common sense, and courage.
1. Support	The first step in great living starts with a picture held in a person's imagination, of what he or she would like to be. Florence Nightingale dreamed of being a nurse; Edison pictured himself as an inventor. Each imagined the future so vividly that they headed for it. Hold a picture of yourself long and steadily enough in your mind's eye and you will be drawn toward it. Picture yourself defeated and that will make victory impossible. Picture yourself winning and that alone will contribute immeasurably to success.
2. Support	The second ingredient is common sense. There is no use in a round peg imagining itself fitted into a square hole. Sir Walter Scott wanted to be a poet and turned to novel writing only when Byron outshone him in his own chosen field. Study yourself; use your head in picking a goal; don't drift.
3. Support	The third ingredient is courage. Real personalities always have the kind of faith that produces courage. Richard Wagner had faith in music and he overcame the world. American medical personnel in Cuba had faith that yellow fever could be conquered and it was. Faith is creative power plus valor.

Activity 12 continued

III. Conclusion
    A. Summary — In summary, I have given you examples of persons in history who have developed strong personalities. I have also given you the three ingredients that influence a personality: imagination, common sense, and courage. Even a moderate exercise of these will produce remarkable results.
    B. Transition statement — I would like to leave each of you with the following thought:
    C. Concluding statement — An individual who concentrates on developing the positive aspects of personality can capitalize on anything life brings. Are *you* capitalizing on life's positive or negative events?

Group Activity: During class, deliver your inspirational message to your classmates.

Individual Activity: Make an appointment with your instructor to plan a specific time to deliver your inspirational message.

Evaluation Form
Inspirational Message

(Points are given to the right of each criterion.)

I. Introduction
   - _____ Gains attention (2)
   - _____ Relates to audience (2)
   - _____ States purpose of presentation (2)
   - _____ Previews main points (2)

II. Body
   - _____ Statement of main points (10)
   - _____ Effectiveness of support (10)
   - _____ Use of transitions between major points (10)

III. Conclusion
   - _____ Summary (2)
   - _____ Transition statement (2)
   - _____ Ends presentation with novel conclusion (2)

IV. Vocal Delivery
   - _____ Rate of speech (____ too slow ____ too rapid) (2)
   - _____ Volume of speech (____ too soft ____ too loud) (2)
   - _____ Conversational style (2)
   - _____ Vocal variety (2)
   - _____ Control of fillers (2)
   - _____ Pronunciation and articulation (2)

V. Physical Delivery
   - _____ Use of gestures (2)
   - _____ Eye contact (2)
   - _____ Correct posture (2)

VI. Personal Qualities
   - _____ General poise and speaker confidence (2)
   - _____ Warmth and friendliness (2)
   - _____ Speaker credibility (2)
   - _____ Conviction to subject (2)

VII. Presentation
   - _____ Provided uplifting message (25)
   - _____ Appropriate visual aids (5)

Activity 12 continued

Option 2 — Employment Interview

Preparation: Consider your life goals in terms of work. Reflect on a position that you would ultimately like to obtain. Choose a company to research that you would actually like to work for, but be realistic in setting this goal. Once you have made this important decision visit your campus placement office, a counselor, or the actual employment office to research the details of the position. In learning about the company, you will want to receive information concerning necessary educational background, specific qualifications, past work experience, job expectations, salary, benefits, and so forth.

When you have received the necessary information, write a letter of application and a resume that would fit the selected job opening. Begin by brainstorming all your past experiences and assets. Make a list including your education, extracurricular experience, work experience, special projects, and personal qualifications. Be sure to list your specific responsibilities from past jobs. Define as clearly as possible the type of position for which you wish to be considered. Remember to survey your list of assets and experiences. These are relevant to the type of job you are looking for. As you organize your material in a letter of application and a resume, be sure that you are credible and ethical, and be prepared to defend why you chose to mention or exclude specific information from your resume. Examples of a letter of application and a resume written by a college student follow.

Activity 12 continued

Mr. Mark Williams
P. O. Box 5493
Lubbock, Texas 79417
April 5, 1975

Mr. John E. Mills
J. E. Mills Trucking Company
21816 Electronic Lane
Dallas, Texas 75220

Dear Mr. Mills,

Marvin Short, Jr., of the Metroplex Traffic Club, has suggested your company to me as an organization interested in high quality motor freight rating and auditing. I feel that my training and experience in motor freight rating and auditing would be an asset to you, and I am very much interested in the opportunities for professional advancement that I would have with the J. E. Mills Trucking Company. I would like, therefore, to be considered for a position in your freight rating and auditing department.

I have been interested in many aspects of the freight industry, from shipping and receiving to rating and auditing, for some time. And, as I have indicated on the enclosed resume, I had the experience of special training in motor freight rating in a course taught by representatives of Time-D.C., Inc.; my aptitude for this work is evidenced by the fact that I was the first student in my class to be employed by Time-D.C. Having advanced steadily in skill and in depth of experience since then, I am now looking for opportunities for further advancement. I feel that working as a freight rater and/or auditor with the J. E. Mills Trucking Company would give me that opportunity.

My present work schedule enables me to be in Dallas any Monday. Would it be convenient for me to come in for an interview on Monday, April 14? I look forward to hearing from you and to the opportunity of working with you in Dallas.

Sincerely,

Mark Williams

Mark Williams

Activity 12 continued

RESUME

Mark Williams
P. O. Box 5493
Lubbock, Texas 79417
(806) 797-8775

Education

Draughon's Business College   Certificate: Motor Freight Rating Specialist.
Lubbock, Texas   Course taught by representative of Time-D.C., Inc.,
January–May, 1973   first to be employed from my class.

Monterey High School   Diploma: June, 1970
Lubbock, Texas
Sept., 1967–June, 1970

Experience

Time-D.C., Inc.   Duties: Rating and Routing (including division of
Lubbock, Texas   revenue) of freight bills from all areas of the country
Title: Rate Specialist, Class B   through a centralized computer system, utilizing
May, 1973–present   IBM 3277 display screens tied into an IBM 370 com-
                                   puter; above average production rate, below average
                                   error rate. Auditing disputed freight bills and cor-
                                   recting or declining as necessary; answering rate
                                   requests from all parts of the country through the
                                   use of teletype and inward WATS telephone line.
                                   Supervisor: Mr. Jack Russell

Hemphill-Wells Department Store   Duties: Receiving freight; inventorying, marking,
August, 1972–April, 1973   and distributing shipments; filing claims; packing
                                   and shipping outgoing freight.
                                   Supervisor: Mr. Red Wynn

Trinity Church   Duties: General office work; daily bus pickup and
Lubbock, Texas   delivery of day school children; maintenance of
Positions: Clerk, Bus Driver   church buildings and grounds.
June, 1970 – July, 1972   Supervisor: The Rev. Alfred Smith

References

Mr. Jack Russell   The Rev. Alfred Smith, Pastor
Supervisor, Rate and Audit Center   Trinity Church
Time-D.C., Inc.   6729 Military Parkway
3718 28th St.   Lubbock, Texas 79410
Lubbock, Texas 79410

Activity 12 continued

Next you will need to formulate two lists of questions. The first list will be questions an employer might ask you, and the second will be questions for you to ask the employer.

One major California company (Flanagan, 1975) has drawn up the following guidelines for forming interview questions. Keep these in mind as you formulate your own questions.

Subject	*Guideline*
Sex	Cannot discuss unless sex is a definite requirement for the position.
Marital Status	Cannot ask if single, married, engaged, divorced, or living with someone.
Children	Cannot ask if applicant has children at home, ages, child care provisions, or future plans for having children. After hiring, numbers and ages of children may be requested for insurance purposes.
Physical data	Cannot ask personal questions regarding height or weight. A physical exam can be required. Physical requirements of the position can be described.
Criminal record	Unless security clearance is indicated, cannot ask about arrests, convictions, or time spent in jail.
Military status	Can ask if applicant is a veteran and, if so, what job related experiences resulted; cannot ask about type or discharge or branch of service.
Age	Cannot ask or estimate age. After hiring, can ask if employee is over 18.
Housing	Can ask how the applicant can be reached; cannot ask about housing.

The following is a list of questions frequently asked by employers during an interview. Use these questions as a guideline for role playing an interview situation.

1. What are your long-range goals and objectives in regard to your vocation?
2. When and why did you establish these goals?
3. How do you plan to achieve them?
4. Specifically, what would you like to be doing five years from now?
5. What kind of salary do you expect to be earning five years from now? Ten years?

Activity 12 continued

6. How much money per year do you feel you need to earn to achieve your personal goals?
7. Which is your first consideration, the money you will earn, or happiness in the job chosen? Explain
8. What causes you to be motivated to do your best?
9. What do you consider to be your greatest strength?
10. What do you consider to be your greatest weakness?
11. Why did you choose the career for which you are prepared?
12. Based on what you did in school, how do you think a professor would describe you?
13. How has college prepared you for this position?
14. What college subjects did you like best?
15. What college subjects did you like least?
16. What grades did you earn in your major field?
17. Is this a good indication of your academic achievement?
18. What were your extracurricular activities in college?
19. What did you learn from participation in these?
20. Do you feel you need additional course work?
21. How much education do you plan to obtain?
22. When would you go for advanced course work if that is your choice?
23. Why do you feel this company should hire you?
24. What qualifications do you have that would make you an asset to this company?
25. How would you describe success?
26. How could you be successful in this company?
27. Describe the relationship that should exist between you and a supervisor?
28. What led you to this particular company?
29. What do you know about this company?
30. What geographic area do you prefer?
31. Are you willing to relocate?
32. Are you willing to travel?
33. Would you be willing to spend six months as a trainee?
34. What have you done that shows that you have initiative and are willing to work?
35. What one accomplishment has given you the most satisfaction? Why?
36. What do you feel has been your most rewarding life experience?

Group Activity: Select a classmate as a partner to role play the employment interview. Take turns acting the role of employer and applicant. As an aid in the role-playing exercise, give your partner the questions you developed as well as your letter and resume. Be prepared to demonstrate to the class your experience in role playing your employment interview.

Activity 12 continued

Before presenting the interview for your instructor consider the following:

1. Have you prepared an introduction of the company? Are you well informed about the employer?
2. Do you know the routine of an interview? Are you prepared enough to be relaxed and use your natural personality?
3. Have you prepared your letter and resume adequately and neatly so the interviewer will be adequately informed about your past achievements and interests?
4. Have you organized your questions and thoughts so you can be relaxed, courteous, natural, and yet professional?
5. Have you checked the interview evaluation sheet to see that you are adequately prepared for the role-playing experience? If so, you are ready to have this interpersonal speaking experience.

Individual Activity: Practice the employment interview by locating someone who has had actual experience in hiring employees. This individual might even be the one advertising the position you selected to prepare for the activity. Explain your assignment to the interviewer and request the interviewer's cooperation. Then give the individual the advertisement, the letter and the resume, and request an appointment for the interview. Before going to the interview review the specifics in the group activity and the textual material. With the permission of the interviewer, make a tape of the interview activity.

Evaluation Form
Employment Interview

(Points are given to the right of each criterion.)

I. Introduction
   _____ Gains attention of class (2)
   _____ Relates to audience (2)
   _____ States purpose of interview (2)
   _____ States background of company (2)

II. Interviewer
   _____ Appears to be ready for interview (3)
   _____ Courteous (3)
   _____ Relaxed (3)
   _____ Specific preparation of questions (5)
   _____ Quality of questions (10)
   _____ Handles salary question tactfully (3)
   _____ Terminates interview smoothly (3)

III. Interviewee
   _____ Appears to be ready for interview (3)
   _____ Courteous (3)
   _____ Relaxed (3)
   _____ Makes good first impression (3)
   _____ Expresses interest in working for company (3)
   _____ Stresses qualifications for particular job (3)
   _____ Reviews past experiences (3)
   _____ Specific with answers (3)
   _____ Handles salary questions tactfully (3)
   _____ Terminates interview smoothly (3)

IV. Attitude
   _____ Speaker's confidence (2)
   _____ General poise (2)
   _____ Energy level and enthusiasm (2)
   _____ Positivism (2)
   _____ Honest and direct (2)

Evaluation Form continued

V.　Personal Qualities
　　　_____ Appropriate dress (2)
　　　_____ Well-groomed (2)
　　　_____ Articulate voice (2)
　　　_____ Eye contact (2)
　　　_____ Correct posture (2)
　　　_____ Control of fillers (2)
　　　_____ Ability to communicate (2)
　　　_____ Rate of speech (2)
　　　_____ Conversational style (2)
　　　_____ Vocal variety (2)
　　　_____ Credibility (2)

Additional Readings in Interpersonal Communication

In addition to books and articles cited in these chapters, the following books are excellent sources for further study of communication.

Alberti, R. E., and Emmons, M. L. *Stand Up, Speak Out, Talk Back.* New York: Simon and Schuster, 1975.

> An expansion of the authors' work, <u>Your Perfect Right</u>, this book presents an assertiveness training program.

Bolles, R. N. *What Color is Your Parachute?* Berkeley, California: Ten Speed Press, 1979.

> In his annually updated book, Bolles attempts to teach the job seeker skills that will be useful no matter how many times the individual searches for work or changes careers.

Horowitz, D. *Fight Back!* New York: Harper and Row, 1979.

> Assertiveness training is brought to the marketplace by informing the reader about dealing effectively with rather than accepting bad service and inferior goods.

Irish, R. K. *Go Hire Yourself An Employer.* Garden City, New York: Anchor Press, Doubleday, 1978.

> This book deals with getting the right job and includes many useful tips on dealing with the job interview situation.

Jongeward, D. *Everybody Wins: TA Analysis Applied to Organizations.* Reading, Massachusetts: Addison-Wesley, 1979.

> Coauthor of several books on applications of TA, Jongeward again provides readable coverage of a practical way to use the theoretical teachings of other authors.

Robertson, J. *How to Win in a Job Interview.* Englewood Cliffs, New Jersey: Prentice-Hall, 1978.

> This book, by the personnel director of a Fortune-100-rated company, deals specifically with the personal interview and the techniques used by interviewers.

Shain, M. *When Lovers Are Friends.* New York: J. B. Lippincott Co., 1978.

> Merle Shain, writer and television commentator, explores the important questions of how to find love, identify the right kind of love, and keep love flourishing.

PART FOUR

Overview

Human beings are very social and require contacts with other human beings to be truly healthy individuals. It is the rare individual who does not seek interactions with others as a course of daily living. Gatherings or groups of people generally elicit favorable associations—parties, planning, achieving, understanding, learning—that reinforce involvements. To demonstrate the value humans place on contact with others, consider the case histories of two men who voluntarily sought adventure and isolation in the wilds.

Ned Roesler (Englebardt, 1978) was a successful executive until age thirty-seven when he chose to become a freelance photographer. At age forty he left friends and family to attempt a 300 mile hike and photographic expedition across the north slopes of Alaska—alone. In his diary on the first night of the trip, knowing that civilization was far away, he wrote, "never felt so lonely in my life." It took him twenty-three days to reach his first stop, a village of about 150 Indians. He recorded his feeling at spotting the village: "The sun reflecting off the village roofs filled me with joy. Soon I would be able to eat, pick up fresh supplies, receive mail, send off postcards and film. And talk to people." He ended the journey nearly dead from exhausting his food supplies. Approximately two days' walk from his final destination he was picked up by helicopter. When he reached camp, "it was his first human contact in 39 days, so he momentarily forgot about his unfed stomach until the pilot pointed the way to the camp kitchen."

The subject of the second case study is Naomi Uemura (Uemura, 1978), a Japanese adventurer who became the first person to reach the North Pole alone. His travels lasted eight weeks as he and his dog team traveled 800 kilometers across the icebound Arctic Ocean. Four days into the trip his camp was ravaged by a polar bear. He writes of being hidden

Small Group Communication

and barely breathing in his sleeping bag as the hungry bear ripped open his tent, "Then my mind turns to my beloved wife in Tokyo. Kimi-chan, help me somehow." Uemura did have the advantage of being able to radio base camp daily to "discuss his progress, to talk about ice conditions, and perhaps just to hear somebody else's voice." He wrote at the end of the dangerous trip that his thoughts went to the "countless people who had helped and supported me, and the knowledge that I could never face them if I gave up."

These two stories, although emphasizing the struggle of two men against the elements, include references to other human beings, to communication, and to companionship. They endured isolation and hardship for the beauty and the challenge but never forgot their associations with and need for other people. Human beings are very social and must spend much of their time with others.

The study of group relationships is essential in a thorough study of the communication process. A study of small group communication is applicable to family situations, informal social groups, organized groups, and many other instances when several people find themselves together. In order to be effective in a group, individuals must be sensitive to their own behavior and the behavior of others. Skill in small group communication can be learned through study and practice.

Attitude Objective: By applying skills and concepts associated with effective group membership, leadership ability, and achievement of group goals, the student will realize more fulfilling and rewarding participation in small group experiences. (*Activities 1–10*)

Knowledge Objective: Given objective test items, the student will recall definitions and concepts related to the following terms and recognize or differentiate among them where appropriate. (*Activity 1*)

I. Small group communication defined
    A. Definition of small group
    B. Small group characteristics
        1. Group size
        2. Group functions
            a. Group qualities
            b. Problem solving group
            c. Learning group
            d. Social group
            e. Therapy group
    C. Joining groups
        1. Reasons
        2. Positive outcomes
        3. Group dynamics
    D. Small group versus individual potential
        1. Properties of groups
        2. Deciding between individual and group
II. Important factors for group participation
    A. Effective group participation
        1. Some techniques
            a. Enhancing communication
            b. Rules for effective participation
            c. Questions to enhance effectiveness
        2. Adverse group behavior
            a. Nonverbal behaviors
            b. Verbal behaviors
        3. Member responsibilities
            a. Member types
            b. Two general responsibilities
            c. Specific responsibilities
    B. Group leadership
        1. Leadership styles
            a. Authoritarian leader
            b. Democratic leader
            c. Laissez-faire leader
        2. Leader responsibilities
            a. Meeting arrangements
            b. Agenda
            c. Facilitator
        3. Leader effectiveness
            a. Decision making
            b. Communication
            c. Motivation

PART IV   Small Group Communication

III. Some applications of small group communication
  A. Brainstorming
    1. Advantages
    2. Suggestions for brainstorming process
  B. Round-table discussion
  C. Small groups in public settings
    1. Panel
    2. Forum
    3. Symposium
    4. Colloquium
  D. Small group presentation
    1. Presentation modes
    2. Planning process

Experiential Objective: The student will participate in small group communication experiences by following instructions for selected activities in the areas listed below. (*Activities 2-9*)

I. Small group concepts
II. Membership rules
III. Therapeutic group
IV. Member roles
V. Leadership
VI. Group versus individual effectiveness
VII. Brainstorming
VIII. Evaluating group effectiveness

Speaking Objective: Following the instructions for the small group presentation, the student will fulfill responsibilities as a group member by preparing a presentation on a selected human development topic or a problem of local, national, or international importance. (*Activity 10*)

CHAPTER 10

Small Group Communication Defined

A small group is defined very generally as a gathering of several people who have some common purpose or who are in some way interrelated. Several examples of small groups would be four couples getting together to play bridge; five people standing on a corner waiting for a bus; seven workers meeting to solve parking problems at their plant; or even ten people, representing various organizations, on a council to plan a large meeting. A more useful definition of small groups will include the concept of communication among those gathered together to seek a common goal. This more restrictive definition would possibly eliminate groups like the one at the bus stop, or people sitting in a physician's waiting room. Thus a small group is better defined as a gathering of several people who, through communication, contribute toward a common goal.

The small group has always been an important means for attainment of human purposes. Probably first in the extended family, then the clan and tribe, the guild, the community, and the state, groups have been formed to conduct government, work, war, religion, recreation, education, and even just to maintain life. Very early in the historical development of the human race it was discovered that groups could perform some tasks more efficiently than individuals, and that certain group procedures worked better than others. This resulted in a body of folk wisdom regarding the selection of leaders, the division of labor, and procedures for making decisions. During the last few decades of human history the scientific community has done much to research small group communication and develop a body of literature useful to all who strive to improve their communication skills.

Small Group Characteristics

Group Size

The minimum group size is defined by some authors as two and by others as three. Because of the emphasis in our society today on interpersonal communication techniques, that is, the interaction of one individual with one other individual, it is probably more useful in studying small groups as a distinct area of communication to say that the minimum size of a small group is three.

The maximum size of a small group varies depending on the characteristics of the members and their purpose in being together. A group ceases to be a small group when individual members are no longer able to communicate with every other member. Two very obvious signs of the loss of small group characteristics are the formation of subgroups or the nonparticipation of some members.

Minimum
Three Members

Optimum
Five to
Nine Members

Maximum
Fifteen to Twenty Members

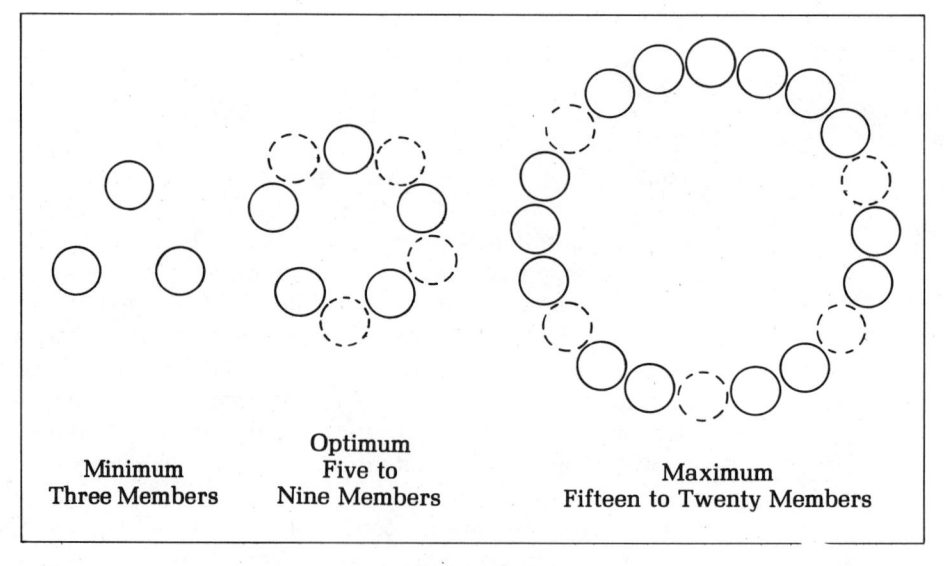

Figure 10.1

Some small groups will function effectively with as many as fifteen or twenty members, but the optimum size for small groups is probably five, seven, or nine. An odd number of members is more effective in case of a split decision because it eliminates the possibility of a tied vote. A small group of five to nine members allows everyone the opportunity to express opinions, provides sufficient input to create ideas for discussion, and allows each member to establish an interpersonal relationship with every other member. Many of the qualities, like cohesiveness, that create optimum small group participation are more readily developed if group size is within the maximum range of eight to ten participants.

Group size affects group performance as well as the satisfaction that each member feels in being a part of the group. Larger groups, for example, take more time to reach decisions, especially if all members express their viewpoints. Factions of the membership may polarize themselves and thus distract the group from the task. Generally, too, dominant members eventually account for most of the input, and in effect create a small group of active participants and a separate group of observers. Even in very large groups, small groups are created to perform certain tasks. Large groups will often elect representatives to governing boards and have many committees to handle specific problems and perform special tasks.

Functions of Groups

An effective small group for most situations is composed of five to nine members who communicate with each other in an attempt to achieve a common goal. This definition can be expanded to include the following qualities (Knowles & Knowles, 1959): members are known and can be identified, members think of themselves as a part of the group and identify with each other, members work together to achieve a common goal, members acknowledge that they need each other's help in reaching their common goal, members form interpersonal communication relationships with each other, and members can behave as a single entity. The common goal, or the idea of a common need or objective, has been expressed throughout the narrowing of the definition of a "small group" and "small group communication." What then are some common goals or functions of groups? Although many small groups will have several functions, most will have a primary function that fits in one of the following four categories: problem solving, learning, socialization, or therapy.

Functions of Groups

1. Problem Solving
2. Learning
3. Socialization
4. Therapy

Figure 10.2

Problem Solving. Small groups that have set a task for themselves that will affect the environment fall into the category of problem solving. Their goal is to carry out the steps it takes to make a change or find the answer to a problem. Examples are numerous. A group of parents who plan and conduct structured after-school activities for their children, a group organized to publish a newsletter for a large corporation, or a group of concerned citizens who organize a clean-up campaign for their neighborhood are all examples of small groups whose goal includes a problem-solving task.

There are numerous models to help groups in their task of problem solving. The most widely known and, perhaps, used model is one formulated in 1910 by John Dewey. He suggested the following steps as a logical process for solving problems.

1. Recognizing the problem—An awareness that something needs to be altered.
2. Defining the problem—A clear statement of the problem as it is perceived.
3. Analyzing the problem—Identifying such factors as causes and extent of the problem to gain greater insight into the problem.
4. Establishing criteria for evaluating potential solutions—Criteria set in advance to help in recognizing the best solutions.
5. Suggesting solutions—Possibilities for solving the problem.
6. Selecting the solution—Applying criteria to select the best solution.
7. Testing the solution—Trying out and evaluating the solution.

The problem-solving group may be well advised to consider a model like the one proposed by Dewey and used for more than half a century, or another similar model for attacking a problem situation.

Learning. The task of a small group oriented toward learning is to share or acquire knowledge. Their direct effect on the environment is minimal since they are not seeking to change things or to create an impact. Their goal is to further their knowledge or impart their knowledge to others.

Small groups of students who meet informally to discuss their field of interest, groups of collectors who meet to share objects from their collections, and professionals who gather to expand their expertise are examples of small groups who meet for the purpose of learning.

Socialization. Social groups generally form because the participants enjoy being with each other as individuals. Social groups are often more selective than other types of groups in admitting new members. Their goals are related to leisure activities that provide enjoyment and entertainment for the members. A group that has a monthly poker game, several individuals who buy season tickets to the theatre, or a group of neighbors who meet occasionally for coffee are examples of small groups whose functions are primarily social in nature.

Therapy. When several people meet for the purpose of self-disclosure, talking through their problems, or trying to improve some aspect of their personalities, the group serves a therapeutic function. A group of neighborhood women, in some cases, might be more a therapeutic than a social group. If their purpose in getting together is to discuss personal problems rather than to talk about more positive aspects of their lives, then it would be logical to classify them as a therapeutic group. Another example of a therapeutic group is a gathering of individuals who are aided in self-disclosure by a professional counselor or psychologist. Therapeutic groups exist in many situations where the group goal is to solve one member's or the group's personal problems.

Joining Groups

People join groups for many reasons. Often their reasons relate specifically to the group goals. Individuals interested in preserving the environment might join a group merely because of the group's specific purpose. People often join groups because they feel that they cannot achieve their goals as individuals; or groups form because of the common motives of several people who discover their similar interests. Individuals will join one group rather than another because they feel that group will be more effective or successful than the other group.

On the other hand, individuals may select groups because of personal values or needs they wish to fulfill. Often the status of a group will be an enticement. If not the group's prestige, it may be the security of belonging to the group or the need to identify oneself with the image that the group creates. Individuals may join groups because they are able to play a role different from other roles they fulfill. A person whose occupation is one of menial labor may be the respected leader of a garden club.

Whatever the motives in acquiring group membership, there is an expected outcome that each individual seeks and that determines satisfaction with the group. A person's self-concept is affected by groups of significance to the individual—family, church, occupation, service clubs, or social organizations. The positions that individuals hold in each group affect the way others react to them, their levels of aspiration, and how they feel about themselves. Membership in a group is generally perceived in a positive light, but may in fact become a difficult burden. Forced participation in a group or heavy responsibilities may make group memberships more a personal liability than a benefit.

Positive Outcomes

When group membership is a good thing, however, there are several incidental yet positive outcomes that occur (Rosenfeld, 1973). One positive outcome sometimes resulting from group membership is the development of a commitment to achieving the proposed outcome. Generally individuals who have been deeply involved in a group decision feel a sense of loyalty and responsibility to each other. Thus a decision of the group is more likely to be enacted than a decision by an individual. Another positive outcome of group membership is the possibility of learning more about one's impact as a communicator. By carefully noting other members' reactions to one's attempts at communication, impact as a communicator can be studied and improved. A third positive outcome that may result from group membership is the opportunity to develop meaningful relationships. Because of the opportunity within small groups to become personally acquainted with all members, communication can exist on a more meaningful, less superficial plane. Last, problem-solving procedures can be learned through group work. By observing the different approaches to a problem suggested by different members, one learns to judge ideas critically and to compromise.

Groups are dynamic in that members are continuously changing and adjusting relationships with each other. Because of the potential for developing close interpersonal relationships, there is a continuous restructuring and readjustment to reduce tensions, eliminate conflicts, and reach solutions to problems. In fact, the term "group dynamics" is widely used in reference to the complex interactions that occur in every group throughout its existence, and which account for the outcomes and decisions agreed upon by the members of the group.

Small Group versus Individual Potential

Properties of Groups

There are many situations where small groups are more effective than individuals in reaching decisions, but small groups are not always the best means of solving a particular problem. A look at some common properties of groups is useful to develop a framework for differentiating between those situations where the individual can be more effective and efficient than the small group. Consider the following properties of groups (Knowles & Knowles, 1959).

1. Background—The history or lack of history of the group influences the way it operates and the confidence placed in it.
2. Participation pattern—Participation among members may vary from none to complete dominance by one member. Generally, groups where all members participate to some extent will exhibit a deeper commitment to the task and outcomes.
3. Communication—The clearness with which members express ideas, opinions, and feelings will be directly related to the effectiveness of the group. When members are unable to understand each other, there is little chance for success.
4. Cohesion—Cohesion refers to the strength of the commitments that hold the group together. There will be less destructive interaction in cohesive groups.
5. Atmosphere—Atmosphere refers to the extent to which group members feel able to be openly and honestly expressive. It will directly affect the ways that members participate.
6. Standards—The set of standards determines what is proper and acceptable behavior within the group. They may be openly expressed or be implicit.
7. Procedures—The methods that groups use to get things done are procedures. All groups must have some procedures. They affect group cohesiveness, atmosphere, and communication patterns.
8. Goals—All groups have goals, their purpose for being. Often goals are vague or merely implicit, sometimes resulting in confusion about what is to be done.
9. Sociometric pattern—Some relationships between and among members of a group are more successful than others. The sociometric pattern refers to the extent of close and not so close relationships that develop. It seems that individuals are more likely to agree with those members they like than those they dislike.
10. Structure—Groups have both a visible and an invisible organizational structure that make it possible to assign tasks and get things done.

These ten characteristics are certainly relevant in differentiating small groups from individuals and make the small group the dynamic force that it can be. They also lead to group ineffectiveness in some situations and the greater effectiveness of the individual.

Deciding Between Individual and Group

Group discussion is most appropriate when a goal can be reached more effectively by the interaction of several people than by the thoughts of a single person. Below is a list of questions (Rosenfeld, 1973) that can be used to decide whether a given situation is more appropriate for group or individual consideration. An answer of "yes" indicates group consideration is important; an answer of "no" indicates the appropriateness of individual consideration.

1. Are many steps required to reach the goal?
2. Is achievement of several goals being attempted simultaneously?
3. Will an appropriate procedure for achieving the goal be difficult to establish?
4. Are the group members likely to perceive the goal as impersonal?
5. Would a single individual be unlikely to have the knowledge needed to reach the goal?
6. Does the plan for achieving the goal demand a division of labor?
7. Are many diverse ideas useful to establish a plan?
8. Are many hours of time required to reach the goal?
9. Will there be some risks that are better shared?
10. Is it likely that group members will be motivated to coordinate their efforts in reaching the goal?

These questions as a whole are probably most appropriate for problem-solving groups; some may be inappropriate for learning-oriented, social, and therapeutic groups.

All in all, groups are an essential force in the achievement of the human causes of survival and enrichment of life. Consider some examples of goals that are more appropriate for individuals than small groups, and vice versa. An individual decision is probably appropriate for selecting personal items that reflect an individual personality, fulfilling routine on-the-job responsibilities for which procedures have been developed, and making a critical judgment when only one knowledgeable person is available. Group consideration is often useful in solving controversial problems, presenting detailed information about a variety of aspects of a certain topic, and planning a charity ball for 2000 people. The usefulness of groups probably underlies the popularity of the phrase, "two heads are better than one."

SUMMARY

A small group is a gathering of three to fifteen or twenty people who come together and rely upon communication processes as a means of achieving common goals. The optimum group size is probably an odd number no greater than nine. Groups serve a variety of functions, but most groups can be classified by their primary purpose: problem solving, learning, socialization, or therapy. People join groups for a variety of reasons. Several common reasons are the group purpose, status of membership, and opportunity to adopt different roles. Many goals can be more effectively achieved through group participation, yet the potential of the individual should not be overlooked. Groups enable human beings to come together to fulfill a variety of social, psychological, and physical needs.

CHAPTER 11

Important Factors for Group Participation

During the early stages of forming a small group, it is important to eliminate any barriers to communication. Early gatherings of the group provide an awareness period when members can begin to know each other, set a clear goal, ask questions, discuss possible barriers, define terms, determine research procedures, select a group leader, establish a plan, and set a definite time line for reaching the goal. Each member of the group should be encouraged to make an oral contribution to the group. Members who hesitate to get involved in the early stages are not likely to contribute later. In addition, to be productive and efficient, leadership patterns must be established within the group.

After effective communication channels are established, deeper discussion of ways to achieve group goals can occur. The current situation, time constraints, and appropriate activities to implement a solution become important topics for discussion. There are seldom single causes or solutions to the sometimes complex problems that arise in achieving group goals. Through effective small group communication, groups can reach goals by proceeding from analysis of the problem to determination of a plan, to its implementation, and eventual evaluation.

Effective Group Participation

Some Techniques

The communication potential of a small group can be enhanced when individuals take some responsibility for interaction among members (Knowles & Knowles, 1959). Group members can encourage each other. This involves being open to what others have to say, praising and indicating agreement when possible, and being responsive to the contributions of all group members. Each member can be a gate keeper and see to it that all members have a chance to make a contribution. This can be achieved by suggesting limits for each speaker or by addressing a member who has not contributed. Group participation is facilitated by paying attention when others express their views. Group procedures bog down when members care to listen only to themselves. Group members can attempt to relieve tension when negative feelings erupt. It is sometimes helpful to ease the situation with humor. It should be obvious by now that communication is the key to effective group participation. Small group work can be accomplished more smoothly when group members express their views clearly, listen attentively to others, and strive to seek a solution acceptable to all.

Often rules make events go more smoothly. Defining rules for effective group participation would be somewhat arbitrary. However, the following list includes six statements that could be called rules for effective group participation (Cassels, 1960). Following the statements are questions that group members might ask themselves as they clarify their purpose and seek to achieve their goals.

1. Define clearly the goals of the group. Time is wasted because of ambiguity surrounding what it is the group is attempting to do. What is the specific group goal? What information or research is necessary before a goal can be reached? What questions must be answered to reach the goal? What terms need to be defined so that all members benefit from the discussion?
2. Determine the power the group has in seeking to achieve its goal. This will affect the decisions to be made. Are there any barriers (e.g., time, money, facilities, authority) to overcome in reaching the goal? What specific factors have interfered with reaching this goal in the past?
3. Make it clear that contributions are expected from all group members. The person who simply nods from time to time might be replaced by a more active participant. Who will be involved in the process of achieving the goal?
4. Allow as many potential outcomes to be discussed as possible. Then begin to evaluate the alternatives and make decisions. What are some alternative ways that this goal might be achieved? What are the advantages and disadvantages to each alternative solution? What obstacles may come up to prevent implementing the plan? What can be done to overcome the obstacles?
5. Do not attach ideas to the person who proposed them. Rather than "Ralph's plan," call it "Plan A." Which solution would be best for the group?
6. Allow members to vary roles from time to time by encouraging flexibility. A group leader, for example, might permit other

members to conduct parts of the meeting where their expertise is especially relevant. How can the solution be put into operation? Who can facilitate the process of implementing the solution?

The rules and questions listed above are not necessarily applicable to all situations but can be considered in the process of achieving the goals of a small group.

It seems then from this analysis that groups can be more effective when the means for achieving the group goal are given careful consideration. Effective communication patterns and a definite plan for achieving the group goal are probably the two most important factors in achieving a successful outcome for a small group.

Adverse Group Behavior

People seem to notice adverse behaviors more readily than effective behaviors. In fact it is all too easy to take effective behavior for granted. Nonverbal cues are especially evident indicators of adverse reactions by members of small groups. Verbal indicators of adverse behaviors are readily definable as well.

Nonverbal Behaviors. Nonverbal cues of dissatisfaction are sometimes sent in obvious ways by those who are not involved with the group and those who disagree with the group. Indicators of noninvolvement include leaning back in the chair, little or no eye contact, fidgeting, and nonexpressive face. This behavior is in contrast to the individual who leans forward, looks at group members, and smiles and nods to reinforce the discussion. Disagreement can be indicated by crossed arms, frowning, and nervous body movements. This is in contrast to nodding the head in agreement and a more relaxed and open body position.

Not listening is certainly an example of adverse group behavior. Before an individual can agree to a solution, it is essential to understand prior messages. The person who constantly asks questions or repeats what has just been said because of failure to listen is certainly a detriment. This is in contrast to the member who seeks to clarify by paraphrasing, or who adds supporting evidence to give credibility to an opinion.

Verbal Behaviors. Verbal tactics aimed at interrupting group progress may be more adverse than the nonverbal tactics. Good examples of this are blocking discussion by bringing in unrelated personal experiences, arguing on a point seemingly resolved, or flat rejection of ideas without a logical reason. Showing hostility or aggression toward specific group members by blaming, criticizing, attacking motives, or deflating egos are other verbal tactics disruptive to group progress. Boasting about personal accomplishments, or calling attention to oneself by excessive talking are other forms of disruptive behavior. Trying to dominate by intimidating other members, withdrawing, whispering to others, and pleading are still other disruptive techniques.

Being an effective group participant is certainly more difficult than being a disruptive one. It takes little practice to acquire the adverse skills listed above. An effective group member may acquire skill in dissipating behaviors that begin to be detrimental to group progress.

Responsibilities of the Group Member

Groups are composed of all types of people, all attempting, it is hoped, to make contributions in their own ways. Many authors have attempted to describe certain types of individuals who seem to surface in numerous small groups. The list can go on and on. A list that seems fairly representative yet not unduly long is given below (Arnold & Hirsch, 1977) with brief explanations of the types.

1. Harmonizer—This person is responsible for keeping things going smoothly, reducing misunderstandings, and reconciling those who have conflicts. A typical statement: "Wait a minute, we've made some progress, let's not lose it, that argument may clear itself up as we proceed."
2. Encourager—The encourager attempts to achieve the full participation of all group members and is generally able to do this by employing outstanding interpersonal communication skills. A typical statement: "Joan, we haven't heard from you yet. What do you think about...?"
3. Clarifier—The clarifier employs descriptive listening skills to facilitate the group by restating or paraphrasing important points during discussion. A typical statement: "That's a good point, Jim. Let me be certain that I have it right. You said..."
4. Initiator—This is the person who suggests new ideas when everyone else is exhausted. A typical statement: "Wait until you hear this. How would it be if we...?"
5. Energizer—This group member is very task-oriented, reminds the group of goals and deadlines, and makes certain that things get done on time. A typical statement: "We've been dwelling on this point for over an hour and I can't see that we're accomplishing anything."
6. Questioner—The questioner often brings up issues that the group has overlooked and seeks information that might prove useful in achieving group goals. A typical statement: "Has anyone done any reading on this that might lend support to what we're deciding to do?"
7. Listener—The larger the group, the more likely it is that it will contain one or more persons who are truly interested in what the group is doing but who make few verbal contributions. This

is generally viewed negatively. However, we've all been in groups where a few listeners would have been appreciated.
8. Tension Reducer—The tension reducer knows the exact place for a joke or a humorous side comment in a small group meeting that is getting tense or dull. A typical statement: "Hey guys, this group reminds me of..."
9. Opinion Giver—This person is extremely well prepared and adept at making meaningful comments that have a sound basis. A typical statement: "Considering that 95% of..., we probably ought to..."
10. Dominator—The dominator uses such tactics as interruptions, long monologues, or long arguments in an attempt to assert authority. A typical statement goes on and on and includes many references to "I."
11. Negativist—One who finds fault with everything, refuses to cooperate, and interjects derogatory comments to make a point is a negativist. A typical statement: "That was a dumb idea. Why can't this group ever be creative?"
12. Deserter—The deserter is indifferent, aloof, and refuses to become involved with the task of achieving group goals. A typical statement (off the subject and in a loud whisper directed to another individual): "Have you seen the movie that just opened at the cinema?"
13. Aggressor—This individual's only goal seems to be to achieve personal status within the group. This is often attempted through boasting, criticizing others, deflating egos, and trying to get attention. A typical statement: "Unlike some others in this group, I am able to grasp the subtle implications of such a decision and recommend that we..."

Do you recognize any of these typical members in the groups to which you belong?

Most group members will, hopefully, fulfill roles that make positive contributions to the group. In general, however, members of small groups have two main responsibilities. The first of these is to be prepared for meetings. This means completing tasks assigned to the individual or the group as a whole before the meeting. It means completing unassigned tasks if necessary to be adequately prepared. Group members can prepare themselves by reading relevant materials, questioning others who might have input, and thinking through relevant issues before meeting with the group. A prepared group member is able to participate. Involvement with and participation in the group is the second general responsibility of group members.

Some more specific responsibilities for effective group membership are given below.

1. Be on a first name basis with members of the small group and remember the names of all members.

2. Be active, energetic, and dynamic.
3. Be willing to share knowledge and experience.
4. Give active nonverbal responses when someone else has the floor.
5. Speak up when you feel strongly about an issue.
6. Ask questions to clarify points of view that are difficult to understand.
7. Do not just sit and listen; propose new ideas, activities, and procedures.
8. Encourage others to participate and get involved; be careful not to dominate.
9. Show respect for the opinions of others even when you do not agree.
10. Try to develop relationships among the ideas presented rather than dwell on independent details.
11. Demonstrate the ability to examine your own personal opinions and prejudices as they apply to the issues, and to change if evidence and reasoning prove you wrong.
12. Evaluate the facts and ideas presented by others rather than merely accept them.
13. Encourage members to undertake worthy projects for which they can enthusiastically share responsibility.
14. Do what you can to keep all members active and involved in group activities.
15. Contribute to such meeting preparations as arranging furniture, serving refreshments, and cleaning up.

If, as a group member, you can perform the fifteen tasks above, you will make a contribution to the final achievement of the group goal that far surpasses that of the average member.

Group Leadership

Some groups function quite well without a leader. These are generally very small groups where all members are motivated and interact well on an interpersonal level. Most functioning groups will have a leader who accepts responsibility for keeping the group organized and productive. The leader of a group may be appointed by some higher authority (e.g., the executive that establishes the committee), may be elected by a larger group that it serves in some capacity, or by the small group itself, or may emerge as group members learn to interact with each other. The leader may serve for a specific term, or an unspecified length of time, or even change with each meeting. The permanent leader gives the group a greater continuity from meeting to meeting. Achieving tasks may be easier as each member and the leader learn specific roles. If leaders change frequently, however, group members feel more equality and more self-motivation since there is no dependence on a single leader. There are several different leadership styles, a number of responsibilities that the leader will accept, and some behaviors that lead to more effective leadership.

Leadership Styles

There are three styles of leadership that can be differentiated: authoritarian, democratic, and laissez-faire. Each has advantages and disadvantages and each is more appropriate than the others in given situations.

Leadership Styles

1. Authoritarian—You will write the letters.
2. Democratic—Who will write the letters?
3. Laissez-Faire—There are some letters to be written.

Figure 11.1. *Leadership styles.*

Authoritarian. The authoritarian leader dominates the group by employing the various instruments of power that are vested with the position. For the extremely authoritarian leader, these powers often include punishment, reward, denial, and intimidation. Group members are viewed by the authoritarian leader as subordinates who are unable to formulate ideas and who are certainly unprepared to make decisions. The authoritarian leader, therefore, dictates all policies. The concepts of persuasion, discussion, and group consensus are unknown to persons who serve such leaders. In fact communication generally takes place only through the leader, with virtually no interaction among members.

Democratic. Although democratic leaders may retain the right to make the final decision, they are interested in working with group members to achieve a collective goal. The democratic leader is not interested in power over others but in bringing out the best that all members have to offer. Responsibilities are distributed to all group members. Decisions are discussed and often made by the group as a whole. The democratic leader is primarily a coordinator or a resource person whose success depends on facilitating the efforts of the entire group in achieving its goal. The democratic leader is accepting of others and is generally an expert in the art of effective interpersonal relationships.

Laissez-faire. Laissez-faire leadership involves a minimum of control or possibly no control at all. The group functions more as a spontaneous group of individuals with a common goal. Laissez-faire leadership generally evolves when the leader is withdrawn, unskilled in the tasks, or believes that direction stifles creativity. It is a rare group that can function effectively in the absence of leadership. Generally, the group will achieve little, or the tasks of leadership will be assumed by one of the more dominant members.

Comparison of styles. From this brief analysis of the three leadership styles, it probably seems that the democratic style is the only one that can be effective. In many situations this is true. However, the authoritarian style has the advantage of efficiency when the time allotted to reach a decision is short. Because of the need for discussion under democratic leadership and the possibility of total floundering under laissez-faire leadership, neither is as effective when time is a factor. Consider the coach of a football team determining a crucial play. Which leadership style would you choose? Without a highly respected person in the role of leader, the authoritarian style often leads to poor motivation, discontent, and lack of individuality among group members. It is probably best, when being authoritarian, to be benevolent and consider group members as human beings with distinct feelings and needs.

Under democratic leadership members are generally more creative and work harder than under the other leadership styles. The group process is more rewarding to members when all feel they have a place. As they learn to know and respect each other, group members under a democratic leader will develop closer, more satisfying relationships with each other. The good feelings of the group may be viewed as more important than achievement of the task. Becoming an effective democratic leader is probably more difficult for most people than becoming an effective authoritarian leader.

Is there no place for the laissez-faire leader? There is in groups that are most likely small and composed of individuals with very similar expectations and working styles. Each member is a leader and each a follower as they work closely together to achieve the group goal. Generally, however, the laissez-faire style leads to the eventual discontent of all members when the group seems to be getting nowhere.

Responsibilities of the Leaders

Leaders may of course delegate responsibilities to other group members. Ultimately, however, the group leader will probably be the one held accountable for certain tasks that must be done to enable the group to proceed. There are two major types of leadership responsibilities: those relating to arrangements and plans for meetings, and those relating to facilitation of group interactions. These will be described in a general context probably more appropriate for the democratic leader than the authoritarian or laissez-faire leader.

Meeting arrangements. The leader is responsible for locating a place to conduct the meeting and for arranging seating to provide an optimum environment. The facility in which the group assembles can enhance the process and possibly the outcome of the meeting. When it is obvious that the planners have given thought to meeting arrangements, group members often feel a greater responsibility toward achieving the tasks of the meeting. Generally, comfortable seating that allows all members to relate interpersonally with all other members will be most suitable. This can be done by arranging chairs in a circle or semicircle, or around a square or round table.

Agenda. The leader should plan the discussion and activities of the meeting prior to the meeting time. This necessitates an awareness of the critical topics to be discussed and advance contact with other officers or committee leaders. It is probably wise to prepare an agenda for the meeting. An agenda is an outline or list of what is to be covered in the meeting. Copies of the agenda can be sent to members in advance or can be distributed at the beginning of the meeting. If agendas are distributed in advance members are better able to prepare for the meeting. Along with the agenda, the leader should distribute copies of other relevant materials. If making copies of the agenda and related materials is impossible, it is extremely important that the leader, at least, have knowledge of the meeting plan and have a copy of important materials.

Agenda for March 1

1. Directer's Report
2. Minutes from February 15
3. Treasurer's Report
4. Social Committee Report
5. Salary Recommendations
6. New Business
7. Next Meeting Date
8. Inspirational Closing

Figure 11.2. *Agenda.*

Facilitator. Once the meeting is in progress the leader's role often becomes that of facilitator. The leader should introduce new members to the group, get each member immediately involved, watch the time and indicate progress, restate opinions for clarity, offer fresh ideas when appropriate, summarize the transactions of the meeting, and provide a transition to the next meeting. The leader is especially important when conflicts arise. The leader might try to get at the source of the problem and get members to talk about the conflict, move on to a new topic, call a recess, or perhaps ask an extremely hostile member to leave the meeting. To facilitate participation of all members, the leader might attempt to

"All those in favor say 'Aye.'"
      "Aye."   "Aye."   "Aye."
              "Aye."   "Aye."

Drawing by H. Martin ©1979, The New Yorker Magazine, Inc.

draw quieter members into the discussion during early meetings (i.e., before the wrong pattern becomes set), be especially attentive when less active members speak, direct questions specifically to less involved members, use eye contact and nonverbal language to get the reluctant member involved, or prevent any one individual from monopolizing the conversation. Leaders must develop individual styles as they fulfill their responsibility for keeping the group moving toward its goals.

Effective Leaders

An effective leader might be defined as one whose group manages to achieve its goals while maintaining good feelings about one another. It is doubtful that significant goals can be reached without all or most group members assuming some responsibility and being accountable for results. Although no recipe for effective leadership has been found, much has been learned and written about leaders. It is probable that a good leader will have abilities in the areas of decision making, communication, and motivation of others. Although many leaders seem to have natural abilities, many effective leaders have studied, learned, and practiced the skills that helped in achieving their success.

Decision Making. In order to be an effective leader it is necessary to be able to make decisions. Too often decisions are made by default. That is, no decision is made but events go on until something that must be lived with occurs. Some helpful hints for making decisions (Engstrom and Mackenzie, 1968) include the following: do not make decisions under stress; base decisions on adequate data; do not put off decisions; consult other people who will be affected by the decision; do not be afraid to make a wrong decision; and do not worry about the decision once it is made. It is important that leaders have confidence in their ability to make decisions. A decision backed by confidence is more likely to succeed than one broached with timidity.

Communication. All groups seem to complain about poor communication. Much has been written about communication and it makes good reading. Many leaders, and others as well, make the mistake of overlooking the essential role of practice. One cannot learn the skill of playing tennis solely from reading; likewise, communication skills must be practiced repeatedly to become a subconscious force in interaction with others.

The human mind often races at two to three times the speed of the spoken word. Thus people continually tune in and out on conversations. Often poor listening habits result in the missing of important details. Some key points for leaders to consider as they listen (Engstrom and Mackenzie, 1968) are the following: evaluate what is being said (i.e., use critical listening skills); consider the credibility of the speaker, and whether statements are supported with evidence; ask questions to confirm the relevance of and to clarify a point; and do not rule out the relevance of a subject because it appears uninteresting.

Leaders are discussion facilitators as well as listeners. In this role they can keep the meeting going or let it bog down and perhaps end in failure. Some hints for improving skill as a discussion leader (Brilhart, 1965) are the following: have a clear understanding of group goals; become skillful in organizing the results of group thinking; remain open minded; be an active group participant; be democratic and consultative; have respect for and sensitivity to others; be self-controlled and show restraint; and share rewards and give credit to the group.

Motivation. The leader's role extends beyond the meeting time and place. The effective leader is able to generate an enthusiasm that carries on after meetings are over to times when members must accomplish tasks on their own. How does a leader get members of a group to do what has to be done? It is, of course, important to be sensitive to and aware of the feelings of others. Some suggestions the effective leader might study in an attempt to eliminate behaviors potentially harmful to the interest and motivation of the group (Feinberg, 1965) are the following: never belittle, as this destroys self-worth and initiative; never criticize a group member in front of others even if tempted under pressure; never fail to give a group member your individual attention; never seem preoccupied with your own interests; never play favorites; never fail to help your members grow; never be insensitive to small things; never embarrass a weak member; and never vacillate in making a decision. To summarize these nine suggestions, the best way for group leaders to motivate group members is to demonstrate a consciousness of individual needs, ambitions, fears, and worth.

The insensitive leader, who is perhaps unintentionally aloof, cold, impersonal, and uninterested in individuals, usually finds it difficult to get group members to exert that extra effort. Some suggestions for what the effective leader might do to enhance motivation among group members (Feinberg, 1965) are the following: let people know where you stand; give praise when it is due; keep members informed of changes that may affect them; perceive people as ends, not means to an end; confirm the feeling that group goals and members are important; be caring, tactful, considerate, and courteous; be willing to learn from others; show through behavior and speech that the tasks of the group can be accomplished by the group members; allow freedom of expression; delegate responsibility; and allow group members to make as many decisions as possible, learn from mistakes, and be proud of successes. The effective leader, therefore, does not motivate through threats or authority but by building the self-concepts and expectations of the group members. Like the comments dealing with leader responsibility, these on group motivations are most likely appropriate primarily for the democratic leader.

SUMMARY

The effectiveness of small groups often depends on the communication skills and contributions made by members and leaders. Group members have two general responsibilities: to be prepared to participate in group activities and actually to participate in a positive way. All small group members must remain alert to what is said and decided as plans are made to achieve group goals. Leaders, whether authoritarian, democratic, or laissez-faire, are responsible for seeing that meeting arrangements are made, for preparing an agenda for conducting meetings, and for facilitating discussion during meetings. Group leaders must possess skill in decision making, communication, and motivation of others.

CHAPTER 12

Some Applications of Small Group Communication

Although small group communication occurs spontaneously in a variety of everyday settings, there are special techniques in group communication settings that can be used for specific purposes. One of these is brainstorming, a technique useful in providing creative alternative solutions for problem solving. Another is the round-table discussion, where a small group comes together to talk about an issue of interest or importance. A third type of activity involves small groups who discuss a topic or make coordinated presentations in front of an audience. Some of the more formal presentations of this type are the panel discussion, forum, symposium, or colloquium. In addition, a small group might form to make a more informal and perhaps creative presentation about some topic of interest to an audience. In this latter case, presentation mode can be varied to provide greater interest and even audience involvement.

Brainstorming

Brainstorming is a special technique used primarily in problem-solving groups. It is one of the most creative ways to generate ideas in a small group setting. It can be applied to any problem if there is a wide range of possible solutions, none of which can be said in advance to be right or wrong. The group simply starts with a problem stated in the form of a question. Each member of the small group, preferably limited to three to five persons, answers with the first thought that comes to mind. One group member, serving as recorder, makes notes on each member's ideas. There is no evaluation of the suggestions during the idea-generating phase of the process. Thus, brainstorming is a technique of quickly generating as many possible solutions as the individuals in the group can think of.

Let's look at an example of the brainstorming process. Picture a group of five elementary school teachers seated at a table brainstorming the question, "What types of equipment should we include in the school's proposal for a creative playground?" Remember, one member of the group is the recorder.

Person 1   I'll start. Parallel bars with ladders at each end.
Person 2: A fort with a wall and a small garrison that can be crawled into.
Person 3: A twisted tube that the kids can crawl and slide through.
Person 4: A sandbox made from railroad ties.
Person 5: Rocking horses, but with other animals like fish, chickens, and elephants.

Person 1: Stacks of tires of different heights in a rectangular area.
Person 2: A slide that twists around and around like a spiral.
Person 3: A raised platform with a ladder leading to it through the middle.
Person 4: A rocket ship with ladders and platforms inside and out.
Person 5: A tall rocket ship with ladders and platforms inside and the spiral slide on the outside.

The process goes on until time or ideas are exhausted. Early in the process, when all members are generating fresh ideas, it is probably better to go around the table person by person. Later, when ideas are harder to generate, people can respond out of turn as ideas come to them.

During the brainstorming process, it is essential that there be no criticism of ideas, either verbal or nonverbal. The wilder, more freewheeling the ideas, the better the process is working. Quantity of ideas is the goal—the more suggestions the better. Combinations of ideas and improvement of ideas are encouraged. If there is creative interaction and spontaneity during the idea-generating session, the alternative solutions to the problem will provide a unique set of potential outcomes.

When the idea generation process is ended, the group should examine the advantages and disadvantages of each suggestion. The least effective should be discarded immediately, leaving a group of plausible alternatives to be discussed, built upon, and improved until a final decision can be made. It is sometimes better to delay the review process for several days. With fresh minds and a new look at the ideas, it is often easier to make a final decision.

Round-Table Discussion

The round-table discussion occurs when a small group of individuals comes together for a formal conversation. The goal is often to reach a solution to a problem or to come to consensus about an attitude or position on a controversial issue. Round-table discussions often occur in educational settings, business and professional environments, and in clubs and organizations. In one sense, a round-table discussion occurs when family members or groups of friends gather for the purpose of discussion. The round-table discussion differs from discussion in general in that there is one specific issue of importance about which the group expects to reach some agreement.

Figure 12.1. *Round-table discussion.*

Since interaction among members is essential for a round-table discussion, individuals in the group must arrange themselves so that eye contact with every other member is possible. Depending on the composition of the group and past experiences together, a leader may or may not be selected. Generally, however, some summary of the outcome will be required. The leader or another designated individual should probably be assigned the responsibility of taking meeting notes and/or summarizing the outcome. And too, a leader or designated individual is sometimes required to keep the group focused on the topic of concern. Leaders designated in advance of discussions will generally make formal statements to introduce the topics and will see that all members have been introduced to each other.

The participants in the round-table generally make no formal preparation for the discussion. That is, members do not make formal remarks as a matter of procedure. Members will often prepare, however, by making certain that they are well informed on the topic to be discussed. In other words, members who are aware of their participation in advance should be prepared to support their positions on an issue with facts and information.

Most of us will find ourselves involved in round-table discussions at one time or another. A common experience is to attend a lecture and be told to form small groups for more personal involvement with the topic. Often groups will seem to "gel" and discussion will be stimulating and relevant. Other times, groups will have trouble getting discussion going.

Embarrassing silence may result because none of the members can think of anything to say.

There are several techniques that group members can suggest or use to get a more vigorous discussion going in a quiet group. First, a member might suggest that all participants introduce themselves and reveal something about their backgrounds. As people become better acquainted, they are more likely to share ideas. Second, it is sometimes helpful to suggest preparing a list. Often people can think of something to add to a list, and too, a list provides a stimulus for focusing the initial discussion. Another suggestion is to make a provocative or controversial statement. This is a sure way to generate some response. However, the discussion may turn into a heated argument instead of an orderly discourse. A fourth suggestion is to address someone with a specific question. This can work well if you know that a member of the group has some relevant experience that might provide meaningful input, or at least form a basis for further contributions by others. Round-table discussions often have time limits and silence proves wasteful.

A buzz group is an adaptation of the round-table discussion that allows members to experience the opinions and thoughts of many individuals in the small group setting. Buzz groups consist of four to eight individuals who meet for short periods of time, approximately three to five minutes. At the end of the time limit, several designated individuals leave the group and join a new group. The rotation process is repeated several times as people are exposed to the thoughts of many more individuals than possible in the round-table discussion. When more superficial but varied input is useful, the buzz group can be an interesting approach to group discussion.

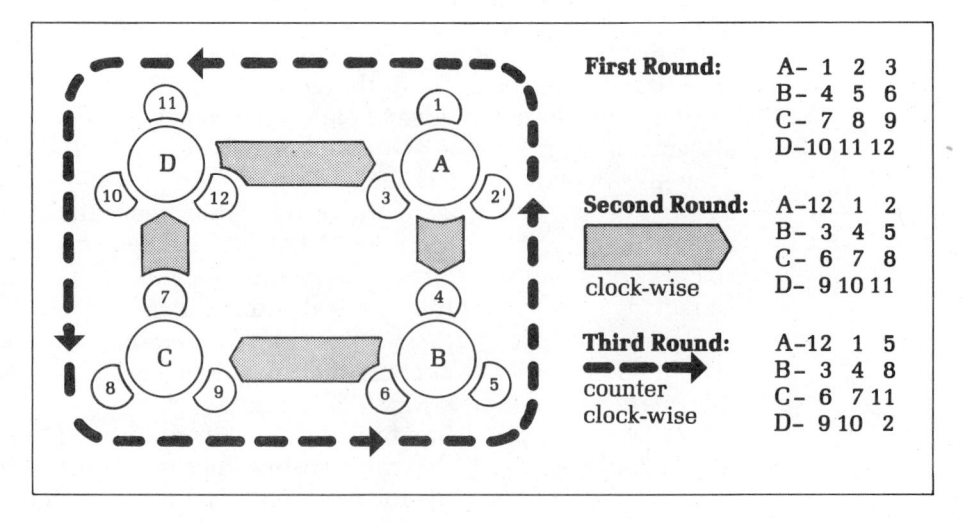

First Round:	A- 1 2 3 B- 4 5 6 C- 7 8 9 D-10 11 12
Second Round: clock-wise	A-12 1 2 B- 3 4 5 C- 6 7 8 D- 9 10 11
Third Round: counter clock-wise	A-12 1 5 B- 3 4 8 C- 6 7 11 D- 9 10 2

Figure 12.2. *Buzz group.*

Small Group Communication in a Public Setting

Many small groups meet privately, that is, they have no audience or observers. These small groups would include club meetings of many types, meetings of committees, social get-togethers, and brainstorming sessions. Some small groups, however, meet in front of an audience. Their ultimate goal is generally to make a presentation or participate in a discussion for the benefit of another group, possibly quite large, that will assemble for the purpose of listening to the program.

Small group presentations can be described by different titles depending on the exact nature of the program. A few of the formal types of small groups that meet in public for the benefit of other groups are panel discussions, forums, symposia, and colloquia. Often these groups will come together for the first time during the presentation. They will have been selected or organized by a program coordinator.

Panel Discussion

A panel discussion consists of a group of speakers (usually four to six) who are well informed on an issue. The speakers are generally seated informally at a table. The success of the panel depends on the spontaneity of the speakers as they react to one another and interact with the audience. A panel discussion will usually begin with a short and possibly prepared message by each of the panelists. The audience then begins participating by directing questions to panel members. It is important that the room arrangement be designed to facilitate the speaker-audience interaction. This can be done by placing the panel closer to the audience than in a more formal speaking situation. A moderator is often used to help direct questions and limit the length of questions and answers. The nature of the messages is often informative.

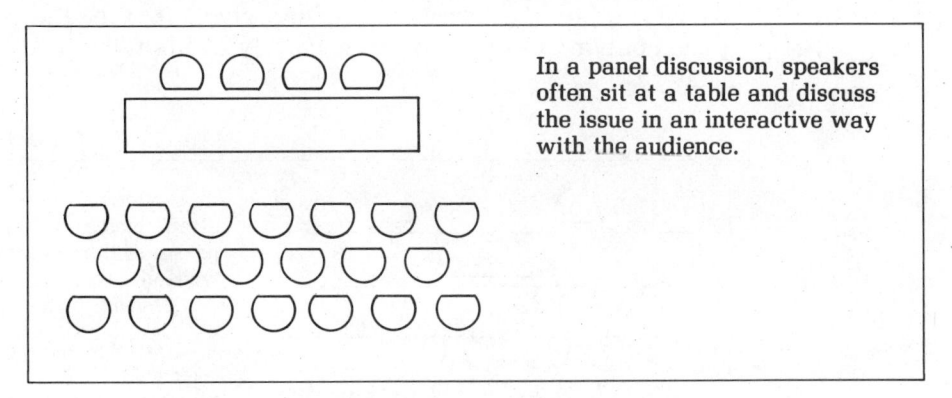

In a panel discussion, speakers often sit at a table and discuss the issue in an interactive way with the audience.

Figure 12.3. *Panel discussion.*

Forum

Audience participation is not an essential part of a forum. The forum is characterized by a group of experts who present their viewpoints on a topic. The speakers may be organized in a debating format with speakers designated to present different sides of an issue. The speakers generally give prepared presentations. Interaction with the audience is primarily for clarification of points and not to develop discussion.

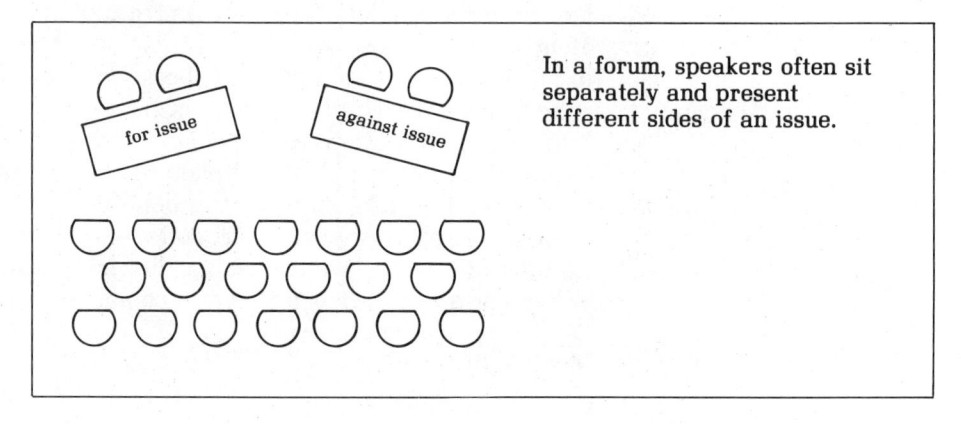

In a forum, speakers often sit separately and present different sides of an issue.

Figure 12.4. *Forum.*

Symposium

Experts on related topics present prepared papers to an audience during a symposium. The subject of a symposium, for example, might be swimming pools. Presentations might include types of swimming pool construction, swimming pool accessories, care of the swimming pool, creating a total outdoor environment for the swimming pool, and maintaining safety around the swimming pool. Often printed copies or summaries of the presentation are given to the audience. Audience participation, if allowed, is generally limited to questions to clarify content.

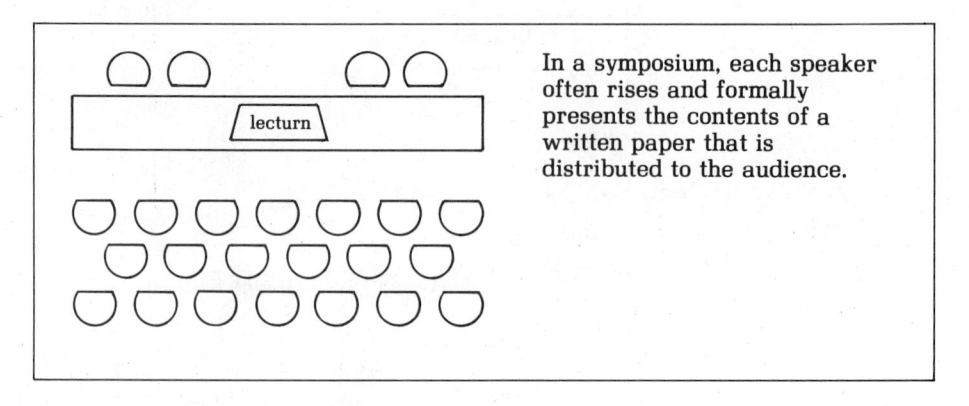

In a symposium, each speaker often rises and formally presents the contents of a written paper that is distributed to the audience.

Figure 12.5. *Symposium.*

Colloquium

A group of individuals assembles to discuss an important issue. Experts in the area of discussion are present to provide details that the discussants need to clarify particular points. Generally a moderator is present to call on the experts when appropriate. The topic of discussion is generally a complex or highly specialized topic of interest to the discussants and audience.

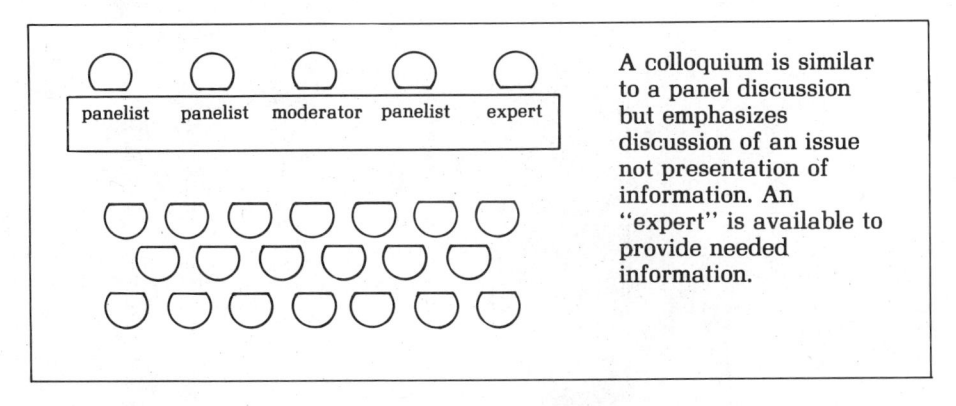

A colloquium is similar to a panel discussion but emphasizes discussion of an issue not presentation of information. An "expert" is available to provide needed information.

Figure 12.6. *Colloquium.*

Planning and Rehearsing a Small Group Presentation

Small groups may also join forces to present more informal programs for which group members rather than outside coordinators are responsible. In this type of presentation the group members themselves work together in private meetings to establish a plan and to assign or accept responsibilities. These presentations may borrow from the format of the forum, panel discussion, symposium, or colloquium, but are characterized by close planning and rehearsal by the group as a whole.

Many authors of communications texts dismiss the small group presentation as a special case of public speaking. They perceive the several speakers as giving independent presentations which rely on the theory and methods appropriate for public speaking. This is true to some extent, yet the small group working together to make a presentation can provide a program of much more variety than an individual can. The program presented by a small group can move faster and audience interest can be held more easily as the program shifts to different speakers and presentation modes. Diversity, variety, and faster pace are easier for the small group to achieve than for the individual public speaker. The choice of presentation modes and a systematic process for planning and rehearsing the program are the two keys to a successful presentation. Creativity and enthusiasm should be taken for granted.

Presentation modes. Presentation modes are the ways the speakers use to present information or provide examples. The innovative small group may develop its own modes of presentation. For the group that needs some ideas, a list of ten common presentation modes is given below. Keep in mind too that many of these can be useful for individual speakers as well as groups.

1. Demonstration—This is the use of actual objects to show the audience what something is or how something operates.
2. Discussion—Discussion is the exchange of viewpoints, usually under the direction of a leader.
3. Lecture—This is an oral presentation of facts or principles with the audience totally passive.
4. Modeling and imitation—The audience listens to and watches a performance with the intention of copying the behaviors and improving skill in a task.
5. Problem solving—A model is followed to arrive at a possible solution to a problem.
6. Role playing—The presenters take on the behaviors of others as they act out events in real or hypothetical situations.
7. Sensitivity training—A group examines their feelings about themselves and each other as they practice communication skills in a straightforward and honest manner.
8. Skill practice session—The audience is given the opportunity to practice skills explained by the group and to receive feedback concerning their performance.

9. Tactile activity—The sense of touch is used to present manipulation or perceptual skills.
10. Visual aids—Material presented orally is made clearer through the use of posters, charts, chalkboard, felt boards, overhead projectors, slides, filmstrips, movies, videotape, or hand-outs.

It is useful for small group members to draw on several of the presentation modes as they prepare and rehearse their program. Again, groups have the advantage over individuals in that some members can work with equipment and props while others are speaking. A balance in varying modes and speakers generally results in a program that more easily holds the attention of the audience.

Preparation. Once a group is formed to make a group presentation, it is necessary to plan, prepare individual parts, rehearse, revise if necessary, and rehearse again. Group members are responsible not only to themselves but to the group as a whole in working toward a successful program. A list of steps suggested for planning and making a group presentation is given below.

1. Become acquainted with all group members.
2. Select a group leader to plan meetings, coordinate activities, and facilitate communication.
3. Define explicitly the goal of the group. What exactly are the instructions, purposes, and expected results of the program?
4. Brainstorm possible ways to achieve the goal. What material should be presented? What presentation modes can be used effectively? How can interest be created and maintained?
5. Determine a solution from among possible alternatives.
6. Individual assignments are agreed on. All members of the group should agree to do a fair share in pulling the program together and presenting it.
7. Individuals complete responsibilities in preparation for rehearsal. It is useful for individuals to prepare notes for use in rehearsals. Members should be flexible in their preparation and ready to adapt remarks spontaneously in case other members present the same material.
8. A rehearsal is held to time the presentation and to make sure that members are prepared and organized. Complete coverage of all material is not necessary, but a brief summary of what each person will say is needed.
9. Changes in the program are made if necessary and part or all of the program is rehearsed again.
10. Individuals polish their parts in preparation for the actual performance. The leader should check with and encourage members to do their best.

11. After the presentation, it is useful for the group to evaluate the experience. Was the preparation complete? How did members relate to each other and accept responsibility?

The group presentation takes time. The group process often takes longer to reach a goal than it would take an individual to reach a similar goal, but it is expected that the product resulting from the group interaction will be worth the extra effort.

SUMMARY

Small group communication skills are useful in many formal and informal settings. Some particularly interesting applications of small group communication are brainstorming, group discussion, and group presentations before an audience. Brainstorming is a technique for generating creative ideas for problem-solving situations. The brainstorming technique allows group members to suggest solutions without receiving criticism. Unusual suggestions are encouraged. Evaluation of ideas occurs at a later time. Group discussions are often called round-table discussions. A round-table discussion occurs when a small group meets with the specific purpose of reaching consensus on the solution to a problem or expressing a common attitude about an issue. Group presentations may be unrehearsed or rehearsed. The panel, forum, symposium, and colloquium are examples of group discussion formats where participants often meet for the first time immediately before the presentation. Their roles are often coordinated by a single leader. The rehearsed group presentation is made by individuals who have met to plan and rehearse their roles. The rehearsed group presentation can incorporate presentation techniques and variety that are impossible for an individual presenter.

Activity 1
Information about Small Group Communication

Preparation: Read the textual material for Part IV: Small Group Communication. Prepare yourself for taking a test on small group communication by reviewing the "Knowledge Objective" included in the overview for Part IV and by answering the practice items given below.

PRACTICE ITEMS FOR PART IV

Instructions: Select the best answer for each item.

1. Groups often form because members are trying to achieve the same
    a. agreements
    b. friends
    c. compromises
    d. goals
2. The minimum size for a group is
    a. one member
    b. three members
    c. five members
    d. seven members
3. Which is most likely to be a therapeutic group?
    a. historic preservation league
    b. weight watchers
    c. garden club
    d. country club
4. A very important general responsibility of a group member is to
    a. arrange for meeting times and places
    b. state an opinion on every issue
    c. prepare to participate adequately
    d. assume a leadership role
5. A group member who uses descriptive listening skills to facilitate discussion could be called
    a. a clarifier
    b. an energizer
    c. an encourager
    d. an initiator

Activity 1 continued

6. *No leader* is considered to be nearly the same as
    a. authoritarian leadership
    b. socialist leadership
    c. democratic leadership
    d. laissez-faire leadership
7. The outline for the discussions and events that are to occur in a meeting is called
    a. an agenda
    b. a program
    c. a guide
    d. a procedure
8. A small group communication situation that encourages quantity, not quality, of solutions is called
    a. rehearsing
    b. decision making
    c. therapy
    d. brainstorming
9. Which type of small group format is used when a group of experts presents independently prepared presentations on related topics?
    a. panel
    b. forum
    c. symposium
    d. colloquium
10. Which step is out of order for preparing and rehearsing a group presentation?
    a. evaluate the experience
    b. select a leader
    c. accept individual assignments
    d. rehearse with group members

Key: 1.d 2.b 3.b 4.c 5.a 6.d 7.a 8.d 9.c 10.a

Group Activity: Attend class and complete objective test items for Part IV: Small Group Communication.

Individual Activity: Make arrangements with your instructor to complete objective test items for Part IV: Small Group Communication.

Activity 2
Important Concepts in Small Group Communication

Preparation: Read the textual material and then recall the information about small group communication that is specified below.

1. Definition of a group:
2. Value of group participation:
3. Advantages of group versus individual problem solving:
4. Six characteristics of a good group member:
5. Reasons why individuals join groups:
6. Responsibilities of a group leader in ensuring effective leadership:
7. Definition of brainstorming:
8. Four rules for brainstorming:

Group Activity: In a teacher-led discussion or in small groups, discuss your answers to the eight items above. Turn this information in to the instructor at the close of class.

Individual Activity: Meet your instructor during office hours to discuss small group communication. Ask questions or make statements to clarify any misunderstanding over the reading material.

Activity 3
Rules for Group Membership

Preparation: Groups are usually organized around rules that govern the conduct of the members. Those rules can be established by custom, as in the case of a sorority or fraternity constitution. A leader may make the rules, as in the case of an authoritative father, or the rules can be agreed upon by a democratic group. Recall several of the groups that you have joined and how the rules were made. Use the instructions below to describe the rules of at least two groups that you have joined in the past. Try to select one group you perceive as successful and another you perceive as somewhat unsuccessful.

1. Description of the size, tasks, and type of organization:
2. Rules enforced by the group:
3. Person or persons in the group who enforced rules:
4. Means of enforcing the rules:
5. Success of group as to individual satisfaction, friendliness, productivity, loyalty, friction, and conformity:

Group Activity: Bring to class your prepared analysis of at least two groups to which you have belonged. In small groups or in a teacher-led discussion, name the group that you feel was more successful. Explain what characterized the more successful group. Was it friendlier and more productive? In what specific ways? Now discuss the group that was less successful. Was that group too large? Was there less direction? In what specific ways did that group lack cohesiveness?

Individual Activity: Describe in writing your perception of why one group was more successful than the other. Explain what characterized the more successful group. Was it more productive and friendlier? Was a definite goal reached because of more direction within the group? Explain what the less successful group lacked. What characterized this group experience? Was the group too large and did it lack direction? Was there a lack of cohesiveness among the members?

Activity 4
Therapeutic Group Situation

Preparation: The same basic plan can be followed when working through an intrapersonal problem or in working through a group problem. This is especially true where there is emotional involvement. The most difficult part of the process is being completely honest with yourself.

For practice in intrapersonal problem solving, try to think of a question that relates to a personal problem that you now have or have dealt with recently. Write a description of the problem. Then answer the following questions.

Problem Questions:
1. What is your goal in regard to the problem?
2. What power do you have in solving the problem?
3. What form do you want a solution to take?
4. What questions need answering before a solution can be reached?
5. Is additional research necessary?
6. What are the barriers that you must overcome?
7. What is unsatisfactory about the present situation? Describe.
8. How serious is the problem?
9. Why did the problem develop?
10. Are you the cause of the problem or did someone else cause it?
11. Who or what has kept the problem from being solved already?
12. What are all the possible solutions as you see them? (Do not evaluate potential solutions now.)
13. What is the ideal solution from your point of view?
14. Does the solution you chose solve the problem?
15. Does the solution create new problems for you?
16. Who must be involved in implementing the solution?
17. Is any money involved?
18. What obstacles could come up in implementing the solution?
19. What approach can you take to overcome the obstacles?

Group Activity: Meet in class with a small group of people to whom you do not mind relating a personal problem. Describe the problem briefly, giving only the facts they must know. Answer the important questions that you prepared for the activity. Give all the possible solutions as you see them. Ask the group members if they have additional solutions. What do they feel is the ideal solution from an objective point of view? Will that solution create new problems for you? Is it better than your solution, and if so why?

Activity 4 continued

Do not spend too long on any one problem so all members will have an opportunity to discuss their problems and solutions. Finally, as a group discuss the therapeutic value of the activity.

Individual Activity: Ask a group of people with whom you feel comfortable to participate in an experiment with you. You may want to select your family members. Describe a problem that you are experiencing as briefly as possible, giving only the necessary facts. Answer the important questions that you prepared for the activity. Give all possible solutions as you see them. Ask the group members for suggestions for additional solutions. What does the group feel is the ideal solution from an objective point of view? Will that solution create new problems for you? Is it better than your solution, and if so why?

After you feel satisfied with the discussion and solution, dismiss the group and write up a description of the experience for your instructor.

Activity 5
An Experience in Observing Roles of Group Members

Preparation: To participate in "Survival II," you must assume responsibility only for yourself. You are one of very few people left in a world destroyed by widespread famine and pestilence. The remaining people know that water, food, and medical supplies are not adequate for all of them. A decision must be made to eliminate at least one-third of the inhabitants or else all will perish.

Before attending class write down as many reasons as you can to persuade the leader and the other memebers of the group that you should be one of those selected to survive. In order to do this effectively, you need to believe in your value as a contributing human being. List all your assets for the group. What special qualities and abilities do you possess that could help the group survive? Do not list any negatives; list only positive characteristics about yourself.

Your goal is to persuade the group of people left that you should be one of those selected to survive.

Group Activity: Meet with the group of survivors of the famine and pestilence. Select a leader. Knowing that one-third of the group cannot partake of scarce resources, determine the number who can survive. Discuss the advantages and disadvantages of selecting each person as one of the survivors on earth. When it is your turn be particularly persuasive in an effort to get the group to choose you. After everyone has had a chance to discuss their own characteristics, the group leader should have the members vote on paper to select the survivors. Voting can be done easily by listing the names of the two-thirds who will survive. After the leader reads the names of the survivors, discuss what the choices reveal about the group's values. What qualities do these people possess that would make each a suitable person to survive under such conditions?

After completing the discussion of survivors, discuss the following questions, which deal with the roles played by each group member. Refer to the text for the "titles" assigned to group members who display various characteristics.

1. How would you evaluate the extent of participation of each member?
2. Was the leader effective in drawing in the more quiet members and checking the dominance of the more verbal members?
3. Which of the membership "titles" best fits each member of your group?

Activity 5 continued

Turn in a summary of your discussion to your instructor at the end of class. Include the list of survivors with the rationale for their selection and the answers to the above questions.

Individual Activity: Choose a group of at least six people that you know outside of the classroom. You may choose a family group, church group, or party group. Explain to the group that you are doing an assignment for class and that you would like them to help you. Explain that each is one of the only people left on earth after a period of famine and pestilence, and because food, water, and medical supplies are limited, only two-thirds of them can survive.

Give the group members 3-by-5 inch cards and instruct them to write down in five minutes as many reasons as possible why they should be one of those selected to survive. Encourage them to be honest but to believe in themselves and not to be modest about their attributes. As the group leader, instruct members to discuss their own characteristics. After all have had a chance to speak in their own behalves, have the members vote on paper to select the survivors. Voting can be made easy by listing the two-thirds who will survive. Read the names of the survivors and discuss what the particular choices reveal about the group's values. What qualities do these people possess that would make each a suitable person to survive under such conditions?

Then discuss the following questions about member participation with your group. Refer to the section in the text that lists "titles" for group participants.

1. How much did each member participate?
2. Did you facilitate communication by drawing in more quiet members and checking dominance of more verbal members?
3. Which of the membership "titles" best fits each member of your group? (Read descriptions to group and decide if anyone fits the role.)

Write a summary of this activity. Describe the group members, the survivors, the rationale for the choice of each, and the answers to the above three questions.

> **Activity 6**
> **An Experience in Observing Leadership**

Preparation: In many group situations a leader either emerges as a dominant force or is selected by the group. Leaders of groups generally fall into one of three classifications: authoritarian, democratic, and laissez-faire.

Authoritarian leaders are extroverted, dominating, and aggressive. They stress the values of discipline, deference to authority, and the outward symbols of status and power. Authoritarian leaders have little, if any, confidence in those they lead and rely on instruments of power to effect their will. Communication among followers is discouraged if not restricted; communication is accomplished almost exclusively through the leader.

Democratic leaders are not interested in possessing power but in stimulating members of the group to participate in group activities. They work as one of the group to achieve collective goals, and enact their roles in such a way as to facilitate effective role behavior in others. They substitute the distribution of responsibilities to every member for personal power over group members. They lead through ability to facilitate others in the attainment of ends.

While they initiate fewer leadership acts than either the authoritarian or democratic leader, laissez-faire leaders are active listeners who sympathetically and lucidly reflect group members' thoughts. They facilitate communication within the group and help bind the group together to strive for a common goal.

"Survival" is a group activity in which leadership roles can be observed. As you participate in the activity, note the qualities of the leader you have selected for your group. Try to determine which category your group and group leader exemplifies.

To participate in "Survival," your group must assume responsibility for the ten inhabitants of the last remaining outpost of humans in a world destroyed by nuclear explosion. The ten people have just realized that life-saving supplies of water, food, and air are adequate for only six of them to survive the three months they must remain in the shelter. A decision must be made to eliminate four of the inhabitants from the nuclear shelter or all ten inhabitants will perish.

The information below is all you know about the ten people.

1. Fifty-year-old scientist—a real ladies' man
2. His twenty-eight-year-old wife—four months pregnant
3. Young physician—has terminal illness; male

Activity 6 continued

4. Twenty-year-old jack-of-all trades—wino; male
5. Thirty-two-year-old architect—homosexual; male
6. Fifty-year-old nurse—too old to bear children
7. Brilliant female—thirty-eight-year-old college professor; never married
8. High-school girl—cheerleader
9. Thirty-year-old nun—studied nutrition
10. Farmer—sixty-five years old; male

Without consulting anyone else, rank the persons in the order that you would have them remain in the shelter. Briefly note the reasons for your selections.

Group Activity: Meet with a group and select one member as leader. Discuss the advantages and disadvantages of each person as one of six survivors on earth. In no more than thirty minutes of discussion, it is the leader's responsibility to see that the group has decided on a list of six survivors. Take five more minutes to discuss and select persons who would compose an ideal group of six survivors. Again, the leader is responsible for seeing that a list is completed.

After completing your list, discuss the following questions, which deal with group interaction and leadership roles.

1. Which of the three styles did your leader display at the beginning of the discussion?
2. Did the leadership style remain the same or change as the discussion progressed?
3. What other leadership styles were displayed?
4. What did your selections within the given survivors and the ideal survivors tell you about your values and those of the other group members?

Individual Activity: Choose a group of people that you know outside of the classroom. You may choose a family, church, or party group. Explain that you are doing an assignment for class and that you would like them to help you. Explain the difference in authoritarian, democratic, and laissez-faire leaders. You will be taking the role of one of these types and you would like the group to tell you which type you display and how effective you are as that type of leader.

Pass out the information available on the ten survivors of the nuclear explosion. Ask each group member to rank the persons in the order that they would have them remain in the shelter, and to briefly note the reasons for selection. As group leader, you should direct a brief discussion of the advantages and

Activity 6 continued

disadvantages of each person as one of the six survivors on earth. At the end of the discussion period it is your responsibility to get the group to select only six to survive in the shelter. After reading the list of survivors, discuss what values are apparent in the group's choices. Finally, ask them to discuss the style of leadership you displayed throughout the discussion. Were you an effective leader? If not, how could you improve in your leadership role? Prepare a summary of the results of this activity in writing. Be certain to include the list of survivors with the reason for their choice and the results of the discussion of your leadership style.

Activity 7
Group versus Individual Problem Solving

Preparation: Before coming to class describe in a paragraph the specifics of a problem that you feel would be better solved by group discussion. Be able to explain why the problem lends itself better to group problem solving than to individual problem solving.

Next, describe in a paragraph the specifics of a problem that you feel would be better solved by an individual. Be able to explain why this particular problem can be solved more easily by an individual than a group.

Label each paragraph as either "Group Problem" or "Individual Problem."

Group Activity: Turn your paper in to a small group leader. Do not acknowledge at this point which paper is yours. The group leader will read one of the problems and the group members will decide whether or not the problem should be group solved or individually solved. After each problem has been discussed, the originator will explain why it was labeled as a "Group Problem" or "Individual Problem."

Individual Activity: Locate at least two other class members who will share their descriptions of problems with you. Make copies of their problems. Then write out the rationale for group versus individual problem solving for your two problems and those you copied from other class members.

Activity 8 Brainstorming

Preparation: Brainstorming is the process of quickly thinking of all the ideas possible in regard to a particular problem, object, or idea. Brainstorming sessions work effectively only if as individuals and as a group you can temporarily avoid evaluating what is said. The goal is for you and everyone involved to feel free to create. Criticism will inhibit the creativity. Brainstorming is a useful skill for an individual as well as a group. For an individual experience in brainstorming take a pencil and notepad and jot down all the ways you can think of to use a tin can. See how many uses you can come up with in ten minutes of time. Remember to avoid personal evaluation of your own ideas.

Group Activity: In class form groups of four to six people. Review the rules for brainstorming. Ask the group to suggest possible uses for a tin can. Ask someone to serve as recorder and to jot down in a brief form all the ideas. At the end of ten minutes stop the group and ask the recorder to read the list. Was the group effective in the session? Were there more ideas from the group than from you as an individual? Do you feel brainstorming is a more useful technique when used with a group?

Individual Activity: Ask your family or a small group of friends to do an experiment with you. Explain brainstorming to them and review the rules. Then ask them to come up with possible uses for a tin can. Ask someone to serve as recorder and to jot down in a brief form all the ideas. Be sure to monitor any evaluations if there is need. At the end of ten minutes stop the group and ask the secretary to read the list. Was the group effective in the experiment? Were there more ideas from the group than from you as an individual? Do you feel brainstorming is a more useful technique when used with a group? Write down your conclusions and include a list of your individual brainstorming and the group's brainstorming ideas.

Activity 9
Evaluating Group Participation

Preparation: The purpose of this activity is to evaluate the effectiveness of presenting a group project or working with a group. After completing a group activity, answer the following questions.

1. What was your group's goal?
2. Did the group reach its goal? How?
3. If not, why not?
4. Did your group use a structured plan in reaching its goal? Describe.
5. Describe the kind of leader that you had and whether you felt the leadership style was effective.
6. What were your most difficult individual responsibilities?
7. Did you feel that you handled all individual responsibilities as well as you could have?
8. Overall, would you evaluate your group as excellent, good, or fair? Justify your rating.
9. Would you enjoy working with this group again? Why?

Group Activity: Bring the answers on your evaluation sheet to class. With the original group, discuss the effectiveness of the group working together as well as the effectiveness of the group activity.

Individual Activity: Talk with at least two members of your original group. The conversations may be by phone or in person, with each alone or all together. Discuss the effectiveness of the group working together as well as the effectiveness of the group activity. Prepare your individual evaluation and summaries of your two conversations in writing.

Activity 10 Speaking Activity

Preparation: Review the following example of a script from a group presentation. It is important to realize that the group prepared the material in anecdotal fashion (i.e., as personal experiences of characters) rather than as factual information. Do *not* conclude that a group presentation must be presented in this way. The tone of the presentation is only one of many details that can be creatively conceived through group participation.

A Group Presentation on Adult Development

Reference: *Passages* by Gail Sheehy

Presentation Modes: Lecture, visual aids, discussion, role playing

Introduction

Entrance of old woman using a walking cane

Music: Yesterday When I Was Young

This is Grandma, she is ninety-four years old and she has come to talk with you today.

Grandma wants to tell you about a book called *Passages* . This book deals with the stages of development we all undergo. But away with this book. I'll just tell you about my life. It seems like only yesterday I was a teenager....

Teenage Passage

Music: Love Potion No. 9

Introduction: What happened to the old days when all I had to do all day was play? My mother was happy to see me playing; it never bothered her. But now all I ever seem to do are things I *have* to do: *have* to do my homework, *have* to go to church, *have* to come in by twelve, *have* to be a good example for my brothers and sisters. Gee, I *never* get to do the things I want to do.

Body: Sometimes I'd like to just throw my arms around my Mom and cry my heart out but other times I hate her and Dad and wish I could run away and live on my own. Oh, how nice that would be! Maybe Bobby and I could get married, get jobs and just do whatever we pleased. I could dress like I wanted, eat whatever I wanted, and stay out as late as I wanted. Gee, I envy my older friends who are graduating from high school. They'll be doing these things pretty soon. But then Dad says he'll get me a car if I graduate and that would really be the greatest!! But

Activity 10 continued

then that's not for a couple of years yet. Meanwhile I've got to live here and take all this trash from them. But then they're not as bad as Jill's parents. She can't date at all, or join after school activities! Now that's the pits! I guess this isn't so bad; I'm even getting my own phone!!

I do have a lot to be thankful for and I'll prove it to my parents by graduating, going to college and being a...a...being what? Well, let's see, I like health and science, maybe a doctor. Do they give doctors time off to get married and have a baby? The patients can't wait, that's for sure. Well, I like children, I'll be a teacher. First grade—too young, I don't think I could stand little kids day in and day out. How about fifth grade? With all the problems with drugs and even teachers getting beat up—NO WAY! I know!! I'll take business administration and take over Dad's business. What about Bobby and our plans for marriage? He wants me to stay home and be a housewife. That would be nice, I guess. To have his meals ready when he comes home and wash and iron his clothes. I do love him so very much. But he's not into college. He wants to go cross country on his motorcycle after graduation.

Oh heck, what am I going to do? I'd better make some kind of decision 'cause here I am a teenager and have no earthly idea what I will do the rest of my life. Maybe I can be both a career woman and a wife. I'll graduate, Bobby and I will get married or else I'll start college first and then get married. Then I'll just work until we have our first baby and I'll stay home for awhile. Then I'll go back to work when he's old enough for a preschool. That's pretty easy, that's what I'll do. At least now I have some idea of what I'll do with my life.

Conclusion: What? Bobby's on the line for me?

Hi! A party on Saturday!! Swimming on Sunday. Yeah, I'd love to go but I'll have to ask permission from you know who. Gee, Bobby, I sure wish I was in my twenties.

Visual aid: Posters showing life patterns of a teenager.

Passage to the Twenties

Music: Boogie Nights

Introduction: Well, here I am. I finally made it, twenty years old. Gosh, it doesn't feel any different. But I am sure it is, at least that's what they say.

Body: Although I had many decisions to make in high school, the ones I make in my twenties will have more bearing on my future activities and goals.

First of all my decision on education. Will I go to college? Where will I go? Why should I go? These are just a few questions I have to answer, and after I have decided what to do, I will probably change my mind a couple of times.

I started at North Texas, then Richland, now Eastfield, and next UTD.

Class Participation: Ask a few students in classroom whether they have attended other colleges and if they feel they made the right decision.

I also must decide on a major field of study. Do I want to be a lawyer, a doctor, an engineer? I need to have some idea of how I intend to make a living for myself. I know that I am only twenty, but now it is time to move out on my own. Get myself an apartment and even wash my own clothes. So many things I haven't done before are now all coming at once. No longer are

Activity 10 continued

my parents there to run to or to work things out for me. How old is twenty-two, twenty-five, twenty-eight, in relation to the rest of my life? I am still young. I am going to take my time and make good decisions. If it turns out to be a wrong decision, I still have time to change.

Conclusion: I'm not going to rush into decisions, I don't think I'm old, not now at least, I'll wait till I'm thirty—then I'll get scared.

Passage to the Thirties

Music: We've Only Just Begun

Introduction: I really thought that at thirty I would have my life together. But now those choices I made when I was twenty just don't seem to fit me anymore. I have some important new choices to make and commitments to be altered or deepened. I now even find it necessary to take a serious look at my marriage.

Body: I just look back now and remember when I was first married. Life seemed so easy then. Do you ever wonder what happened to those happy ever after endings?

When we were first married, it was the agreement that I would stay home, be a good housewife and have children. He would go out and be the bread winner of the family. I didn't have to go out into the world in any full sense.

But my husband adapted himself to the outside world and he became successful in his work. He became confident in himself and no longer in need of someone to support his efforts at advancement. So, therefore, he decided he wanted me to be more of a companion—he wanted more than a wife and mother. He suggested that I go to school and take a few courses.

Can you imagine how helpless and confused I felt? After seven years of feeling safe and secure in my home, I felt threatened. It was like he was trying to get rid of me, as if he was kicking me out of my own house. Just thinking about it brings back the horrible memories of that conversation.

Role Playing:
  Husband: Kathy, don't you want more out of life than just sitting at home? I think maybe you should go to school and take a few courses.
  Wife: But Bob, my life is devoted to the children and my home.
  Husband: But I want you to be more than a wife and mother, I want you to be a companion for me.
  And so forth.

Can you imagine how I felt? So confused. I wasn't sure that I could cope with this change. How could I be pushed out into a world that I knew nothing about?

Men don't realize just how much time it takes to care for the home, care for the children, and by all means have dinner prepared when he comes home from a long hard day at the office.

I wonder if he has ever stopped to think of what I gave up when I married him. I gave up my ambitious career plans to be the type of wife that he said he wanted me to be. But now almost seven years have passed, and his idea of what he wants in a wife has changed.

I knew that if I didn't act on my own impulse to broaden during this passage that the problem would double. But I felt that devoting the time, love, and discipline necessary to

Activity 10 continued

make it work would invite a jealous backlash from my husband. So, I retreated instead to the safety of my childhood and tried to reel him back in to me. He sensed that as a trap. That led to the other woman. He used the excuse that she fortified his masculinity. But since I was dependent on my husband and I had the children to think of, I tried to overlook the problem. My whole effort was to hang on to the arrangement although it was filled with hate.

Conclusion: Just what do you do in a situation like this? Divorce isn't always the answer.
 You really have to stop and ask yourself—Have I failed in everything, in being a good wife and a good mother? Or have I just messed up my whole life making wrong decisions?
 Should I tear up the life that I spent most of my twenties piecing together?

Middle Age Passage

Music: Days of Wine and Roses

Visual Aid: corsage, bud vase with one rose, flowered hankie

Introduction: At forty, you're not getting older, you're just getting better.

Body: I no longer have the career decision problems that I had at twenty. I know where I am going. My decision has been made about my career whether it's right or wrong. If it's wrong I can make the best of it or I can even change it. Hindsight is better than foresight at forty. I don't have to worry about raising the kids anymore as I did in my thirties. They're grown and gone off on their own. It's too late to worry about whether I brought them up right or not. They are already grown and I don't have the problems of decision making and child rearing anymore. Now we look forward to traveling, retirement, and maybe paying off the mortgage.
 "Empty Nest Syndrome" is a problem for some couples. They sometimes feel it's a time for rediscovering each other. Some couples feel glad to have the kids gone. Others feel lonely. If one parent is glad they are gone and the other is sad about the new freedom, divorce can easily occur. Yes, that's what is happening to some friends of ours.
 Me, I am glad to have the freedom. I might take a trip or I might stay home with a drink and just relax. At forty and fifty, your life has been set. You have made your decisions, your mistakes, your successes.

Questions to audience:
 When you go home with a problem, do you feel your parents are answering you with what they would do if they were your age again? Are they putting themselves in your shoes or are they answering with the experience and morals of today?
 Oh, at forty and fifty life isn't all a bed of roses. We see younger couples coming home with their dates and start remembering those days from our own pasts.
 It's a time for renewing commitments to one another; accepting the values of today as opposed to the values of our twenties.

Questions to audience:
 Do you all see these changes in your parents? Do you all consider that they have problems, too? Are your parents glad their children are gone? Are they lonesome and brooding?

Conclusion: I would like to conclude by reading you this poem: "Postscript" by Sandra Hockman.

Activity 10 continued

Conclusion

Old woman enters again

Well, my life has been an open book before you. I'm the sum total of what I have lived—my dreams, my hopes, my thoughts. Yes, ninety-four is wonderful. Son, take me home now—nice talking to you.

Another example of one speaker's part in a presentation based on a human development book follows. This example is given to demonstrate a more formal and factual group presentation. The group who prepared this latter presentation based their report on the actual content of the book rather than an interpretation of the content. As each member made a formal presentation, other members facilitated and contributed to the use of several presentation modes.

Parent and Child Ego States

Outline	*Script*
I. Introduction	
A. Attention device	"It is indeed a desirable thing to be well descended, but the glory belongs to our ancestors." *Plutarch*
B. Relate to the group	Think back for a moment to your ancestors. How do you remember them? Look into yourself. Do you find their characteristics intricately woven into your being?
C. Statement of purpose	Let's do a little exploring! We'll explore together two ego states. I hope to lead you to a simple, concise understanding of the Parent and Child ego states that are undeniable parts of each one of us.
D. Preview of main points	
1. First main point	First, I'll define the Parent ego state. I'll cite the characteristics of the Nurturing Parent and the Critical Parent.
2. Second main point	The interesting, often frustrating Child ego state will be tackled next. The Natural Child, the Little Professor, and the Adapted Child are all a part of you and me. I'll discuss just what part these ego states play in our lives.
E. Transition statement	I invite you to be introspective for the next few minutes, examining the fibers of your mental makeup.
II. Body	
A. First main point	For better or worse, parents serve as models and are imprinted on the brains of their children.

Activity 10 continued

1. Support — The Parent ego state is the incorporation of the attitudes and behavior of all the emotionally significant people who serve as parent figures to the child. Not only Mom and Dad, but grandma, the babysitters, a favorite aunt or uncle, and others. Gestures, postures, stances, and many forms of body language are incorporated from parental models.

   Presentational modes:
   (group members demonstrating)
   - Mother's stance while scolding.
   - Grandma looking down her nose while responding to a question.
   - Dad's authoritarian desk banging for emphasis.

2. Support — The Nurturing parent is sympathetic, protective, nurturing.

   Presentational modes:
   (group members demonstrating)
   - "Come on honey, you're tired. I'll carry you for a while."
   - "Let Mommy kiss it and make it all well."
   - Were your parents nurturing? Do you see these nurturing tendencies in your actions?

3. Support — The Parent ego is filled with opinions about religion, politics, tradition, sex roles, life styles, child rearing, and all the facets of cultural and family scripts. These opinions are often irrational, may not have been evaluated by the Adult ego state and may be prejudiced. Thus the critical parent is alive and well!

   Presentational modes:
   (visual aid, transparency)
   - "Children should be seen and not heard."
   - "Kids should respect their elders."
   - "Boys shouldn't wear long hair."

   When transacting with other adults, the Critical Parent can be seen.

   Presentational modes:
   (group members demonstrating)
   - Wife to husband: "Men can't change diapers. That's a woman's job."
   - Patient to head nurse: "Who ever heard of a male nurse?"
   - Worker to worker: "I don't think he's going to be right for the job. Look how wide apart his eyes are set."

4. Transition — You and I have our own unique Parent ego states. These states can at times help us and other times hurt us. Awareness of the Parent gives us more choice in our behavior and enhances our chances of becoming winners and raising our children to be winners.

Activity 10 continued

B. Second main point — Now, we'll move from the Parent to the Child ego state. The Child ego state is the inner world of feelings and experiences and adaptations. The Child is the foundation of a person's self-image. Your feeling of being a winner or loser is likely to stem from your Child ego state.

1. Support — The Natural Child feels free and does what he or she wants to do. The Natural Child is affectionate, impulsive, sensuous, uncensored and curious. The Natural Child can add warmth, charm, and zip to your personality. However, the Natural Child has another side. He or she may be fearful, self-indulgent, self-centered, rebellious, and aggressive. When these characteristics remain unharnessed in adulthood they can be self-defeating.

Presentational mode:
(role playing by group members)

When Mary was a little girl, if she couldn't have what she wanted, she would respond in this manner (action of tantrum). As a grown woman, Mary was a competent secretary and in line to be a personnel manager. However, when her request for certain vacation dates was denied, Mary reacted in her Natural Child ego state in this manner (adult tantrum). Mary's superior was not impressed. He submitted a negative report and Mary not only failed to get the desired vacation dates, she failed to get her promotion. Mary's behavior was self-defeating.

The healthy, happy person allows the appropriate expression of the Natural Child each day.

2. Support — The Little Professor is that part of the Child ego state that is innately intuitive, creative, and manipulative. He or she figures things out and often believes in magic. The Little Professor is that smart little kid in each of us. When you feel intuitive, experience a moment of genius, create for the fun of it, or manipulate someone else to get what you want, the Little Professor is involved.

People who express creativity purposefully use their Little Professor in conjunction with their Adult ego state.

Activity 10 continued

Presentational mode:
(role play)

With an active Little Professor, a person can manipulate a spouse, parent, teacher, boss, or friend. See if you can spot the Little Professor's manipulative powers at work in this scene. This husband is coming home very late from work. Surprise! He's remembered flowers, presents, and the right amount of sweet talk.

Husband: "You look lovely, dear. The house is so clean. Can I do anything for you?"

This wife reads her spouse well and seizes on the opportunity to spend the evening dining in her favorite restaurant instead of slaving over the hot stove. She also gets a little extra cash from hubby in his moment of vulnerability for that new dress she's been wanting.

Wife: "Well, I went shopping today and saw this beautiful dress and I didn't have time to cook dinner, so I would like to go out to a nice restaurant."

See how the Little Professor manipulates? Are any of us guilty of this type of manipulation at times?

3. Support

The Adapted Child is the trained child who develops socially but sometimes feels very not-OK. Some adaptation of natural impulses is essential. However, some parental training is unnecessarily repressive.

Presentational mode:
(role play)

Jay whines over a spat with a friend. Mother responds. "Shut up! I'll give you something to really cry about if you don't."

Devona asks a childish question.

Child: "Mommy, why can't I take a bath with my clothes on?"

Mother responds.

"I can't stand it! You're driving me right up the wall. Don't ask me another dumb question!"

This training is unnecessarily repressive. When natural expressiveness becomes overly inhibited, the child may learn to feel not-OK and follow patterns of complying, withdrawing or procrastinating.

As you can readily see the Adapted Child is very often troubled. This is true when a child born to win develops the loser image,

Activity 10 continued

		and acts not-OK. Life can be pretty miserable if the overly Adapted Child, in the search for approval, loses sight of authenticity as a person.
	4. Transition	What activates the Child ego state? Very often it is activated by another person coming on with a strong Parent.
	Presentational mode: (interact with the class and discuss feelings)	Kassie! Really! Sit up straight and pay attention! You're not even listening to my speech! (How did this make you feel, Kassie?)
III.	Conclusion	
	A. Summary	Are you feeling overwhelmed by the complexity of the person you are? I hope that you have gained a little insight into the Parent and Child ego states.
	B. Importance of message	If you would enjoy a little deeper analysis of the real you, I would recommend reading *Born to Win* by James and Jongeward.
	C. Closing	Next, Susan will help us understand why we act the way we do.

Now complete your preliminary preparation for either Option 1 or Option 2.

Option 1: Human Development
The purpose of the speaking activity is to inform the audience of the content of a human development book. The instructor may suggest a book or your group may choose one from the text's reference list. To prepare for this activity purchase and review a copy of the book before the next group meeting.

Option 2: Local, National, or International Problem
The purpose of the speaking activity is to select the best possible solution to a local, national, or international problem of interest to the group. This will be accomplished by individual preparation and group interaction. To prepare for this activity read *U.S. News and World Report* or any news magazine, and cut out an article to take to class that you feel would be an interesting topic for problem-solving discussion

Group Activity:

Option 1: Human Development
During class become a member of a group, choose a leader for the group, and discuss the part each person will take in the group project. Familiarize yourself with the book to enable you to select a portion for your part of the group presentation. Review the presentational modes in the text and consider which of these could be used in your presentation.

Activity 10 continued

During the next meeting participate with your group in the preparation of an outline for the group presentation. In your plan be sure to include any visual aids and equipment needed as well as at least four presentational modes to be used during the group presentation. To ensure success for the performance of the whole group, accept responsibility for your individual role. At the end of class your group should prepare a written plan detailing the responsibilities of each member of the group.

Before the next class meeting outline your part of the presentation on the front of 3-by-5 inch cards. On the first card include the following information for your instructor.

Your Name _____
Title of book _____
Pages of the book to be covered in your presentation _____
Presentational modes to be used _____
Equipment needed _____

After turning in your cards to your instructor meet with the group to discuss procedure. Review the evaluation form included at the end of this activity to be certain that you are adequately prepared for the presentation. Briefly rehearse your part with the group to build confidence, perfect timing, and to avoid repetition of key items. After the final group meeting continue to rehearse your part of the group presentation as you would any speech. On the day of presentation be adequately prepared to fulfill your responsibilities as a group member. Take an active and enthusiastic part in the presentation to ensure your group's success in this project.

Option 2: Local, National, or International Problem
During the first meeting the group will need to select a discussion problem that the students feel is challenging, interesting, and can be solved. As a group you will need to consider the time that you have to solve the problem, the information available, and the the expertise of the individuals involved in the process. When a general area has been decided on, you need to phrase a question so that there will be open and productive discussion. Finally, during this meeting the group will need to choose a leader to be in charge of the group's preparation and presentation.

As an individual and as a group discuss and answer on paper the questions below.

Statement of the problem:
1. What terms within the problem need to be defined?
2. What is unsatisfactory about the present situation?
3. Why did the problem develop?
4. Who is involved in or affected by the situation?
5. What previous action has been taken to solve the problem?
6. Why didn't it solve the problem?

Activity 10 continued

7. What specific factors have kept the problem from being solved already?
8. What are the basic causes of the problem?
9. What criteria must the solution meet?
10. What are possible solutions to the problem (use the brainstorming technique)?
11. Which solution solves the problem?
12. Which solution eliminates the cause?
13. Which solution does not create other problems?
14. Which is the very best solution overall?
15. Who would be needed to put the solution into action?
16. What is the cost, time, and energy involved in implementing the solution?
17. What plan can be implemented to put the solution into action?
18. What obstacles might be encountered?
19. What plan might be used to overcome the obstacles?

After the initial research and preparation, individuals, with the help of the group leader, will need to decide on a particular topic for the presentation. Review the presentational modes in the text and consider which of these could be used to clarify and create interest when presenting your material to an audience. Participate with your group to prepare an outline explaining the organization of your material. This outline should specify the order in which each person will speak as well as a topic or heading to be covered. You will probably want to cover to some degree the questions answered in your research. In your outline be sure to include any visual aids and equipment needed as well as at least four presentational modes. To ensure success for the performance of the whole group, accept responsibility for your individual role. At the end of the class the group leader should prepare a written plan detailing the responsibilities of each member of the group.

After completing the outline and assigning responsibilities, plan to meet with your group a final time to complete preparation for your presentation. Review the evaluation form included with the activity to be certain that you are adequately prepared for the presentation. Briefly rehearse your part with the group to build confidence, perfect timing, and to avoid repetition of key items. After a final group meeting continue to rehearse your part of the group presentaiton as you would any speech. On the day of presentation be adequately prepared to fulfill your responsibilities as a group member. Take an active and enthusiastic part in the presentation to ensure its success before an audience.

Individual Activity: Because of the requirement of group interaction and presentation to an audience, there is no equivalent individual activity suggested.

Evaluation Form
Group Presentations

(Points are given to the right of each criterion.)

Group Evaluation

I. Presentation modes (5 points each; 20 points total)
   _____ Demonstration
   _____ Discussion
   _____ Lecture
   _____ Modeling and imitation
   _____ Problem solving
   _____ Role playing
   _____ Sensitivity training
   _____ Skill practice session
   _____ Tactile activity
   _____ Visual aids

II. General comments (3 points each; 30 points total)
   _____ Was a group goal established? (3)
   _____ Was there meaningful interaction among group members? (3)
   _____ Were conflicts dealt with effectively? (3)
   _____ Was there commitment to the group and its decisions? (3)
   _____ Was there communication from the group to the audience? (3)
   _____ Did each individual accept responsibility as a group member? (3)
   _____ Did the group succeed in getting the audience actively involved? (3)
   _____ Did the group seem enthusiastic over the project? (3)
   _____ Was the group well prepared? (3)
   _____ Were the presentation modes used well coordinated? (3)

Individual Evaluation

III. Attitudes toward group participation (4 points each; 20 points total)
   _____ Brought new ideas and activities to the audience. (4)
   _____ Shared knowledge with the group and the audience. (4)
   _____ Shared opinions with the audience. (4)
   _____ Directed discussion to the goals of the group. (4)
   _____ Encouraged fellow members to participate and to do well. (4)

IV. Presentation (3 points each; 30 points total)
   _____ Poised and confident (3)
   _____ Use of gestures (3)
   _____ Eye contact with audience (3)

Evaluation Form continued

_____ Correct posture (3)
_____ Conversational style (3)
_____ Speaking rate (3)
_____ Volume of speech (3)
_____ Vocal variety (3)
_____ Control of fillers (3)
_____ Pronunciation and articulation (3)

Additional Readings in Small Group Communication

In addition to books and articles cited in these chapters, the following books are excellent sources for further study of communication.

Barker, L. L. *Groups in Process: An Introduction to Small Group Communication.* Englewood Cliffs, New Jersey: Prentice-Hall, Inc., 1979.

> *The reader of this informative book will gain further insight into effective communication in small group situations.*

Hughes, C. L. *Goal Setting.* New York: Amacorn, 1965.

> *An explanation is given on how to establish goals and subgoals at all levels of an organization, and how to harmonize individual and organization goals in the process.*

Shaw, M. E. *Group Dynamics: The Psychology of Small Group Behavior.* New York: McGraw-Hill Book Company, 1975.

> *A thorough coverage of small group processes as they relate to reaching group goals.*

Trecker, H. B., and Trecker, A. R. *Working with Groups, Committees and Communities.* Chicago: Follett Publishing Company, 1979.

> *This is a practical book for those who are heavily involved in "committees"—identifying needs, developing leadership, making decisions, and evaluating outcomes.*

PART FIVE

Overview

Opportunities to speak in front of groups are feared and avoided by many people. Often people who have long feared expressing themselves in the speaker-audience situation find after experience that such fears are unfounded. Any experienced speaker will admit to feeling some nervousness in speaker-audience situations, but all have learned to deal effectively with anxiety.

In thinking about speaker-audience experiences and feelings, consider the testimonies of several "successful" students of public speaking.

> *No matter what profession you plan to go into, you are going to have to communicate. A communication course really helps conquer that sick, tense feeling you get before you make a speech. The world's number one fear is speaking in front of an audience. A communication course helps you make that the number three fear.*
>
> *I was afraid and nervous the first day I walked into class. After each speech, I became more confident of myself... This course helps very much in becoming relaxed and confident of yourself when making a speech. The best cure for "speechphobia" is a communication course.*
>
> *Being somewhat reserved, I thought giving a speech would be quite difficult. Yet, after only a period of about four months, I found that a speech can be quite easy as well as fun to give. Taking a communication class turned out to be an enjoyment and a learning experience.*
>
> *I could always talk in front of a few people, but I froze in front of a crowd. After my experiences in a communications course, I feel fairly confident when I talk in front of a large group.*
>
> *I think we need to know how to communicate well with people today. The future is full of changes and you never know when you might have to give a speech. It could be in other classes or at a banquet, or you might be top salesperson of the year or the recipient of an award.*
>
> *In the career I am planning, I have to communicate well with the public. I have to be dominant but also soft spoken at times. I think that everyone should take a communications course.*

Speaker-Audience Communication

Of the many students asked how they felt about the speaker-audience situation, none expressed greater anxiety after learning how to prepare and deliver such messages. The speaker-audience situation can be a rewarding one in both the personal and professional areas of living. As one student so wisely commented, the future is unknown. The time to learn is today. Then the challenges of tomorrow can be readily met no matter how unlikely future public speaking prospects may seem.

The material on speaker-audience communication is intended to build on communication skills already acquired. You will learn how to prepare a message for presentation to a large group, and you will experience the anxiety of anticipating the experience and the positive rewards of successfully making the presentation. Afterwards you too will be able to offer testimony about the value of communication.

After studying the material on speaker-audience communication, the reader should be able to demonstrate acquisition of the following behaviors.

Attitude Objective: By applying the skills and concepts associated with speaker-audience communication, the student will feel confident about abilities to make a formal presentation to a large group. (*Activities 1–10*)

Knowledge Objective: Given objective test items, the student will recall the definitions of the following terms and recognize examples or differentiate among them where appropriate. (*Activity 1*)

    I.   Planning speaker-audience messages
        A.   Types of messages
            1.   Informative
            2.   Persuasive
            3.   Entertainment
        B.   Preparing the material
            1.   Setting
            2.   Topic
            3.   Gathering material

                a. Personal experiences
                b. Interviews
                c. Experiments
                d. Courses
                e. Mass media
                f. Library search
            4. Ordering material
                a. Topical
                b. Chronological
                c. Spatial
                d. Causal
                e. Comparison/contrast
                f. Problem solution
            5. Supporting material
                a. Example
                b. Statistics
                c. Testimony
II. Delivering speaker-audience messages
    A. Organizing the message
        1. Introduction
        2. Body
        3. Conclusion
    B. Delivering the message
        1. Modes of presentation
            a. Impromptu
            b. Extemporaneous
            c. Manuscript
            d. Memorized
        2. Visual aids
            a. Speaker
            b. Charts
            c. Overhead and opaque projectors
            d. Chalkboard
            e. Models and objects
            f. Handouts
            g. Slides, etc.
        3. Rehearsal
III. Informative speaking
    A. Types of informative messages
        1. Description
        2. Demonstration
        3. Definition
        4. Reporting
    B. Developing informative messages
        1. Audience needs
        2. Common learning principles
        3. Methods of explanation

PART V   Speaker-Audience Communication 297

               a. Definition
               b. Synonym
               c. Antonym
               d. Analogy
               e. Negation
               f. Classification
               g. Rephrasing
         C. Evaluation of informative speeches
    IV. Persuasive speaking
         A. Types of persuasive messages
             1. Expected behaviors
             2. Purpose of the message
             3. Classification of topics
         B. Developing the persuasive message
             1. Audience characteristics
             2. Gaining listener acceptance
                 a. Awareness
                 b. Dissonance
                 c. Resolution
                 d. Reinforcement
                 e. Action
             3. Persuasive speaking outline
         C. Evaluation of persuasive speeches
         D. Receiving the persuasive message
             1. Critical listening
             2. Fact versus opinion
             3. Intent of the speaker

Experiential Objective: The student will participate in speaker-audience experiences by following instructions for selected activities in the areas listed below. (*Activities 2-4, 6-9*)

              I. Outlining public speeches
             II. Using the library
            III. Practice in informing an audience
            IV. Persuasion
             V. Practice in persuading an audience

Speaking Objective: Following the instructions given for Activities 5 and 10, the student will prepare and present informative and persuasive speeches. (*Activities 5 and 10*)

Optional Speaking Objective: Following the instructions given for Activities 11 and 12, the student will prepare and present entertaining and impromptu speeches. (*Activities 11 and 12*)

CHAPTER 13

Planning the Speaker-Audience Message

During a lifetime most individuals are on the receiving end of the speaker-audience message many more times than they are on the sending end of the message. Not only should an effective communicator be prepared to deliver messages to an audience, but the effective communicator must develop skill in receiving such messages. As sender, the communicator has the responsibility to present a thoughtfully prepared message designed specifically for the audience, the occasion, and the setting. As receiver, the communicator must avoid irresponsible messages and evaluate carefully those messages meant to change the listener's values, beliefs, or behaviors. A knowledge of speech preparation and practice in speech delivery can do much to enhance a communicator's skill in sending and receiving speaker-audience messages. To begin, consider several ways that the speaker-audience situation can be differentiated from interpersonal and small group communication: (1) characteristics of the listener, (2) advance preparation of the message, and (3) formality of the delivery.

Those who gather to listen to a speaker-audience message generally perceive their role more as receivers of the message than as participants in an interactive process where they both send and receive messages. Although unusual circumstances might produce an audience composed of a single listener, the audience will generally number above the fifteen that is considered maximum for effective small group interaction. The audience size results in the listeners' expectation that they will be able to say little, if anything, during the speaker's presentation. The lack of opportunity to speak is quite a reversal from the expectation in interpersonal or small group communication.

The messages in many speaker-audience situations are prepared in advance and even rehearsed to produce the best presentation possible.

Advance preparation is important because the speaker wishes to make an impact with a specific audience in a given amount of time and set of circumstances. Unprepared speakers will often ramble so much that the audience fails to grasp the intended message. Although speakers will sometimes prepare messages before interpersonal or small group interactions, these situations are generally more spontaneous.

The setting in which a speaker-audience message occurs is generally somewhat formal. In most situations the message is prepared with thought given to grammar and the omission of slang and colloquial words and phrases. The speaker is generally set apart from the audience so that each listener can both see and hear the speaker. Much can be done to make the setting somewhat intimate, but the separation of the speaker and audience and the prepared message make the situation appear more formal than the usual casual setting associated with interpersonal and small group communication.

In considering speaker-audience communication the key is planning. Planning a message for each specific situation is a must. In developing an effective and appropriate message, it is important to be aware of the special characteristics of the different types of speeches that can be presented and to give consideration to the setting, topic, and the gathering and ordering of material.

Types of Messages

Students of public speaking will hear references to informative, demonstration, ceremonial, entertainment, inspiration, eulogy, motivational, introduction, tribute, presentation, acceptance, and many other types of speeches. In any public speaking situation, however, most messages can be classified according to their intent to inform, persuade, or entertain. The more specific categories listed above will generally fall within one of the three major categories. And sometimes the same speech will include segments to inform, persuade, and entertain.

SPEAKER-AUDIENCE MESSAGES

Purpose of Speaker	Response of Listener
1. To Inform	1. Acquire Knowledge
2. To Persuade	2. Change Behavior
3. To Entertain	3. Experience Diversion

Figure 13.1. *Types of message.*

Informative

When the purpose of the message is to add to the listener's knowledge it is an informative message. Such messages would include a demonstration of how to operate a new type of machine, an introduction of a visiting dignitary, a lecture on child psychology, a news program on television, or the findings of a committee appointed to investigate fringe benefits for employees of a company. In all these examples the speaker is seeking to provide information that listeners will retain as part of their stores of knowledge.

Persuasive

When the purpose of the message is to bring about some action or change some belief on the part of the listener, it is a persuasive message. Such messages include product advertisements presented on television, political speeches to create support for a given candidate, motivational pitches to exercise for good health, inspirational encouragement to become a better person, appeals to donate time or money to good causes, or reasons for taking a certain stand on an issue. In all these examples the speaker is seeking to convince or motivate the listener, and is hoping the listener will react in ways that support the message objective.

Entertainment

The purpose of a speech to entertain is diversion—it is not to impart knowledge or provide a rationale to acquire certain beliefs or take specific actions. The speech to entertain should not be confused with the stand-up comedian's performance or a humorous monologue. Although it will frequently produce laughter or wild applause, this is not a requirement. The speech to entertain might include a description of a mountain climbing expedition, the perilous adventures experienced as an undercover police detective, and humorous stories about children in a preschool. The speech to entertain will occupy the minds of the listeners but will not obligate them to retain any knowledge or consider beliefs or actions. Facets of the speech to entertain can be very useful in creating interest or attracting attention in informative and persuasive speeches.

Others

Hopefully, the speech types mentioned above and those the public speaker will hear mentioned in the future can be classified as speeches to inform, persuade, or entertain. The demonstration speech, where a procedure is actually shown, is an informative speech. However, if the ultimate purpose is the sale of the object being demonstrated, the speech would include persuasive elements as well. The eulogy, a formal speech praising someone who has recently died, is most likely informative in nature. Likewise, introductions of or tributes to someone are likely to be informative. Speeches to motivate and inspire will probably contain elements of persuasion to change behavior or perform some action. The ceremonial speech, traditionally made to celebrate some event, will be informative or persuasive if given in a serious vein, or entertaining if given lightly. The speeches accompanying presentation and acceptance of awards can be either informative or entertaining depending on the occasion.

It is difficult to determine the nature of a speech by its title. The important point to consider is the special techniques public speakers can use to enhance the informative and persuasive aspects of their messages. These will be discussed in more detail in the last two chapters. The purpose of this chapter is to inform the reader about some general principles of speech planning and preparation, and to persuade the reader that public speaking skill can be enhanced by giving attention to these principles.

Preparing the Material

Adequate preparation for delivery of the message is extremely important. Unprepared speakers may alienate their audiences as well as damage their own self-concepts. It is the exceptional person who can consistently address new audiences without prior preparation. Consideration must be given to the setting, topic, gathering of materials, ordering of materials, and supporting materials.

Setting

Each occasion for public speaking will involve a speaker, an audience, a time, a place, and a purpose. Before beginning work on the organization of the message, a thorough analysis of these factors is important. To be effective the message must be tailored to the setting.

Speakers know themselves well and should consider their own backgrounds, interests, and experiences as they prepare their messages. It is important to ask, "Is this speech suited to me? Do I know enough about the topic? Can I relate to the needs of the audience?" Audiences often appreciate getting to know the speaker as well as learning the message. Ideas discovered through research can be more meaningfully presented when they are related to the experiences of the speaker and the audience. It is important too to display a positive attitude about the speaking experience. Making excuses or mentioning shortcomings has only a negative effect on the message.

Setting = Speaker + Audience + Time + Place + Purpose

Figure 13.2. *Setting.*

The message must be adapted to the audience. Would you deliver the same message on "home insulation" to a junior high school science class, a neighborhood association of home owners, the local chapter of the home builders' association, and the national society for insulation research? Hopefully, you would tailor your message to suit the background, knowledge, and experience of each group. The good speaker will find out as much as possible about the audience. The presentation must not be so simple as to be boring, or so complex that it cannot be understood. It is a good idea too to have information about the receptiveness of the audience toward the topic. Since speakers will probably receive a more favorable response from audiences whose views are similar to their own, the message can sometimes be developed in ways that will make audience attitude more favorable. Each audience will be unique and will require special consideration in message planning. Such characteristics as size of the audience, age and sex of the audience members, educational backgrounds and socioeconomic factors, memberships and affiliations, experiences with the topic, and values and interests are often relevant to message planning. How do speakers learn audience characteristics? They ask questions and more questions until they learn enough to prepare a message to gain the attention and hold the interest of the audience.

The time and place will affect the preparation and delivery of the message also. The speaker has a responsibility to others sharing the same program to stay within the time limits agreed on in accepting the speaking responsibilities. Lack of attention to time can result in a rushed, possibly flustered, conclusion to the speech. The place in which the speech is delivered has an effect also. Characteristics of the location can affect the use of visual aids, the speaker's attire, the distance between speaker and audience, and the comfort of the speaker and audience. Often a request by the speaker for changes in the setting can make a possibly unpleasant atmosphere more suitable.

The purpose of the speech will affect the message. It will often determine whether the topic is presented in an informative or persuasive manner. Speeches are a part of many different occasions in our society. As a guest speaker at the monthly meeting of an organization, you may decide it will be more appropriate to develop an informative message. On the other hand, you may be selected to deliver a persuasive message to the membership of your own organization on the importance of consistent attendance; or you may be invited to speak as a recognized expert on a subject and discover that a persuasive message would immediately alienate your audience. Purpose, like other considerations discussed above, is important in planning a message that will be worthwhile and interesting for the audience and rewarding for the speaker.

Topic

Once an analysis of the setting is complete, the next step in speech preparation is determining the topic. What exactly will be the subject covered by the speech? The topic statement represents the goal of the speaker. It is essential for guiding the speech development and determining if, in fact, the message fulfills the initial purpose. Once determined, the topic statement or speech objective is not set in cement—it can be modified or discarded. Its importance may be expressed by considering the following question: If you do not know where you are going, how will you know when you have arrived? The topic statement tells you where you want to go, and a comparison of the prepared message with the topic statement tells you if you succeeded in getting there.

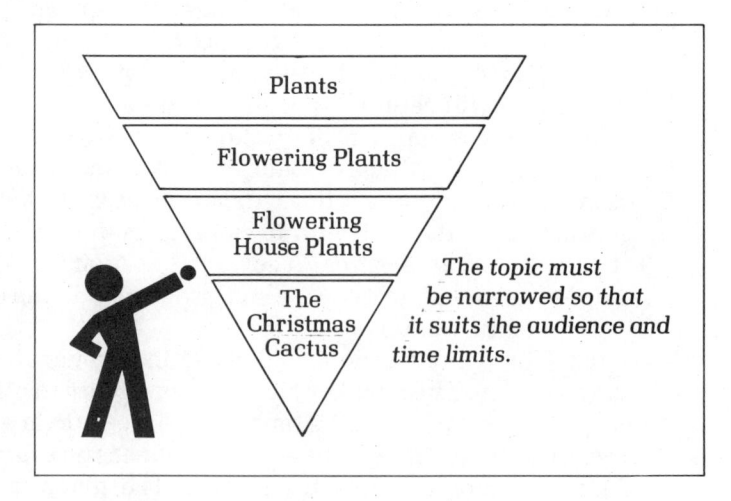

Figure 13.3. *Topic.*

In beginning topic selection it is common to be very general, but eventually the topic must be narrowed to suit the setting and especially the restraints of time limits. Another important advantage of a narrower topic is that it can reduce time in researching materials and it can help in organizing ideas. The speaker's interests and those of the audience may relate to the great leaders of World War II. Volumes have been written on this topic. To narrow such a general topic, a speaker might consider leaders of a specific nationality, of a specific campaign, or even one leader as he or she functioned in a specific situation. A good topic is like a good photograph—the image must be sharp and clear. Several specifics may be more meaningful to the listener than vague generalities. Some examples of general areas and topic statements are given below.

> *General:* Auto tune-up
> *Topic statement:* The audience will understand the importance of spark plug gap and timing as it relates to fuel economy.
>
> *General:* Shakespeare
> *Topic statement:* The audience will recognize the relevance of *Midsummer's Night Dream* to modern society.
>
> *General:* Photography
> *Topic statement:* The audience will realize the value and simplicity of recording their lives in photographs.

Gathering Material

Once a topic that fits the parameters of the setting is selected, gathering materials for preparation of the message is the next task. There are many ways to gather materials and most good speeches will include several of these. In fact, in public speaking and other communication situations, the more knowledge at the speaker's command, the more interesting the message will probably be. Some of the more common sources for gathering information are review of personal experiences; conversations with others; conducting experiments; courses taken; mass media—television, films, magazines, and newspapers; and library search.

Personal experience. Speakers will often prepare a public message based on experience they have had. In fact, many speaking invitations are made because of the knowledge and experiences for which individuals are known. As a potential source of information on a topic, it is useful for the speaker to review direct personal experiences and perceptions that relate to the topic.

Interviews. Other people are good potential sources of information in preparing a public message. Conversations with acquaintances are a good way to develop ideas and increase knowledge of the topic. Appointments can be made with people in the community to gather information from knowledgeable people. It is wise to prepare specific questions in advance of an interview. The initiator of the interview should be prepared to take responsibility for getting the kinds of information needed. (See the section in Chapter 7 that relates to the interview process.) Telephoning and writing letters requesting information are two other means of gathering information from others.

Experiments. Conducting experiments may seem too sophisticated for the public speaker. Experimentation does not always require years of dedicated work or intricate equipment, but can be quickly and easily done for some topics. Consider the topic relating to auto tune-ups given above. As an experiment, the speaker might adjust the spark plugs on several cars in several ways and compare the approximate miles per gallon for each car with the miles per gallon when spark plugs on the cars were set appropriately. Other simple experiments can often be devised to provide useful and interesting information for a public speech.

Courses. The public speaker can learn each day while taking advantage of the many learning experiences available. Information presented by instructors, news media, performers, and writers, encountered as a routine part of life, can be useful in preparing a public message. Attention to available learning opportunities can lead you to a special program on campus or in the community, to a news program or film, or to a recently published article relating to the topic. This type of information is up to date and gives credibility to the speaker.

Library. Library search probably comes first to the mind of the speaker who is gathering material for a message. It is useful and important to supplement other types of information with support from journal articles, books, and reference materials. Within a very short time, the speaker who is familiar with library use can systematically collect a list of sources relating to the topic. The speaker who does not learn efficient ways to use the library will expend much more time and energy and possibly discover nothing of relevance. And too, the skills learned to find speech materials in the library will be useful in other academic, professional, and personal quests for materials.

As speakers gather materials, their goal is to become informed about the topic. They must read widely and study carefully so that the presentation reflects thoroughness and credibility as they present information or seek to persuade. In reviewing materials, it is important to be selective and to make notes that will enable recall of important ideas, figures, statements, or examples. It is important to be aware too that all written and spoken words are not necessarily dependable. It is necessary to question each source and consider the qualifications and honesty of the author or speaker, to determine whether similar information is available from other sources, and to decide if conclusions are justified from the rationale presented. It is a good idea too to document notes with the source—author, title, date, and page numbers, for example—so that the original material can be easily obtained for future use or checking of details. It can be quite embarrassing to admit in front of an audience that the source of one's information is not available.

Ordering Material

As speakers gather material, they will often begin to see some order to it. Relationships will become apparent among the random bits of information gathered from various sources. There are several particularly useful ways to arrange material for a speech: topical, chronological, spatial, causal, comparison/contrast, and problem solution. By using one or a combination of these orders, a speech can be developed logically and will be more understandable when delivered.

Topical. When parts of the message are organized on the basis of similarities and each component is explained before going on to the next, the order is topical. If all topics are equal in weight their order makes little difference. If topics differ in their importance, ordering will be especially critical to the impact of the message on the audience. The topical order might be used in an informative speech on cats by discussing one breed before discussing another.

Chronological. If information is organized from a beginning to an ending point by numerical logic, a chronological order has been used. The ordering may be based on the steps in a process or a sequence of events. A speech to describe major events occurring in a specific period of time could be presented in chronological order from earliest to latest.

Spatial. When the development of a message is organized around a specific point of reference and follows a logical progression, the speaker has used a spatial ordering. Examples of spatial ordering are left-to-right, top-to-bottom, north-to-south, and center-to-outside. The spatial order would be particularly useful to describe a place or an object.

Causal. When the relationship of events is shown as cause and effect, a causal ordering has been used. This is particularly useful in persuasive messages when it can be shown that events can be altered by taking action or changing behavior. Causal ordering would be useful to describe the events that lead to various types of traffic accidents.

Comparison/Contrast. If a message is presented by describing similarities and differences between several related objects or events, the comparison/contrast ordering has been used. Specific examples of how the objects or events are alike and unlike should be given. An informative presentation about different brands of a product might be made using comparison and contrast of each brand on several characteristics.

Problem Solution. When a message presents an unacceptable situation and a way to improve it, the problem solution format is being used to present the message. It is important that the situation, the problem, possible solutions, and recommended solutions be included. By clearly developing a plan of action, the speaker will enable the audience to understand the reasoning and to accept the recommended solution.

As speakers consider topics and the nature of messages, it is important to keep in mind the ways the materials can be most effectively ordered. As material is gathered, yet another aid will be available for weeding out unneccessary information. And too, as the message is prepared for presentation, the pieces will tend to fall together.

Supporting Materials

As ideas for speech content begin to develop, it is wise to seek support for the message through the use of examples, statistics, and testimony. Support materials represent information from sources other than the speakers themselves. Appropriate use of support will make the message more credible. The ideas expressed will be backed up by sources other than the speakers' opinions or interpretations and will, therefore, become more believable to the audience.

Example. An example supports the message of the speech by providing a specific instance or illustration of the point being made. It adds interest to the message by allowing both the speaker and audience to use their imaginations as they seek to understand an idea. Examples should be used often in most speaking situations to clarify, provide diversity, and gain acceptance. Examples may be given without elaborate detail. The use of a list will often provide a brief example that is concise and to the point.

> *Opportunities for higher education abound in our area. There are four state-supported universities within sixty miles, two large community college systems, and at least five well-known private colleges and universities.*

More detailed examples are useful when a specific aspect of the message is difficult to understand. Detailed examples provide depth of meaning and are often complete enough to tell a story. The length of the speech has much to do with the elaboration of an example, however. The extent of detail of an example must be kept in proportion to the length of the speech. Generally, a speech that introduced one point and concluded with a detailed example would be ineffective in getting the total message to the audience.

Both brief and detailed examples may be either factual or hypothetical. A factual example is one based on an actual occurrence. It need not include every detail of what occurred; it can be edited to fit the message. A hypothetical example originates in the speaker's

©1978 United Feature Syndicate, Inc.

imagination and is recognized as a fictional example by the audience. It represents something that could exist or could have happened and is designed to help the speaker make a point. Both real and hypothetical examples are useful speaking tools. Since it actually occurred or existed, a factual example is likely to have more credibility with the audience. The hypothetical example, however, is likely to have more relevance for and be more interesting to a particular audience.

Statement: There are many ways to earn college credits without attending traditional classes.

Factual example: R. Jacobs earned thirty hours credit by passing formal examinations on course content.

Hypothetical example: Imagine a student who was able to earn credit by exam, complete independent study courses, take self-paced options of courses, and never enter the classroom.

Statistics. A second type of support material is statistics. Statistics are summaries of numbers of events, objects, or persons that are similar in some way. Speakers will often use statistics to summarize examples too numerous to mention individually. Statistics are useful for clarifying ideas and helping an audience visualize the size or extent of some occurrence. Percentages and whole numbers are probably the most commonly used statistics in general public speaking. It is probably better to round off those numbers the audience is expected to retain after one hearing. The wise speaker will use statistics sparingly, as too many are hard to comprehend and are difficult for the listener to relate to the main points of the message. Statistics should not be used to impress the audience. Speakers must be certain that they know the meaning of statistics used in their presentations. Statistics may sound impressive, but to be impressive they must relate to the message.

Testimony. A third type of supporting material is testimony. Testimony refers to information, ideas, or opinions that originate from a source other than the speaker. Few speakers find themselves the sole authority on a topic and most audiences realize that speakers take material from books, periodicals, television, films, and so forth. Such material is either presented exactly as it was originally written or is restated in the speaker's own words. The exact replication is called a quotation; the restatement, paraphrasing. The quotation is appropriate when the original source has stated something in a way that particularly fits the message. When quotations are used, they should be brief (e.g., several sentences) or the listener may be unable to comprehend the meaning intended by the speaker. Longer materials that deserve inclusion should probably be paraphrased. Paraphrasing results in better comprehension and condensation of material through paraphrasing will permit more than one source to be used. Testimony, whether a quotation or a paraphrase, is especially useful to gain acceptance for a point or to add clarification. Just be certain that credit is given to the originators of unique and specific testimony. A speaker who attempts to take credit for another's ideas will quickly lose credibility with the audience.

In using the three types of supporting materials—example, statistic, and testimony—areas of the speech requiring support must first be determined. Then, as support materials are selected, sufficient sources must be reviewed to allow selection of appropriate and credible materials. Third, support materials must be presented to make ideas clear, interesting, and acceptable to the listeners. And last, the speaker must determine if the message is too heavily dependent on one type of support or one particular source. Consideration of such factors may lead to the discovery of more appropriate examples, statistics, and testimony. Recall too the very important consideration in selecting support materials —they do not necessarily fit the message merely because they sound good.

SUMMARY

The speaker-audience situation can be differentiated from interpersonal and small group communication by the role of the listener, advance preparation of the message, and formality of the delivery. Generally, public speeches can be classified as informative—the presentation of content; persuasive—an attempt to change opinion or behavior; and entertaining—an opportunity to enjoy a message. Some speeches contain elements of all three.

The format for delivery of the speaker-audience message generally permits the originator the opportunity to plan and prepare for optimum presentation. The setting, the topic statement, and the gathering and organizing of material are important considerations in preparing the message. Setting involves the audience, time, place, and purpose for the speech. The topic statement provides the focus of the speech. Gathering materials requires search and selection of materials suitable for developing the topic statement. Organizing the materials involves arranging them in a manner that optimizes audience understanding of the message. Inclusion of supporting materials such as examples, statistics, and testimony provides credibility for the message.

CHAPTER 14

Delivering the Speaker-Audience Message

Once the topic has been researched, materials have been gathered and ordered, and adequate support has been developed, the speaker's efforts must turn to delivery of the message. It is very useful to prepare a speaking outline that includes all the parts necessary to make an effective presentation. After the material is organized in outline format, the presentation mode must be selected, visual aids prepared if appropriate, and rehearsal must begin. When a well-planned speech is developed around an appropriate outline and rehearsed until it is adequately learned, a speaker's success is only a matter of having a positive attitude about the experience.

Organizing the Message

Most speeches are presented in three parts: the introduction, the body, and the conclusion. In very simple terms, the audience is first told what they will be told, then they are told, and finally they are told again what they were told. To prepare the message, it is suggested that the body be developed before the introduction and the conclusion.

Body

The body of the speech is composed of statements of the main points and supporting materials. A good speech states a few ideas well. Regardless of the length of the speech, two to four main ideas are usually sufficient. Given more time for presentation, it is better to develop the main points in more depth or with more supporting material than to increase the number of points to be made. Close attention must be paid to the wording of the main points. They must be concise and clear enough for the audience to understand, and they must be vivid enough to make the audience remember them. It is useful to make the listeners feel that each main point applies to them in some way; that is, to help the listeners identify with the message. If the topic relates to social security, for example, it would be inappropriate to address a group of young adults in the manner a group of retirees would be addressed. Last, as the main ideas are stated, it is often suggested that a similar sentence structure (i.e., similar wording) be used for each so that the listener will readily perceive the progression from main point to main point.

Once the main ideas are stated and ordered they must be supported. A message is more likely to be remembered if the important points are reinforced by illustrative support materials. When the speech is on a topic the audience finds generally acceptable, examples in the form of illustrations, personal experiences, and comparisons will be most useful for lending support. There will be less need for testimony and statistics. When the audience is totally unfamiliar with, or against the message to be presented, examples, testimony, and statistics will all prove useful. The important point to remember in developing the body of a speech is to limit main points to two to four and to provide as much supporting material as time permits.

Introduction

Once main points and support materials are determined, the next step is to develop an introduction to capture the attention of the audience. The introduction is a lead-in to the message. Its purpose is to capture the undivided attention of the audience, to explain exactly what the speech will be about, to point out the value of the message, and to preview the main points.

Gaining the attention of the audience is perhaps the most difficult of the four purposes of the introduction to accomplish. Personal experiences are often good for gaining attention. For example, in requesting funds for charity, the speaker might reveal personal help received from that charity. Humorous stories are effective if they fit the audience and the occasion, are relevant to the material, and set the desired tone. Illustrations such as stories, pictures, or slides, can be used to gain attention if they create an image of the topic presented. A story that begins, "Picture yourself on a dark road on a rainy night with a flat tire..." makes the audience want to know what will happen next.

Speakers often use rhetorical questions to gain attention. These are questions that create interest but have no expected response from the speaker or audience. The speaker might begin by asking, "What will you do when our sources of energy are depleted?" The purpose of a rhetorical question is to get the audience thinking, to make the audience curious, to involve the audience, and often to draw the audience closer to the viewpoint held by the speaker. A direct question is one that the audience is expected to answer. A speaker will sometimes gain attention by eliciting brief responses from the audience. This technique can be used to create audience involvement with the message and to gear the message more directly to audience needs and interests. When time is limited, however, the direct question can occupy much more time than the speaker intends.

Unusual or dramatic devices gain attention through the element of shock. The speaker who uses such devices must be careful not to overshadow the intended purpose of the speech. The objective of the speech will be lost if the audience remembers only the drama and forgets the message. A last suggestion for gaining attention is to use quotations by famous people. It is important that quotations be read slowly, and that important words and ideas be stressed. Whatever the attention-getting device, its selection must be based on the audience, the message, and the setting.

A speech will contain only one central idea, and it can be derived from the topic objective or statement. The audience should never have to guess the intent of a speech; it should be easily understood and immediately obvious. To point out the value of the message, a statement of the specific relevance of the message to the audience is a very effective device. It is necessary to make the audience feel that the message is important to them in some way. The preview of main points can serve to reveal what will be emphasized in the body, and often serves as an effective transition from introduction to body of the speech.

Conclusion

The conclusion is as important as the body and introduction. Since the last thing said by the speaker may be remembered the longest, a strong and effective conclusion is needed. The purpose of the conclusion is to provide a brief summary or reminder of the main points, to reemphasize the value of the message, and to close the speech with a meaningful sentence that leaves the listener convinced that the message was worth hearing. It is often useful to include parts of the introduction in the conclusion. Many of the introductory techniques, like humorous stories, personal references, examples, and quotations can be used to end the speech. If the conclusion has been effective there will be no need to tell the audience that the speech is over. If the speech has been effective, you will know that the audience was sincerely pleased to have heard your message.

The introduction and conclusion of the speech are essential components of an effective presentation. It is unwise to prepare only the body with the idea that the introduction and conclusion can be developed as you begin and end the actual presentation. Once the three parts of the message have been prepared it is useful to outline the speech. The following outline is a very general format that could be used in most speaker-audience situations.

```
            I. Introduction of the Speech
               A. Gain attention of the audience.
               B. State the purpose of the speech.
               C. Relate the speech to the audience.
               D. Preview the main points.

           II. Body of the Speech
               A. Main Idea
                  1. Supporting Material
                  2. Supporting Material
                  3. Etc.
               B. Main Idea
                  1. Supporting Material
                  2. Supporting Material
                  3. Etc.
               C. Main Idea (Optional)
                  1. Supporting Material
                  2. Supporting Material
                  3. Etc.
               D. Main Idea (Optional)
                  1. Supporting Material
                  2. Supporting Material
                  3. Etc.

          III. Conclusion of the Speech
               A. Summarize Main Ideas
               B. Emphasize Value of Message
               C. Close the Speech
```

Figure 14.1. *Outline of speech.*

Delivering the Message

All speakers feel some anxiety as the time draws near for the presentation of their messages. The experienced speaker has learned, however, that preparation is the key to minimizing the anxiety felt prior to speaking, to maximizing the enjoyment of making the presentation, and to ensuring a feeling of satisfaction for a job well done. In preparing to present a speech, consideration of modes of delivery, use of visual aids, and rehearsing the message are important.

Modes of Presentation

There are four basic modes of presentation available to the speaker in the speaker-audience situation: impromptu, extemporaneous, manuscript, and memorized. They progress from little or no time in preparation to the completely memorized presentation. The situation and skill of the speaker determine the mode to be used. A beginner of average skill does well to plan ahead for preparation and rehearsal time.

Impromptu. In the impromptu mode, the speaker must rely on knowledge acquired from past study or experience. There is little or no preparation time and ideas are organized as the speaker communicates to the audience. When speakers become adept at impromptu speaking, their skill can be used to advantage in answering questions or volunteering ideas. Impromptu speaking allows spontaneous and natural expression that can effectively reveal sincere feelings. When someone has been called upon to "say a few words," an impromptu speech has been requested.

Extemporaneous. Extemporaneous speaking is used more often than impromptu speaking because it allows a communicator time to prepare the presentation. The speaker can prepare an outline or notes from research on the topic. Advantages of extemporaneous speaking are the following: (1) notes can be used to provide security to the speaker during the presentation; (2) information needed to express the central idea can be clarified; (3) information to support the main points can be documented; and (4) because of practice with the outline or notes, the speaker can communicate more directly and spontaneously than if a script is read or a memorized speech is repeated. Disadvantages of extemporaneous speaking are the following: (1) there is generally no record of what has been said; (2) the speaker can lose track of the flow of thoughts and appear to ramble; and (3) the speaker who has not adequately rehearsed may refer too frequently to notes or even forget what to say.

Manuscript. In the manuscript mode of delivery the material is written out. This offers the advantages of providing a complete record of what has been said and of the selection of language to express the message exactly. The disadvantage of the manuscript mode is the lack of interaction, through frequent eye contact, of the speaker with the audience. And too, it requires the ability to read effectively from the written page. The speaker must attempt to be spontaneous and energetic while reading. In the manuscript mode it is especially important that the speaker employ vocal variety, gestures, and eye contact to communicate with the listeners. The manuscript mode is especially appropriate when many exact quotations are to be used. The president of the United States uses this mode frequently because his words must of necessity be very carefully chosen.

Type	Preparation	Verbatim
1. Impromptu	No	No
2. Extemporaneous	Yes	No
3. Manuscript	Yes	Yes
4. Memorized	Yes	Yes

Figure 14.2. *Modes of presentation.*

Memorized. The speaker using the memorization mode completes the research and writing and then memorizes the speech. This is probably the most difficult and least used mode because a communicator knows that forgetting any one idea will destroy the entire speech. In the extemporaneous and manuscript modes, the speaker has something to rely on—in the memorized mode, only memory. Often speakers are so preoccupied with what will come next that they fail to communicate and totally destroy the objective of the message. An advantage of the mode, however, is that the speaker is well rehearsed and can maintain good eye contact with the audience. Other advantages are the use of exact wordings, quotations, and examples, and exact timing of the length of delivery. For effective delivery a memorized speech should appear to be an extemporaneous speech delivered without notes. This results in a more natural speaker who is better able to relate to the audience.

Overall, the best mode of speech delivery is the extemporaneous. The speaker has thoroughly researched the topic and prepared the message but is able to be flexible. Good eye contact can be maintained and a conversational manner can be used for delivery. More skilled extemporaneous speakers are able to react to the nonverbal messages of the audience. The extemporaneous message involves memorized ideas, not memorized words. In short extemporaneous speeches, it is best to avoid using any notes at all; in longer speeches, a short outline sequencing the ideas can be used. Eventually, speakers usually gain confidence using this mode and feel free to give up lengthy note cards that seem so essential at first.

Visual Aids

The delivery of a speech can often be enhanced by using visual aids. Visual aids are materials such as charts, models, films, or even the chalkboard. They permit the listener to see as well as hear and thereby increase understanding of the message. Too often, speakers fail to use a visual aid to clarify points and their impact is lessened.

Speakers themselves are possible visual aids. They can use movement and dress to help the audience understand the message more clearly. Through gestures and movements the speaker can demonstrate

CHAPTER 14   Delivering the Speaker-Audience Message   319

the size and shape of objects, or the correct way to swing a tennis racket. Using dress to enhance the verbal message, a speaker might demonstrate proper attire for disco dancing or skiing in extremely cold weather. Using themselves as visual aids is limited only by the creativity of the speakers.

Charts.   Probably the most widely used visual aid for smaller audiences is the chart, graph, sketch, drawing, or picture displayed on a stand or easel. It has the advantage of being easy to prepare and set up. It does require some practice, however. It is quite easy, when several are used, to mix them up and fumble to find the appropriate image. Its major disadvantage can be the difficulty the audience sometimes has in seeing it. If the image is too small, all the apologies the speaker can render are useless. Also, it is helpful to the audience to print or draw with dark inks on very light backgrounds, and to place the image so that it is completely still during viewing.

Screen.   For larger audiences the same effect can be achieved by using overhead and opaque projectors to show the image on a screen. The overhead projector can be used with charts, graphs, sketches, or drawings placed on a transparent film. Generally the image is created on a sheet of 8½-by-11 inch paper and transferred to the "transparency" by using a special piece of easily operated equipment. The opaque projector can be used with pictures or charts without transfer to the special film. Although the overhead requires more preparation than the opaque projector, it is much easier to use during the presentation. Both have the disadvantage of requiring bulky equipment and the possibility of equipment failure.

Chalkboard. The chalkboard is a medium that is generally available to most speakers. In fact, it may suffer from excessive and improper use. Too often speakers will turn their backs to their audiences and spend several minutes writing or drawing on the board. To use the chalkboard effectively, the speaker must develop a style of maintaining eye contact and message delivery with the audience while briefly jotting down notes or diagrams. The right-handed speaker should assume a sideways stance to the left of the writing area and maintain eye contact and voice projection by looking over the right shoulder. It may be a better strategy to arrive early, prepare the chalkboard, and cover the written message until the appropriate moment in the presentation. Again, audience size will affect the visibility of the chalkboard message.

Models. Models and objects are sometimes useful visual aids. They are a necessity for many demonstration speeches. If the object itself is too large to be brought before the audience, the use of a model can overcome this difficulty. A model, however, may be difficult and time consuming to create. Smaller audiences can often benefit from close examination of the object. For larger audiences, the speaker again has the difficulty of making certain that the entire group can see the object or model.

Handouts. Handouts, or materials the audience receives and can take with them, are often useful. Handouts can include materials prepared by the speaker or materials the speaker is able to collect from agencies and businesses. Each member of the audience should receive a copy of the materials. To keep the audience from reading handouts while the message is being delivered, they should not be distributed until speech content makes reference to them. If the audience is larger than anticipated, the speaker will often be embarrassed by two few hand outs. If the audience is much smaller than anticipated, there may be no use for possibly costly materials. The speaker may wish to have back-up posters or transparencies if the size of the audience is an unknown.

Film. Slides, filmstrips, movies, and videotapes are another category of visual aid that speakers will sometimes use to complement verbal messages. These media have in common the need for projection equipment, a darkened room for viewing, and possible breakdown during use. Most visuals of this type will be accompanied by audio materials. They lend a very professional tone to a presentation but are often quite expensive and lengthy. For the average speaker, slides with personal narration will be the most readily available of the visual aids in this category.

Any point that can be made clearer by the use of a visual aid should probably not be made without one. The visual aid, however, should be carefully prepared in advance. There are few things more irritating to an audience than a speaker who does not know how to run equipment, has to shuffle through a stack of posters, or addresses the chalkboard instead of the audience. The list below outlines some important considerations for using visual aids in a speaker-audience situation.

1. Keep the aid simple—do not confuse yourself or your audience.
2. Use two or more simple aids rather than one complicated aid.
3. Make the visual aid twice as large as seems necessary.
4. If using more than one visual aid, number them consecutively.
5. Place the viewing point of the visual aid in the center of the audience's viewing area.
6. Keep the aid at the eye level, or slightly higher, of the audience.
7. Do not block the view of the aid by standing between it and the listener.
8. When showing visual aids consecutively, allow time for the audience to view each one completely.
9. Look at the aid only when making specific reference to it.
10. Reveal the aid at the specific time when it coincides with the speech content.

The audience will benefit from good visual aids. The speaker will benefit too, since they serve as reminders of what should be said and help relieve tension.

Rehearsal

By now it should be obvious that preparation is the key to a successful speaker-audience presentation. Preparation includes rehearsal or practice in delivering the message. Practice does not mean merely reading your outline several times or memorizing your main points. It means standing up and speaking the message and using the gestures and visual aids just as if there were an audience assembled. A good method for rehearsing the extemporaneous speech is given below.

1. Complete your outline of introduction, main points, supporting materials, and conclusion.
2. Study the outline until you have no problem remembering the sequence of ideas.
3. Once the outline is committed to memory, begin presenting the speech to some friendly objects in your surroundings. Use your visual aids.
4. Go over and over those areas that cause you problems.

5. Once the problems are overcome, find some friendly volunteers (e.g. friends, family) to listen to your performance. Use your visual aids.
6. If you have the opportunity, practice your delivery in the room where the actual presentation will be made.
7. As you become more and more adept at delivering the message, begin concentrating less on the message itself and more on the audience.

As speakers practice their extemporaneous speeches, they should vary the words used to express the message. Any major changes in message should be made early in practice. A speaker who is involved with the message will be more likely to involve the listeners. Practicing vocal variety will aid audience involvement. If an emotional point is being made the speaker's voice should reflect this. If a point needs to be made emphatically, the speaker's voice should be louder and more abrupt. Above all, practice in changing rate, pitch, and inflection is important to develop a good delivery of the message. A speaker should be sure that words can be distinctly and easily understood without making the presentation appear memorized by speaking in a continuous monotone. A conversational style should be developed; gestures and movements should be natural. Members of the audience must feel that they are being spoken to directly.

What about stage fright? Nearly all speakers experience stage fright to some extent, but find that they can successfully present a speech. In fact, as speaking experiences increase, the ability to handle the anxiety increases until many people find speaking to an audience enjoyable. Early in speaking experiences, however, it is hard to accept the idea that one can do an adequate job of presenting a message to an audience. It is imperative to prepare, to rehearse, and to think about the satisfactions and rewards the experience will bring. In fact, successes are likely to result in the seeking out of speaking opportunities!

SUMMARY

There is more to speaker-audience communication than knowing a subject and/or pulling materials together. The information, thoughts, and ideas must be arranged in an organized manner and then delivered in the most effective way. We have all experienced the discomfort of listening to an "expert" who did not deliver the message in a meaningful way. We might forgive such individuals by saying, "he is a well-known scientist," or "she is a learned scholar." Most of us, however, are not so renowned and simply make a poor impression when we fail to prepare adequately to deliver a speaker-audience message.

Nearly all speaker-audience messages can be effectively organized by using the format of introduction, body, and conclusion. It is best to limit the body of the message to two to four main points and expand the message by incorporating varied and appropriate supporting materials. Mode of delivery—impromptu, extemporaneous, manuscript, or memorized—must be considered in preparing to present the message. Extemporaneous is generally the best approach since it requires preparation but allows for flexibility. Visual aids like charts, models, and films are helpful in presenting some aspects of the speaker-audience message. They must be selected to complement, not detract from the message. Last, in preparing to deliver a speech, rehearsal is important to help the speaker gain confidence and project a positive self-image.

CHAPTER 15

Informative Speaking

An important purpose of communication is to collect and provide information. When the giving of information that will be useful to the listener becomes the primary purpose of a speaker, the resulting speech may be classified as informative. People like to know things and they are curious. It is the fun of telling people something they do not know that makes informative speeches popular.

Part of the task in developing an informative message depends on the ability to avoid vague, ambiguous, misleading, or unproved statements, and to use examples, illustrations, statistics, quotations, and paraphrasing to support what is said. Care must be taken to avoid statements of feelings and opinions. Learning to select and present relevant information is a valuable skill to acquire. The aim of an informative speaker should be to add to the knowledge of the listeners, to give them useful information. The informative speaker must explain and clarify material that is vital to the understanding of the topic. The information must be accurate, objective, and clear. The response from the listeners should be one of understanding and interest in what was said.

Some authors feel that all speeches include some exchange of information, whether they are labeled informative, persuasive, or entertaining. The persuasive speech includes information as background to gain listener acceptance; the entertaining speech adds information to the purpose of passing time pleasantly. The distinction then between an informative speech and the transfer of information lies in the purpose of the message. The purpose of an informative speech is to have the listener receive, comprehend, and retain the message. Clarity and the creation of interest while providing useful information should be the goals of the speaker. There is no question of listener acceptance and no attempt to convince or stimulate the listener. When the listener must be convinced or stimulated to accept the message and act on it, the speech is persuasive in purpose even though it includes information. If the informative message is not retained but is merely a pleasant means of passing time, the message would more likely be classified as entertaining. An informative speech will have a focus and provide valuable information to be retained and used by the listener.

In developing informative speeches, many skills discussed in the previous chapters will be needed. To expand further the ability to deliver effective informative speeches, it is useful to become familiar with several specific types of informative messages, some special considerations in developing informative messages, and some evaluation criteria to apply to informative messages. An example of an informative speech will be provided to demonstrate concepts presented earlier in the chapter.

Types of Informative Messages

Although informative messages have been discussed as one of three types of speeches, achieving the goal of an informative speech, that is, increasing useful knowledge, can be fulfilled in several ways. Consideration of the various ways to inform an audience may give added direction to the preparation of informative messages. There are four common ways to approach an informative speaking situation: (1) description, (2) demonstration, (3) definition, and (4) reporting. As these are discussed, it should become obvious that there is much overlap between categories and that a single speech could easily include several of the four types.

1. Description
2. Demonstration
3. Definition
4. Reporting

Figure 15.1. *Types of informative messages.*

Description

Description is common in everyday conversation and reading. As listeners learn about the characteristics of a place, an object, an organization, or a process, they seek to recreate it in their imaginations. It is the vividness of details that determines how closely the listeners' mental images match the actual place, object, organization, or process. In an informative speech that emphasizes description, it is particularly important to determine the audience's familiarity with the topic. The audience that has greater experience will benefit more from specific details, whereas the audience with less experience requires more general information.

In describing a place, an object, an organization, or a process, the speaker might use personal observations to create the description, or rely on other sources to create an image that is then recreated for an audience. The National Gallery of Art in Washington, D.C., a famous Van Gogh painting, the Association for Patrons of the Gallery, or the best way to tour a museum might provide informative speaking topics for one who has been to the museum, seen the painting, supported the organization of patrons, and made the tour, as well as one who used library search, interviews, and other sources to create an image for the listener. The following is a list of some informative speaking topics that rely on description.

>The varied terrain of the state of Texas
>America's palace—a tour of the Biltmore mansion
>My day at Disney World
>The unique characteristics of the steel-belted tire
>The teeth of the shark
>The sculpture of Henry Moore
>The Society for the Prevention of Cruelty to Animals
>How your heart and lungs work together
>Applying for financial aid in college
>Creating an old-fashioned Christmas

Demonstration

When the object or process can be shown directly to the audience the need to create verbal images is significantly reduced. A speech that informs by showing or by doing is a demonstration. The purpose of the spoken message is to introduce and clarify the demonstration. Demonstrations are often used in advertisements for products or to teach skills in fields like cooking, athletics, and carpentry. The demonstration may be used in more creative ways as well. For example, it might be used to reveal the absurdity of a process or to prove the correctness of an unlikely idea. The demonstration is especially effective for topics that would be difficult or impossible to describe, for audiences that especially benefit from visual stimuli, or when a special impact needs to be made. Some examples of demonstration topics are given below.

>The New Magic Cook 21-in-1 kitchen gadget
>An inside look at a Swiss watch
>The fine design of American silver
>How to tune your guitar
>The Heimlich Reflex—saving lives
>Anyone can pound a nail
>You don't think your pocket could be picked?
>Recognizing a counterfeit twenty
>What is a hot dog really made from?
>How to fix your hair for that special party

Definition

Definition, of course, is explanation of the meaning of a word. Many definitions include descriptions of places, objects, or processes. To distinguish the definition speech from the descriptive speech, it is confined to the definitions of ideas—concepts and constructs. Concepts and constructs are intangible and cannot be seen or heard. They are experienced. Examples of such ideas would include love, trust, fear, intelligence, sophistication, and insecurity. There are many observable behaviors associated with such constructs. A hug is a behavior associated with love, but a hug in itself is not love. We use the observable behaviors to help define the concept or construct. There are concepts and constructs associated with specific fields as well as human experiences. Examples would include gravity, refraction, and inertia. Such ideas are generally operationally defined, that is, defined in terms of events or behaviors, so that people who use the words will attach similar meaning to them. Informative speeches will often provide such operational definitions of ideas so that an audience will acquire a better and more useful understanding of a particular concept or construct. Some examples of informative speeches to define are listed below.

      The meaning of self-esteem
      Reality versus fantasy
      Intimacy versus isolation
      Photosynthesis—the key to life

A better life through complex numbers
State and trait anxiety
Who are our neighbors?
Empathy—can you recognize it?
What is articulation in speaking?
Implications of cognitive style and learning

Reporting

The fourth type of informative speech is reporting. Reporting should be viewed as a very objective process. The speaker is, in a way, the intermediary between an event and the telling of an event. A report should be based on the direct relay of an observation from one source to an audience. Judgment and critical analysis, if they occur at all, are left to the listener. The subject might be a personal experience; a problem or critical issue; or a book, movie, or exhibit, as well as specific occurrences.

Many topics appropriate for the informative report could easily become persuasive topics. If the speaker takes a position on one side of an issue rather than gives a balanced treatment of all sides, the speech purpose becomes persuasive. In considering nuclear power plants, for example, an informative speaker would do nothing to convince the audience to favor or disfavor the issue. Some examples of informative speeches to report are given below.

My day as an elementary school volunteer
An experience—twenty-four hours of blindness
Ways to secure your home or apartment
Apartment dwellers versus absentee landlords
Eliminating smallpox from the face of the earth
The films of Sylvester Stallone
The King Tut exhibit in retrospect
Jimmy Who? His rise to power
Tornadoes, hurricanes, and blizzards of 1978
Progressive country music appeals to all

Informative speaking can be fun and a learning experience for speaker as well as listener. Remember, sharing useful knowledge is the purpose. An informative speech makes no attempt to change the listener's attitudes, values, or behaviors. The message should be so neutral that listener acceptance is of no concern to the speaker.

Developing the Informative Speech

Audience Needs

In informative speaking, the prior knowledge of the listener is extremely important in formulating the message. The speaker must consider the audience's present knowledge of the topic so that this knowledge can be adequately built on. Knowledge of special audience interests is helpful in selecting supporting materials. Too often the audience fails to understand a message because of inadequate background, or becomes bored with the message because of its simplicity. Audiences may be generally informed on the topic, basically uninformed, or a combination of informed and uninformed. The last, of course, is the most difficult of the three for which to prepare. Because the speaker-audience setting allows little opportunity to determine audience needs at the time of presentation, investigation of audience characteristics must be done prior to preparation of the message.

Spending time on elementary generalities wastes both speaker and listener time if the audience is generally well informed on a topic. To provide adequate and appropriate stimuli for the knowledgeable listener, it is suggested that the speaker present new information, introduce a different facet of the subject, or discuss it in relation to a similar area. The knowledgeable listener will appreciate a presentation that builds on current understanding yet stimulates further thinking.

The uninformed listener should not be classified as stupid. There are many topics of which we all have little knowledge. A good informative speech can be a stimulus in creating new interests. The uninformed listener requires the basics, the fundamentals, the elementary. It is wise to limit coverage of the topic to a narrow aspect and use repetition to reinforce learning. The most important thing for the speaker to avoid is the demonstration of a superior attitude or a tendency to talk down to the audience.

The audience with a mix of informed and uninformed listeners is the most difficult for which to prepare. The message must include the generalities as well as the specifics. The correct balance is challenging but difficult to achieve. The speaker can subtly introduce the basics in the guise of a review as a means of ensuring that all listeners have a common background. The specifics might be introduced as unusual applications or interesting asides. However the goals are accomplished, the message must be prepared in a positive way so that all listeners find satisfaction in receiving the content.

Common Learning Principles

Much has been done in recent years to discover ways to facilitate human learning. An informative speaker is a teacher whose goal is to provide the opportunity for acquisition of information. Some general principles of effective teaching are briefly listed below.

1. Make the atmosphere pleasant. If the experience is enjoyable the learner will be more likely to pay attention than to drift away with seemingly more interesting private thoughts.
2. Open the presentation with an attempt to motivate the learner. Unless the learner's attention is caught, most of the message will be lost. Continue relating the message to the learner's needs

and interests. Help the message fit into an already established area of the learner's mind.
3. Information can be more readily acquired when it is presented in an organized manner. It has been discovered that learners themselves will attempt to organize material that is presented in an unorganized fashion. The impact of an informative speech will be greater if the organization is provided by the speaker. Review the ways of ordering material (i.e., topical, comparison/contrast) presented in Chapter 13.
4. Teach the principle underlying your message. Do not merely cite many specific examples. The principle may appear as one main idea of the informative speech and some of the specifics as supporting details. The demonstration speech dealing with the twenty-one-function cooking aid might be presented under principles of blending, chopping, grinding, and slicing, with the twenty-one functions as specific examples of each.
5. Introduce information in small amounts. The human mind needs time to deal with facts and figures and cannot assimilate too much at one time.
6. Use repetition to help the learner retain relevant information. The more often a thing is heard, the more likely it is that it will be remembered. In speaker-audience communication, it is suggested that the central idea be repeated at least three times—in the introduction, body, and conclusion.

These six points sound simple but form the basis for much of the information-giving aspects of public speaking.

Methods of Explanation

Speakers generally develop quite detailed knowledge of their informative speaking topics. Their search for materials is often a learning experience. Because of their familiarity, they sometimes prepare their messages without considering the way explanations familiar to them will sound to the listener. In other words, the speaker will generally have a more sophisticated command of the topic than the audience. To be certain the audience grasps the meaning of the message, the informative speaker must clearly explain words and phrases essential to the message.

Definition is the most common method of explaining words and phrases. The purpose of the definition for clarification is to explain complex words and phrases in terms the audience is more likely to understand. The definition should be brief, probably a single sentence, and should be stated in the speaker's own words (i.e., not the dictionary's words). Listener comprehension will be decreased considerably if the audience misses key points because of unfamiliarity with the terms used. It is particularly important to clarify complex or technical terms and terms that have different meanings depending on usage. An example of a definition to clarify content is given below.

> A *greenhorn* is an inexperienced person who can be easily fooled into believing something that is untrue.

Several other ways to clarify the meaning of speech content are expressed in the following list.

1. Synonym—A synonym is a word that has basically the same meaning as another word. *Infuriate* and *enrage* are synonyms.
2. Antonym—An antonym is a word that has basically the opposite meaning as another word. *Infuriate* and *soothe* are antonyms.
3. Analogy—Analogy clarifies an unfamiliar word or phrase by comparing it to something that is familiar. Remember the analogy used in an earlier chapter to describe an effective speech? *An effective speech is like a clearly focused photograph.* Analogies are either literal or figurative. A literal analogy is a comparison of things in the same categories. *Polyester carpeting has many of the qualities long valued in wool carpeting.* Figurative analogies compare things in different categories and, therefore, provide some of the more creative visual images. *That movie was as exciting as watching two snails run a mile.*
4. Negation—Negation means explanation by describing what the word or phrase does not mean. *Rehearsal of your speech does not mean memorizing the outline.* (Remember?)
5. Classification—Classification relates the word or phrase to other words or phrases that form a more general set. *An informative speech is one kind of speaker-audience message.*
6. Rephrasing—Rephrasing means stating the same thing in different words. It offers the listener several ways of relating one idea to another idea with which they have had prior experience and it serves as reinforcement just as repetition does. It can be boring, however, if the speaker overuses it. Consider the following two sentences as acceptable examples of rephrasing. *Supporting materials add credibility to your message. When you use examples, statistics, and testimony, what you have to say will be more readily accepted by your audience.*

During preparation and rehearsal of an informative speech, it is important to pay attention to the words and phrases used. Speakers are wise to ask themselves if they would have understood the words and phrases before they developed the message, and to ask their friendly listeners during rehearsal to point out difficult words and phrases. To confuse in an informative message is certainly not to impress.

Evaluation of Informative Speeches

Many times listeners accept a message and give little, if any, thought to the quality of the message. Some speakers secretly hope that their listeners are among that group of people that fails to consider the worth of the message. Well-educated persons, however, should develop skills that enable them to evaluate activities in which they participate, and they should use credible evaluations received from others as a means of personal improvement.

There are a number of criteria or points to consider in evaluating an informative speech. Many relate to vocal and physical delivery and personal qualities of the speaker. These are important in all speaking situations. Other criteria relate to the general speaking outline with appropriately prepared introduction, body, and conclusion. Criteria of major importance in considering informative speeches are listed and described below.

1. Does the message provide the listener with useful information?
2. Does the message present the information in a nonbiased way? That is, was the speech informative, *not* persuasive?
3. Was the supporting material relevant to the main points?
4. Did the supporting materials help to maintain the listener's interest in and attention to the message?
5. Was the supporting material adequate enough to establish listener confidence?
6. Were visual aids used where appropriate?
7. Were visual aids of acceptable quality?
8. Was repetition used sufficiently to reinforce the main points?
9. Did the message deal with one central idea?
10. Did the message include two to four main ideas?

These criteria should be applied to informative messages as final preparation is completed. They can be applied while listening to others' informative messages. Consider them while reviewing the following example of an informative speech and the example of an evaluation form for informative speeches.

Example of Informative Speech

A well-written informative speech, "The Mystery of Dreams," is provided for review. The example is presented along with the general speaking outline. Read the example carefully while considering each component and the informative, unpersuasive nature of the message.

An Informative Speech

The Mystery of Dreams

Outline	*Script*
I. Introduction	
A. Opening statement to gain attention	For years, small groups of dedicated individuals have tried to unravel the mysteries of the dream world. One of the most intriguing questions studied by these researchers is, "What causes dreams?"
B. Connecting statement	Views held about the nature of dreams have differed vastly throughout the centuries and through various cultures.
C. Statement of main purpose	I plan to inform you about dreams and their interpretation.
D. Preview of first main point	...to describe the nature of dreams.
E. Preview of second main point	...to talk to you about Sigmund Freud's studies on the interpretation of dreams.
F. Preview of third main point	...and finally, to introduce three approaches to understanding dreams.
G. Relate speech to audience	The study of dreams can be a fascinating subject and one that contributes to a greater understanding of self.
II. Body	
A. Statement of first major division	Whether one believes that dreams are real experiences in which we leave our bodies during sleep, or whether one thinks dreams are inspired by God or by evil spirits, one idea is not controversial: the view that all dreams are meaningful and significant.
1. Support	Meaningful because they contain a message which can be understood if one has the key for its translation. Significant because we do not dream of anything that is trifling.
2. Support	To contribute to an understanding of the nature of dreams, something must be said about the "condition of sleep" and the effect of this condition on our mental activity. Erich Fromm, the author of *The Forgotten Language*, describes sleep as "a condition of chemical regeneration of the organism; energy is restored

	while no action takes place and even sensory perception is almost entirely shut off." Psychologically, sleep suspends the main functional characteristic of waking life: man's reacting toward reality by perception and action. This difference between the biological functions of waking and sleeping is, in fact, a difference between two states of existence.
B. Statement of second major division	Sigmund Freud's interpretation of dreams is the earliest, the best known, and the most significant contribution of modern science to dream interpretation.
1. Support	Freud's dream interpretation is based on the same principle as his psychological theory: the concept that we can have strivings and feelings and wishes which motivate our actions and yet we have no awareness of them. He called this "unconscious," and by this he meant that not only are we not aware of them, but also that a powerful "censor" protects us from becoming aware of them.
2. Support	A greater understanding of the unconscious led Freud to a discovery which shed light on normal behavior. It permitted him to explain an error like forgetting or a slip-of-the-tongue which had puzzled many observers, and for which no explanation had been found. This phenomenon of suddenly not being able to remember something was studied very carefully by Freud. We would forget maybe because the subject reminded us of some fear, anger, or other emotion. As Nietzsche once said, "My memory says I could not have done it. My memory yields."
3. Support	Freud thus came to the assumption that the essence of dreams is the hallucinatory fulfillment of irrational wishes; their function is the preserving of sleep. This explanation is understood more easily in those instances where the desire is

		not irrational and where the dream is not distorted, as is the case with the average dream, according to Freud.
4.	Support	For example, assume that someone has eaten a very salty meal before going to sleep and feels very thirsty during the night. He may dream that he is in search of water, finds a well and drinks great quantities of the water. Instead of waking from his sleep to satisfy his thirst, he gives himself hallucinatory satisfaction by the fantasy of drinking water and that permits him to go on sleeping.
C.	Statement of third division	There are three approaches useful to consider in attempting to understand dreams.
1.	Support	The first approach suggests that all dreams are expressions of the irrational and asocial nature of man.
2.	Support	The second approach suggests that dreams are revelations of unconscious wisdom, transcending the individual.
3.	Support	The third approach suggests that dreams express any kind of mental activity and are expressive of our irrational strivings as well as of our reason and morality; they express both the worst and best of ourselves.
4.	Support	These three theories are by no means recent. A brief survey of the history of dream interpretation shows that the recent controversy about the meaning of dreams contains discussions which have been going on for at least the past three thousand years.
III. Conclusion		
A.	Summary	In summary, you have heard briefly about dreams and their interpretation, and, also, about the research that has gone into dreams and dream interpretation. Finally, you heard about three approaches to understanding dreams.
B.	Importance of message	Dreams and their interpretation are still very controversial subjects. If

C.	Transition statement	one can find the time, dreams can be a most fascinating subject to study and one that relates personally to every one of us. In closing, I would like to leave each of you with the following thoughts.
D.	Refers back to introduction	How real are dreams?
E.	Closing statement	How far does our unconscious mind go?

Reference sources:
1. *The Interpretation of Dreams,* by William Stekel, M.D.
2. *The Forgotten Language,* by Erich Fromm.
3. *Some Must Watch Some Must Sleep,* by William C. Dement.

Example of Evaluation Form

The evaluation form following this chapter includes many criteria that audiences of informative speeches might use to judge the worth of messages they hear. Speakers who are planning informative messages might use the form as a checklist to evaluate their own messages. An instructor could use the form or a modification of the form to provide feedback to student speakers.

SUMMARY

An informative speech has the specific purpose of providing the listener with information. Because of the enjoyment and excitement associated with sharing knowledge, informative speeches are very popular. To inform requires clear and vivid description as material is explained and clarified. There are several types of informative messages: description, demonstration, definition, and reporting. Audience needs are important considerations in developing informative messages at the appropriate level of difficulty. Listeners must not be bored by a message that they have often heard before, or confused by a message that assumes prior experience with the topic. A speech becomes persuasive when a speaker shares feelings and opinion in an attempt to change the listener's behavior.

Evaluation Form for Informative Speeches

I. Introduction
   - _____ Attention-getting device
   - _____ Statement of central idea
   - _____ Preview of main points
   - _____ Importance of message

II. Body
   - _____ Statements of two to four main points
   - _____ Relevant supporting materials
   - _____ Interesting supporting materials
   - _____ Adequate supporting materials

III. Conclusion
   - _____ Summary of main points
   - _____ Importance of message
   - _____ Strong and/or novel ending

IV. Visual aids
   - _____ Appropriateness of aids
   - _____ Ability to use aids
   - _____ Quality of aids

V. Presentation
   - _____ Useful information
   - _____ Informative, not persuasive
   - _____ Sufficient repetition
   - _____ Adequate transition between parts

VI. Personal qualities
   - _____ General poise and speaker confidence
   - _____ Expression of warmth and friendliness
   - _____ Rapport with audience
   - _____ Speaker credibility

VII. Vocal delivery
   - _____ Rate of speech
   - _____ Volume of speech
   - _____ Vocal variety
   - _____ Control of fillers (ah's, er's, you know, etc.)
   - _____ Tonal qualities (enthusiasm, sincerity)
   - _____ Pronunciation and articulation
   - _____ Conversational style

Evaluation Form continued

VIII. Physical delivery
　　　　　——————— Use of gestures
　　　　　——————— Eye contact
　　　　　——————— Correct posture

———————————————————————————————————————

CHAPTER 16

Persuasive Speaking

The goal of the persuasive speaker is to have the listener take action on an idea or issue, accept or strengthen a belief, or change a point of view. A persuasive message generally includes some information that serves as a background for the true purpose of the speech. The remainder of the persuasive message is designed to create a feeling of discomfort in the listener. The discomfort may result from embarrassment over graying laundry, from the desire to possess some very appealing item, from guilt over a belief, or from a realization that something is perceived by an authority figure to be wrong. If the persuasive message is effective, the listener feels compelled to eliminate the discomfort by changing to a different brand of detergent, by buying that appealing item, by changing the belief, or by correcting what was perceived as wrong.

Persuasion is a part of everyone's life at all levels of communication and in many different situations. At an interpersonal level, persuasion is sometimes used in asking permission to do something or in getting someone else to do something. In small group communication, many attempts are made to gain acceptance for recommendations or actions to be carried out by the membership. In the interactive environment of interpersonal and small group communication, the speaker is often placed in a defensive role as others attempt to refute the underlying rationale of the request. In the more formal speaker-audience situation many of the same types of persuasive messages occur, but generally the speaker receives the attention of the audience during the time allotted for delivery of the message. Since most individuals deliver and receive many persuasive messages, it is useful for everyone to know effective ways to classify, prepare, evaluate, and receive them.

Types of Persuasive Messages

Persuasive messages can be classified in three ways: according to the type of behavior expected from the listener, the purpose of the message, or the nature of the topic. Possible behaviors resulting from persuasive messages are adoption, continuance, discontinuance, and deterrence. The purposes of the message are either to stimulate or convince. Two classifications of topics for persuasive messages are policies and problems, and beliefs or values. The three classifications for persuasive messages will be reviewed with examples of topic statements that reflect each category.

Types of Persuasive Messages

1. Expected Behaviors
    A. Adoption
    B. Continuance
    C. Discontinuance
    D. Deterrence

2. Purpose of Message
    A. Stimulate
    B. Convince

3. Types of Topics
    A. Solutions to Problems
    B. Values and Beliefs

Figure 16.1. *Persuasive messages.*

Expected Behaviors

Persuasive messages are intended to have some effect on what the listener will do or believe. Some persuasive messages are presented with the purpose that the listener will *adopt* the belief or action being expressed. The speaker's message is intended to become part of the listener's value system. For example, adoption is intended when the speaker encourages the listener to accept the government's policies to curb inflation. When the message is aimed at maintaining some behavior or attitude, *continuance* is sought. At a meeting of a weight reduction group, a speaker might urge members to continue working toward their goals of slimness by following their diets. The goal of the message would have been *discontinuance* had the speaker discussed those habits that lead to overweight. Persuasive messages of *deterrence* warn against potentially negative outcomes. The speaker hopes to change behaviors or beliefs before a negative situation occurs. Messages urging smokers to give up their habit before permanent lung damage occurs are examples of messages of deterrence. Some further examples of persuasive topics focusing on the behaviors of adoption, continuance, discontinuance, and deterrence follow.

> Individualism—why be afraid to be different?
> Develop your own physical fitness program
> Four ways that you can help decrease the crime rate
> Parents keep it up—childhood diseases are nearly gone
> Preservation of our American heritage must not be stopped
> Let's keep our first place in nuclear armaments
> Give up your biggest contribution to pollution, your car
> The increase in teenage alcoholism must end
> Everyone needs to fight pornography
> Don't lose your family in a home fire
> Recognize these signs of drug abuse before it's too late
> Avoid possible nuclear contamination—stop those power plants

Purpose of Message

The speaker can consider persuasive messages in relation to their intent. Some persuasive messages are intended to *stimulate*. These messages have the purpose of motivating listeners to some action that is consistent with their existing beliefs and values. Most successful students, for example, realize that studying is an important part of achieving academic goals. However, some students who would not argue about the value of studying would benefit from stimulation to study. More students who are unsuccessful might benefit from a persuasive message on the value of studying. They need to be *convinced* that studying is worthwhile. The persuasive message to stimulate is directed primarily toward specific actions or behaviors; that to convince, toward values and beliefs. Several examples of topics relating to both are given below.

> Everyone must conserve energy
> Attend your place of worship every Sunday
> Join the armed forces and see the world
> Our energy is a valuable resource
> The value of church attendance
> The importance of the U.S. armed forces

Classification of Topics

Persuasive topics are sometimes classified as relating to solutions to problems or to values and beliefs. Many situations arise where groups of all sizes come together to agree on a solution to a problem of mutual concern. Small groups may discuss the solutions informally; large groups may recognize speakers who formally present their views to the group.

The nature of the solution is such that speakers will employ techniques of persuasion to gain acceptance for their views. The suggested solutions will nearly always relate to some specific action to be performed in the name of the "group," whether it numbers two or 2000. The other category of messages relates to values and beliefs. These messages attempt to bring the listener's values and beliefs in line with those of the speakers. The immediate result may not include an observable action, but a change might occur within the listener. Such changes are generally subtle and will often require continued persuasive messages over an extended period of time. A speaker may argue in favor of the death penalty with the intention that the listener will accept specific arguments and support the same viewpoint. Any change will be unobservable unless the members of the audience take some action like writing to their state's governor. Some examples of problem-solution and belief-value topics are given below.

> To beat inflation, we must freeze prices and wages
> Call your dentist today and save your teeth
> How you can halt the decline of the inner city
> Synonyms—murder and abortion
> The value of cultural differences among neighbors
> The importance of patience in everyday living

Developing the Persuasive Speech

The persuasive message might be considered an extension of an informative message that seeks to gain listener acceptance. As it is in developing the informative message, consideration must be given to audience characteristics. In addition, it is important to be familiar with some ways of gaining listener acceptance and to understand appropriate modifications of the general speaking outline when applied to persuasive messages.

In preparing persuasive messages, it is important to recognize that persuasion is different from coercion. Coercion is different from persuasion in that it leaves no alternatives. It forces the listener to accept the message. Persuasion can be dangerous, too, if listeners are convinced or stimulated to do something that they do not want to do. The best defense against a persuasive communicator is the recognition that persuasive techniques may distort the truth and be unethical, that a choice between alternatives exists, and that you can say no.

Audience Characteristics

To be effective, the persuasive speaker must develop a message that allows the listener to be accepting. This requires a careful analysis of the audience background and values. For example, it might be ineffective always to assume that an audience has deep religious beliefs. Religious references as supporting materials would have less impact with some groups than with others. In fact, an audience inclined to accept a persuasive argument might reject the message entirely because of the wrong choice of supporting materials. A group of working mothers, for example, might not hear a message on the benefits of reading to young children if it were introduced with the assertion that working mothers typically fail to read to their children.

Persuasive speakers are sometimes undecided about whether or not to present both sides of an appeal. If time restrictions permit, there are audiences for which hearing both sides will benefit the speaker's purpose. These are listeners who are known to react unfavorably toward a specific viewpoint or who are likely to hear the other side from another speaker. When the audience strongly favors the other side of the argument, the speaker's credibility will be improved if the audience sees that the speaker has considered the opposite view. If it is known that the audience will be likely to hear the other side, it is useful to present the other side and then immediately show why it should be rejected. When several speakers are scheduled to follow each other, it will generally be advantageous to be the last speaker—that is, to make the last impression.

For some audiences presentation of only one side of an issue is probably better. When the listener is known to favor the message, as in the persuasive situation intended to stimulate, it may be more useful to develop only one side of the issue. When the persuasive speaker is fairly certain that the listener will hear only one side of a controversial issue, it may be advantageous to present only one viewpoint. Also, if the message intends an immediate action on the part of the audience—for example, a financial contribution—the message will generally be more effective if only the speaker's side is presented.

The point to consider in preparing the persuasive message, as well as any other message, is how it will be perceived by the audience. Many speakers think only of their own reaction and feelings. Speakers are wise to put themselves in the place of the audience and ask themselves what the message is saying to them.

Gaining Listener Acceptance

Persuasive messages include a recommendation for some change or action. Some goals of persuasive speaking that require major changes or actions will require a series of messages delivered over a long period of time. The antismoking campaign of the American Cancer Society is an example of a series of related messages continuing over an extended time. Other persuasive messages are intended to have immediate results. The persuasive message, whether alone or in a series, will generally include the following five components: (1) awareness, (2) dissonance, (3) resolution, (4) reinforcement, and (5) action.

Awareness. The awareness step of the persuasive message is designed to gain the listener's attention. Also, the awareness phase of the persuasive message is necessary to call the listener's attention to a

1. Awareness
2. Dissonance
3. Resolution
4. Reinforcement
5. Action

Figure 16.2. *Parts of the persuasive message.*

discrepancy between what the speaker favors and what the listener favors. It is the initial attempt of the speaker to cause discomfort in the listener. The more obvious the awareness of the discrepancy, the more the listener will pay attention. Awareness may be developed through a shocking statement or visual aid, a rhetorical question, a specific example, a literary quote, or any other means that attracts the attention of the listener.

Dissonance. Dissonance is a strong feeling within an individual that something is wrong. There is a lack of harmony between two forces that include behaviors and/or attitudes. For example, a health foods advocate can create a great deal of dissonance by implying that people are poisoning themselves through what they eat. When dissonance is created in the listener, the speaker has gone beyond gaining attention and making the listener aware of a situation. The listener feels a great deal of tension. Nonverbal messages from the audience can be useful indicators that dissonance has been created.

Resolution. The resolution phase of a persuasive message tells how to reduce the tension or discomfort being felt. The attitude or desire to follow through with the speaker's intention is established. The speaker should inform the audience how to overcome any barriers that stand in the way of relieving the tension or discomfort. It is helpful to present an actual plan that the listener is likely to accept with gratitude.

Reinforcement. The reinforcement step in the persuasive message motivates the listener by describing the positive outcomes likely to result from acceptance of the speaker's message. The reinforcement will often refer to the future and the positive rewards the listener is likely to receive. Listeners visualize in their minds the suggested behavior and feel satisfaction. The nonverbal message of the audience after the reinforcement step should be very different from that resulting from the creation of dissonance.

Action. The action step is a specific command the speaker can use to end the message. This will generally be brief and suggest an immediate behavior or value change. It gives the listener a specific task to perform. It is more effective if it can be tied to the listener's daily routine. To improve the probability that the action step will be performed, it should not require too much extra effort on the part of the listener.

Consider the following example of the five steps of persuasion.

1. Awareness: Police files are full of descriptions of children in our own community who are physically and psychologically harmed by their parents—sometimes to the point of death.
2. Dissonance: Consider the worst tortures you can and imagine experiencing such treatment from the persons in your life you trust and depend on.
3. Resolution: Observant citizens of the community can significantly reduce child abuse by being responsible enough to report suspected cases to authorities.
4. Reinforcement: If you improve the life or even save the life of one abused child, you will have made a significant contribution to your community and to society in general.
5. Action: When you suspect child abuse, pick up your phone and call XXX-XXXX, your child welfare office.

These five statements with appropriate introduction, transitions, supporting materials, and conclusion, could become an effective persuasive message.

Persuasive Speaking Outline

The general public speaking outline presented earlier is not abandoned in persuasive speaking. A persuasive speech, like an informative speech, requires an introduction, body, and conclusion. Within this format, the steps of persuasion—awareness, dissonance, resolution, reinforcement, and action—must be incorporated. Generally the awareness step will be included in the introduction; dissonance, resolution, and reinforcement will be a part of the body; and the action step will be the last statement of the conclusion. These are generalizations, of course, and a creative speaker might very well develop an innovative format that includes the five persuasive steps in other locations within the introduction, body, and conclusion of the speech.

To demonstrate several ways of developing persuasive messages, possible outlines for a problem-solution message and a values message will be presented.

Problem-Solution Outline

I. Introduction
   A. Create awareness of problem—awareness
   B. State the problem (central idea)
   C. Relate problem to audience
II. Body
   A. Nature of the problem (main idea)—dissonance
      1. Causes of problem (support)
      2. Effects of problem (support)
      3. Extent of problem (support)
   B. Solution to the problem (main idea)—resolution
      1. Procedure to be followed (support)
      2. Realistic expectations (support)
      3. Success in similar situations (support)
   C. Outcomes to be expected (main idea)—reinforcement
      1. Elimination of problem (support)
      2. Advantages that will result (support)
III. Conclusion
   A. Problem restated
   B. Summary of important points
   C. Challenge audience
   D. Ask for action—action

Values Outline

I. Introduction
   A. Gain audience attention
   B. Describe the value, the ideal (central idea)—awareness
      1. What it is
      2. Why it is important
   C. Relate problem to audience
II. Body
   A. Absence of value (main idea)—dissonance
      1. Familiar example (support)
      2. Statistics (support)
      3. Testimony (support)
   B. Benefits of the value (main idea)—resolution
      1. Familiar example (support)
      2. Personal experience (support)
   C. Audience adoption of value (main idea)—reinforcement
      1. Procedure to be followed (support)
      2. Rewards to be realized (support)
III. Conclusion
   A. Description of value restated
   B. Summary of important points
   C. Challenge audience
   D. Ask for action—action

In using these outlines, remember that they are merely guidelines. Every speech will be unique and require its own adaptation of the general speaking outline.

Evaluation of Persuasive Speeches

The evaluation of a persuasive speech is similar to that of an informative speech. In any speaking situation, the personal qualities of the speaker, vocal delivery, and physical delivery are important considerations. Adequate preparation and rehearsal is one way to ensure success on these criteria. The message itself and the appropriate visual aids require consideration also. Some questions of major importance in evaluating persuasive messages are listed below.

1. Does the message create discomfort in the listener? That is, was the speech persuasive, *not* informative?
2. Did the speech make the audience aware of a discrepancy between listener and speaker?
3. Was dissonance created?
4. Did the speech provide for resolution of dissonance?
5. Did the message demonstrate a positive outcome from accepting the message?

6. Did the message provide the listener with an appropriate action to perform or attitude to adopt?
7. Did supporting materials relate to audience beliefs and values?
8. Were visual aids used appropriately to support the speaker's goals?
9. Was listener interest maintained throughout the message?
10. Was the speaker ethical in developing the persuasive message?

These criteria should be considered in preparing persuasive messages and in listening to those of other speakers. Consider them while reviewing the following example of a persuasive speech and the example of an evaluation form for persuasive speeches.

Example of Persuasive Speech

A well-written persuasive speech titled, "The Need to Sterilize Your Pet," is provided for review. The example is presented along with the general speaking outline. Read the example carefully as the components and the persuasive nature of the message are considered.

A Persuasive Speech

The Need to Sterilize Your Pet

Outline	Script
I. Introduction	
A. Gain attention (posters)	While all of us were eating breakfast this morning, there were probably hundreds, maybe even thousands, of kittens and puppies just like these (posters) being put to sleep, just in this state alone.
B. Create awareness	There is a definite need in the United States to make people aware of this growing tragedy—if only people understood the necessity of having their animals spayed and neutered.
C. Relate to audience	I don't suppose many people even think about this sort of thing until it's too late and their dog or cat becomes pregnant. What will happen to their offspring? Will they be sent to the animal shelter to meet an inhumane *death*?
II. Body	
A. First main idea	Many people believe that having their pets sterilized is too expensive.
1. Support	Since the new spay and neuter clinics

CHAPTER 16   Persuasive Speaking   351

			have opened, it doesn't take much to help save the lives of very innocent animals.
	2.	Example	I worked with a woman two years ago helping to get local clinics started. We went door to door trying to get petitions signed so that the city would put them into operation. The biggest resentment we received came from the veterinarians—they were afraid of losing many of their customers—when actually they wouldn't be losing any because most people wouldn't pay the amount they wanted *anyway!*
	3.	Personal experience	Before the clinics opened, it cost me $35 to have Fritzie, my female cat, spayed. Price used to be the problem; the only reason now for owners to delay sterilizing their pets is laziness.
B.	Second main idea		There are other reasons, too, for avoiding the responsibility of creating unwanted animals.
	1.	Example	Another great copout people use is "Well my cat is a Tom—why do I need to have him fixed?" This is even worse. If one male cat roams the neighborhood he can bring problems to two or three families at a time! The same situation exists for male dogs.
	2.	Example	Many people say, "I enjoy kittens and puppies around the house." But what happens to them after they have started to grow up? Do owners find them a good home or take them to the animal shelter to be "adopted"? And what if owners do find them a good home—do the people who take them have them sterilized?
C.	Third main idea		On a recent news report coming from New York City, a dump truck was shown pulling up to the back of the animal shelter and men were shown throwing hundreds of dead animals into the back of it.
	1.	Support	This is happening everywhere—simply because the animal population is way overcrowded. Why do

                                                                                   we—decent human beings—allow this to happen? Don't these poor unsuspecting animals have a right to live?

        2. Personal experience   I went to the animal shelter recently to get some information about sterilization of pets. While I was there I went back and looked at the animals. There were at least four female cats each with five or six kittens, just waiting to be adopted. Do you honestly think they will *all* be adopted? This was a small place. What do you think the total would be if you added up all of the shelters in the state? The problem is compounded considerably with the addition of dogs.

III. Conclusion
    A. Central idea restated   The biggest reaction to this kind of situation is—so what if I do have mine spayed or neutered, how will that help? It will be a big help because so many people won't, even if it is absolutely free. That is why it is up to you to help keep the population down.

    B. Plant idea in memorable way (posters)   When I look at kittens and puppies like these, and see them in animal shelters—I can't help but think of the movie "Holocaust." Although theirs is not a gas chamber—a pressure chamber is so much more humane—what is the difference—they both equal death.

    C. Action   So please, don't let your pet's offspring become a statistic in your nearby animal shelter; have him or her spayed or neutered. I did and I hope you'll do the same.

Example of Evaluation Form

The evaluation form following this chapter includes many criteria that audiences of persuasive speeches might use to judge the worth of messages they hear. Speakers who are planning persuasive messages might use the form as a checklist to evaluate their own messages. An instructor could use the form or a modification to provide feedback to speakers.

Receiving the Persuasive Message

Because persuasive messages intend to bring about behavioral change, the receiver must develop skills that permit rational choices rather than blind following of suggested actions. One way to resist persuasion is to not listen. This approach, however, eliminates the possibility of receiving beneficial persuasive messages and willingly adopting suggested behaviors. Rather than not listen, it is useful, in receiving persuasive messages, to rely on critical listening skills.

Critical listening skills (see Chapter 4) enable the listener to assess the ideas and supporting materials that form the basis of a persuasive message. Critical listening involves more than merely receiving and understanding a message; it means evaluating and judging the message. By listening critically, the receiver of a persuasive message can decide whether or not to be made uncomfortable by the speaker, and whether or not to reject the suggested action. In listening critically to a persuasive message, two considerations are particularly relevant: analysis of fact versus opinion and intent of the speaker.

Fact and Opinion

Fact. Facts are certain. There is evidence available that lends unquestionable proof to the truth of a fact. For example, it is a fact that there are fifty states in the United States, that the earth is round, and that Dallas, Texas, is not a seaport. Something accepted as a fact at one point in time may be shown to be incorrect at a later date. For example, it was once accepted as a fact that the earth was flat. There are several tests that can be applied to help in verifying statements as facts: (1) Is there any evidence against the statement? Or can it be verified as truth? (2) Do other already established facts agree? (3) Do the experts in the area confirm it as fact? Sometimes speakers who are seeking to persuade by whatever means they can make nonfactual information, or opinion, seem factual. The conscientious listener must analyze persuasive messages carefully to determine if statements are supported by evidence sound and sufficient enough to judge them factual.

Opinion. A sound opinion is a judgment based on the best available, although unverifiable, information; the three criteria used to judge whether a fact exists cannot be shown to be true. When evaluating materials, the speaker and listener must be aware that all that is written is not fact. Opinions based on the best information available are useful and acceptable as support for a speech, but should be presented as such. Both speaker and listener must guard against the use of unverified facts and unsound opinions. The dishonest persuader can be quite effective in making a lie appear to be an informed opinion or even a fact. The speaker or listener must consider the source and the soundness of statements used in preparing or listening to messages intended to persuade.

Intent of the Speaker

When listening to a persuasive message, it might be wise to ask the following question: What does the speaker have to gain by my performing the suggested action? Many persuasive messages are delivered for the well-being of the listener, but many others are based on a profit motive. Advertising is a multimillion dollar business with the sole purpose of convincing individuals to purchase one product or service rather than another. Advertising agencies rely on psychological research and the power of suggestion to sell products. They can present their messages via the powerful channels of visual as well as audio media. How often do individuals buy products, visit places, participate in activities, and generally behave in ways that are not in their best interest? As a consumer and as a listener, consider the intentions of the speaker before accepting the message. Become sophisticated and remember that many persuasive messages have more than one side to consider before important decisions are made.

SUMMARY

The persuasive speech has the specific purpose of changing the listener's behavior. Persuasive speeches are designed to convince the listener to adopt a belief, continue a behavior, or avoid a potentially negative outcome. Persuasive speeches attempt to convince individuals to change values or beliefs or stimulate them to some action based on current values and beliefs. Persuasive speeches are often directed toward a specific solution to a problem or toward specific values and beliefs. Effective ways to develop persuasive speeches are: to create an awareness of the purpose; to create dissonance, that is, discomfort; to offer a suggestion for eliminating dissonance; to show the positive outcome resulting from eliminating dissonance; and to indicate a specific action for removing dissonance. In developing effective persuasive speeches, the speaker must include supporting materials that are ethical and honest. The receiver of a persuasive message must develop skills in critical listening.

Evaluation Form for Persuasive Speeches

I. Introduction
 _____ Attention-getting device
 _____ Central idea presented
 _____ Relate message to audience

II. Body
 _____ Dissonance created
 _____ Resolution of dissonance
 _____ Reinforcement of solution
 _____ Support relates to personal experiences

III. Conclusion
 _____ Central idea restated
 _____ Summary
 _____ Challenge to audience
 _____ Action step

IV. Visual aids
 _____ Appropriateness of aids
 _____ Ability to use aids
 _____ Quality of aids

V. Presentation
 _____ Persuasive, not informative
 _____ Adequate transitions between parts

VI. Personal qualities
 _____ General poise and speaker confidence
 _____ Relates to audience values
 _____ Rapport with audience
 _____ Speaker credibility

VII. Vocal delivery
 _____ Rate of speech
 _____ Volume of speech
 _____ Vocal variety
 _____ Control of fillers (ah's, er's, you know, etc.)
 _____ Tonal qualities
 _____ Pronunciation and articulation
 _____ Conversational style

VIII. Physical delivery
 _____ Use of gestures
 _____ Eye contact
 _____ Correct posture

Activity 1
Information about Speaker-Audience Communication

Preparation: Read the textual material for Part V: Speaker-Audience Communication. Prepare yourself for a test by reviewing the "Knowledge Objective" included with the Overview for Part V and answering the practice items given below.

PRACTICE ITEMS FOR PART V

Instructions: Select the best answer for each item.

1. How many topic statements form the basis for a good speech?
   a. one
   b. two to four
   c. at least five
   d. as many as time permits
2. Which is a description of a persuasive speaking topic?
   a. recognizing the danger signs of cancer
   b. method for developing effective listening skills
   c. necessity for banning nuclear power plants
   d. how proper exercise can improve your health
3. When speakers state the numbers of products sold during a period of several years, they have presented
   a. an example
   b. a quotation
   c. a statistic
   d. a speech
4. The purpose of dissonance in a persuasive speech is to
   a. entertain the audience
   b. make the audience uncomfortable
   c. provide information for the audience
   d. introduce specific examples to the audience
5. An effective poster will be
   a. complexly designed
   b. written rather than printed
   c. made on a colorful background
   d. twice as large as seems necessary

Activity 1 continued

6. "The Meaning of Love" is most likely the title of an informative speech based on the technique of
    a. description
    b. demonstration
    c. definition
    d. reporting
7. Which method of explanation has been used when an unfamiliar word is compared to something familiar?
    a. synonym
    b. analogy
    c. negation
    d. rephrasing
8. An audience uninformed about the topic of a public speech must receive
    a. basic information about the topic
    b. different facets of the subject
    c. specific uses for the information
    d. unusual applications of the information
9. A purpose of a persuasive speech is to
    a. debate
    b. quote
    c. discuss
    d. convince
10. When should the audience be told about both sides of an issue in a persuasive speech?
    a. The next speaker is likely to present the other side.
    b. The audience is ignorant of both sides.
    c. The time allowed for the presentation is very short.
    d. The speaker is only pretending to be for one side.

Key: 1.a 2.c 3.c 4.b 5.d 6.c 7.b 8.a 9.d 10.a

Group Activity: Attend class and complete objective test items for Part V: Speaker-Audience Communication.

Individual Activity: Make arrangements with your instructor to complete objective test items for Part V: Speaker-Audience Communication.

Activity 2
Outlining in Public Speaking

Preparation: Using the outline make a statement about one of the controversial topics listed below. Be prepared to present your ideas to small groups.

I. Introduction (personal reference, humorous story, picture, quotation, question, etc.)
II. Central idea (your purpose)
III. Body (a major point to be explained)
IV. Summary (summarizes main idea)
V. Conclusion (closing statement)

Possible topics for discussion are listed below.

1. Women should receive equal pay for equal work.
2. Marriage is an institution that primarily benefits males.
3. Religion and faith in God are what made this country great; if we lose these we lose everything.
4. Parents should give their children the freedom and encouragement to live their own lives; giving direction and control will stunt self-expression.
5. People who seek government assistance are basically parasites; they live off the work the rest of us do.

Group Activity: In class form a group with people who have outlines that deal with the same topic that you have chosen. Choose a leader to be in charge of the group. Present your outline orally to the group. Ask for criticism of the ideas that you presented and determine how your outline could be improved. Listen to everyone's ideas on this topic. After each has had a turn, the group leader should put all the ideas together with the group to make a longer outline to produce a final speech. Turn in the group outline at the end of the class.

Individual Activity: Take your outline to an English instructor and ask the instructor to mark any corrections or suggestions on the outline. Turn in the original and corrected outlines to your instructor.

Activity 3
Learning to Use the Library

Preparation: Learning to use library resources is an important skill. There are five exercises below designed to help you increase your familiarity with library resources. Go to the library you plan to use to prepare your speeches and complete the five exercises. Be sure to ask either the librarian or your instructor for help if needed.

1. Find a circulating book (one that can be checked out) on the subject of gardening. List the following information about the book.
    Call number:
    Title:
    Author:
    Publisher:
    Place of publication:
    Year of publication:
2. Find a book written by Mark Twain. List the following information about the book.
    Call number:
    Title:
    Publisher:
    Place of publication:
    Year of publication:
3. Find a magazine article on the National Football League. Give the information requested below.
    Title of article:
    Author of article:
    Name of magazine:
    Date of publication:
    Page numbers:
4. Locate the date the first United States citizen walked on the moon and give the headline from the *New York Times* on that date.
    Date:
    Headline:
5. Using the reference collection, locate a map of the United States. Give the following information.
    Call number:
    Title:
    Publisher:
    Date of publication:
    Page number:

Activity 3 continued

Group and Individual Activity: Find another class member who has completed this activity. Compare your answers (most will probably be different) and experience. Write a one-paragraph summary of your library experience.

Activity 4
Presenting an Informative Message to a Small Group

Preparation: Locate a single source and use it to prepare an informative message of about three minutes in length. Be certain that it includes an introduction, body with supporting materials, and a conclusion. Outline the message on 3-by-5 inch note cards and prepare to present it to a group of two other persons. You may use the cards for the presentation.

Review the following evaluation sheet as your prepare your message.

Group Activity: Work together in groups of three to evaluate informative speeches. Listen and be prepared to give constructive criticism after hearing each speech. Evaluate each speech as though it were a finished product. After listening to each speaker, write out two copies of the evaluation. Give one copy to the speaker and the other to the instructor. The instructor can review the evaluation and note any difficulties the student may be having. After listening to the other speakers, present your speech and then collect evaluation sheets from your listeners. If time is left, orally evaluate the speeches and discuss ways in which each of you might improve before presenting an informative speech to a large audience.

Individual Activity: Ask three people from your class or three friends or family members to listen to your informative speech. Instruct them to evaluate your speech as though it were a finished product. Give each a copy of the evaluation sheet and ask them to give you constructive criticism that might improve your speaking. After the evaluation sheets have been filled out, ask them to give oral criticisms of your speech.

Student Evaluation Sheet for Informative Speeches

Speaker's name: _____

Topic: _____

1. What is your overall reaction to the introduction?
2. What is your assessment of the main points discussed?
3. What is your evaluation of the supporting materials?
4. What is your overall reaction to the conclusion?
5. How easy was it to follow the organization of the presentation?
6. What do you think about the way the speaker spoke?
7. What personal qualities of the speaker enhanced or detracted from the presentation?
8. What is the major area of improvement you believe the speaker should concentrate on?

Activity 5
A Speech to Inform

Preparation: Instructions follow for delivering a number of different types of informative speeches. These include the following:

1. Description or demonstration,
2. Definition,
3. Report of personal experience,
4. Report on a famous person,
5. Report on a book,
6. Report on a thought-provoking article, and
7. Report of a problem situation.

Your instructor will give you special instructions about which type of informative speech you may present and an acceptable time limit for presenting your message.

As you research a topic, remember to document your sources for further possible reference. After you have selected and researched a topic, complete an outline of your speech. To develop a format for your outline, use examples presented in the text and included with this activity. Transfer the outline to 3-by-5 inch cards and practice your speech until you are prepared to deliver it. As you practice work toward eliminating the cards or reducing them significantly. Be certain to include appropriate visual aids.

If you are using visual aids, keep in mind the following points:

1. Do not hand out visual aids while you are speaking.
2. Do not speak to the aid when using it. Maintain eye contact with the audience.
3. Practice with the aid when you are rehearsing your speech.
4. Keep models covered until you are ready to use them. After using them cover them again.
5. When writing on the blackboard or on poster board, use large, clear, simple diagrams. Make sure the drawing can be seen by everyone.

Informative Speech to Describe or Demonstrate
The purpose of this speech is to convey descriptive information to the audience in an interesting way from subject areas like the following.

An organization: For example, a labor union, a traffic safety program, the Federal Reserve System, a beehive, the New York Stock Exchange, the Peace Corps, the

Activity 5 continued

  electoral college, the scout organization, a college fraternity, the National Labor Relations Board, the European Economic Community, and so forth.

A place: New York, Berlin, the Canal Zone, Saigon, the French Riviera, Paris, Jerusalem, New Orleans, San Francisco, Rome, Florence, Moscow, London, Stratford-on-Avon, a famous monument, a cathedral, and so forth.

A historical event: A famous battle, the rise of Hitlerism, the Arab-Israeli war of 1967, recent stock market trends, a famous trial, the fight for civil rights, a presidential election, and so forth.

A process: Making perfume, making elderberry wine, using the card catalogue, raising vegetables, navigating a commercial airliner, studying, collecting coins, collecting stamps, building a plant terrarium, collecting butterflies, building stage scenery, refinishing old furniture, and so forth.

An object or mechanism: A computer, a vacuum cleaner, a human organ (heart, lungs, etc.), a printing press, a watch, a camera, a shotgun, a hi-fi set, a slide rule, or any other invention.

If your speech topic is a description of an organization or place, you may want to use a spatial ordering of material by describing the relationship of various parts to the whole. A comparison/contrast ordering of material would be useful, too, in telling your listener how the organization or place is like one that might be more familiar or easier to visualize.

If your speech topic describes a historical event or a process, you may want to use a chronological order. You would begin at the beginning of the process or event and follow through the succeeding steps until you reach the end. Because one step logically follows another, you should have no difficulty remembering your material, particularly if you have rehearsed it.

If you choose to describe an object or mechanism, you may want to use a topical ordering of material. Begin by mentioning the origin and common uses of the device and then explain the device by (1) pointing out its theoretical basis, (2) describing its various parts, (3) showing how its parts interact and function as a unit, and (4) demonstrating how the device functions as a whole in a larger system.

Example of an Informative Speech to Describe

Amish People (or the Plain Folk)

Outline	Script
I. Introduction A. Opening statement to get attention	Sixteen is the special age for teenagers of this unusual group of people.

Activity 5 continued

    B. Connecting statement — When these particular young people reach sixteen they are given a courting buggy and a beautiful spirited horse.

    C. Statement of main purpose — The main purpose of my speech is to inform you about the Amish people or the Pennsylvania Dutch as they are sometimes called.

    D. Preview of first main point — I will begin by giving a brief history of the Amish.

    E. Preview of second main point — ...by sharing some of their unique and unusual customs.

    F. Preview of third main point — ...and, finally by describing their contributions to this country.

II. Body
    A. Statement of first major division — The history of the Amish goes back nearly 400 years.

        1. Support — The Amish were born from the religious turmoil of the Anabaptist movement in the sixteenth century in Switzerland. They did not believe in war or any other violent act. Because of this they were often subjected to a violent death. In one town there were so many Amish caught, who were considered to be heretics, that a huge bonfire was built in the Town Square to accommodate all the offenders. To make things easy, these people were tied to long ladders and dropped one by one into the flames.

        2. Support — Approximately 300 Amish came to America before the Revolutionary War. After the American constitution was ratified, they came in larger numbers.

        3. Support — The Amish people settled not only in Pennsylvania, but in many areas of North America. Wherever they chose to settle, because of their shrewd judgment of land and methods of farming, they were always successful in producing above-average crops.

    B. Statement of second major division — Life for the Amish is very simple.

        1. Support — The home is the pulse of their life. Their house is plain, curtainless, and without pictures on the walls. The kitchen is very large. Simplicity and cleanliness are the order of these homes. Color is captured by the vivid colored rugs, pillows, afghans, quilts, and glassware.

Activity 5 continued

2. Support — The red, one-room school house is still in use among the Amish where they go through the eighth grade. That is considered enough education for the Amish young people. These schools are usually taught by a young unmarried lady who has an eighth-grade education. Until the first grade children speak German. English is learned in the school and in the fourth grade the students begin to learn high German.

3. Support — An unmarried man is clean-shaven. When he marries he grows a beard. Most weddings are in November after the harvest. The husband and wife do not live together until spring. However, every weekend the young husband collects his bride from her parents' home and visits family members for the weekend. This is a festive time and gifts are given to the young couple. Then on Sunday evening or Monday morning the young man returns his wife to her parents' home. This continues until the spring when the young couple have collected enough gifts, and they are ready to set up housekeeping themselves. The entire first year is spent mainly building a relationship with one another. This custom comes directly from Deuteronomy 24:5, "When a man takes a new wife, he shall not go out with the army, nor be charged with any duty; he shall be free at home one year and shall give happiness to his wife who he has taken."

4. Support — The Amish women and girls wear long dresses of solid colors. Men's hats must be black felt in winter, and straw in the summer. The dimensions of the brim and crown are strictly regulated.

5. Support — None of the things we simply take for granted are used by the Amish. There are no conveniences, automobiles, tractors, electricity, refrigeration, radio, central heating, or hot and cold running water in homes. These plain people worship in private homes, using German as the common language.

Activity 5 continued

    C. Statement of third division — The Amish are hard workers.
       1. Support — Next to the Bible and his religion, the land is the most important thing in an Amish man's life. He knows that this land may one day be in the hands of his great-great-grandsons. They regard themselves not as landowners, but as guardians of the land for future generations. They are careful to give back what they take from the land.

       2. Support — The teen-age boys are instructed in the essentials of prosperous farming. By the time a young man is seventeen or eighteen he has the basics of animal husbandry, crop rotation, and farm finances equivalent to a college agricultural student.

       3. Support — The Amish till miles of black earth, which yields one of the lushest agriculture bounties of an unirrigated county in the nation.

       4. Support — Their farms are among the most prosperous of any in the nation. Each year extra land is planted and the produce is canned, preserved, and given to charitable organizations. In fact, most of the food used by the Amish is produced on their own farms.

       5. Support — There is virtually no divorce among the Amish. They are hard working, thrifty, prosperous, and there is no need for welfare.

       6. Support — Because of their unique customs and lifestyle, the Pennsylvania Dutch country of Pennsylvania draws four million visitors annually, creating a large tourist trade for the area.

III. Conclusion
    A. Summary — You have heard about the Amish, their history, their culture, and their contributions to this country.

    B. Important message — These are people of the earth, who regard themselves as guardians of the land for future generations.

    C. Transition statement — I would like to leave you with the following thought.

    D. Closing statement — The Amish, within their communities, exemplify love, nonviolence, goodness, and simplicity. Their unity comes from within the community.

Activity 5 continued

Informative Speech to Define a Concept
In an informative speech define an abstract concept. Some suggested topics are: democracy, courage, academic freedom, beauty, existentialism, romanticism, communism, pride, puppy love, humor, common sense, self-reliance, autonomy, liberalism, conservatism, prejudice, anxiety, anti-Semitism, nationalism, idealism, materialism, and culture.

In writing a speech of definition, consider the following ideas.

1. When possible explain the derivation of a word. The word "democracy" comes from two Greek words, *demos*, meaning "people," and *kratein*, meaning "rule." Thus, the two words together mean "rule by the people."
2. Give a brief history of the word. Show how the meaning has changed or how the present day meaning relates to the old meaning.
3. Give concrete examples to illustrate the concept.
4. Compare or contrast the concept with other closely related concepts.
5. Cite the views of various writers.
6. Explain common misconceptions about the concept.
7. Explain what the concept does not mean.
8. Be objective in explaining the concept. *Do not allow personal prejudices to distort the definition.*
9. Do not be overly technical in explaining the concept.
10. Vary your sources of information. Do not use series of encyclopedias or dictionaries.
11. Research the word. Paraphrase quotations that you found. Remember to mention the source even when paraphrasing.
12. Be as specific as possible.

Example of an Informative Speech to Define

Plea Bargaining

Outline	Script
I. Introduction	
A. Opening statement to get attention	Guilty or not guilty is not the question. The question, however, is justice or injustice.
B. Connecting statement	Is America selling herself short? Are we living in a land where justice is just a game?
C. Statement of main purpose	Plea bargaining is a part of our judicial system that many know little about.
D. Preview of first main point	I would like to begin by informing you what plea bargaining is.

Activity 5 continued

    E. Preview of second main point   ...by explaining to you why we plea bargain.
    F. Preview of third main point   And finally, by informing you of the choices you have in a plea bargaining situation.

II. Body
    A. Statement of first major division   Plea bargaining is an agreement made between the prosecuting attorney and the defendant. The defendant agrees to enter a plea of guilty, and in return the prosecuting attorney agrees to recommend a particular sentence to the judge. The key word here is "recommend" because the court is not bound to any agreement made.

        1. Support (definition)   Another way to explain plea bargaining is to tell you that it is an agreement made outside of court which does not require a trial by jury.

Following are two famous plea bargain cases which will make the plea bargaining process easier to understand.

        2. Support (example)   Spiro T. Agnew was a plea bargain case. His part of the "deal" was to plead guilty and resign as vice-president of the United States. In return, the court held him accountable for only one count of tax evasion.

        3. Support (example)   John Dean was also a plea bargain case. He agreed to turn state's evidence and in return the court held him responsible for only one count of obstruction of justice.

        4. Support
           Visual aid:
           (charts or posters with statistics)   The two examples may lead you to believe that only the rich and powerful use plea bargaining as a tool. This is not necessarily so. The charts show that the majority of all cases are handled by plea bargains.

The next chart shows the way the case loads of the United States District Criminal Courts are handled. Of all cases reviewed by these courts in the five states, 85% are handled by plea bargains, 5% of the cases are dismissed, and only 10% ever get to trial.

    B. Statement of second major division   Plea bargaining has benefits for the defendant, the court, and the average tax-paying citizen.

        1. Support   The defendant is benefited by plea bargaining for three main reasons. (1) The penalty is often lessened from a felony to a misdemeanor. (2) The sentence is shortened. If you plead guilty, the court will often give

Activity 5 continued

                                        you a better "deal" because you saved the court the time, trouble, and money involved in a jury trial. If you are facing a sentence of three to ten years, you may get three years if you plea bargain. If you go to court, the jury may give you ten years. (3) If you turn state's evidence, the charges could be dropped completely.

      2. Support — The courts are benefited by plea bargaining because of the time element involved. A jury trial takes anywhere from eight to twelve hours. A plea bargain takes only twenty minutes. Plea bargaining is a tool used to keep the court dockets from becoming too overloaded.

      3. Support — The average tax-paying citizen is benefited by plea bargaining. Without plea bargaining there would be need for more judges and more courts, which means more tax dollars.

  C. Statement of third division — In a plea bargaining situation, you have three choices to make.

      1. Support (handout for visual aid) — You may initiate the plea bargaining process by filling out one of the two forms I am passing around.

      2. Support — You can accept the plea bargain offer given to you by the prosecuting attorney.

      3. Support — If you believe you are innocent, it is your constitutional right to demand a trial by jury. An attorney cannot force you into a plea bargain.

III. Conclusion
  A. Summary — In summary, I have tried to inform you as to what plea bargaining is—a settlement made outside of court which does not require a trial by jury. I have also tried to show you why we plea bargain—the defendant is often offered a better "deal." The court saves time and the public saves money. And finally, I have tried to show you the choices you have in a plea bargaining situation. You may (1) initiate the plea bargain, (2) accept an offer, or (3) demand a trial by jury.

  B. Value of message — I would just like to say that plea bargaining is a tool used in our American justice system. It has advantages and disadvantages. If any of you are ever in a court situation, you will

Activity 5 continued

C. Closing

know the choices you have. Just remember, make the choice that is best for *you*.
I would like to leave each one of you with the following question. It was better stated by Bob Dylan in his song "Hurricane." "Are we living in a land where justice is just a game?"

Informative Speech to Report on a Personal Experience
The goal of this speech is to report on a personal experience to an audience. The message should have a specific purpose and should make the audience think as well as feel. The experience you relate could point up some insight about people or could suggest a moral. A moral to a story could be that those who lie chronically will not be believed even when they tell the truth. Your story may be a simple experience; it does not need to be dramatic or unusual. The most natural organization for this kind of speech is generally chronological order. Avoid talking about a series of events, such as places visited on a trip. Concentrate on one incident or key event. You may want to choose a frightening experience, an embarrassing incident, an educational experience, or an eye-witness account of something you have seen.

After choosing your subject you will need to outline your experience. The following references to the general public speaking outline might be used to help in organizing your material.

I. Introduction: the setting of the experience
II. Body: the elements of the experience in chronological order
III. Conclusion: the significance of the experience

Remember, be certain that your experience includes an insight or a moral so that the audience will realize the significance of the experience.

By using narrative details, you should be able to bring the audience immediately into the experience. The events should be told in the sequence in which they occurred. Use language that will describe the incident as vividly as possible. Try to make your audience feel as if they had been present. Appeal to their senses of sight and sound. Your goal might be to arouse in them the same feelings that you experienced. Do not be inhibited as you express your feelings and recreate the experience.

Activity 5 continued

Example of an Informative Speech to Report on a Personal Experience

The Brown-Eyed, Blue-Eyed Experiment

Outline	Script
I. Introduction	
A. Opening statement to get attention	To be abused by another human being is a devastating experience.
B. Connecting statement	It doesn't matter at what age this happens—from the time a child is old enough to understand until one is elderly—it is a crushing and hurtful thing.
C. Statement of main purpose	The purpose of my speech is to inform you of an experiment conducted in a college class which brought to my memory painful experiences from the past.
D. Preview of first main point	I would like to begin by giving you an outline of the classroom experiment.
E. Preview of second main point	Then I want to share with you several personal experiences from my childhood years.
F. Preview of third main point	Finally, I will share with you how I handled that classroom experiment.
II. Body	
A. Statement of first major division	The experiment was conducted in a psychology class. Our professor decided that the blue-eyed people in our class were to be the master race; and the brown-eyed people, the minority group.
1. Support	It was decided that the minority group must bring candy and gum to the "superior" race; they were to type an extra set of notes to be given to a blue-eyed person. Each brown-eyed person was to sit in a designated place and to speak only when recognized by a "chosen" member of the "master" race.
2. Support	I did not toss the idea aside lightly, but talked at length with family members and classmates. Several felt, as I did, that the experiment could get out of hand—by that, I mean tearing up textbooks.
B. Statement of second major division	As I thought about this over and over from Wednesday until Friday, old memories reared their ugly heads. As a small child, from five to twelve years of age, I remember being

Activity 5 continued

                                                      verbally and physically abused by my classmates. My brothers and sisters were as well.

1. Support   One time when my brother John was five and just starting school, Mother purchased new shoes for her three older children and when she got to John the money was gone. Knowing it would be just a short time before she would be able to get John's shoes, she decided to send him to school barefoot. The kids tormented and shamed John, and jumped on his little feet.

2. Support   I wore braids for a short period of time and one afternoon after school, as I neared the end of our road a band of young classmates jumped from behind trees and pulled my hair. Then they proceeded to pull me up the road by my braids.

3. Support   Many noon times when the snow was just right to pack a good, hard snowball, our family was prevented from going home at noon for lunch. A group of boys filled the hard packed snowballs with rocks, and as we began our walk home we were literally pelted with these "home-made bombs."

4. Support   Just twice do I ever remember getting even. Once two of us got one of the ring leaders alone and held him, while our oldest sister, who had long fingernails, plunged her hand in his mouth and dug his gums. Another time, Iris, a girl my age and three times as large, was standing by the side of the road. Behind her was a deep ditch filled with slush. Iris had beaten my little body more than once, and that day as she stood there a plan rapidly took shape in my mind. We were on good terms, or so Iris thought, and when she was completely relaxed, teetering on the edge of the ditch, I suddenly put both hands on her chest and pushed her with all my might. It was so completely unexpected that she fell right into that deep ditch of slush. She was soaked from head to toe and floundering like a walrus.

Activity 5 continued

C. Statement of third major division	All these memories surfaced as I contemplated the upcoming experiment to be held in my class.
1. Support	When the day came I was so over-wrought from mentally reviewing the happenings in my life as a child, and what might happen in class, that I *skipped class*.
2. Support	The following class period I dreaded going to class, yet determined to give an account of why I failed to participate in the experiment.
III. Conclusion	
A. Summary	In summary, I have tried to inform you of the incredible emotional and physical pain human beings can and do inflict upon one another.
B. Important message	In conclusion, I would like to say that my experiences have helped me to be more sensitive of the feelings of others.
C. Transition statement	And I would like to leave you with the following thought.
D. Closing statement	It doesn't cost one penny to be kind, and those who we count as being important to us are the ones who take time to encourage, and in a thousand little ways to be thoughtful on an individual basis.

Informative Speech to Report on a Famous Person
The goal of this speech is to give a brief biographical sketch of a famous person's life. In preparing for the speech you should complete the following tasks.

1. Read a biography of a person, living or dead, who interests you.
2. As you read, list the major forces or interests that seemed to shape the person's life. Be particularly aware of significant factors in the person's life (e.g., a specific belief or attitude, an insecure childhood, a specific talent, or an influential person who helped shape his or her life).
3. Look at each period in the person's life and choose events that support your overall judgment of the person.
4. Since this is a brief biography, insignificant dates and minor events should not be considered. When outlining your speech, use personal sayings, conversations, excerpts from letters, various idiosyncrasies, and quotations by the person.
5. Using the outline, orally rehearse the speech. Be familiar enough with any quoted material so that you can maintain eye contact with your audience.

As you deliver your informative biographical sketch before your audience, remember to include only those materials that illustrate your dominant theme and do not include extraneous material. Since your time is limited, be careful not to dwell too long on any

Activity 5 continued

one story or event from the person's life. Be enthusiastic about your subject and try to motivate your audience to want to know more.

Example of an Informative Speech to Report on a Famous Person

Mark Twain

Outline   *Script*

Outline	Script
I. Introduction	
A. Attention-getting statement	"Man is the only animal that blushes—or needs to!"
B. Connecting statement	These are words characteristic of a man who depended on the quirks of humanity for his livelihood.
C. Relate to audience	The man is Samuel Langhorne Clemens—the writer of such popular books as *Huckleberry Finn*, the *Prince and the Pauper*, and *Tom Sawyer*. Mark Twain: known to the world as a humorist, yet a man who suffered countless personal tragedies.
D. Statement of main purpose	I'd like to tell you a little about this man and some of the events that changed his outlook on life.
II. Body	
A. First main point	Mark Twain's childhood and life experiences formed the basis for his writing.
1. Support	Sam Clemens was born November 30, 1835, in Florida, Missouri.
2. Support	He lived there for only a short time before he and his family moved to Hannibal, where Sam was to spend the greater part of his childhood.
3. Support	It was in Hannibal that he experienced many of those things that formed the basis for his later works.
B. Second main point	Many of Twain's stories dealt with happy times, like rafting down the Mississippi. There were tales about bad times too, and there were some tall tales that expressed personal tragedies in a humorous way.
1. Support	For example, he tells of an old wino, a very dear friend, who was shot down on Main Street in broad daylight as the entire town looked on.

Activity 5 continued

    2. Support   He tells also of two missionaries who were boiled and eaten by the savages they were trying to save. This was not normally the custom in that area, but the savages, when questioned, said they were sorry, and that they had tried missionaries every other way and hadn't found any use for them yet.

    3. Support   Possibly the most tragic tall tale of all is about Mr. Wheeler, the distinguished owner of the local carpet factory, who was caught by his own machinery and pulled through in less than a minute. His wife, who loved him dearly, bought the piece of carpet in which his remains had been woven. She wouldn't allow Mr. Wheeler to be folded, so they rolled him up and planted him end on end like a monument.

  C. Third main point   All these tragedies contributed to Twain's bitterness as an old man. Perhaps, though, the greatest effect was made by the deaths, over the years, of different family members.

    1. Support   His wife, two daughters, and a brother all died within three years of each other.

    2. Support   Twain was terribly saddened by their deaths, but he always commented that even had he been able to bring one or all of them back he wouldn't have done it. He felt that each person is born with one possession which outweighs all his others—his last breath.

III. Conclusion
  A. Transition statement   Mark Twain died in 1910, an embittered and disillusioned old man.

  B. Summary   He left the world with a legacy of his personality, humor, and insights into human nature.

  C. Closing statement   His popularity can best be summarized by the inscription on a monument erected in his honor in Hannibal, Missouri. It reads "He was a lover of humanity, and the whole world mourned when he died."

Informative Speech to Report on a Book
The purpose of this speech is to present material from one book and is usually referred to as a book review or lecture-recital. Choose a book that really interests you. Read the book and choose a theme to develop. Phrase the specific purpose or theme

Activity 5 continued

carefully and keep this in mind as you search for material. Choose quotations from the book to amplify and clarify your theme. If the meaning of the quotation is not clear, you will need to paraphrase it or explain briefly how it relates to your conclusion. Alternate brief commentaries with brief quotations rather than presenting long quotations. Be careful that the quoted material does not comprise more than 50% of the speech. Type the material on notecards or in a manuscript and rehearse with the quotations until you are completely familiar with the author's words.

Possible ideas for speeches are listed below.

1. The Jazz Age as seen in F. Scott Fitzgerald's *Tender Is the Night*.
2. Mark Twain's humor in *Innocents Abroad*.
3. Dostoyevsky's concept of punishment in *Crime and Punishment*.
4. Thomas Wolfe's view of America in *You Can't Go Home Again*.
5. Ernest Hemingway's attitude toward the sea in *The Old Man and the Sea*.

In order to be an effective interpretive reader you must have a complete understanding of your material and reflect this in your voice. Vary your rate, pitch, and volume. Use proper phrasing and meaningful pauses. Use a variety of facial expressions and gestures to help get messages across to the listener. Although you have not memorized the material, you must maintain steady eye contact with the audience as you speak and read.

Example of an Informative Speech to Report on a Book

Will There Really Be a Morning?
An Autobiography by Frances Farmer

Outline *Script*

I. Introduction	
A. Opening statement to get attention	Who has the right to decide whether or not people are mentally ill and should be put some place where they cannot harm themselves or others or whether or not they are capable of functioning in our society?
B. Connecting statement	This was one woman's question to herself over and over as she spent seven years of her life in a mental institution.
C. Statement of main purpose	The main purpose of my speech is to relate briefly her story as told by Frances Farmer in her autobiography *Will There Really Be a Morning?* The book was published by Putnam's Sons in New York in 1972.

Activity 5 continued

      D. Transition — Should Frances Farmer have been placed in a mental institution after being classified as a schizophrenic? She didn't think so!

II. Body
    A. Statement of first major division — This autobiography relates one of the most terrifying self-analyses of schizophrenia ever to be recorded.

        1. Support (definition) — Schizophrenia in its simplest definition is a person's inability to deal with frustration. The person becomes withdrawn and has a complex communication problem.

        2. Support — Acknowledged as one of the world's most beautiful women and critically acclaimed as an actress, Frances Farmer fell from stardom headlong into the terror-ridden world of the insane.

    B. Statement of second major division — She was released after seven years of horror.
        1. Support — Many of these years were spent in animal cages in the ward in which she was destined to stay.

        2. Support — The only thing which kept her going while in the mental institution was the hatred for her mother who put her in the institution.

        3. Support — When leaving the institution, she tried to sever all connections with the past by going to California where she spent three years as a motel clerk.

    C. Statement of third major division — She was discovered and persuaded to appear on "This Is Your Life" which eventually brought her back to her first love, the stage.

        1. Support — Her appearance on television did bring her back to the world of acting she knew before she was sent to the institution.

        2. Support — Frances Farmer completed her novel describing all the nightmares of her life a few days before she died of cancer of the esophagus.

III. Conclusion
    A. Summary — Frances Farmer reaffirmed that despite the twisted nightmare journeys, life itself is something of value and a reason for survival.

    B. Closing statement — Her message is important: if any of you are ever put in the position of having to make a decision as serious as placing someone in a mental institution, know beyond a reasonable doubt that this is the course of action to take and be certain that proper help is given.

Activity 5 continued

Informative Speech to Report on a Thought-Provoking Article

The purpose of this speech is to inform the audience of a thought-provoking article from a reputable journal like *Saturday Review, Harper's, Atlantic Monthly,* or *New York Times.* Do not choose an article that has already been summarized. Choose a well-researched article in which the author draws responsible conclusions. Do the following to prepare for the speaking assignment.

1. Read the article to get general meaning.
2. Read the article again slowly. Look up difficult words and concentrate on parts you do not understand.
3. Read the article through a third time and outline the material on note cards. If you plan to use direct quotations, transcribe the quotations to the cards or plan to read from the work itself. In an informative speech of this type it is a good idea to select key passages from the article that substantiate your main points. However, do not let more than one-third of your speech be directly quoted material.
4. Since the content of the speech will be limited by time available, you will not be able to cover all the points of the article. Go over the outline that you have made of the article and decide the most important points. What can be omitted without destroying the author's purpose?
5. Outline the speech again keeping only the necessary material and quotations. Rehearse the speech with notes in hand and put the ideas in your own words. When reading the author's words, maintain audience contact. When reading directly quoted material, hold the cards or magazine up to a level that facilitates reading but does not block you off from the audience. Read all quotations with feeling, understanding, proper emphasis, and eye contact. Remind the audience that you are presenting only the views of the author and not your own. Make comments like "As the author concludes . . ."

Some additions to the general speaking outline are suggested below.

I. Introduction
    A. Title of article, source, name of author, date of publication
    B. The significance of the article
II. Body: a summary of article
III. Conclusion
    A. Summary of author's main points
    B. Quotation from article

Activity 5 continued

An Example of an Informative Speech to Report on an Article

Will the Government Raise Your Child?

Outline	*Script*
I. Introduction	
A. Title of article, source, name of author	"Will the Government Raise Your Child?" is an article from *Moody Monthly*, by Gary Hardaway, a free-lance writer living in Fremont, California. The article was published in November of 1979.
B. Significance of the article	It raises the question: does the government have the final say as to how a child is educated, disciplined, and supervised?
II. Body	
A. First main point	There are those who would seek to establish government as the Great Guardian of our children.
1. Support	Dr. Mary Jo Baine, Assistant Professor of Education at Wellesley College believes ". . . the fact that children are raised in families means there is no equality. In order to raise children with equality, we must take them away from families, and communally raise them."
2. Support	In 1972, the Minneapolis Declaration of Feminism advocated a similar position: ". . . with the destruction of the nuclear family, children must be seen as the responsibility of the entire society, rather than the individual."
B. Second main point	During the past ten years, laws and court cases have done much to take away parental rights once considered fundamental. Consider these facts:
1. Support	Your teenager can obtain contraceptives and abortions without your knowledge.
2. Support	In many states teenagers may run away from home, as a result of a law passed in 1974.
3. Support	Schools across the country ignore objections of parents regarding teaching on homosexuality, abortion, and morals.
C. Third main point	In 1978, a twenty-five member United States National Commission was created, drawing representatives from social welfare and child care causes.

Activity 5 continued

      1. Support — At a meeting in August, 1978, the Commission defined its broad purposes: "Eliminate... discrimination against children," "encourage... responsible self-expression," "encourage attitude supportive of cultural pluralism," "promote understanding and appreciation of differing cultural and societal roles."

      2. Support — The goals of the commission seem lofty, but what do they really mean? Does "discrimination against children" mean failing to rent to families with kids or does it place its emphasis on the discipline a parent uses to curb disobedience? "Cultural pluralism" might refer to the rich variety of ethnic heritages which flavor our history. It could also provide a disguise for homosexuality, pornography, sexual communes and other life styles.

   D. Fourth main point — Many child advocates argue that they are uniquely qualified to judge what the needs of family members are and how they can best be met by government activity.

      1. Support — Senator Orrin Hatch of Utah mailed out thousands of letters preparing his readers for possible United States Commission recommendations.

      2. Support — He alerted them to watch for suggestions promoting:
         1. The right of children to sue their parents.
         2. The right of children to choose their own family.
         3. A minimum wage for household chores.
         4. An equal rights amendment for children.
         5. Government take-over of all responsibilities concerning children.

      Most of these ideas are praised in the book, *The Children's Right Movement*, 1977, edited by Ronald and Beatrice Gross.

III. Conclusion
   A. Summary of author's main points — Mr. Gary Hardaway has written an article with the intent to educate American parents of a movement in our country which has already gained the attention and support of politicians in the highest offices in our nation, and whose ideas are being passed into law by our federal government.

Activity 5 continued

    B. Quotation from article   The final principle in the UN Declaration of the Rights of the Child proclaims, "the child shall be protected from practices which foster racial, religious or any other form of discrimination." That could include those children who have been taught old-fashioned moral and religious standards based on God's Word, the Bible.

Informative Speech to Report on a Problem Situation

The purpose of this speech is to report on a problem situation or issue. You will be focusing objectively on a problem situation or issue of political, social, or economic significance. The goal is to explore the nature and dimensions of a problem without trying to formulate a workable solution for it. The speaker spells out the problem in some detail without inserting personal judgments concerning causes or solutions.

While noncontroversial subjects tend to lend themselves more readily to informative speech topics, controversial subjects can be persuasive or informative depending on the approach the speaker takes. Informative and persuasive speeches both require careful explanation or background, but persuasive speeches are intent on convincing an audience and not merely on informing them. Many of the techniques used in informative and persuasive speeches are basically the same. Each provides explanations and evidence and draws conclusions from these. In an informative speech, the writer would describe the content of the problem, indicate the growth of the problem, the people who are directly involved, and some of the consequences of the problem on others. A persuasive speaker goes a step further and usually advocates a change or the acceptance of a new policy.

In writing the informative speech to report on a problem, keep the following suggestions in mind.

1. What is the significance of the problem?
2. What is the extent of the problem?
3. Does the problem seem to be getting worse or better?
4. Do you have concrete evidence and specifics to support these conclusions?
5. Have you been specific in indicating the source of the evidence?
6. What are some social, political or economic consequences of the problem?
7. What factors have contributed to the problem?

Choose a topic that interests you and go to the library to do research. Suggested topics might be: unemployment, poverty, apathy in politics, high school dropouts, air or water pollution, juvenile delinquency, alcoholism, abortion, censorship codes, foreign trade, plea bargaining, inflation, the Ku Klux Klan, the American Communist party,

Activity 5 continued

atomic power, the outer-space program, civil rights, labor unions, suicide rate, cults, and extremist groups.

An Example of an Informative Speech to Report on a Problem

Military Power of the United States

Outline	*Script*
I. Introduction	
A. Opening statement to get attention	When we think of America, we often think of the trite phrases that describe America. These terms include: "America the Beautiful," "Home of the Brave," and "Land of the Free." After all, we have been told that America is the richest, most democratic, and the most powerful nation in the world.
B. Connecting statement	If you believe these cliches, then you are a dreamer.
C. Statement of main purpose	The purpose of my speech is to try to truthfully inform you about the last cliche mentioned, which is the rank of the United States as a military power.
D. Preview of first main point	I will begin by informing you of the defense build-up between the United States and our most formidable foe, the Soviet Union.
E. Preview of second main point	I will also compare the budgets for defense between the two countries.
F. Preview of third main point	And finally, I will discuss the atrocities of a nuclear war.
G. Importance of message	Hopefully, my message will help you understand America's plight and its efforts to recover.
II. Body	
A. Statement of first major division	The defense build-up by the Russians during the past fifteen years has been unbelievable. The United States has also increased its build-up, but on a much slower pace. SALT II has done little to ease the situation. Secretary of Defense Harold Brown said: "It would be a mistake to believe that a SALT II agreement... will solve our defense problems or end the strategic nuclear competition."

Activity 5 continued

       1. Support — The Russians have passed us in the area of research and technology more than any other area. They spend 75% more on military research than we do.

       2. Support — The CIA estimates the Soviet's armed forces to be three times that of the United States.

       3. Support — With these two items being built up, their weaponry has also substantially increased. This is quite alarming considering the country is at peace.

       4. Support — The United States has increased military build-up in some areas, but has cut other very important areas. For example, the United States once had a missile that could defend the states from a Soviet missile. They have been abandoned. Interceptors that could intercept Soviet manned bombers have also been cut back.

   B. State of second major division — The main explanation for the Soviet Union's massive military build-up is of course due to their increase in military spending.

       1. Support — The Russians outspend the United States by 25% to 45%. Their outlays have passed the United States every year since 1971.

       2. Support — The United States has planned to spend 1.5 trillion dollars in defense spending over the next ten years compared to two trillion dollars that has been spent since 1945.

   C. Statement of third major division — With the Soviets becoming militarily superior to the United States in recent years, is nuclear war a possible threat? Of course it is. The facts toward this grow daily.

       1. Support — General David Jones, Chairman of the Joint Chiefs of Staff, said: "They have a doctrine which considers nuclear war as thinkable. . . We consider nuclear war as unthinkable."

       2. Support — Our defense in case of an attack is also far inferior to that of the Soviets. Their industry is spread out. They have a complex civil defense system. They even have systems to protect farm animals and food. They also maintain a defense that would shoot down incoming nuclear warheads.

       3. Support — Americans like to think that a nuclear weapons build-up would only lead to MAD (Mutual Assured Destruction). There is one small

Activity 5 continued

	problem. The Russians do not believe in MAD.
4. Support	As stated earlier, the Russians consider nuclear war as thinkable. And why not? Estimates say that only nineteen to twenty million Russians would die compared to 120 to 180 million Americans if a nuclear war was launched today. Their value of life is much different from ours.
5. Support	It is not coincidental that the Soviets became deeply committed to defense shortly after the Cuban missile crisis. They were ousted by a superior military power earlier. And it is not coincidental either that the United States is accepting Soviet combat troops in Cuba. It is hard *not* to accept them when you are no longer superior.

III. Conclusion
    A. Summary — In summary, I have tried to inform you about the United States' inferiority as a military power both in defense build-up and budgeting. I have also tried to explain the truths of a nuclear war.

    B. Importance of message — Obviously, the military power of the United States affects all of us.

    C. Transition statement — I would like to leave you with this thought.
    D. Refers back to introduction — Do we still live in "America the Beautiful?"
    E. Closing statement — Or do we live in a MAD, MAD, MAD world?

Group Activity: Give a copy of the outline of your speech to your instructor when it is your time to speak. Go to the front of the room and begin to inform your audience. Attempt to capture their attention by pointing out the significance of the information you are about to convey. Limit the subject to what can be covered easily in the time allotted. Do not try to cover too many points or expect the audience to learn too many ideas in a single presentation. Keep in mind the importance of reinforcing main points. Repeat key words, phrases, or statements either in the same or different words. Be careful not to omit any material needed for a clear understanding of your subject. Explain any technical words unfamiliar to the listener. Appear confident when you speak. Use your visual aids to help you summarize or reinforce facts and information. Deliver your speech with confidence, eye contact, and vocal variety. Your goal should be to transfer your interest in your subject to your audience.

Activity 5 continued

Individual Activity: Make an appointment with your instructor to evaluate your speech. Give your instructor a copy of your outline. To improve your presentation follow the suggestions included with the group activity. At the conclusion of the speech, review your specific strengths and weaknessess in public speaking techniques.

Evaluation Form
Informative Speech

(Points are given to the right of each criterion.)

I. Introduction
   _____ Attention-getting device (2)
   _____ Statement of central idea (2)
   _____ Preview of main points (2)
   _____ Importance of message (2)

II. Body
   _____ Statements of two to four main points (2)
   _____ Relevant supporting materials (2)
   _____ Interesting supporting materials (2)
   _____ Adequate supporting materials (2)

III. Conclusion
   _____ Summary of main points (2)
   _____ Importance of message (2)
   _____ Strong and/or novel ending (2)

IV. Visual Aids
   _____ Appropriateness of aids (2)
   _____ Ability to use aids (2)
   _____ Quality of aids (2)

V. Presentation
   _____ Useful information (20)
   _____ Informative, not persuasive (20)
   _____ Sufficient repetition (2)
   _____ Adequate transition between parts (2)

VI. Personal qualities
   _____ General poise and speaker confidence (2)
   _____ Expression of warmth and friendliness (2)
   _____ Rapport with audience (2)
   _____ Speaker credibility (2)

VII. Vocal delivery
   _____ Rate of speech (2)
   _____ Volume of speech (2)
   _____ Vocal variety (2)
   _____ Control of fillers (ah's, er's, you know, etc.) (2)
   _____ Tonal qualities (enthusiasm, sincerity) (2)
   _____ Pronunciation and articulation (2)
   _____ Conversational style (2)

Evaluation Form continued

VIII. Physical delivery
        _____ Use of gestures (2)
        _____ Eye contact (2)
        _____ Correct posture (2)

Activity 6
Persuasion to Change Bad Habits

Preparation: Write a description of a bad habit that you would like to overcome (e.g., smoking, eating, spending money, taking pills).

Group Activity: Attend a class for a small group activity in persuasion. The class will divide in groups of four and go to separate areas. While in groups, members will verbally describe habits that they know are bad for them. The groups will select one person's problem for role playing. The person whose problem has been selected will leave the room and the other three persons will devise a situation to demonstrate an unfavorable outcome of the problem. The person will return to the room and join in the role-playing exercise but will not know what the group has planned. The role playing should be persuasive enough to make the person realize what will happen if a change of behavior does not occur. If time permits, the group should select other members to role play outcomes for their problems. Finally, the group should discuss the persuasiveness of the role-playing solutions. Were the solutions effective in helping the individual solve the problem?

Individual Activity: Ask a group of your friends to gather and talk about the bad habit that you want to overcome. Ask the group to help you role play an outcome for your problem. You will need to leave the room and the others will devise a situation to demonstrate an unfavorable outcome. You will return to the room and join in the role-playing exercise but will not know what the group has planned. The role playing should be persuasive enough to make you realize what will happen if you do not change your behavior. Write a description of how the role playing affected you. Did the conclusion make you want to change your behavior? Was the group persuasive enough? Why?

Activity 7
Analysis of a Persuasive Situation

Preparation: Select a persuasive situation such as a film, television documentary, newscast, advertising campaign, political campaign, or commercial. Consider the creators as persuaders who are selecting and emphasizing details in ways designed to sway your opinion. A good persuader will contrive situations and events that seem harmless and require little effort or concentration on the part of the viewer. Be objective as you survey the situation; analyze the motives of the creators and the devices set up to convince the viewer of a point of view. After you choose a persuasive situation to analyze, write a summary or description of the situation. Answer at least eight of the following questions as fully as you can using specific examples whenever possible.

1. What was the purpose or message of the persuasive situation?
2. What common premises were apparent (values we seemed to share, basic beliefs, things we believed in before or things that the persuader thought we believed).
3. Was dissonance produced by a violation of basic beliefs or shared values? How was this done?
4. Did acceptance of the message alleviate the dissonance? Did you feel differently about anything afterward?
5. What attention devices were used to focus your attention, voluntarily, involuntarily, or in anticipation, on what the persuader wanted to emphasize?
6. What basic needs were appealed to?
7. How did the situation produce an emotional response in you? Were you motivated to accept the message because of your emotional response? When you experienced a feeling-response, did you participate vicariously in the situation?
8. What attempts were made to gain viewer involvement? Did you remain aloof from the action? Were any traits of your own recognizable in the situation? How did you feel if you recognized yourself?
9. Were any group appeals made? Did you identify with any of the groups? If so, did you feel pressured to accept the message because of the group identity? Analyze your feelings about negative reference groups if they were used.
10. What did the persuaders use as symbols of their message? Look for objects, scenery, climate, color, analogies, ways of speaking. Identify what the symbols represented.
11. Did the situation provide you with an awareness that you did not have before viewing it? Did it make you want to say, I never thought of it that way before?
12. Did the situation motivate you toward any action, or did it only suggest a change in belief?

Activity 7 continued

13. If you already believed in the central message, consider the ways in which your belief was reinforced.

An example of answers to these questions follows.

Example of Persuasive Activity

The following questions are answered in relation to the Avis car rental commercial.

1. The purpose of the persuasive situation is to get you to rent your car from Avis.
2. Common premises are that the man needs to rent a car and he needs to rent it quickly.
3. Dissonance is produced because people assume you don't have to run through airports to rent cars. Avis shows this by making fun of the Hertz commercial.
4. It alleviates the situation in that Avis shows you are supposed to walk through airports, not run.
5. Attention devices used are the man sprawled on the floor with papers everywhere saying he was running to rent a car when the man he was going to jump suddenly raised up.
6. Basic need appealed to is the desire or need for a car when access to your own is not possible.
7. You are motivated to accept the message because the message makes sense and it makes fun of the Hertz message.
8. No attempts are made to gain viewer involvement just to persuade you to rent from Avis.
9. No group appeals are made (except to that "group" that rents cars).
10. Symbols used are just typical airport conditions with the reference to the Hertz commercial.
11. It doesn't provide you with new awareness; it just reinforces your belief of what you already know.
12. It motivates you to rent from Avis.
13. It reinforces your belief by just making an apparent example of the obvious.

Group Activity: In class orally summarize the persuasive situation that you have analyzed. Using the information and specific examples in the questions as guidelines, discuss the motives of the persuaders. Have they been successful in convincing the viewer of their point of view? Were you swayed to their opinion? Why? Why not?

Individual Activity: Find at least one other person with whom to discuss the persuasive situation that you have summarized. Write a one-paragraph summary of the other person's impression of the persuasive situation.

Activity 8
A Rationale for a Persuasive Topic

Preparation: Compare the two speeches that follow. The same topic—advertising—is briefly presented as an informative speech and as a persuasive speech. Note the different manners in which the two messages have been prepared.

An Example of an Informative Speech

Advertising

Outline	Script
I. Introduction	
A. Opening statement to get attention	What does this ad mean to you? To a housewife this advertisement could be a way for her to save money. To a salesmanager, it could help sell a product. And to an accountant, it is just another cost to the business.
B. Connecting statement	Businesses use advertising to retain loyal customers, to retrieve lost customers, and to recruit new customers.
C. Statement of main purpose	Just what are the methods by which businesses develop advertisements to sell their products?
D. Preview of main points	I hope to answer this question for you as I describe the types of selling appeals and techniques used to attract attention to a product.
II. Body	
A. Statement of first major division	Advertisers use two basic approaches to appeal to consumers: emotional and rational.
1. Support (show ad)	Emotional purchasing is subjective and impulsive in nature and has a strong appeal. For example, a woman won't buy a dress because she *needs* it but because she wants to be recognized. Rational purchasing is weighing out the advantages and disadvantages of the various products. For example, when a man buys a car he may choose a Chevy because he feels it is a better car; however, the style

Activity 8 continued

	he chooses within the Chevy line might still be strictly emotional.
2. Support	Using these two basic consumer motivators, the advertiser expands them and turns them into selling appeals.
3. Example (show ad)	This can be done by making the consumer believe that he *deserves* the item. (Life is tense—you need a pick-me-up—you need to be pampered.)
4. Example (show ad)	This can be done, also, by making the consumer believe everyone is doing it. (Sinning is less sinful in groups.)
5. Example (show ad)	And last, it can be done by giving consumers excuses for enjoying themselves. (Sinning is in style.)
6. Transition	By using these appeals the product should sell.
B. Statement of second major division	There are two basic categories of techniques used to attract attention to a product: claims and appeals.
1. Support	Claims focus the attention on the product and what it can do for you. It appears to be rational.
2. Support	Appeals zero in on your emotions, your fears, desires, and cherished beliefs.
3. Examples (show ads)	Some examples of claims are the following: Benefit—what it will do for you, New—has to be new or improved, Tests show—proven tests show your product is better, and Take it from me—if stated with experience and confidence.
4. Examples (show ads)	Some examples of appeals are the following: Family—if you care about your family you'll use our product, Self-image—emphasis on user, Snob appeal—few or exclusive, Bandwagon—everyone's using it, Youth—makes you feel or appear youthful, Love—become more attractive to opposite sex, and Patriotism—love or support your country.
5. Transition	These are just a few of the techniques used by the advertising world.
III. Conclusion	
A. Summary	Many hours of time and labor and money went into these advertisements and what for? To

Activity 8 continued

	make us more aware of the products and services that are available. The advertisers explain to us the differences between products and give us the necessary information we need to make choices.
B. Importance of message	It has been proven that more people seek out the advertised brand than the unadvertised—because the consumer feels it has more value.
C. Closing statement	So next time you see a commercial on TV or see an ad in a magazine, I hope you will be more aware of its purpose so that *you* can decide how it will affect you.

An Example of a Persuasive Speech

The Seduction of Advertising

Outline	*Script*
I. Introduction	
A. Gain attention	Have you recently flipped through a magazine such as *Mademoiselle, Cosmopolitan,* or *Lady's Home Journal*? Do you realize that you are being seduced by the countless shiny ads displayed on the pages of these and most other magazines?
B. Examples	The vast majority of the magazines we pick up and browse through or read today are literally filled with very attractive advertising. These ads may be selling every possible type and brand of cosmetics, cigarettes, cigars, liquors, wines, automobiles, articles of clothing, and jewelry.
C. Emphasize central idea of speech	An important point to realize is that these ads were created with one thing in mind—to sell the product shown. There are many ways to do just this. These advertisements may be very seductive, even fraudulent, and sometimes are a put-down to the viewer or prospective customer.
D. Leading question for transition	Is it possible to develop new ways of looking at advertising? Is this desirable? Is it something you wish to cultivate within yourself?
II. Body	
A. First main idea	Many people have researched the advertising business and have demonstrated that it is possible to learn how to develop an objective

Activity 8 continued

                                          eye when viewing the advertised object. A book titled *Subliminal Seduction*, written in 1974 by Wilson Bryan Key, presents very thorough research on this topic. If you have not read this book I think you really must in order to understand just how many ways the consumer is being seduced.

1. Support (visual aid)   Consider this: there is an ad for Racquet Club Cologne for men. It suggests that if you wear this cologne you will play tennis or racquet ball to a different advantage. You will be a very handsome and rugged athlete and a very sexy man. The ad reads, "Crisp. Stylish. Exhilarating. Your most effective weapon." You won't just smell good—you will be wearing a weapon.

2. Support (visual aid)   A prime example of another kind of seduction is described by Wilson Key in his book. Almay's nail polish ad shows a man and a woman toasting each other with glasses of white wine. Wait! There's more. Here in the base of the woman's glass if you look closely you will see a photographic trick. The woman's fingers reflected through the glass have been photographed to show a nude image nestled in the base of the glass. You may think this really outlandish, but if you really look at the photograph you will see it. Key stated in his book that many ads use this method of subliminal sexual suggestion to sell the product.

3. Support (visual aid)   As a final example consider this model pictured in two ways. On the first page no makeup—all her supposed flaws are pointed out. Her hair is dull and messed up. You can bet that special lighting was used in the photograph to make her look flat and dull. On the second page she is made up to perfection with cosmetics and naturally looks gorgeous. The copy under the ad suggests that this woman is not acceptable in her natural state—she must be made up in order to be attractive. Many cosmetic advertisers use this technique of telling women that they are not attractive if they do not use the advertised product. The visual and emotional gimmicks are hard to

Activity 8 continued

    B. Second main idea

        1. Support

        2. Support

        3. Support

        4. Support

III. Conclusion
    A. Central idea restated

    B. Plant idea for action

    C. Action

---

turn down. This type of manipualtion is a real insult to women.

I know from a great deal of personal experience about the techniques of advertising. I worked for eight years in the advertising industry as a commercial artist, a copy writer, an audio visual production manager, and an account executive.

The main concern was always to sell—to put on the very best promotion in order to sell the product.

In all these years in advertising I became very cynical because I felt that the advertiser was concerned for the customer only as a buyer and never as a person.

Countless gimmicks were used and sometimes very unscrupulously. Townhouse rooms were made to look larger by photography and copy could be written to such an alluring degree that many flaws of a product were ignored or intentionally covered up.

The problem with all these advertising techniques and their influence on our lives is that they are manipulative and seductive. None of us want to be manipulated. Our individuality is unique and this type of advertising is a threat to our own uniqueness. Most of us care about ethics and being honest.

It has been illustrated to you in this presentation the seductive and manipulative means by which advertisers display products. And, it is very important to learn to cope with and be critical of these elements in our lives.

When you see an advertisement with a beautiful person, an attractive home, or a liquor promising all sorts of good things you must remember that other messages may also be present. These messages may be giving you an illusion. A perfume cannot give you the man of your dreams or a life lived happily ever after.

So learn how to develop this objective eye. Learn to take care of your own individuality and uniqueness. The advertiser cannot seduce you unless you allow this seduction.

Activity 8 continued

Examine the topics for a persuasive speech listed below. Select a topic of your choice or choose one from the list. Write a short explanation (i.e., one paragraph) to show its appropriateness as a persuasive speaking topic. Include the means by which you would create dissonance and the action step you would suggest. Then give an explanation of how you might use the same topic as the subject for an informative speech.

Persuasive Topics

1. Insecticides and Pesticides—Poisoning the Nation: See Rachel Carson's *Silent Spring*.
2. A Plea for the Liberal Arts: In the age of science we are becoming splinter men. Overspecialization is dangerous to the democratic philosophy.
3. A New Public Morality: Are Americans any more "immoral" than their forefathers or has the change in attitudes made it seem to be so?
4. The Migrant Workers: The story of the miserable lives of exploited workers who are imported for profit.
5. A New Look for Segregation: Years after the Supreme Court decision there is still the question—can social attitudes be legislated?
6. Living under the Bomb: See Philip Wylie's *Triumph*. Find an analogy in Athens or other nations that lived under pressing danger. What has this done to our social fabric, mores, etc.?
7. The Puff of Profit: The reaction of tobacco companies to the medical evidence against smoking seems to be somewhat dishonest. We ban the cranberries but not the Camels.
8. A Second Offense: The number of sex crimes is increasing. There are many examples of a sex criminal who is released from prison ten times worse than before.
9. The Insurance Scandals: Alarming increases in number of medical malpractice suits and dishonesty in adjusting auto insurance have occurred.
10. Morality of our Politicians: What should men like Representatives Mills of Arkansas and Hays of Ohio do when they commit misdeeds? What should their constituents expect them to do?
11. In Memory of. . .—Or the Cost of Dying: An analysis of current funeral customs —the pagan ceremony, the prolonged suffering, the profit exploitation by unethical funeral directors. Examine the practices of other cultures.
12. The Measure of a Man: Society today judges men by false standards. People in the past did this also, but the men we remember as great today are not the ones always honored in the past.
13. Censorship: It is more harmful to deprive people of the freedom to choose what they will read and see than it is to prevent obscene literature. Who is to decide

Activity 8 continued

       what is acceptable? Find examples of books such as *Huckleberry Finn* that have been banned in the United States.

14. Outmoded Moral Concepts: Laws on birth control, divorce, abortion, and euthanasia should be brought up to date. The evils of the present system are greater than those that would accrue by changing the laws.
15. Pornography: There is a massive amount of vulgar literature being sold at a profit. Take the view that this is aimed at poisoning our youth and is a problem that each individual should fight to correct.
16. Mental Illness: Mental illness should be treated as a medical disease, but society has attached a social stigma to it. Discuss the paradox today that society sends patients to hospitals to be cured, and then refuses to accept them back into society.
17. Tranquilizers: The American people increasingly depend on pills to avoid facing the problems of life. We must learn to face problems constructively.
18. The Danger to the Far Right: Ultra-conservative groups who claim to be anticommunist do more harm to American freedom than they do to help it.
19. The Value of the Radical Right: Radical groups may not always be right. In fact, they may do some harm. But to prohibit their existence would be a major step toward tyranny of the government. Who would decide which groups are undesirable? Point out that progress has often been stimulated by groups that were considered "radical."
20. Individualism: People today are afraid to be different. Point out the progress that has been made by individuals who dared to be different.

Group Activity: Read your topic to the class and present your rationale for classifying the topic as persuasive. Review the means of producing dissonance and the action step. Discuss with the class the types of discomfort and actions that would be the most effective for developing effective persuasive speeches. Then explain how the same topic might be used for preparing an informative message. Finally, discuss and compare the two examples.

Individual Activity: Locate a friend or relative who will discuss your persuasive topic with you. Discuss your rationale for classifying the topic as persuasive, your way of producing dissonance, and your suggested action step. With your partner, try to improve these. Then present your rationale for changing the persuasive topic to an informative topic. Finally, compare the two examples included with this activity.

    Write out your topic and one paragraph about it along with a summary of your discussion with your partner.

Activity 9
A Mini-Persuasive Speech

Preparation: An outline for a mini-persuasive speech is included below. Refer to that outline and then formulate ideas on a subject of your choice. Write a statement beside each of the headings in an attempt to sway the listener to your point of view. The idea may be researched later in more depth and used for a longer persuasive speech.

Mini-Persuasive Speech Outline

I. Gain attention:
II. Establish credibility:
III. Establish common premise:
IV. Produce dissonance:
V. Reduce dissonance:
VI. Personal experience:
VII. Action:

To help in your preparation, an example of a mini-persuasive speech is given below.

United Way

Gain attention: Have you ever played the card game solitaire? Then you know how badly you want that one card that will make you a winner.
Establish credibility: United Way gave the winning card to 631,432 people last year. As a United Way contributor and a volunteer for three and one-half years, I know what my United Way dollars do. (Give several examples.)
Establish common premise: Do you know for sure that you or someone in your family will not need a United Way agency next year?
Produce dissonance: Would you say no to a retarded child when he asked you to teach him to tie his shoe? If you do not give to United Way, you've done just that.
Reduce dissonance: So decide to give. There's really no question about it. Your gifts will decide which agencies will function next year.
Personal example: I've seen the joy on the faces of the parents of a six-year-old boy when they were told at the Collier Center that their child was not mentally retarded, but only had a severe hearing disorder.
Action: When you are asked to give, give freely. You might be giving the winning card to yourself or someone in your family.

Group Activity: Present your mini-persuasive speech in class. If time permits ask class members for ideas on making more persuasive statements. Do you feel this subject is interesting enough to research in depth and make into a detailed six- to eight-minute persuasive speech? If not, where is the topic lacking? Turn in a copy of your mini-persuasive speech.

Activity 9 continued

Individual Activity: Using the statements prepared to follow the outline, attempt to persuade a friend or family member to your point of view. At the end of your short speech, ask for criticism of your ideas. How could you write the speech to be more persuasive? Write out a copy of your mini-persuasive speech and a one-paragraph summary of your experience in presenting it.

```
┌─────────────────────────────────────────────────────┐
│                      Activity                       │
│                         10                          │
│                 A Speech to Persuade                │
└─────────────────────────────────────────────────────┘
```

Preparation: Your instructor will give you special instructions about the type of persuasive speech you are to prepare and an acceptable time limit for presenting your message.

After you have selected and researched a topic, complete an outline of your speech. Be sure to include quotations, personal experience, examples, and statistics as support. Use the format presented with the persuasive speech example in the text and the persuasive speech example included with this activity. Transfer the outline to 3-by-5 inch cards and practice your speech until you are prepared to deliver it. As you practice work toward eliminating the cards or reducing them significantly. Be certain to include appropriate visual aids.

Example of a Persuasive Speech

Abolish the Death Penalty

Outline	*Script*
I. Introduction	(Show a transparency of Roman soldiers at Christ's cross.)
A. Attention device	Without capital punishment, how would society protect itself?
B. Specific example	Jesus Christ was a victim of capital punishment. Today his memory is respected. He was innocent.
C. Relate to audience	That one supreme example should make you shiver at the thought that today the death penalty is still used.
D. Central idea	Capital punishment—a ritualistic, uplifted, accepted, cruel example of man's inhumanity to man—must be stopped forever.
E. Transition	Let me tell you why.
II. Body	
A. First main idea	The death penalty is not more effective than imprisonment as a deterrent. The death penalty is not a deterrent to crime.
1. Common value	We all want to feel safe in society, but having the death penalty is not a way to ensure this.
2. Dissonance	Comparisons show that in abolition states, the homicide rate is only about one-third to one-half as high as it is in the other states. If executions prevent crimes, then after an

Activity 10 continued

	actual execution the homicide rate should drop. However, no significant difference was found in this respect in a study of homicide rates sixty days prior and sixty days subsequent to five executions in Philadelphia. European states which have abolished the death penalty have lower homicide rates than states which retain the death penalty. The Scandinavian countries, which have abolished the death penalty, have homicide rates about one-half as high as England, which retained the death penalty until recently.
3. Transition	So, capital punishment does not reduce violence in society.
B. Second main idea	Capital punishment does lessen people's respect for human life.
1. Quotation	Marc Ancel in *The Problem of the Death Penalty* said, "Capital punishment has a demoralizing effect on the public, the prisoner, and the entire prison atmosphere." He suggested that capital punishment might actually "constitute a morbid stimulus to crime."
2. Personal example	I know myself that I learn quickly by example.
III. Conclusion	
A. Summary	Do people learn to kill other people from the example set by the state? Dr. Karl Menninger said in his book *The Crime of Punishment*, "I know that there is not a particle of preventive value in the wreaking of vengeance and anger in the quick elimination of this one wretch."
B. Central idea restated	Dr. Menninger wrote the following also: "Eliminating one offender who happens to get caught weakens public security by creating a false sense of diminished danger through a definite remedial measure. Actually, it does not remedy anything, and it bypasses completely the real and unsolved problem of how to identify, detect, and detail potentially dangerous citizens."
C. Present idea in memorable way	Imagine the horror of a person about to be executed. Realize the irreversibility of capital punishment. Think about the death of an innocent person. Accept that this vengeance

Activity 10 continued

                                          by the state does not lessen violent crimes. Consider that you are really less safe living in a culture that practices capital punishment. Capital punishment solves nothing, but it may cause trouble.

   D. Action step   Do not join in the useless violence. Do not be guilty yourself. Decide and fight against capital punishment!

Group Activity: Attend class to present your persuasive speech. Give your instructor a copy of your outline.

Individual Activity: Make arrangements with your instructor to present your persuasive speech. Give your instructor a copy of your outline.

Evaluation Form
Persuasive Speech

(Points are given to the right of each criterion.)

I. Introduction
   _____ Attention-getting device (2)
   _____ Central idea presented (2)
   _____ Relate message to audience (2)

II. Body
   _____ Dissonance created (2)
   _____ Resolution of dissonance (2)
   _____ Reinforcement of solution (2)
   _____ Support relates to audience values (2)
   _____ Support relates to personal experiences (2)

III. Conclusion
   _____ Central idea restated (2)
   _____ Summary (2)
   _____ Challenge to audience (2)
   _____ Action step (2)

IV. Visual aids
   _____ Appropriateness of aids (2)
   _____ Ability to use aids (2)
   _____ Quality of aids (2)

V. Presentation
   _____ Persuasive, not informative (40)
   _____ Adequate transitions between parts (2)

VI. Personal qualities
   _____ General poise and speaker confidence (2)
   _____ Relates to audience values (2)
   _____ Rapport with audience (2)
   _____ Speaker credibility (2)

VII. Vocal delivery
   _____ Rate of speech (2)
   _____ Volume of speech (2)
   _____ Vocal variety (2)
   _____ Control of fillers (ah's, er's, you know, etc.) (2)
   _____ Tonal qualities (2)
   _____ Pronunciation and articulation (2)
   _____ Conversational style (2)

Evaluation Form continued

VIII. Physical delivery
 _____ Use of gestures (2)
 _____ Eye contact (2)
 _____ Correct posture (2)

> **Activity**
> **11**
> **Speech to Entertain**

Preparation: Using a subject of your choice prepare a five- to six-minute speech to entertain. Suggestions for topics are listed below.

1. Women
2. Dating
3. Television commercials
4. Liars I have known
5. How not to study
6. Getting married
7. Hippies
8. Being the youngest in the family
9. Sex education in the schools
10. Being myself

Many subjects can be approached in an entertaining way. The speech to entertain can be informative, stimulating, even convincing as long as these goals are not the chief aim of the speaker. The example included is an informative speech on Burma Shave signs. This speech catches the attention and interest of an audience by developing a trend of thought about a chosen topic. The subject will not necessarily make the listeners laugh out loud. It may bring only smiles of amusement and still be classified as a speech to entertain.

When organizing your thoughts you will want to put ideas together in an entertaining way. The audience should see that a definite trend of thought has been developed yet should not feel that they must recall facts or consider changes in behavior. Techniques that you may want to use are exaggeration, juxtaposing incongruous statements (e.g., appending a frivolous afterthought to a serious statement), using humorous or unusual figures of speech, making a play on words by using clever phrasing and puns, telling humorous anecdotes, and using humorous examples.

In delivering a speech to entertain, you must approach your subject with more objectivity and less emotional involvement than you do in a serious speech. When you speak to entertain there is a feeling of thoughtful fun that you must catch and transfer to the listener.

In creating humor, you must strive to achieve a comic sense or spirit of fun and realize what might be laughed at. Humor can come as a result of an intellectual turn of a phrase. The line must then be projected in a witty way that communicates its humor. Audiences often laugh at incongruities. These are extremes that exist and you as a speaker will need to emphasize the difference between the expected and the actual.

Activity 11 continued

Laughter can also be provoked when the audience has experienced the situations presented. As a speaker, you would try to get the audience to visualize the happening and think that "something like this has happened to me." Through wise selection and emphasis your voice and gesture should communicate the comic. You will need to learn the technique of exaggerating without being too obvious. Humor should seem easy and spontaneous. You should vary your line of delivery as well as your gestures and movements.

Finally, an entertaining speaker must possess a good sense of timing. You should allow time for the audience to savor the thought. You may point out a humorous line by pausing before the line. Less humorous lines can have a faster pace. Never obviously wait for laughs. When the audience does laugh you should wait until the laughter begins to die down. If you do not wait, the audience will be afraid to laugh for fear of missing something. Remember too that you must never break character and laugh with the audience. Some famous comedians do this but it is incorrect for the public speaker.

Until you actually deliver the speech and see the audience reaction you will not know whether or not your speech is entertaining. Much depends on how your speech is delivered. The only assurance of success you will have is in your preparation. Your effort and ability to select a topic, organize, and rehearse the speech to entertain will be rewarded by the warm reception of your listeners.

Example of a Speech to Entertain

Burma-Shave Signs

Outline	Script
I. Introduction	
A. Opening statement to get attention	"Henry the Eighth/Prince of Friskers/Lost five wives/But kept/His whiskers."
B. Connecting statement	This little jingle has been seen by the side of highways by many people. Numerous other jingles like it have also been seen. They are what are known as Burma-Shave signs. Signs like these are on many highways all over the country, helping motorists enjoy their trips as well as advertise Burma-Shave.
C. Statement of central idea	The background of these signs is an interesting anecdote in American merchandising.
D. Preview of first main point	I will begin by describing the Burma-Shave Company and how it was started.
E. Preview of second main point	I will then tell you how the Burma-Shave signs came into being.

Activity 11 continued

    F. Preview of third main point   Finally, I will give you a few examples of some of the jingles.

II. Body
    A. First major division   The Burma-Shave Company was founded by Clinton Odell, a retired owner of an insurance organization. The company originally manufactured a liniment, the essential oils of which came from Burma. Clint combined the word "Burma" with the Latin word vita, meaning life or vigor, for the name of his new company. The liniment, however, was a very odorous one and did not sell well enough to keep the business going.

                                                              Meanwhile, one of Clint's sons, Allan Odell, was traveling in England and discovered that many of the men there were using a brushless shaving cream. Allan felt that this would be a good product for their company to manufacture, thus the birth of Burma-Shave.

    B. Second major division   Burma-Shave was such a new idea that it did not sell well in America. One day while driving along a highway, Allan was trying to think of new ways to advertise their product. While driving, he saw a series of signs telling about a filling station down the road. Allan believed that the Burma-Shave Company could use the same kind of advertising. The advertising experts said it wouldn't work. You had to sell shaving cream with statistics, testimonials, and smiling, well-shaven faces. Clint, however, decided that anything was worth a try and agreed to spend $200 for the first set of road signs. They appeared in September, 1926, near Lakeville, Minnesota. Allan wrote the first jingle which read, "Cheer up/Face/The war/Is/Over."

                                                              Allan and his younger brother, Leonard, took the job of installing the signs. Leonard drove a truck loaded with freshly painted signs and the necessary tools for setting them up while Allan raced ahead in a car to find a likely spot and an amiable farmer willing to rent the space. By the time Leonard arrived, Allan had talked the farmer into the deal, and the

Activity 11 continued

    C. Third major division
       (visual aid: posters with jingles)

brothers went to work. The $200 gamble paid off. Sales jumped from almost zero to $68,000 in one year.

By 1965 there were over 7,000 sets of Burma-Shave signs dotting highways all over the country. Each set consists of six signs spaced about 100 feet apart. Souvenir hunters used to carry off entire sets of jingles so they are now bolted to fence-high iron or wooden posts.

Sites for all Burma-Shave signs are leased from farmers at an annual cash rental. The farmers show a genuine loyalty toward the signs. They protect them from farm animals, guard them against souvenir hunters, and repair broken ones.

Burma-Shave jingles are very catchy. Examples of a few of them are: "Are your whiskers/When you wake/Tougher than/A two-bit steak?" "A peach/Looks good/With lots of fuzz/But man's no peach/And never was." Wives called their husband's attention to signs such as "He played/A sax/Had no B.O./But his whiskers scratched/So she let him go." Farther down the road the husband had his turn and read aloud: "Soon shaving brushes/Will be trimmin'/Those screwy hats/We see on women."

Safety experts soon pointed out the fact that the signs helped to slow down drivers. Burma-Shave took the hint, and wrote such jingles as: "Don't take a curve/At 60 per/We hate to lose/A customer" and "Past schoolhouses/Take it slow/Let the little/Shavers/Grow."

The Odells didn't realize how seriously some people took their jingles until one series of signs suggested: "Rip a fender/Off your car/Send it in/For a half-pound jar." Dozens of tiny fenders from toy cars poured into the Minneapolis office, and jars of Burma-Shave were dispatched. But the big surprise came when they began to receive crates containing real, ripped-off fenders! Of course they sent the half-pound jars to these people also.

Activity 11 continued

                        Another motorist responded to the sign which read: "Free, free/A trip/To Mars/For 900 empty jars." He sent a letter to the Odells saying that he had 898 jars saved up and would report any day now for his free trip. The Odells hastily replaced the signs with: "If a trip to Mars/You'd earn/Remember, friend/There's no return."

                        Jingles are selected annually from contests open to both professionals and amateurs. Jingles in poor taste are never accepted. Though many of those submitted would undoubtedly amuse many motorists, others might be offended. A few examples of the jingles that were "censored" are: "If wife shuns/Your fond embrace/Don't shoot/The iceman/Feel your face." "Listen, birds/Those signs cost/Money/So roost a while but/Don't get funny." "My man/Won't shave/Sez Hazel Hus/But I should worry/Dora's does."

III. Conclusion
    A. Summary   In summary, I have told you how the Burma-Shave Company was formed. I have also told you how the Burma-Shave signs originated. Finally, I have given you a few examples of the Burma-Shave jingles.

    B. Closing statement   In closing, I would like to say that Burma-Shave signs have become a national institution in the United States. They are seen by millions of motorists all over the country. These signs have well served their purpose, not only to advertise Burma-Shave, but to make traveling more enjoyable to many people.

Group Activity: Give a copy of the outline of your speech to your instructor when it is your time to speak. Attempt to capture the attention of your audience as you present your speech to entertain. Remember your goal is to provide an enjoyable experience, not to encourage the retention of information or to bring about behavioral change.

Individual Activity: Make an appointment with your instructor to evaluate your speech. Give your instructor a copy of your outline. At the conclusion of the speech, review your specific strengths and weaknesses in presenting a speech to entertain.

Evaluation Form
Entertaining Speech

(Points are given to the right of each criterion.)

I. Introduction
   _____ Attention-getting device (4)
   _____ Preview of central theme (2)
   _____ Preview of main points (2)

II. Body
   _____ Two to four main points (2)
   _____ Relevant supporting materials (2)
   _____ Interesting supporting materials (2)
   _____ Adequate supporting materials (2)

III. Conclusion
   _____ Summary of main points (2)
   _____ Strong and/or novel ending (4)

IV. Visual aids (if appropriate)
   _____ Appropriateness of aids (2)
   _____ Ability to use aids (2)
   _____ Quality of aids (2)

V. Presentation
   _____ Entertaining message (20)
   _____ Not informative or persuasive (20)
   _____ Adequate transition between parts (4)

VI. Personal qualities
   _____ General poise and speaker confidence (2)
   _____ Expression of warmth and friendliness (2)
   _____ Rapport with audience (2)
   _____ Speaker credibility (2)

VII. Vocal delivery
   _____ Rate of speech (2)
   _____ Volume of speech (2)
   _____ Vocal variety (2)
   _____ Control of fillers (ah's, er's, you know, etc.) (2)
   _____ Tonal qualities (enthusiasm, sincerity) (2)
   _____ Pronunciation and articulation (2)
   _____ Conversational style (2)

Evaluation Form continued

VIII. Physical delivery
      _____ Use of gestures (2)
      _____ Eye contact (2)
      _____ Correct posture (2)

Activity 12
Impromptu Speech

Preparation: An impromptu speech is given with little, if any, preparation. The speaker is called upon to inform, persuade, or entertain, and is given no time for the usual outlining, let alone search for supporting materials. The topic, of course, must be one upon which the speaker has adequate background to present a credible message. The speaker should attempt to follow the general speaking format of introduction, body, and conclusion with two to four main points and supporting statements. Impromptu speaking can be fun as well as challenging. Experience with impromptu speaking can make that statement, "we'd like to hear a few words from you about . . .," much less threatening.

Select one of the following options for a two-minute impromptu speech.

Option 1: Childhood Event

To choose a subject look back over your childhood and select an event that made a special impression on you. What is it? Do you remember a special birthday? Your memorable Christmas? Your childhood sweetheart? A day in school? An incident with a special friend? The day you went camping?

Specific topics might be one of the following.

1. A lesson I learned in school
2. The thrill of getting a special present
3. A specific day at school
4. A humorous thing I said as a child
5. A favorite teacher
6. An incident involving a father, mother, sister
7. An unforgettable character I met growing up

Think briefly about the incident that you are going to talk about. You must not attempt to cover too much in your talk. Limit yourself to one incident. The objective of this talk is to give you experience speaking before a group and to develop your self-confidence.

In preparing your impromptu message just think through the incident in chronological order. Do not write out what you are going to say. Above all do not attempt to memorize it. You are simply going to talk for two minutes about an experience from your early life.

Activity 12 continued

When your time to speak comes you should not even think about making a talk. You should simply chat with the audience for two minutes in a spontaneous, natural, relaxed way as you would relate a story to someone over a coke. To develop the ability to speak effectively, you will conquer your fear and develop courage sooner if you will choose a subject with which you are very familiar. Remember to be yourself as you relate this incident to us. Do not try to be anything other than what you are.

Option 2: Learning a Lesson
Choose a subject based on an incident in your life that taught you a lesson. The speech might be about a lie you once told or the day you skipped school. When making the talk you will want to use specific facts and actions that produce images in the minds of the audience. Good speakers try to get their listeners to see what they are saying. They do not talk in colorless generalities and without enthusiasm.

Specific topics might be the following.

1. An encounter with the law
2. A scary experience
3. An embarrassing experience for me
4. How I offended someone
5. A crisis in my life
6. A tragedy in my life
7. A disappointing day
8. Something I wish I'd never said

When it is time for you to make your two-minute talk you will need to answer the following questions in some detail.

1. The circumstances—who was involved, when did it occur, where did it happen, what happened, and how did it happen?
2. What effects did the incident have on you?
3. How did you feel about the incident?

In telling the incident be sure to relive it and even act it out for the audience. Be as energetic and enthusiastic as you possibly can be. In order to make a successful talk of any kind you must be enthusiastic. Enthusiasm does not mean that you are loud or shout at the audience. You speak with intensity and animation. You have the life and energy that result in a more attractive personality. Genuine enthusiasm is one of the secrets of success in any project, but it is certainly necessary in successful speaker-audience communicaton.

Option 3: Frustrating Incident
Choose a subject based on an incident that made you angry. You will need to relive that experience before the audience with all the fervor you felt when it happened.

Activity 12 continued

Specific topics might be the following.

1. I ran out of gasoline
2. I was convinced "honesty is the best policy"
3. When persistence paid
4. The day I was robbed
5. An experience as a hitchhiker
6. When I broke something
7. I was cheated
8. I was jilted
9. I was criticized
10. A mistake I made

When it is your turn to speak before the group you will want to be prepared. You should have selected an incident that made you excited or frustrated. The story may be any incident from your business, your school, your community, your family, or among your friends that irritates you. Be certain that you choose a subject that has enough material to last for two minutes. Begin your talk with a specific example. Start by telling us what, when, where and how you became angry or excited. What did you do and how did you do it? Be enthusiastic and act out your experience as much as possible to help the audience relive it with you.

Group Activity: When it is your turn, present your impromptu message to your audience. To make it an effective experience, do not "cheat" and memorize your speech. If you do, in all likelihood your audience will know that the message was prepared in advance. It is generally more difficult to make a memorized message appear impromptu than to muster the courage to make an impromptu speech.

Individual Activity: Make arrangements with your instructor to present your impromptu speech. Do not "cheat" and memorize the message. Your instructor will be able to recognize a memorized message.

Additional Readings in Speaker-Audience Communication

In addition to books and articles cited in these chapters, the following books are excellent sources for further study of communication.

Carnegie, D. *Quick and Easy Ways to Effective Speaking.* New York: Simon and Schuster, 1977.

> Dale Carnegie is famous for helping individuals develop confidence in their public speaking ability. Students of communication will find much of his approach like that of other authors.

Culligan, M. J. *How to Be a Billion Dollar Persuader.* New York: St. Martins Press, 1979.

> Successful executive Culligan, responsible for two billion in sales in his lifetime, discusses making the most of presentations, using research effectively, follow-up, concept and product persuasion, do's and don't's of public speaking, and much more.

Gilbert, M. A. *How to Win an Argument.* New York: McGraw-Hill, 1979.

> One approach to winning arguments is based on communication skills and effective development of supporting materials.

Linver, S. *Speak Easy.* New York: Summit Books, 1978.

> The speaker's total image as it impacts the communication is covered. The reader is encouraged to evaluate personal qualities as they relate to the "spoken image."

Sarnoff, D. *Speech Can Change Your Life.* New York: Dell Publishing, 1978.

> This book provides another persuasive message on the value of gaining adequate speech communication skills.

Stone, J. and Backner, J. *Speaking Up.* New York: McGraw-Hill, 1977.

> This book is written for women who find themselves unprepared to speak effectively in meetings and to make presentations. It covers impromptu and prepared speech making to both large audiences and smaller groups.

Final Activity
Speech Communication Skills Inventory

Preparation: As you complete this course in speech communication, you have a set of feelings about your present skill in various speaking situations. As stated in Activity 2, Part I, it is an interesting exercise to record these feelings and to compare them with the feelings about your speech communication skills expressed as you began the course.

For each statement below, rate yourself as you feel at this moment. Indicate your feelings by circling the appropriate number to the left of the statement.

1 = very strong   2 = strong   3 = don't know   4 = weak   5 = very weak

Think carefully and be honest with yourself. These results are for you alone.

1. 1 2 3 4 5   I feel good about myself when meeting people.
2. 1 2 3 4 5   I feel adequate when I talk to people.
3. 1 2 3 4 5   I project a positive self-image.
4. 1 2 3 4 5   I use words that are well suited to my listener.
5. 1 2 3 4 5   I use correct grammar.
6. 1 2 3 4 5   I find the right words to express my thoughts.
7. 1 2 3 4 5   I use natural gestures when speaking.
8. 1 2 3 4 5   I understand nonverbal feedback from others.
9. 1 2 3 4 5   I look at people when I talk to them.
10. 1 2 3 4 5   I give others a chance to speak.
11. 1 2 3 4 5   I listen attentively to what others have to say.
12. 1 2 3 4 5   I say words clearly when I speak.
13. 1 2 3 4 5   I am comfortable in conversations with others.
14. 1 2 3 4 5   I let others know my true feelings.
15. 1 2 3 4 5   I consider the feelings of others.
16. 1 2 3 4 5   I am open in considering others' opinions.
17. 1 2 3 4 5   I am comfortable admitting that I don't understand.

Final Activity continued

18.	1 2 3 4 5	I contribute when I participate in small groups.
19.	1 2 3 4 5	I work well in group activities.
20.	1 2 3 4 5	I am relaxed when I give a speech.
21.	1 2 3 4 5	I hold the audience's attention when I give a speech.
22.	1 2 3 4 5	I am able to write an organized speech.
23.	1 2 3 4 5	I am able to convince others to accept my opinion.
24.	1 2 3 4 5	I use evidence to back up what I say.
25.	1 2 3 4 5	I appear to know what I am talking about.

Group Activity: Go back to Activity 2, Part I, and compare the two sets of ratings you gave yourself on each item. Hopefully you will have gained confidence in many of the skills included on the rating form.

To gain an overall impression of your improvement, total all the points you gave yourself on the first rating and total all the points you gave yourself on the second rating. Amount of improvement will be indicated by the difference in the two scores. (Since strong skill is given a rating of 1, remember that the lower score will be the better score.)

Finally, with your classmates discuss those areas where you gained the most confidence and those areas where you still need to improve your self image.

Individual Activity: Go back to Activity 2, Part I, and compare the two sets of ratings you gave yourself on each item. Hopefully you will have gained confidence in many of the skills included on the rating form.

To gain an overall impression of your improvement, total all the points you gave yourself on the first rating and total all the points you gave yourself on the second rating. Amount of improvement will be indicated by the difference in the two scores. (Since strong skill is given a rating of 1, remember that the lower score will be the better score.)

Finally, make an appointment with your instructor to discuss those areas where you gained the most confidence and those areas where you still need to improve your self-image.

References

Adell, A. W. Values clarification revised. *The Christian Century*, 93: 687-688.

Adler, R. and Towne, N. *Looking Out/Looking In*. New York: Holt, Rinehart and Winston, 1978.

Arnold, W. E., and Hirsch, R. O. Small group communication. In W. E. Arnold and R. O. Hirsch, eds, *Communicating Through Behavior*. St. Paul: West Publishing Company, 1977.

Bach, G. R., and Wyden, P. *The Intimate Enemy*. New York: Avon, 1968.

Barnlund, D. C. Toward a meaning centered philosophy of communication. *Journal of Communication* 12: 197-211.

Berne, E. *Games People Play*. New York: Grove Press, Inc., 1964.

Berne, E. *Transactional Analysis in Psychotherapy*. New York: Grove Press, 1961.

Berne, E. *What Do You Say After You Say Hello?* New York: Grove Press, 1972.

Bloom, L. Z., Coburn, K., and Pearlman, J. *The New Assertive Woman*. New York: Delacorte Press, 1975.

Brilhart, J. K. *Effective Group Discussion*. Dubuque, Iowa: Wm. C. Brown Company Publishers, 1974.

Cassels, L. You Can Be A Better Leader. *Nation's Business*, June 1960.

Christie, A. *A Murder Is Announced*. New York: Dodd, Mead and Company, 1950.

Dewey, J. *How We Think*. Boston: D. C. Heath and Company, 1910.

Eisenberg, A. M., and Smith, R. R., Jr. *Nonverbal Communication*. Indianapolis: The Bobbs-Merrill Company, Inc., 1971.

Englebardt, S. L. Alone Across Alaska. *Reader's Digest*, July 1978, 70-75.

Engstrom, T. W., and MacKenzie, A. *Managing Your Time*. Grand Rapids, Michigan: Zondervan Publishing House, 1968.

Fast, J. *Body Language*. New York: Pocket Books, 1970.

Feinberg, M. M. *Effective Psychology for Managers*. Englewood Cliffs, New Jersey: Prentice-Hall, Inc., 1965.

Fensterheim, H., and Baer, J. *Don't Say Yes When You Want to Say No*. New York: Dell Publishing Co., Inc., 1975.

Filley, A. C. *Interpersonal Conflict Resolution*. Glenview, Illinois: Scott Forsman, 1975.

Flanagan, W. How to Keep Bias Out of Job Interviews. *Business Week*, 26 May 1975, 77.

Gordon, T. *Parent Effectiveness Training*. New York: Peter H. Wyden, Inc., 1970.

Hall, E. T. *The Hidden Dimension*. Garden City, N.Y.: Doubleday Inc., 1966.

Hall, E. T.: *The Silent Language*. Greenwich, Conn: Fawcett Publications, 1959.

Harris, T. A. *I'm OK—You're OK.* New York: Harper and Row, 1967.

Howe, L. W., and Howe, M. M. *Personalizing Education: Values Clarification and Beyond.* New York: Hart Publishing Company, Inc., 1975.

James, M., and Jongeward, D. *Born to Win: Transactional Analysis with Gestalt Experiments.* Reading, Massachusetts: Addison-Wesley, 1971.

Jourard, S. M. *The Transparent Self.* New York: Van Nostrand Reinhold Company, 1971.

Kenyon, S. J., and Knott, A. T. *A Pronouncing Dictionary of American English.* Springfield, Mass.: G and C Merriman Company, 1953.

Knapp, M. L. *Nonverbal Communication in Human Interaction.* New York: Holt, Rinehart and Winston, Inc., 1972.

Knowles, M., and Knowles, H. *Introduction to Group Dynamics.* New York: Association Press, 1959.

Lazarus, A. *Behavior Therapy and Beyond.* New York: McGraw-Hill Book Co., 1971.

Luft, J. *Of Human Interaction.* Palo Alto, Cal.: National Press Books, 1969.

Maslow, A. H. *Motivation and Personality.* New York: Harper and Row, 1954.

Masten, R. *Speaking Poems.* Carmel, California: Sunflower Ink, 1977.

Meininger, J. *Success through Transactional Analysis.* New York: The New American Library, 1973.

Molloy, J. T. *Dress for Success.* New York: Warner Books, Inc., 1975.

Molloy, J. T. *The Woman's Dress for Success Book.* Chicago: Follett, 1977.

Narciso, J., and Burkett, D. *Declare Yourself—Discovering the ME in Relationships.* Englewood Cliffs, New Jersey: Prentice-Hall Inc., 1975.

Nierenberg, G. I., and Calero, H. H. *How to Read a Person Like a Book.* New York: Cornerstone Library, 1971.

Patton, B. R., and Giffin, K. *Interpersonal Communication: Basic Text and Readings.* New York: Harper and Row, Publishers, 1974.

Powell, J. *Why Am I Afraid to Tell You Who I Am?* Niles, Illinois: Argus Communications, 1969.

Rosenfeld, L. B. *Human Interaction in the Small Group Setting.* Columbus, Ohio: Charles E. Merrill Publishing Company, 1973.

Simon, S. B., Howe, L. W., and Kirschenbaum, H. *Values Clarification: A Handbook of Practical Strategies for Teachers and Students.* New York: Hart Publishing Company, Inc., 1972.

Smith, M. J. *When I Say No, I Feel Guilty.* New York: Bantam Books, 1975.

Sommer, R. *Personal Space: The Behavioral Basis of Design.* Englewood Cliffs, N.J.: Prentice-Hall, Inc., 1969.

Steiner, C. M. *Scripts People Live.* New York: Grove Press, 1974.

Uemura, N. Solo to the North Pole. *National Geographic,* September 1978, 298-325.

Whorf, B. L. Science and linguistics. In J. B. Carroll, ed., *Language, Thought, and Reality.* Cambridge, Mass.: MIT press, 1956.

Index

Boldface page numbers represent activities.

Action step, 347
Adell, A. W., 164
Adler, R., 206–207
Agenda, 249
Aggressiveness, 154
Alberti, R. E., 225
Appearance, 113–114
Arnold, W. E., 244–245
Articulation, 112
Artifacts, 97–98
Assertiveness, 153–155, **197–199**
Assertive rights, 153
Audience needs, 302–303, 329–330, 344–345
Authoritarian leadership, 247, 273
Awareness, in persuasion, 345–346

Bach, G. R., 174
Backner, J., 416
Baer, J., 153, 154–155
Barker, L. L., 292
Barnlund, D. C., 37
Behavioral flexibility, 166, 173, **201**
Beir, E. G., 140
Berkowitz, B., 70
Berne, E., 177, 187–189
Bloom, L. Z., 153, 154
Body language. See Body motion
Body motion, 92–93, 100–102, 105–109, **126–127**, 318–319
Bolles, R. N., 225
Brainstorming, 255–256, **277**
Brilhart, J. K., 251
Burkett, D., 148–150
Buzz group, 258

Calero, H. H., 98–102
Carnegie, D., 416
Cassels, L., 242–243
Chain
  branching, 87
  gossip, 87
  single-strand, 87
Chalkboard, 320

Charts, 319
Christie, A., 169–170
Civikly, K., 140
Coburn, K., 153, 154
Collet, P., 140
Colloquium, 261
Communication
  chains, 86–88
  channel, 9
  defined, 3–47
  definition of, 2–4, 7
  encounter, 12, 14, 28, 31
  exchange, 8–11
  function of, 17
  process, 37, 177, 251
  skills inventory, **50**
Conflict resolution, 173, **206–207**
Credibility, 38, 45, 306–307
Culligan, M. J., 416

Decision making, 18, 250–251
Decoding, 10
Defensiveness, 43
Definition, 328–329, 331–332
Delivery systems, 12–14
Demeanor, 113–114
Democratic leadership, 247
Demonstration, 262, 327
Description, 326–327
Descriptive listening, 167, 170, 172, **202–204**
Dewey, J., 234
Discussion
  group modes, 256–261
  speaker-audience mode, 262
Dissonance, 346
Distance, zones of, 94
Distractions
  avoidance of, 88–89
  environmental, 86
  physiological, 86
  psychological, 86
  semantic, 86
  social, 86
Drawling, 96

421

Ecroyd, D., 70
Ego state
 adult, 180-181
 child, 179-180
 parent, 178-179
 stroking, 186
 whole personality, 181-182
Eisenberg, A. M., 92
Emmons, M. L., 225
Empathy, 170, 172, **205**
Employment interview, 157-160
Encoding, 8
Englebardt, S. L., 226
Engstrom, T. W., 251
Entertaining message, 18, 303
 speech, **406-412**
Environment, 98
Explanation, 331-332
Extemporaneous speaking, 317
Extrasensory perception, 27
Eye contact, 108

Facial expressions, 108-109
Fact, 353
Fast, J., 100
Feedback, 10
Feelings
 denial of, 148
 not owned, 148
 owned, 148
Feinberg, M. M., 251, 252
Fensterheim, H., 153, 154-155
Filley, A. C., 174
Film, 320-321
Flanagan, W., 220-221
Forum, 259-260
Free information, 151, 155

Gestures, 107-108
Giffin, K., 142
Gilbert, M. A., 416
Goals, 231, 237
Gordon, T., 168-169, 174
Grooming, 113
Group dynamics, 236, 237. *See also* Small group
 facilitator, 249-250
 leaders, 250-252, **273**
 members
  adverse behavior of, 243-244
  participation of, 241-243
  responsibilities of, 244-246
  roles of, **271**
  types of, 244-245
 participation
  evaluation of, 278
  rules for, 242-243
 relationships, 227
 versus individual, 237-238, **276**

Hall, E. T., 94
Handouts, 320
Harris, T. A., 177
Hearing, process of, 77-78

Hirsch, R. O., 244-245
Horowitz, D., 70, 225
Howe, L. W., 165-166
Howe, M. M., 165-166
Hughes, C. L., 292

Impromptu speaking, 317
 speech, **413-415**
Informative message, 17, 301
 presentation to small group, **361**
 speaking, 325-339
 speech
  evaluation of, 333, 338-339
  example of, 334-337
  presentation of, **363-388**
 topics, 392-398
Interpersonal communication, 16, 142-191
Interview, 155-160
Intrapersonal communication, 15
Irish, R. K., 225

James, M., 177
Johari window, 40-41
Jongeward, D., 177, 225
Jourard, S. M., 150

Kenyon, S. J., 112
Kirschenbaum, H., 165-166
Knapp, M. L., 92
Knott, A. T., 112
Knowles, H., 233, 236, 241-242
Knowles, M., 233, 236, 241-242

Laissez-faire leadership, 247-248
Language
 acceptable usage, 31
 communication process, 31
 considerations in use, 30, 31, 33, **59**
 dialects, 32
 formal, 31
 general American, 32
 operational, 148-149
 regional influences, 30
 slang, 31
 standard, 31
 symbols, 31
Lazarus, A., 150-151
Leadership
 responsibilities of, 248-250
 small group, 246-252
 styles of, 247-248
Learning, 234-235
 principles, 330-331
Lecture, 262
Letter of application, 157-158
Library, use of, **359-360**
Life scripts, 178, 190
Linver, S., 416
Listeners
 getting to know, **52**

helping the, 105–113
Listening, 77–89, 243
    active, 78–80
    characteristics, 80–81
    critical, 79–80, 84–85, **120**, 353
    discriminative, 80, 85, **119**
    empathic, 171–172
    habits, 81–82
    improvement, 82–89
    log, **124–125**
    myths, **117**
    passive, 78
    process, 77–78
    questionnaire, **121–123**
    serious, 79, 82–84, **199–220**
    social, 79, 82–84, **119**
    types, 78–80
Loser, 190
Luft, J., 40, 41

Mackenzie, A., 251
Manuscript presentation, 317
Marsh, P., 140
Maslow, S. H., 17
Masten, R., 2, 142
Meaning, 7, 28
Media, 14
Meeting arrangements, 248–249
Meininger, J., 177
Memorized presentation, 318
Messages. *See also* Noise
    conflict of, 98–99
    distortion of, 85–89
Model, communication, 8–11, 16
Modeling, 262
Models, 320
Molloy, J. T., 97–98
Morris, D., 140
Motivation, 251–252

Narcisco, J., 148–150
Newman, M., 70
Nichols, R., 140
Nierenberg, G. I., 98–102
Noise, 11, 99–100
    physical, 11–12
    psychological, 11–12
Nonverbal behaviors, 243
    communication, 13, 91–102, 190
    messages
        awareness of, 99–100
        implications of, 98–102
    symbols, 72–73, 185
Note-taking, 85

Opinion, 353
Originator, 8
O'Shaughnessy, M. O., 140
Owning feelings and thoughts, 147–150, **194–196**

Panel discussion, 259

Paralanguage, 96, **130–131**
Patton, B. R., 142
Pausing, 96
Pearlman, J., 153, 154
Perception, 22–27, **58**
    of self. *See* Self-concept
Personal experience, 314
    space, 94–95, **128**
Persuasion, 18
    to change bad habits, 389
    components of, 345–348
Persuasive message, 302, 341–355, **399–400, 401–405**
    situation, analysis of, 390–391
    speaker, intent of, 354
    speech
        development of, 344–349
        evaluation of, 349–350
        example, 350–352
    topics, 343–344, **392–398**
Physical characteristics, 96
Pitch, 96, 111
Posture, 105–106
Powell, J., 150–151
Presentation modes, 262–263, 317–318
Problem/solution, 348
Problem-solving, 233, 262
Pronunciation, 112
Psychological games, 178, 187–189, 190, **211**
    stoppers for, 189
Public speaking. *See* Speaker-audience message

Question
    direct, 314–315
    rhetorical, 314
Quotations, 310, 315

Rate, 96, 111
Receiver, 9
Rehearsal, 263–264, 321–322
Reinforcement, 346
Reporting, 329
Resolution, 346
Resume, 159
Rhythm, 96
Robertson, J., 225
Roesler, N., 226
Role playing, 262
Rosenfeld, L. R., 140, 236, 237
Round-table discussion, 256–258

Sarnoff, D., 416
Screen, 319–320
Script analysis, 190
Self-concept, 37–47, **60, 62**
    effects of, 42
    feedback, 44
    improving, 44
    intrapersonal, 46

private self, 39-41
public self, 39-41
Self-confidence, 43, 45
Self-disclosure, 150-153, 155, **194-196,** 235
Self-fulfilling prophecy, 41
Self-image. See Self-concept
Sensation, 21, 27, **56**
   selective attention, 22
   sensory adaptation, 22
   receptors, 21-22
Sensitivity training, 262
Skill practice, 262
Shain, M., 225
Shaw, M. E., 292
Shirley, J. L., 140
Simon, S. W. 165-166
Small Group. See also Group
   benefits of, 236
   characteristics of, 232-235
   communication, 16
   concepts, **267**
   definition, 231
   functions of, 233-235
   joining, 235-236
   membership, **268**
   presentation, 261-264
   properties of, 236
   size, 232-233
Smith, M. J., 151-152, 153, 155
Smith, R. R., Jr., 92
Socialization, 235
Sommer, R., 94
Speaker, 4
Speaker-audience communication, 16, 299-354
Speaker-audience message
   body, 313-314
   central idea, 315, 331
   characteristics of, 299-300
   conclusion, 315
   delivery of, 316-322
   gaining attention, 314
   gathering material for, 305-307
   introduction, 314-315
   main points, 313-315
   ordering material for, 307-308
   organization of, 313-316
   outline for, 316, 348-349, **358**
   planning of, 299-311
   preview of main points, 315
   setting, 302-304
   summary, 315
   support materials for, 308-310, 313-314, 316
   time and place, 303
   types of, 300-302
Speaking, fear of, 294-295
Speech communication, 13, **54**
   material
      causal order of, 307
      chronological order of, 307
      comparison/contrast order of, 307
      courses, 306

      examples, 308
      experiments, 306
      interviews, 305-306
      library, 306-307
      personal experience, 305
      problem solution order of, 308
      spatial order of, 307
      statistics, 309-310
      testimony, 310
      topical order of, 307
   topics, 304-305
Stage fright, 322
Steiner, C. M., 177
Stevens, L. A., 140
Stone, J., 416
Strokes
   conditional, 186
   negative, 186
   positive, 186
   unconditional, 186
Stroking, 185-187, **210**
Structural analysis, 177, 178, 190, **208-209**
Swift, J., 72-73
Symbols, 8, 28
Symposium, 260

Tactile activity, 263
Therapy, 235, **269**
Thomson, D. S., 70
Touching, 95, **129**
Towne, N., 206-207
Transactional analysis, 177, 182-185, 190
Transactions
   crossed, 184
   parallel, 183
   ulterior, 184-185
Trecker, A. R., 292
Trecker, H. B., 292

Uemura, N., 226

Valens, E. G., 140
Values, 163-166, 349
   clarification, **199-200**
Verbal communication, 13, 243-244
   symbols, 72-73
Visual aids, 263, 318, 321
   images, 28
Vocal expression, 109-113
   quality, 112-113
   variety, 322
Volume, 110

Whorf, B. L., 31
Winner, 190
Words, 28
Written communication, 13
Wyden, P., 174

Zigler, Z., 70